THE AMAZING ADVENTURES OF BOB BROWN

THE AMAZING ADVENTURES OF BOB BROWN

A REAL-LIFE ZELIG WHO WROTE HIS WAY THROUGH THE 20TH CENTURY

CRAIG SAPER

ESE

Empire State Editions
An imprint of Fordham University Press
New York 2016

Fordham University Press also publishes its books in a variety of electronic formats. Some content that appears in print may not be available in electronic books.

Visit us online at:
www.fordhampress.com
www.empirestateeditions.com

Library of Congress Cataloging-in-Publication Data
available online at catalog.loc.gov.

Printed in the United States of America
18 17 16 5 4 3 2 1
First edition

Contents

Introduction 1

1 When the Artist Became a Fiction Factory, 1907–17 5

2 A Pulp Nonfiction Adventure Story: Once Upon a Time, 1886–1907 49

3 Free Love, Free Verse, and Free Radicals in the Avant-Garde, 1913–17 71

4 Exile, Escape, Empire, and World Travels, 1917–28 111

5 Expatriate Avant-Garde in the South of France, 1928–32 147

6 Let There Be Beer, Wine, Snacks, and Radical Social Change, 1932–40 195

7 *Saudade* and Going Home Again: The Amazon, Hollywood, Brazil, and Manhattan, 1941–59 241

Acknowledgments: The Making of a Biography 269

Notes 277

Index 295

THE AMAZING ADVENTURES OF BOB BROWN

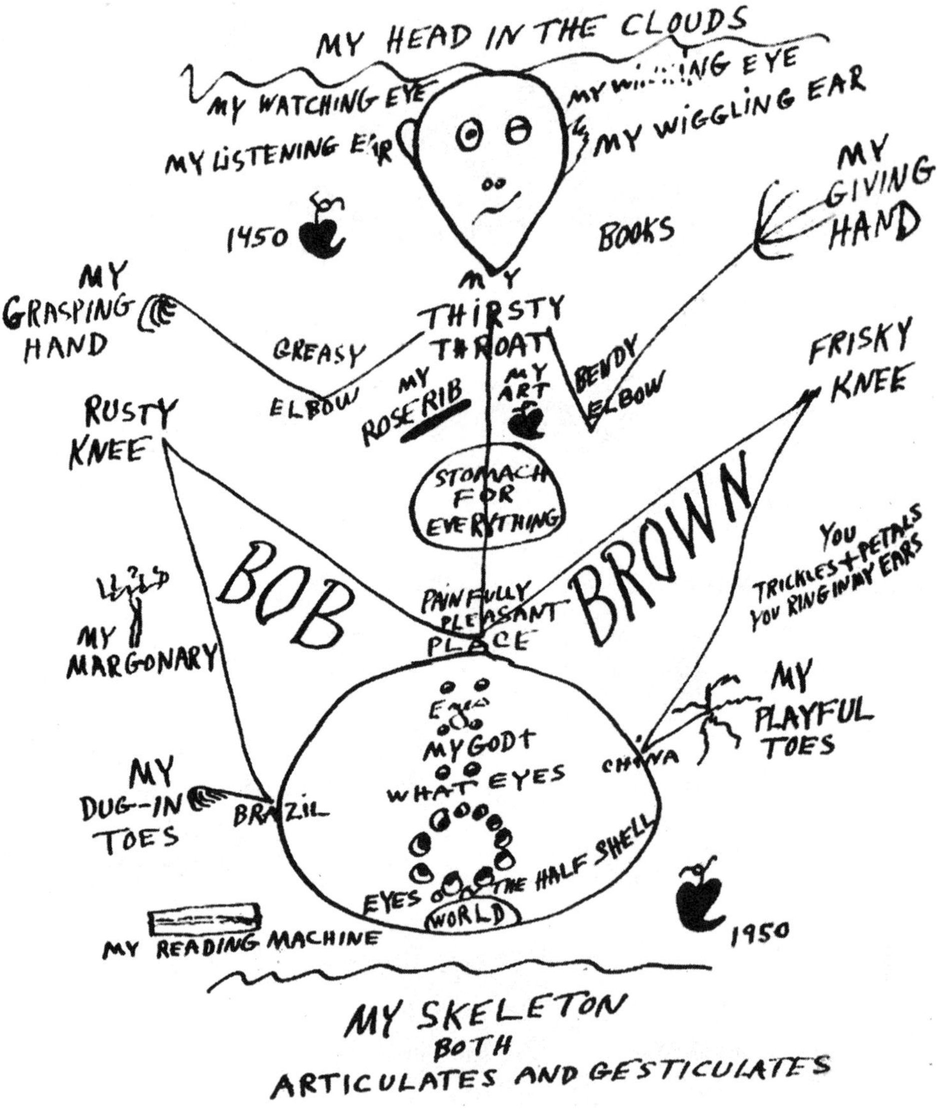

Bob Brown's 1959 selfie poem "I Don't Die! No Flies on Me!" (an autobiographical selfie-visual-poem by Bob Brown, 1959 [reprinted in the new Roving Eye Press edition of *1450–1950* in 2015])

Introduction

> Bob had been not just one person,
> but Bob^1, Bob^2, Bob^3, etc.
>
> —*Walter Lowenfels*[1]

The title character of Woody Allen's mockumentary *Zelig* transformed his appearance and personality, chameleon-like, depending on the situation in which he found himself, and the name now defines that postmodern personality type who morphs into multiple roles. The Zelig character type also illuminates an apt, even if comically absurd, illumination of the quintessential American ethos of self-invention and reinvention. For Robert Carlton Brown II (1886–1959), self-invention began at age seven, and his pulling himself up by his bootstraps would culminate in Brown's becoming one of the most successful writers and publishers of the first half of the twentieth century. But Bob was not just one person.

He was a bestselling short-fiction writer for the pulps, writer of the stories for the first serial movies made (e.g., *What Happened to Mary*, 1912), and later a Hollywood treatment writer (writing one treatment about switched babies and mistaken identity). That was Bob^1. Besides his great success in contributing to American popular culture, he was a central character in the avant-garde arts, both among the expatriate writers, publishers, and artists in France and among the Imagist poets in Greenwich Village and the artists' colony near Grantwood Village on the New Jersey Palisades near the town of Ridgefield. That was Bob^2. Besides his importance among the vanguard, he was also an entrepreneur and owner of multiple business ventures, and he was a world traveler circumnavigating the globe first class, a wealthy international publisher, an art and artifact collector, a philanthropist, and a Wall Street stock trader. That was Bob^3. He was also a Communist commune worker, an instructor at a radical college, and curator of a museum exhibit that included trenchant criticism of another of Bob's lives as a gourmet-cookbook writer. That was Bob^{4}. He was also a book dealer throughout much of his life, a co-owner of a restaurant, an impresario of Webster Hall parties, an important food critic, a cookbook and travel guide writer, and an advocate for drinking beer and cooking with wine. That was Bob^{5}. His friends and mentors included cultural figures from Marcel Duchamp and Man Ray to H. L. Mencken and O. Henry to Nancy Cunard and Gertrude Stein to William Carlos Williams and Mina Loy. Brown not only wrote in every imaginable genre, from pulp fiction squibs to modernist poetry to "proletarian realism" to gourmet cookbooks and many more, he lived his life in different genres, and his work is often footnoted in a wide array of books. His massive network of friends has led some to see Bob^{6}'s importance as a minor figure in a hundred other biographies. He moved from wealth to forced poverty and back again. He shifted from being a public figure to sometimes fleeing into obscurity. Bob Brown was a true cosmopolitan and multicultural citizen of the world, having lived in one hundred different cities (not just visited, but lived on, five continents).

Here is a list of just the cities *outside* the United States.

Amsterdam
Athens
Bahia
Barranquilla
Begawan
Belgrade
Berlin
Brussels
Bucharest
Budapest
Buenos Aires
Cairo
Cape Town
Cape Verde
Caracas
Cologne
Colombo
Copenhagen
Corfu
Domingo City

Frankfurt
Genoa
The Hague
Halifax
Hamburg
Havana
Helsinki
Hiroshima
Hong Kong
Istanbul
Java
Kharkov
Kiel
Kobe
Kyoto
Leningrad
Lima
Lisbon
London
Lucerne

Madrid
Marseilles
Mexico City
Milkan
Montevideo
Moscow
Munich
Nagasaki
Nagoyn
Naples
Odessa
Osaka
Palermo
Para
Paris
Pernambuco
Pircue
Prague
Progresso
Recife

Rice	Seville	Turin
Rio de Janeiro	Shanghai	Valencia
Rome	Singapore	Valparaiso
Rosario	Sofia	Venice
Rostov	Stalingrad	Vera Cruz
Rotterdam	Stockholm	Vienna
Salina Cruz	Sumatra	Warsaw
Santiago de Chile	Tangiers	Yokohama
Santiago de Cuba	Tehuantepec	Yucatan
Santo	Tokyo	Zululand
São Paulo	Trieste	Zurich

This is a story that follows its subject from pulp fiction factory to stock trader and ticker-tape reader to patron and impresario of vanguard arts to a war-resisting exile to international publishing mogul to Surrealist inventor of what Bob Brown called a "Readies" style of preparing texts for his reading machine to activist curator and teacher to Hollywood hack and lush libertine to prolific cookbook writer and beer-cure champion to visual poet and *éminence grise* of the Beat Generation poets to a now-prescient designer of a precursor to e-readers and new forms of publishing to many more serendipitous discoveries and star-crossed losses. This biography is also an argument about transliteracy, publishing platforms, and information design and distribution. Brown's lifelong passion for publishing in every imaginable form, genre, and medium is instructive for anyone who seeks to appreciate the rapid changes in reading and publishing today. To fully understand and appreciate Brown's notion of processed texts and tele-vistic distribution and his prescient perspective on new forms of electronic literacies, we need to see Brown's reading machine, and his description of himself as a fiction factory, in the larger context of his other work as a publisher and writer. Brown's work and multiple careers illuminate, for contemporary culture, what is now called transliteracy, or reading on multiple platforms. His work as a publisher did not simply package poetry and essays; for Brown, printing, publishing, and distributing books and magazines was a type of literature by design.

As a fiction factory, he cranked out a thousand stories, making him one of the wealthiest writers of the day.

1

When the Artist Became a Fiction Factory, 1907–17

I was a fiction factory.

—*Bob Brown*[1]

We were a bunch of word-pirates writing pulp fiction [. . .]. We didn't call it pulp, back there before the war [. . .]. [W]e had no name for it. Loosely we referred to our work as doing blood-and-thunder.

—*Bob Brown*[2]

Bob Brown poured forth fiction, lively, swift-moving and enthralling fiction, at a pace that made [him a fortune]. It wasn't so bad being a pulpwood hack.

—*Berton Braley*[3]

[. . .] they were machines for making jokes. A button machine makes buttons, no matter what the power used, foot, steam or electricity. They, no matter what the motivating force, death, love or God, made jokes.

—*Nathanael West*[4]

As soon as Robert Carlton Brown arrived in New York, he unpacked his "haymaking" Oliver No. 5. He'd likely purchased the typewriter in Chicago at the company's main headquarters and showroom. In anyone else's biography the typewriter's specific mechanics would not appear at all, but its design and specific machinations would influence Robert's later avant-garde projects, and the typewriter itself played a key role in the modernist visual poetry Brown began producing in the early 1910s. The Oliver brand had inverted U-shaped type bars that swung down from two towers on each side of the machine, striking the ink ribbon, as it was lifted up and unrolled from spool to spool. The upright type bars looked like metal wings waiting to lift the machine off the ground. The Oliver was among the first "visible type" machines introduced.

Previous machines were "blind" writers, meaning that the typists could not see the results until after they had typed the text (similarly, in the 1980s, the first generation of electronic typewriters displayed only one line before the typist pressed a button to print those few words). New machines, like the Oliver, introduced before the turn of the twentieth century, focused the typist on the few centimeters visible between the two towers of type bars, but in that space one could now see what was being typed. It's difficult to imagine now, when typing commonly allows a view of the entire page (on a screen), that "visible type" once meant seeing just a small fraction of one line.

Typewriters epitomized the bureaucracies created to manage the industrial revolution in the late nineteenth century and the emergence of office culture in the twentieth century. The typewriting machines removed reproduction and writing from their connection to the voice and allowed for every business and government to have what we might call today a personal word processing machine. Printing no longer needed to be reserved for permanent and important documents and books or mass-produced newspapers; now it could serve a more ephemeral smaller-scale purpose for business memos, for directives, and for the freelance writer sending out stories and reports. As early as 1898, another unintended use for the typewriter appeared: a visual art machine. The No. 5 introduced the backspace option and, with it, the start of typewriter art. Something intended to produce rapid transcripts in multiple copies by secretarial pools in service of large systems of organizations could also produce a unique typed visual poem by one artist. The recognition that one person now had a type of press increasingly changed publishing. For publishers today, the size of the publishing company, its means of printing, and the typical print runs continue to determine how one describes the press. Typically a small press produces limited runs of under a thousand. A press smaller than small is called a "fine press." Following along that spectrum, a typewriter owner who self-publishes either art or texts might have begun to think of his work as a "personal press" imprint.

The early typewriter artworks were produced in promotional contests for secretaries to demonstrate their dexterity in working on these machines. The Oliver Company sponsored these contests, and the most famous results were portraits that used type-strike intensity (depending on how hard one pressed the key) and character choice (e.g., which letter, number, or dingbat one chose) to produce remarkably realistic shading and figuration. The practice of making typewriter art eventually led to a whole variant of concrete and visual poetry mostly since the 1950s. Brown started to compose abstract typewriter art in the 1920s but never published the results. His abstract pieces look similar to the concrete and visual typewriter artworks produced thirty or forty years later.

Robert moved into a furnished room located on the corner of West 4th Street and West 12th Street in Greenwich Village. He delighted in the address's seeming impossibility: Streets run parallel to one another, and 4th should be about eight blocks away from 12th. How they could intersect, he didn't know, but the corner still looks today much as it did when he arrived. The four-story walk-ups were sweltering in the summers, and the apartment was dusty and cramped, but Robert positioned himself in front of the window and started pounding out stories.

He had come to New York on the advice of Bob Davis, the editor of all Munsey magazines. Munsey was one of the dominant pulp fiction publishers in an era when their popular magazines, including titles like *Ocean*, *Railroad Man's*, *The Scrap Book*, *All-Story*, *The Cavalier* (which eventually absorbed *Scrap Book*), and weekly versions of the last two, dominated the media landscape. They were called "pulps" because of the low-grade pulp paper they were printed on, as opposed to the "slicks" or "glossies" (also sometimes called "smoothies") with glossy multicolored covers. These magazines dominated all other forms of fiction for decades, and the style began to characterize modern American fiction. Brown described his stories, and by extension most of the magazine stories, as often "crammed full" with "a little light Falstaff, a hunk of heavy Hamlet, a great deal of Dickens."[5] The editors demanded that Bob churn out high-quality stories at the rate of a pulp machine; and although pulp fiction would later figuratively describe the low quality of the writing itself, in the first two decades of the twentieth century the best short fiction was found in those magazines. Although most pulps appealed to a young male audience, the most popular smoothies had women readers of *Ladies' World*, *Women's World*, and *Ladies' Home Journal*. Munsey also published newspapers, and its editors would eventually ask Robert to write for those as well. So, while Robert began his career writing jokes and detective stories for young

He was filled with the push and hustle necessary to churn out high-quality stories at the rate of a pulp machine.

men, he would also find huge success writing for women's magazines like *Ladies' World*.

When Robert visited the Munsey offices, on the top floors of the Flatiron building (175 Fifth Ave), he would sit under pictures of famous contributors to the magazines on the wall behind him facing the editor and the windows. Davis, the editor, would stare at the writer and occasionally look up at the pictures of the great writers, sigh longingly, and then gaze down again at the writer as if to suggest how far the young writer would have to go even to be worthy to sit under the watchful gaze of these greats. As if this were not enough, behind the editor were mottos on placards reminding the writer that "This Is My Busy Day—Cut it Short," and "Find a Man for the Job not a Job for the Man," and other axioms all chosen to make the writer feel small, insignificant, and replaceable.[6] In 1907, Robert took it as a challenge as Davis began the grueling mentoring process.

In 1903, Davis had introduced O. Henry's (pen name of William Sydney Porter) short stories as the editor of a special issue of the *New York Sunday World* magazine. Around 1911, Davis featured Edgar Rice Burroughs's Tarzan stories; eventually most of Burroughs's works appeared under Davis's editorship. Davis's specialty was what he called "pseudo-science" fictional pieces, and he encouraged the young Robert Brown's interest in imagining futuristic gadgets couched in adventure stories.

Davis had urged Brown to move to New York to become what the pulp editors called a "ready writer"—ready and able to write the needed genre of story and to fill word quotas in the pulp magazines. Decades later, Brown would pick up on this moniker to name the texts prepared for Brown's reading machine "readies" (the neologism could be pronounced as *ree-deez* as an allusion to reading and, years later, to bringing reading into the age of the talkies; it can also be prounced *reddies*, alluding to ready and to Reddy, one of Brown's nicknames). Like Brown, Davis was constantly generating more plot ideas than he could actually write, and the two quickly began thinking of ways to build their inventiveness into a business. Davis, already a respected celebrity at least among publishers and writers because he edited so many pulps, had a unique vantage of American fiction from the turn of the century until 1920. While at Munsey's he managed 40,000 manuscripts annually submitted to the publications under his editorial direction and "considered himself a conduit through which most of the fiction written in the United States passed."[7] He was also famous for reading all the submissions himself and infamous for harshly criticizing writers, even those whom he regularly published. If one did not live up to his standards, he would exclaim, "Rotten! r-r-rotten! Here, take it away!" He might tell a writer that he planned to put the (rotten) story in a strongbox so that he could later pull it out, the way a parent might pull out embarrassing baby pictures and show the now-successful writer his or her inauspicious beginnings.[8] So, if Davis did read 40,000 stories as an editor, then he read more than a hundred stories a day. Still, he found time to start an advertising business, on the side, with the young Robert Carlton Brown.

Davis devised a plan whereby instead of placing short humorous pieces in the magazines he edited, he would sell advertising ideas directly to companies. He brought in Brown from Chicago to help generate the short ditties and memorable catchphrases Brown had already begun building his reputation on in business magazines and newspapers. Magazine advertising had existed long before, but, in the year they started their business, newer means were being employed to reach a mass audience: Planes flew over the city promoting a Broadway play, New York City made arrests over supposedly obscene advertisements on trolley cars that used anatomically correct bulls in the illustrations, and research-driven books about advertising's effectiveness began to appear.

The new advertising venture needed a name. Davis suggested Thomas Hardy. Hardy was not only still publishing fiction in 1908, and a celebrity; he had published serialized stories in the nineteenth century that originated the term *cliffhanger* in a story about secret marriages and daring rescues: *A Pair of Blue Eyes* (Hardy, 1873) with editions, just in the nineteenth century, in 1885, 1889, and 1895. Thomas Hardy invented the bread and butter of Davis and Brown's career. Davis wanted to use the name in honor of Hardy's connection to pulps and in winking acknowledgment of the controversial and popular "fits of love" sections of Hardy's *Jude the Obscure* (1895). *The New York Bookman*, with which both Davis and Brown were very familiar (and that Harry T. Peck, who was, fifteen years later, in 1910, involved in a real-life sex scandal, had edited), published an editor's review of *Jude* that claimed it was "simply one of the most objectionable books that we have ever read in any language whatsoever."[9] Choosing a name for the business that connected it to this string of associations was just the sort of scandalous inside joke the pulp writers loved. The name alluded explicitly to Hardy as one of the key innovators in high-quality, if salacious, adventures that made pulp fiction popular, and then to the claims against Hardy's supposedly obscene novel, *Jude the Obscure*, because of the adultery and sex, by reviewers including Peck's well-known dismissal of Hardy's novel as "Jude the Obscene," and finally to Peck's own adultery and sex scandal that was in the news just as Brown and Davis were starting their company. Brown later used the name, as an allusion to "*the* Thomas Hardy," self-consciously, in the serialized stories in *Pearson's Magazine*, starting in 1910, soon after Davis and Brown ended their partnership; the main character in those stories, the sleuth Christopher Poe, used the pseudonym Thomas Hardy whenever he worked undercover.[10]

The Thomas Hardy Company (an example of a precursor to the advertising agencies) started selling catchphrases (what an advertiser today would call copy) like one for Barking Dog tobacco with the slogan "It doesn't bite!" Another catchphrase, "A Caress in Confection," promoted a chocolate "Soul Kiss" made by Huyler's, a very successful candy company; Brown was familiar with the Huyler promotions department from the company's 1904 World's Fair coin. Huyler's employed Milton Hershey, who later started his own eponymous candy company that specialized in chocolate Kisses. The Thomas Hardy Company also worked for Joseph M. Gaites, the Broadway producer, on creating an advertising idea for his hit summertime musical *The Three Twins*, which opened on Broadway in 1908. The musical, filled with disguise, mistaken identity, love affairs, and memorable melodies like "Yama Yama Man," also had a "faceograph machine" that presumably could identify the true identity of the three eponymous characters. In the end, the three men are proved to be unrelated: Two look like each other, and the third is in disguise. The machine was a fictional face-reading machine. The musical, especially the facial-recognition machine, left a lasting impression on Brown.

Besides advertising, Davis and Brown considered working for the film industry, but Davis had lost a fortune in the late 1890s when he and several partners started the American Sportagraph Company using a miragraph camera to make nickelodeon movies of boxing matches. "Miragraph," Davis explained, is Latin for "wonderful pictures." Davis's company was the first ever to film a boxing match, but when an unexpected knockout ended the fight after only twenty-eight seconds, the film was unmarketable and the company folded. In 1913, Davis wrote a two-reel screenplay for a Mutual Film production to star the champion boxer Bob Fitzsimmons, and although the film was never made, Davis published a well-received biography of Fitzsimmons thirteen years later.[11] Bob was itching to write for the fledgling movie industry too.

The Thomas Hardy advertising partnership failed to generate enough income to keep it going, and it folded about a year after starting. Other advertising agencies had very different luck; one in particular was also closely connected to Robert Brown. Bruce Barton, who'd grown up with Robert and was the editor of their high school's newspaper, often rejected the jokes and catchphrases that later launched Brown's career as a writer. Barton also started working as a publicist and advertiser around the same time as the Thomas Hardy group started making advertisements. Bruce, unlike Robert, had many successes in advertising; eventually Barton cofounded BBDO, one of the most successful advertising agencies ever, with one of the B's in the company's name standing for Barton. Barton wrote a bestselling religiously oriented self-help book called *The Man Who Nobody Knows* (1925), portraying Jesus as a business executive. The book's huge success led to Barton's being called, to his regret, "the man who everybody knows."[12] Brown resented Barton's success and especially Barton's mix of Christian fundamentalism with advanced capitalism that continues to fuel today's Republican Party. Robert Brown took a road less traveled. Many years later, in 1920, Davis abruptly left Munsey's to start his own literary agency, but back in the 1910s, he was part of the world's largest publishing machine.

Although Robert's advertising venture did not succeed, his career as a writer continued to draw positive attention from editors interested in this very young talented writer. Robert would continue to pitch his plotlines, or go over drafts, for Davis's various Munsey-published magazines, or do the same for other publishers, like Street & Smith Publications' magazines. As he sat on the editorial offices' waiting room benches he traded ideas with those who sat with him. They were all rising stars, including two whom Robert Brown had known in college in Madison, Wisconsin: Horatio Winslow and Berton Braley. Bert, a popular poet among the magazine readers, considered his own work on the pulps "not as an inspired art, but as a practical craft—as carpentry with words."[13] Braley and Brown rejected the romantic myth of the inspired artist, and, while Bert would describe the craft as artisanal, Robert saw it as an industrial process.

Starting in July 1911, ads for *Munsey's Magazine* included Davis's own "I Am" poems, in which the poem's narrator would speak from the perspective of an inanimate object; the first object Davis chose was a printing press. Robert also started thinking about an "I Am" poem, casting himself as a writing machine. He thought of his typing with wiggling fingers that would attract words to land on sheets of paper through the machine; he kept returning to the image of the wiggling fingers intermingling with typewriting machines, his image of wide-scope explanation, throughout his multiple careers especially in his avant-garde book, particularly in the subtitle of his 1931 book, *Words: I but bend my finger in a beckon and words, birds of words, hop on it, chirping*, with the subtitle printed in microscopic 2-point type. The technique of wireless telegraphy, demonstrated at the 1904 World's Fair (where Robert had worked before moving to New York), allowed writing to travel long distances instantly to a waiting reader decoding the long dashes and dots. Now pulp fiction writers began imagining a future in which machines narrated their own stories and where images traveled through space tele-visually; decades later, Robert would include aspects of these communication technologies in his designs for a reading machine and the processed texts called readies. It all seemed far-fetched at the time, but Robert started building a career on writing about the far-fetched; soon he would be on improbable adventures similar to his characters' adventures.

Because Robert had received few rejections, he knew he had a formula for getting published. He also looked around the waiting rooms and quickly realized that there was a relatively small group of writers, which never numbered more than 300 and usually much fewer (under a hundred), who wrote more than half, and often much more, of all the pieces in the pulps. He could name nearly all of the writers in New York. Another thousand or so writers from around North America and England produced the remainder. In a later period, but with a similar need for content for the pulps, the editors needed "200 million words a year to fill these magazines."[14] Even at one to two cents a word, Robert figured out that he could make a handsome living, if, and only if, he could produce a constant stream of tens of thousands of words. He had to become one with his typewriting machine—rapidly wiggling fingers on keys; eyes on papers and type; ears listening for the carriage return warning bell; the demands of a pulp fiction mind orchestrating the entire production.

For a year or so, from 1908 to 1909, Robert lived in cheap apartments and "ate at even cheaper cafeterias."[15] When he wasn't typing his stories, he was drinking and talking about stories with his fellow writers. Their conversations were not limited to those present in the flesh but included the "ghosts of all the heroines and villains [. . .]. Little Nells shivered in threadbare shawls outside the swinging doors, waiting for fathers who never came home. Wraiths of murdered men floated in our cigar smoke. Red-thumbed detectives strolled through in search of escaped zebra-striped convicts. Cops lurked in corners with lengths of rubber hose."[16] It was a lively time, with the bar filled with the best fiction writers all drawn to New York to try their hand at making a living per word. They greeted Rabelais as he "came in, arm in arm with François Villon. Boccaccio and Casanova showed up sometimes, to our old dandy's dear delight. We bought Poe many a drink and discussed with him the latest murder in the Rue Morgue. Sam Johnson shuffled through in his greasy bathrobe. Salvation Army lasses and austere George Eliots gave us the wink. Gaboriau and Gautier rubbed elbows with us. Those were swell days for literary guys."[17] Robert spent all day typing out stories as fast as he could, and then all night reading, drinking, and talking about his life as a fiction machine in the magazine industry.

Even his identity was literary and poetic, as Brown claimed to use many pen names. By 1910 these included Anthony Wright, Orville Updike Kidd, Nathanial O. Buddy, Carlton Roberts, Peter P. Durham, Shadow Steve, Martin Mydham, Hartridge D. Tyler, and H. E. Twinells and John S. Brackett, the last two of these mentioned in this biography's second chapter, on Brown's childhood and adolescent years in Chicago. He used these names to avoid the appearance that only a few writers produced all the stories in an issue of a pulp even if that was very often the case. In one issue of *Smart-Set*, with new editorial leadership, Brown apparently wrote the majority of the stories, allowing the magazine to survive through the transition. Sometimes editors would create "house names" that they would assign randomly if one writer had two or more stories in one issue. Other times, particularly productive authors would have a few names they would use to avoid overexposure.

When Brown entered the editorial offices of Street & Smith, he would sit in a stall facing an editor of a particular magazine: for example, the editor of *Buffalo Bill, Diamond Dick, Popular, People's Magazine*, or other Street & Smith magazine editors. Each editor would either go over drafts with Robert or give him a new assignment. After finishing working with one editor, he would get up from his chair and move to the next stall, switching with another writer. The separation between each magazine was just a makeshift divider, and the flimsy divisions between magazines applied to editorial policy as well. The editors working on the approximately thirty-five pulp titles at Street & Smith often moved the stories among the different magazines if they needed to fill space in one title.[18] Brown and other writers liked to call the lone president of Street & Smith, Ormond Gerald Smith, the Smith Brothers, Ormond and Gerald, jokingly confusing the publisher with the two cough drop makers.

It was at one of his visits to Street & Smith that Brown met William Wallace Cook. Cook was already a famous fiction writer and, much later, the author of a writer's guidebook, *Plotto.* He intended the book as something besides "a mechanism that yields a cut and dried plot by the mere use of a thumb index."[19] Instead, he wanted to suggest plotlines that demonstrated his general theory of narrative composition. For Cook, every narrative had a protagonist with a "purpose" who had to confront an "obstacle" (either successfully overcoming the obstacle or not). Cook specialized in science fiction and westerns and wrote 66,000 words a week for years. Given that rate of production, he appropriately named his autobiographical account of his writing life *The Fiction Factory* and used a pen name, as he had done many times before in the pulps. One of the first pen names Robert Brown used was Julia Edwards for his work for the *New York Weekly*, perhaps so that he'd feel more comfortable writing about marriage and domestic situations, which were the focus of those articles, rather than the cowboys and science stories he had usually written. For his autobiography he used the name John Milton Edwards.

Cook was already planning to mentor Robert in the "fiction factory" method before they had even met. Soon Robert was calling Cook

William Wallace Cook, the inventor of the plotto and fiction factory methods.

"Uncle Bill." Although Bill was regarded as a straight arrow, "sober among the soaks" in Brown's phrase, Cook had a fascination with, even a fetish about, the most decadent corners of city life. He lived most of the year with his wife in rural Marshall, Michigan, halfway between Ann Arbor and Kalamazoo. During his long visits, of between one month and six weeks, twice a year to New York, Cook lived as near as he could to what he called the dregs of society. He drank in stories, characters, and situations around him as he nodded and smiled at the prostitutes, or when he bought drinks for grifters or "panelhouse punks" (slang for a criminal who would rob brothel customers from behind a moving panel in the wall). He interviewed "bunco-steerers" (swindlers or card sharps—in card lingo, mechanics) who seemed eager to tell him their tricks. They would keep lockers at Grand Central, or at the newly constructed Penn Station, to store their disguises. When the next greenhorn arrived from out of town, they could quickly prepare for their charade. In his time spent with Robert, Bill would teach the young writer about writing fiction based in the streets and often involving a criminal element.

They produced multiple serials for Davis and for Street & Smith. When Cook came to town, the editors and publishers would take him to long working dinners, and they treated him with an appreciative excitement usually reserved for new discoveries whom they wanted to seduce into becoming part of their stable of regular writers. Cook, like Davis, was unbelievably productive and intellectually generous, and they both thought of the young Brown as a promising up-and-comer who needed paternal guidance about freelance writing.

The life of young writers was a struggle and brought them into contact with colorful material for their stories. The low rents and cheap food in the Village allowed pulp writers to start their careers and regularly consult with their editors. The situation of the writers changed little for two decades, and one, ironically, described how he "could dine sumptuously for around nine cents per meal [in the 1920s]. A hamburger steak made of meat-flavored sawdust cost four cents, a good hard roll was a penny, coffee two cents (made from dishwater with a dash of chicory)."[20] The first few months in New York were not that different for Brown, but with Cook's help Robert would soon find some financial success.

The day after Brown first met Bill Cook, on a "sweltering day in July," one of the hottest summers in New York City on record, Bill showed up at Brown's austere furnished studio apartment in the Village. He was impressed with the young Brown's natural talent, and he wanted to lend a helping hand to writers who showed promise. As Cook surveyed the young writer's grimy existence, he started to think of ways he might help. Brown kept typing away, in his undershirt, by the opened window. Cook had wished that when he was young and struggling someone had helped him by giving him guidance about writing, providing financial backing, or simply helping him get a start in life.

Just as he paced over to Brown, who was still typing furiously, the solution came to him. He closed down the lid of the Oliver, and Brown looked up, mumbling the story to try to keep it in his memory before it dissipated like a balloon letting out its air and flying about the room.

"Pack up, Bob, you're moving uptown to my room," Cook said in his fatherly voice. Robert, who could never resist a father figure, listened intently to the deal.

"I've got a brass bed going to waste and the place is big enough to hold a prize fight in, or write a hundred thousand word serial," he explained with delight.

"But my week isn't up here. I can't afford to lose any rent right now," he protested as Cook started stacking "manuscripts, Thesaurus, type-paper and carbon" with "pearls of sweat plopping down on them from his big, bald chin." Robert continued to protest even as he also started to pack up his belongings. He'd decided he wanted to get out of the apartment even if he couldn't afford to leave a week's worth of rent on the table.

Robert got into the taxi and moved uptown to Cook's luxurious room for the rest of the month. It was in the middle of Broadway's Great White Way, so named because the colored lights blew out too fast and so the theater owners used white lights, and Brown broke out in song to celebrate, singing the chorus of "Give My Regards to Broadway" as they got closer to the brownstone on West 44th Street very near Broadway.

The "luscious Renoir-haired landlady," the third wife of Bob Fitzsimmons (the world champion boxer), greeted them. Julia Gifford had an on-again, off-again, relationship with the boxer, and in that month, during the writers' stay, she was separated from him only to reunite for travels to England and, then, Australia and New Zealand (they were finally divorced in 1915).

Brown remembered the house as "soon to be torn down to make way for the Astor Hotel," but that seems unlikely since the Astor had been built five years before in 1903 and opened in 1904. Cook's rented room in the house was lavishly furnished and included Fitzsimmons's exercise equipment and punching bags; it was the boxer's spare room and gym. The two brass beds were absurdly baroque, with the "wondrous execution" of the brass tubes seeming to undulate, which delighted Brown. It was like sleeping under "a spectacular Arc de Triomphe of brass-beddom." He remembered the rest of the furniture as "overstuffed as boxing gloves" and the bathroom filled with "silver plated plumbing to shame the brass." For all of his experiences, he was still a twenty-two-year-old kid, and this place left him breathless.

He bumped his head on a punching bag, tripped over a stuffed canvas practice dummy, and started to realize that his stay in Fitzsimmons's old gym-spare-room might not be a holiday. Sure enough, the next morning Bill woke Robert at 6:00 A.M. with a "slap or two on his tummy." Cook had already taken his shower, and now he pushed Brown into the shower to start the day. They would go for an unbelievably hearty breakfast in Times Square, including "butter cakes, wheat cakes, corned beef hash with an egg astraddle, Adam and Eve on a Raft, and Wreck 'em! kippers and bacon, sometimes chicken livers," and, after that "day laborer's" meal, they started working by 7:00 A.M. Precisely because of pulp stories (and, later, Hollywood movies), a minor mythology exists around remarkably idle writers' waiting for the muse to strike. Instead, Brown worked as something like an athlete paid during training camp at the fiction factory gym.

Bill Cook paid the young Brown "twenty-five dollars a day [about $550 in present-day funds], furnished the typewriter paper," and started the workouts. Working at least six days a week, Brown saw the financial up side of a disciplined approach to writing. Still, the grueling requirements, with 32,000 words a week, made it a constant challenge to stay focused. In a thinly veiled description of Robert Brown, Cook later wrote that the young writer "spoils an otherwise fine character by [. . .] straining for a so-called Bohemian effect." He believed that Robert was "doped and shanghaied" but that he would eventually "escape to more creditable surroundings." Although he was able to produce quantity and quality for the pulps for a few years, Brown later escaped from the conventional work life of pulps, embracing what Cook called "wildly unconventional" bohemia.[21] But Brown took the driving work ethic with him even as he threw convention to the wind. Cook thought of fiction writing as a business, similar to "running a newspaper, a bank, or a factory," and similarly Robert started to implicitly and embryonically think of reading and writing as mutable mechanized processes rather than as a natural analog of thought.[22] Brown had little time to fully develop these thoughts as he furiously tried to keep up with his mentor's output of words on the page; they both raced to type stories, meet the word counts demanded by the publishers, and become one with their machines.

It was a weird scene. Cook had blue eyes made larger by his gold spectacles and an unusual mustache. It was un-dyed but nevertheless "rainbow"-colored with "flecks of gray, but also blue, red, and brown" in the mix. The printed words seemed to sputter in beads of sweat off Cook's rainbow mustache onto the page with the clickety-clack as a soundtrack. Bill would occasionally whip out a handkerchief and dry the perspiration from his face and fingers. He thought like a printer because he had, earlier in his career, typeset his own stories, and he would obsess about the visual mechanics of the final product and always produce "a sheet of copy without a single typographical error or erasure." He would type with two fingers but still produced, in a sweaty six-hour day, about thirty full pages. Robert's mind wandered off to an early description of a printed page as "a trickle of type running through a wide meadow of margin," and he saw the scene with the mustache serving as the wide meadow and the sweat as the trickle of type. To keep up the pace, Brown at first used up pages with lines with one-word dialogue. "Yes," he said, and "No," she answered, with each word taking an entire line, but the final product looked like a few scraps left on a dirty white plate, rather than a complete page ready for an editor's eyes.

Counter to the intensity of typing out the stories, Cook always began in a rocking chair in front of the typewriter, thinking. He would plan the story out in his head beforehand as he rocked calmly, and then when he started typing he would almost become one with the machine. When they weren't typing, Cook explained what he called his "plotto" method, which he would not refine and publish as a book until a decade later.

The plotto system combines three overlapping indexes of suggested plots. First the writer picks a general plot or master plot—for example, the vague but inclusive "Seeking by craftiness to escape misfortune." Then the writer picks, out of ten or twenty choices, the more specific situation.[23] For example, after the writer chooses the general schema, she or he might choose the following line (with the layout appearing with the indexing numbers before the line). Other parts of the code include *, **, or *** for the sections of the multipart conflicts in each plot (with the * after the first part of the conflict, ** after the second, etc.); capital letters for main characters (e.g., A, male protagonist; B, female protagonist; A-6, male officer of the law and B-6, female officer of the law); and a complicated numbering system that correlates to the narrative types of each plot. It was like what Hollywood producers would decades later call a "high concept," a one-line description of a plot under the category mystery (the suggestions each function as both before and after plotlines and base plotlines): "A [the code for the male protagonist] sells his shadow for an inexhaustible purse."[24]

Taken as a list of what Cook calls "suggestions," not formula, the plotto method functions as a combinatorial system that generates story ideas. Some of Cook's suggestions seem unintentionally Surrealist; for example, "1398 A. [Cook's code for a protagonist] investigating a psychic problem, finds that he must place his faith in so called 'automatic writing.'"[25] At its most abstract, the plotto method asked writers to follow a series of steps to create a story: Decide on a main character with a certain characteristic (choosing from a relatively large set of options); then, put the character in a specific situation (choosing from a list of suggestions); and, finally, choose a resolution (from an index of possibilities). The general themes were organized under clichéd phrases: Love's Beginnings; Love's Misadventures; The Marriage Proposal; Love's Rejection; Craftiness; Simulation; Mystery; and, many more.[26] In E. L. Doctorow's *Ragtime*, set at the same time as Brown's years as a popular writer, the budding-filmmaker character invents one of his own plotlines. He announces the plot summary as "The Thoughtful Butcher," alluding to the formulaic aspect of early cinema. Plotto is a system of often-shopworn plots and clichés that, in its comprehensiveness and systemization, resembles computer programs that promise to help writers produce scripts, or stories, by combining suggested plots, conflicts, and characters. A sampling of Cook's suggestions gives a sense of their breadth.

56

(38) (766)
B is convinced that several eligible men are in love with her ★ B is unaware of the fact that she is the victim of egotistical self-deception ★★ (65) (86) (184) (194a)

71

(**a**) (250) (1095) (101a)
A seeks to escape annoying manifestations of love ★ A, in order to escape annoying manifestations of love, pretends |1| that a wax figure, X, is his invalid wife; |2| pretends that he is married; |3| pretends that he is engaged to be married (2c)
(24a, b, c, d)

(**b**) (143) (145)
B, in order to escape annoying manifestations of love resorts to simulation (83) (84a) (58a, b, c)

1386

(**b**) (903) (ll43b)
A, a young artist in needy circumstances. has a picture rejected by a customer, B★ A, a needy young artist with an ordered picture left on his hands, discovers in the picture a map locating buried treasure ★★ (1394) (1399) (1403)

(21) Falling Into Misfortune Through Mistaken Judgment

1330

(853) (900-★) (1150)
A. dabbling in things he does not understand, seeks to accomplish wonderful results ★ A, involving himself recklessly in matters he

does not understand, succeeds only in making himself ridiculous ★★(231) (513) (900★-★★) (1111b)

1257

(721) (938)
A, a sculptor, models a bust of B (908) (1067-★) at B's order ★ B, displeased with the work of a sculptor, A, destroys a bust in an angry outburst ★★ (1256) (1395)

1143

(**a**) (778 ch A to A-5; 1217a ch A to A-5 & A-8 to A) (1144 ch A to A-5)
A is a connoisseur of precious stones and has a valuable collection ★ A. in order to protect his collection of valuable stones against robbery, displays replicas of them, comparatively worthless, to would-be customers ★★ (729) (1166a ch A to A-5)

(**b**) (903-★) (1370b ch A to GF-B) (1370c ch A to F-B)
A, an artist, is hired by B to paint a miniature; and into the miniature he is to weave an intricate series of lines which constitute a concealed map of great importance (903★-★★) (1444)

The plot lines capture the dramatic tension so common in Hollywood movies and pulp fiction before:

728

A digs a pit for a tiger trap and baits it with a quarter of bullock meat ★ A constructs a concealed trap, and a person dear to him, CH, falls into the trap and cannot escape (622 ch SN to CH) (591 ch B to CH; 179a ch B to CH) ★★ A constructs a deadly trap and, by accident, falls into it himself ★★★ (875b) (1319b ch A-2 to A)

(31) Living a Lonely, Cheerless Life and Seeking Companionship

910

(736 ch B to D-A) (1105 ch B to D-A)
A seeks happiness in being the pal of his daughter, D-A, and in making her happy ★ A is ultra old-fashioned, and his daughter, D-A, ultra modern ★★ (1067 ch B to D-A) (1151 ch B to D-A)[27]

As you can see above, before and after the plot lines the plotto method includes a series of numbers. The writer chooses one of those numbers from the group from the three listed before the line and one from the group after. The plotto method intends for the writer to make all the choices by reading all the choices first, not just by picking a number randomly and then deciding; as an experiment a writer could choose a number randomly. The potential author picks one of those lines from the three offered, and these have extra bits of plot, which he or she can decide to use or not to use. The numbers lead the writer to another index in the book, which supplies more specific situations as follows from these small and incomplete excerpts:

1027

A, hard pressed for money, is beguiled by the devil into an unwise proceeding.

1418a

A, while engaged in an important enterprise, drinks from an enchanted water and falls asleep.

1433

(b) A has a dream so vivid that it seems a part of his waking experience.[28]

Finally, taking one example these are the three choices for the writer to conclude the story:

1354a

A. discovers a magic method for realizing all his wishes but at the expense of years of his life for every wish granted.

1357

A. discovers a magic method that allows him to live forever, but his magic fails him and he dies.

1367

A. is investigating psychic phenomena; A. meets with disaster when illusion becomes reality through the overthrow of his reason.[29]

The intense mornings at the fiction factory "gym" would end after five or six hours of work using a less systematic prototype of Cook's plotto method (that he did not publish or complete until about a decade later). After a light lunch, they "just loafed" or had friends over. The two men made an unlikely pair: the one married, straitlaced, a teetotaler, looking older than his forty years, laughing at the foibles of the characters surrounding him with a "demonical toad chuckle" but always systematic and organized and, just wanting to live his rural midwestern life even in New York, detached from his decadent surroundings; the other young, gregarious, out for a good time, filled with wanderlust, always thirsty for a cold beer, and titillated and seduced by the adventure plots he was writing.[30] One of the newfound friends who would spend afternoons with Cook and Brown was an unemployed chorus girl who lived directly across the back alley on West 45th Street. Cook, portrayed by Brown as fatherly and innocent of the sexual tensions, tagged along on dates to Coney Island or a saloon, drinking ginger ale while Robert and his chorus girl drank ale. Later, as Cook hit the bed snoring and ready to awake before 6:00 A.M., Robert would watch the chorus girl's striptease across the alley as she pretended to get ready for bed with her lights on and the curtains up, discreetly noticing if Robert was watching. Brown claimed that both he and Cook were "monogamously married to our typewriters," but the story's overlapping plotlines (of writers living in a boxer's gym, literally sweating over their typewriting machines as they banged away at their stories, learning the ropes of plotmaking, and an unconsummated voyeuristic affair with a chorus girl) make the simple plot as steamy as a pulp fiction romance with a machine-age twist. After one month living with Cook and working in what Brown called the fiction factory, with its algorithmic instructions to crank out stories, Brown was able to increase the pace of his publishing and became a publishing juggernaut of his own.[31]

Just listing some of the titles Brown published in 1908 alone gives a sense of the breadth and quantity of his publications. These are Robert Carlton Brown's publications for *The Gray Goose* in 1908: "Peg's Trousseau," "The Eye of the Sunken Ship," "The Alley-Baby and the Forty Mothers," "The Great Black Way," "The Making of an Anarchist," "Bill Bean's Bump of Observation," "The Car and the Call," "Sensational Shirley Jones," "The Watchman at Falls Bridge," and many more in other pulps. Although from a contemporary perspective Brown seems unbelievably productive, it was not unusual for the select group of pulp writers to write more than a million words a year.[32] The challenge was learning how to write that much, that fast, and with high enough quality that editors, who were publishing the likes of O. Henry, Willa Cather, or Edgar Rice Burroughs, would publish it.

In the fall of 1908, Frank Munsey, the owner of the Munsey publishing empire, took an interest in Robert's career and decided to send him to London. Robert brought his mother, Cora, with him to England and Europe, and Cora continued to cheerlead and coach Robert as he wrote and published. He also had wanted to bring his fiancée, whom he had met while boarding in her house in Madison, Wisconsin, while attending one year of college before dropping out to start earning a living as a writer.

His fiancée's family insisted that Robert return to Madison first and get married before they lived together in London or anyplace else. Brown left for London without his fiancée, and later, at the end of his stay in England and tour of Europe, he returned to Madison and got married.

Munsey wanted Robert to continue writing for the pulps and Munsey-owned newspapers, especially the *Boston Journal*, which he had recently bought and wanted to turn into a cash cow. He also wanted Robert to continue his informal learn-as-you-go pulp writing education. Robert was sent to work with a team of writers based in London to learn what they then called, in English newspapers, "feuilleton" or serialized stories. The French were also using the term to refer to a genre of writing at which Robert had already proven himself successful. The feuilleton meant short column-filling pieces of epigrams, literary trifles, and joke-like squibs. After spending nearly a year in London, he learned more about the serialized form and he added the experience to his growing catalogue of set-places and detailed descriptions. Among the most important of the London-based writers was Elizabeth Miller. She influenced Brown greatly as a writer and also in terms of his politics and personal life. Miller (known among her chums as Mabel) was famous for an essay she wrote at the turn of the century explaining the absurdity of a set of protocols insisting that women ride sidesaddle.[33] In clear and straightforward terms she argued that the woman should decide to ride the horse any way she chose, not follow some archaic notion of propriety. The whole question might now seem trivial, but it reflects the cultural shift occurring in parallel to the political suffragist movement. Pointing to the arbitrary constraints of a paternalistic culture, the "new woman" movement had emerged in the last decade of the nineteenth century, and in the first two decades of the twentieth century it was an increasingly mainstream perspective. As the movement influenced popular culture, it also became, in turn, a consumerist-feminism that shared a *Cosmo*-girl attitude toward issues like "Where Is the Source of Beauty?"[34] In the article with that title, Miller answers that inner beauty and contentment make the difference, and the older woman is often more beautiful than one whose face betrays youth's lack of age-won wisdom. The popular magazines became one of the major venues for this criticism of Victorian patriarchal values. They portrayed heroines as economically independent with jobs of their own, self-reliant, physically active, often divorced or single, and, to a lesser extent, sexually aware. The young Brown was getting his education.

All of this independence was often couched in romantic adventure stories. The titles of Miller's many novels captured both of these aspects of the "new woman" attitude. A small selection of these suggestive titles, somewhere between Harlequin romances and more daring perspectives, is instructive: *His Forbidden Wife* (1920), *Her Mad Infatuation* (1924), *In Love with Herself* (1927), *Temporary Wife* (1932), *Circus Lady* (1935), *No Man's Daughter* (1936). Her self-confident heroines and emotional relationship-centered plots make her work a precursor to what critics, often dismissively, now call "chick lit," and for Brown they were a clear model of his writing, especially in the wildly popular stories about a young heroine that he started publishing in 1912. Miller's stories often included the stock characters of modern romance like the young divorcée trying to warn her inexperienced friend to avoid the handsome ne'er-do-well, and Brown borrowed this "new woman" feminism to build characters in his fiction; he was less interested in the vestiges of romance and fashion than in the character's motivation, as in many of Miller's stories.

In 1908 and 1909, Miller published in *The Argosy*, *The Scrap Book*, *The All-Story Magazine*, *The Live Wire*, *Railroad Man's*, and various newspapers. All of these were Munsey magazines, and she tended to tailor the articles to the niche audiences of each of these venues; so, *The Scrap Book* had an audience of women interested in "I Must Not Weep" (November 1907), while *Railroad Man's* had an audience of men interested in railroad stories like her "On the 'Eureka.'" (August 1908). Gender identification of the narrators of these stories and articles was fluid, and, although Miller did not use any, the pen names helped writers address different audiences. Brown was instructed to also publish in these magazines, and he also recognized how Miller's perspective (and gender identification) shifted depending on the audience. This was somewhat similar to Bill Cook's use of a female-sounding name when publishing in specific magazines or on topics thought to appeal to women only. Robert started to think of stories with strong and lithe female protagonists; one idea that started to percolate in Robert's mind began with a young girl who functions autonomously and daringly to solve crimes and rescue herself, and with whom the reader identifies. He also started to think of stories that dealt with disguise, murder, drugs, and just a hint of sexuality, but the major lessons Brown took away from his time in London was how to write serialized stories, as well as the feminism of his friends.

Benefiting from Mabel's influence and her incredible productivity, Robert wrote serials, and many short stories, for Munsey's *Argosy* and *The Gray Goose* and various newspapers, including "Sailing in Circles." He also wrote a now lost novel, *Bramble Hill*, which became his first, and one of his two, unpublished manuscripts. Mabel and Bob understood that they were writing for what they called in England at the time readies, scratch, or cash, and the group saw their typewriters as readies machines printing out money per word. Perhaps a less explicit lesson from his stay in London concerned the publishers' increasing use of new technologies for the British papers. Harmsworth's *Daily Mail*, used telegraphic means to collect stories from its New York office and, more important, to allow the paper to print an edition in Paris. These transmissions included not only text but also pictures. Brown would remember this use of technology, as he dreamed of a time when one could beam all literature wirelessly around the world. Frank Munsey, famous as a miserly and cutthroat businessman, whom one commentator claimed that "nobody liked," had long before used high-speed printing presses to print on pulp paper; this method drove the price of a magazine down from twenty-five cents to ten cents.[35] The push toward increased efficiency eventually led to electric transmissions of news, and that, in turn, would lead to radio programming and later television. The very genesis of the pulps ultimately spelled the demise of the printed versions of pulp fiction by the late 1940s, with radio, television, and movies taking over those pulp-type stories. In 1909, the transmission system reinforced the reach and power of the booming newspaper and magazine businesses, especially including Frank Munsey's businesses, rather than suggested a system that would eventually shift the fiction business empires away from the printed magazines and papers.

While Brown was still in England, he started to publish in *Pearson's Magazine*, the publication that had published Upton Sinclair, George Bernard Shaw, Maxim Gorky, and H. G. Wells. Brown's detective stories would follow the exploits of a distinctly American version of Sherlock Holmes. In reference to that American heritage of the detective genre, he named the protagonist Poe. The titles of Brown's own short stories suggest the recurring motifs of stunts, miracles, tricks, exoticism, and mystery: "A Sleep-Walking Stunt" (*The Gray Goose*, May 1909), "A Ten-Dollar Miracle" (*Munsey's*, June 1909), "The Handle to My Name" (*The Argosy*, October 1909), and many more.

After leaving London, Robert returned to Madison, Wisconsin, as planned, intending to marry his sweetheart, the niece of Chauncey Williams, the publisher who served as a cultural-father figure for Brown in Chicago. There was some confusion about which niece he intended to marry. When he arrived, Katrina Fox insisted that she was engaged to marry Robert. She produced the beautifully bound book, *House of Content*, that Robert had written for her as proof that he had proposed only to her. Robert liked this scenario very much. Cornelia Lillian, the second-oldest Fox sister, known as Lillian, also insisted that she was engaged to marry Robert. The mothers of both Robert and the Fox sisters intervened, and they sided with Cornelia Lillian's claim; they argued with Katrina but in the end insisted that Robert marry Lillian. In any case, the younger sister eventually bitterly consented to let her sister marry Robert, and Brown was married to Cornelia Lillian Fox in 1909. Phil Spooner, the son of one of Wisconsin's U.S. senators at the time, was the best man, and, although it was a big, elegant wedding with distinguished guests, the groom walked down the aisle in a tuxedo he'd borrowed from a fellow writer from New York. Another of the Fox sisters, Anna Myra, traveled to Europe with the newlyweds.

After getting married and going on their honeymoon in London and Europe, they returned to New York. In the winter of 1910, Robert increased his productivity in writing stories and ended his failed business partnership with Davis. In the spring of 1910, Lillian had to have two operations for appendicitis and "complicated female trouble," and Robert had to nurse her back to health slowly over three months. After her recovery, Lillian was eager to start painting, and she was as interested in the art scene as was her husband. She started to explore what the city had to offer, but with the summer's heat, she and Robert desperately wanted to get away from the sweltering asphalt. They planned a camping trip to Far Rockaway, where they could spend all day, and night, at the beach. They expected to spend most of August camping and enjoying the beach, but they both got sunburned, and Robert's many ailments from the sojourn cut the vacation short to three days. Robert joked sardonically that he suffered from "varicose veins, gout, chilblains, bad legs, foot trouble, and several allied complaints. Hardly able to crawl, but we had our vacation. Thank God!"[36]

Instead, on July 29, 1910, they went to Coney Island. They met Frederick Arthur Dominy, a fellow writer and mentee of Bill Cook's, and talked about old times and the current writing business. Dominy wrote about hunting and practical guides for outdoorsmen with a focus on the undeveloped areas of Long Island. His "Shooting the Wily Snipe" describes crouching in a blind waiting for the snipe the way Brown described pub crawls, studio visits, and Coney Island as "a whole lot of fun."[37] Brown wrote to Bill Cook, whom he called Uncle Billie in that letter, and recounted the (fictionalized) scene of the trip to Coney Island. He describes how "Dominy had his fortune told by a lady who assured him that a dark woman was on his trail, that a fair-haired female would do him dirt, that a cross-eyed wench was laying for him and that a mulatto had a brick in her mitten awaiting his slightest advance. Dominy said he was very sorry, that it must be somebody else, he'd left his harem at home. Truth, Billie, so help me, as I never tell the same lie twice."[38]

In the same letter to Cook, Brown confessed that he would continue to write short stories rather than switch to writing for the stage or movies. That decision probably meant that he would not ask to write the treatments for the movies, or the play, adapted from his stories. If he had written those early scripts, his life might have taken a different course. Often the early scriptwriters eventually became producers or directors. He might have moved to Hollywood in the late 1910s instead of the late 1930s. Perhaps if he had moved to Hollywood and joined the film industry, he never would have associated with the political and artistic radicals of the Village, but he decided to keep exploring literary pursuits even as his writing experiments would keep confronting the newer technologies like movies, television, and other machines. He later claimed that he had "always been movie-minded," but he had not yet entered the movie industry.[39] He was on the cusp of the movie industry. Although he eventually wrote prose short stories about the movies appearing in theaters each week, he never wrote a script or made a movie. Instead, he would take that movie-mindedness with him to his later modernist avant-garde work.

In the same letter to Cook, Brown gossiped that Howard Dwight Smiley, a fellow writer and, like Cook, from rural Marshall, Michigan, had written to Brown asking for money. Although Brown felt insulted by the request, did not give Smiley the money, never answered the letter, and ended the friendship, the incident also indicates that other writers considered Brown successful enough to ask him for money. Robert, at this time only around twenty-five years old, published "Plot Your Progress Curve," in *Everybody's Magazine*; it was an article that summarizes his life and many accomplishments. Soon Robert had made enough money from writing to leave New York in the early spring of 1911. He first traveled south, with his wife and mother in tow, through Alabama, with a stop to visit his writing colleague and old friend Berton Braley, who was visiting the Fairhope single tax colony (a community founded on a cooperative structure that would influence Robert's thinking a quarter-century later). After the stop at Fairhope, they traveled west to New Orleans.

In the middle of what tourists now call the French Quarter, and what was called then the Creole Quarter, they learned what it meant to experience Creole cuisine, drink French wine (instead of beer), and absorb the romantic charms of the architecture and markets; he thought of the extended visit as research on the scenes and scenarios for his pulp stories. For living accommodations, he rented rooms across from the Old Absinthe House on Bourbon Street, and, for writing, a studio above a restaurant near Old Ursuline Convent. With his mother, if not Lillian, he also became particularly interested in food markets, produce, and the famous cooking; soon Robert and Cora, his mother, became gourmands and appreciators of the gumbo, Creole dishes, crabs, and French wines at Antoine's and La Louisiane. They became so fascinated by cooking and recipes that they bought up the remainder of the signed copies of Lafcadio Hearn's *Gombo Zhèbes: Little Dictionary of Creole Proverbs* (1885) and gave them as gifts. Hearn, famous as a popular writer who captured, and helped create, the image of New Orleans, especially the Creole Quarter, as a place more similar to a Caribbean capital than a southern city in the United States, also must have served as a model for Robert and Cora for the type of cookbooks that they would start publishing decades later with prose descriptions of customs and cultural practices surrounding the recipes; they started files of recipes and descriptive histories of cuisines and foods.

While in New Orleans, Robert began thinking of ways to incorporate the city into his works as a setting for mystery. Here is how the autobiographical experience appears later in his fiction as the "quaint French Market, which he loved. Passing slowly through the fish-market first," he soon found "fat Pompanos, chubby 'Reds,' and beautiful, shapely Sea-Trout. Tubs of crabs, crawfish, and turtles made him hungry for a good Creole gumbo." He described the market as this "little down-at-the-heels public trading-place in the Creole Quarter." As he walked through the market, "looking for lagniappe," the free tastes or a small extra gift you get when you buy something, he saw "piles of green plantains, cocoanuts [*sic*], coops of chickens, and heaps of green vegetables, all mixed together into a crisp, colorful, peppery Southern salad." Cutting through Chartres Street, Robert Brown would have "sauntered along absorbing the atmosphere," like a character in one of his stories, "stopping to enjoy glimpses of green courtyards through doorways, and finding picturesque street-scenes unexpectedly at corners; quaint iron-bordered balconies and dark, foreign charcoal-shops."[40] Robert decided to scout for other locales for his fictional character, Christopher Poe, to visit.

He went off alone to Mexico and then to the Caribbean. Lillian and Cora slowly made their way back to New York. After a short stay in Mexico City with colorful bullfights, cockfights, and *señoritas* (some of whom were being pimped by their mothers for a few *pesos* a night), he traveled to Cuernavaca as the Mexican Revolution against Porfirio Díaz heated up and spread. Here is a fictionalized account of his travels in the Poe stories.

> A minute later the dusty train came to a stop at a little adobe village consisting of a hollow square of baked mud houses glaring in the sun; a scattering of maimed, ragged natives running along beside the train, begging piteously in high-pitched voices, "Un centissime, señor, un centissime I" and a handful of native women with large, shapely small-necked water-bottles of pottery, catching scalding water from the waste-pipe of the high-shouldered steam-engine.[41]

Brown visited a wealthy German-born painter there, supposedly named Richard Nord (although no records exist of such a painter), whose profits from the colorful market scenes that tourists bought allowed him to buy a *hacienda* with a large crew of laborers. When the Zapatistas came to take over the *hacienda*, Nord and Brown jumped on the train that was leaving the station. As they looked back at the town, they saw the English teashop owner shot dead in the street. Seeing the woman lying in the dirt, Brown decided that it was time to leave Mexico. He decided to spend time in Cuba, Santo Domingo, and Puerto Rico (where he visited his wife's relatives, who had bought timberland there).

He thought of these travels to the Caribbean as another World's Fair with a carnival celebration, catching "gigantic fish," marveling at the interior's natural and cultural wonders. Apparently, political turmoil followed Brown to Puerto Rico, but this time as something of a farce with one president seeming to assassinate the next every day, and visitors watching this unfold while sipping champagne. Most likely, Robert and other foreigners talked about the political turmoil from *the year before* rather than witnessed any executions or inaugurations. As he made his way back to New York, Lillian traveled to Holland in September 1910 to study painting in Middelburg, Zeeland, Holland, at a time when a second-generation Hague School naturalism was still the dominant force in art before De Stijl modernism moved art toward abstraction. Her aesthetic concerns, much like those of the painters of the Chase School in New York, focused on conveying light within an improvisational impressionism. Her interest in painting would lead her family on at least one more European adventure in a couple of years.

Once again back in New York City, Brown would play poker in his writing studio all night with his friends Berton Braley (who later chronicled the life of freelance magazine writers), Leslie Quirk (a popular writer who judged his literary success by the ability to sell his stories), and Horatio Wilson (who was connected to the wealthy Guggenheim family through his wife, Rosalind Mae Guggenheim). Rosalind was also Brown's writing student who later published under the pseudonym Jane Burr. Other writers, like Don Marquis and Homer Croy, sometimes sat in on games. Brown would regularly lose, and his losses would motivate him to write the next day a "six thousand word story and sell it . . . for a cent a word," leaving him with a profit instead of a loss. The losses at cards kept him from gambling in his work. Instead of trying to get as much as ten cents at better magazines, he decided not to risk wasting time with rejections. By this time, Robert was writing for a larger audience than a young vaudeville writer, Cecil B. DeMille, who was not yet in the film business; when DeMille left New York in 1913, to make his first moving picture in a Hollywood garage, he marked the start of the fiction-writing world's slow shift from the East to the West Coast. When Brown later returned to writing popular fiction in the 1930s, he moved to Hollywood and looked up his old writing chums, who were then producers. With his success, he started to act as an agent for others, including his mother, Cora, who was selling articles and preparing for her later career as a cookbook writer. He also became a friend and mentor to Ann Watkins. Watkins was Theodore Dreiser's literary secretary when Dreiser was editing the progressive *Delineator* magazine.

Watkins later became a high-profile literary agent for Sinclair Lewis. According to Brown, Ann would call him to get rid of the pestering Fritz Krog, a protégé of Dreiser's. After Brown's intervention, Krog, desperately in love with Brown's wife, Lillian, started following Brown around with a gun to scare, threaten, or perhaps kill Brown so that Krog could marry Lillian. It seems like fiction, but Dreiser wrote about Krog's obsession with Ann, and his subsequent insanity, in "Emmanuela," with the title character a thinly veiled version of Ann Watkins.[42] Once again Brown found himself living in a reality with the contours of fiction. Robert traveled to Europe to spend time with his wife, and soon Lillian was pregnant.

In 1911, the couple decided to have the baby in Madison so that her family could help. While in Wisconsin, Robert learned to grow tomatoes on his in-laws' farm and would, more than two decades later, during the Great Depression, write a cookbook about growing one's own vegetables. On July 11, 1911, Cornelia Brown was born. During the birth and Lillian's recovery, Robert spent time with Katrina, his wife's younger sister, whom he had courted as a freshman in college. They shared the same fantasy of running away together to some South American retreat, but in the end, Robert's new family moved back to New York (and he never saw Katrina again). Robert's immaturity and irresponsibility seemed out of character to those who knew him as a conscientious old pro at writing genre stories. His Christopher Poe detective stories were a critical and popular success, generating a loyal following and a bestselling series and novelization. Even with a small family to support, he continued to want to try his hand at painting and visual art, but his wife repeatedly reminded him of his obligations.

One can imagine Brown's having his main character exclaiming, "Opium! Imagination! Murder!" as the banker-sleuth, Christopher Poe, solved yet another case with help from Mr. Burns, his sidekick. Robert would lift his hands from the typewriter keys, read a few lines aloud, and keep typing. The keys would catapult through the air the sweat dripping from his forehead. His fingers seemed to move as fast as a machine. Strange words and phrases would pop onto the paper with each machine-gun burst of sound: "hoptalk," "burnese," "white stuff," and "brassing up the rag." Reams of completed pages would sit to one side, and as he finished one page, he would quickly grab a new piece of paper from an unused ream. His spacebar-flattened thumbs, smudged with black ink, pounded out a rhythm to the return bell's melodies. Robert would often chuckle to himself that his readers would soon know much about the tools, tricks, and procedures of the private detective but nothing about the writer's formulae, machines, and techniques.

Robert's short stories about the millionaire banker-detective received good reviews when they were republished as a novel, *The Adventures of Christopher Poe*, in 1913, which quickly became a bestseller. The reviews' descriptions of the book—"ingenious yarns, with some surprises and any number of hair-breadth escapes"—made it the type of book to "while away the time on a tedious journey, or keep the reader awake and attentive until late into the evening."[43] His most famous banker-sleuth would offhandedly comment on why the criminal might have a "dead-white face," by explaining to the perplexed police detectives, that "maybe he took burnese or the white stuff. If that's the case, we may hear some hoptalk somewhere. Those gervers often let something slip in brassing up the bundle of rag."[44] The drug slang for cocaine, burnese; for heroin, white stuff; gerver is a safe-cracker; and preparing the opium, brassing up the rag, makes the underworld an exotic locale and also suggests a series of secret codes that the sophisticated detective, reader, or writer should know. In fact, Poe uses similar shorthand to communicate with his sidekick/fellow banker, Mr. Burns.

Brown also started thinking about his other, even more popular serial, about a spunky waif, Mary Craig, who, like an earlier version of Nancy Drew, gets caught up in threatening action and adventure. He was now among the top-three bestselling fiction writers in the United States. Although his Mary stories became popular movies starting in 1912, Brown misremembered in the late 1940s the Poe stories' also becoming movies, but there is no record linking those stories individually or the character's name or the specific plots to any silent film (but whether there was a film made from his stories remains an open mystery).

Others have illustrated how modernist writers read pulp fiction detective novels for inspiration. For example, while William Faulkner was writing *Sanctuary* and even *Light in August*, he was likely drawing on pulp fiction for inspiration, as he was, at the time, an avid reader of pulp magazines like *Black Mask*.[45] It is much less common to find one author *writing* both avant-garde modernist texts and pulp fiction. "The hard-boiled male, a relatively positive and stable site of reader identification, becomes celebrated for his rugged individualism and opposition to all forms of collectivity, whether existing or imaginary" in hard-boiled novels and "modernist works drawing on that tradition."[46] Brown saw himself as enacting the model of individuality that his fictional characters represented when he argued that one should "be free verse."[47]

Christopher Poe, on the boards of banks, solves crimes that involve his banks, but unlike the stereotype of the dull, unimaginative banker, Poe utilizes arcane facts about every criminal subculture and seedy neighborhood to put himself in the middle of the criminal action. Likewise, Brown resembled Poe: Robert had increasing wealth from publishing stories, his success in the stock market, his travels, and his voluminous encyclopedic knowledge. They also shared an interest in code systems. Christopher Poe, on his way to the South Station, wires a message, in cipher, to his sidekick and fellow millionaire banker, Mr. Burns.

> Canvas opium dives catering to foreign criminals. Watch for tall, white-faced Englishman with close-cropped hair, tenor, decided stoop. Send Volume H and suit of slops by my man to Grand Central at 11:12. I'll run across you.[48]

In his travels, Robert thought of himself as a collector, more like an ethnographer or participant-observer than a tourist; rather than visit exotic locales with all of the comforts of home and without living among the people, Brown traveled to absorb and digest cultures and customs: living in, not just visiting, places. Using the common trope of popular fiction of the era, to *exoticize* New York City (and cities in general), the popular writers applied an explicit Orientalism in order to romanticize the huge migration of people from rural to urban areas as well as the enormous numbers of immigrants giving the cities character. O. Henry, the most famous short-story writer in the United States (who chose the pen name perhaps to hide his past as a convicted bank embezzler), coined the phrase "Baghdad-on-the-Subway" to describe New York in one of his short stories first published in *McClure's*, "A Madison Square Arabian Night," and unwittingly marked the effort to imagine the city as the setting for criminal intrigue, colorful markets, street performers and hawkers, the strong smell of foods from a thousand places, and crowded, chaotic adventures.[49] For Brown, Orientalist urban fantasies meant wanting to live as cosmopolitan globe-glider and become exotic and mysterious while delving into romantic, irrational adventures. Brown did not seek to patronize and, literally, conquer these marginalized characters, but to become one of the wanderers on an adventure to a thousand places.

In the *Poe* novel, all the chapters or episodes are about the same length—averaging 30 pages, with 200 words per page (or about 6,000 words); at the current rate at the time, Robert was making the equivalent of more than $2,500 for each story or close to the equivalent of $35,000 for the whole series. (That doesn't include any of the other series or short stories he was publishing in that same year.) The novel form sold for $1.25, equivalent to more than $25 today. This was not an inexpensive book; Brown profited from its sales both when it appeared in the American edition of *Pearson's* and also as a separately published novel. Brown was particularly pleased that, when a British pulp published his Poe stories, they were greeted favorably as the American lineage of the Sherlock Holmes stories (which were still being serialized throughout the years Brown was publishing Poe). *Pearson's* was a more prestigious magazine than other pulps, like *Argosy*, to begin with, and publishing in both the U.K. and the United States added to the prestige. The U.S. *Pearson's* would sometimes run its stories in other U.K. magazines, like *The Royal* or *Novel*, but Brown's name does not appear in any of these pulps from 1910 through 1915. However, it could well have appeared in some British venue. He also published some of the Poe stories in *College World*, another New York–based pulp.

Christopher Poe's adventures began as serialized stories from 1910 through the publication of the novelization of the series and finally with a couple more stories, after the novel's ending, that appeared up to 1915. The plots of each episode follow the same formula. First, the crime is described in O. Henry–esque third-person reporter's style. Here is a passage from an O. Henry story first.

> Pulling out from the wall a folding-bed, Jimmy slid back a panel in the wall and dragged out a dust-covered suit-case. He opened this and gazed fondly at the finest set of burglar's tools in the East. It was a complete set, made of specially tempered steel, the latest designs in drills, punches, braces and bits, jimmies, clamps, and augers, with two or three novelties, invented by Jimmy himself, in which he took pride. Over nine hundred dollars they had cost him to have made at— [elision of the fabricator's or store's name in the original, perhaps to make it seem like a censored police report], a place where they make such things for the profession.[50]

Compare that passage with this one from the Poe stories:

> His inspection produced the astonishing facts that the outer door had been drilled through, evidently by hand, in just the spot where the tumblers could be thrown; but the metal of the inner door, by far the more important of the two, had been melted by a powerful electric current. It was a curious combination, wholly unprecedented. (Brown, 1913, 9)

Both passages describe the thief's process and the precise mechanisms of the safe, list the mechanisms and tools, and insinuate the virtuosity of the professional safecracker. Next, Poe announces in cryptic form a hypothesis. Then, after these descriptive set-ups, Poe and his sidekick set out to solve the case. They describe in great detail colorful street scenes, markets, and places. The investigation may take them to a few cities or to various neighborhoods in Manhattan. During the investigation the reader also collects the facts (e.g., some ashes in an ashcan near a back door) and probably starts quietly guessing how it all fits together. Finally, confronting the criminal usually involves some action or fight until the criminal is subdued. As the dénouement, the details of the crime and steps to Poe's solution are explained to the criminal, sidekick, and police.

> He cut through the alarm plate in the outer door of the safe, and sent in the proper signal to the insurance company at five-fifteen. In penetrating that plate before signaling the insurance company to set the alarm, he knew the opening of the safe could not be registered. He had then gone to work on the inner door with his electric drill, which he had concealed in his pail.[51]

In a similar manner, O. Henry describes how the safecracker performed the deed.

> In a minute Jimmy's pet drill was biting smoothly into the steel door. In ten minutes—breaking his own burglarious record—he threw back the bolts and opened the door. (O. Henry, 172)

Each episode of the Poe stories ends with a happy return home, and sometimes one additional revelation. Although both O. Henry and Brown mastered the form, had similar prose styles, used details to add naturalism and realism to their writing, and made a fortune selling stories, now middle school English literature anthologies and classes include only O. Henry stories. Robert Brown is missing.

What happened to Brown? His fame and influence as a writer earned him a place in *Who's Who* of 1912, the same year that the first Manhattan Horn & Hardart Automat opened. The Automat, an instant and enduring success for decades through the early 1960s, allowed the customer to choose the food he or she wanted, say a slice of pie, from a restaurant-size vending machine that was a wall of automatically opening small containers with windowed doors, continually refilled from within. Robert, both fascinated by the mechanization and also repelled by the homogenization, visited frequently until he left the States. Although both hugely successful in 1912, both Automat and Robert Brown are mostly forgotten for similar reasons: The technologies that made them success stories—that the user could conveniently and inexpensively pick up a mass-produced pulp magazine or slice of pie—also pushed the artisan (writer and cook) behind the scenes and out of the profit stream.

In the midst of Brown's success, *McClure's* editor, Charles Dwyer, bought Brown's *What Happened to Mary* serialized stories about a young girl's struggles to make her way and succeed in life without the help of any paternal protection from parents or husband. The editors and publisher loved the idea and thought it perfect for a revamped *Ladies' World*. Bought in 1912 by McClure Publications, publishers of *McClure's* magazine, where Willa Cather was publishing her stories and serving as an editor until 1912, *Ladies' World* became a full-fledged magazine with full-color covers with the success of Brown's stories. Dwyer, who had become an editor at *Ladies' World* in 1905, and Frank Lewis, who had recently bought a controlling share of the magazine from Hearst Publications, helped negotiate the deal with Thomas Edison's production team, including Charles Brabin, the producer, and Horace G. Plimpton, the scriptwriter for the films, the latter of whom, like Robert Brown, had various

The *What Happened to Mary* series was simultaneously released as serialized movies and in *Ladies' World* magazine.

pen names and spellings of his name in print. Dwyer mentions Plimpton in his description of the deal but leaves Robert Brown out of the story.[52] Brown pulled together the first installment, and, after that issue appeared, the editors approached a producer, Horace G. Plimpton, at the Thomas A. Edison Kinetoscope Company. The editors and producers talked about a scheme to "tie in" the magazine's publication with the release of the films, and later some historians would consider the *What Happened to Mary* deals the first example of a tie-in.[53]

Sales of the magazine reached a million copies a month when his

"What Happened to Mary" mystery stories became a runaway success in film, with screenings in 20,000 theaters, and as a play. It singlehandedly allowed *McClure's* to convert their pulp magazine into a slick or smoothie with a four-color cover and drawings by artists, especially Gibson. To put the circulation numbers in perspective, remember that the total population of New York City at the time was only 4.7 million, and the total U.S. population was 92 million. The magazine was reaching at least 1 percent of the total U.S. population directly, and if it landed in family households, or was shared, then the impact was far greater; it's safe to say that *Ladies' World*'s impact was greater than that of later women's magazines. The magazine was sold for five cents a copy, the equivalent of about a dollar today. The tie-in also allowed the publisher, McClure's, to function as a production company through the 1910s, not only with Edison but with other studios as well. McClure's *Ladies' World* suddenly represented the ethos of feminine self-confidence, much as the reimagined *Cosmopolitan* did starting in the late 1960s. The subtitle of another story printed in the same September issue as episode two of the Mary stories read: "But She Beat The Men at Their Own Game"; another column's title asks, "How Shall I Do My Hair?"[54] Although much of the magazine is filled with fashion advice, homemaking rules, an advice column, and advertisements geared toward homemakers, mothers, and women's beauty products, the possessive in the magazine's title tells the subtle story. This was not a world of pretty maternal ladies; this was a ladies' world.

The August 1912 issue included Brown's first installment and advertised,

> ONE HUNDRED DOLLARS FOR YOU IF YOU CAN TELL
> "WHAT HAPPENED TO MARY"

The already fine line between marketing and fiction writing had disappeared in what one film historian calls a "lowly sales gimmick," and another described the contest as an ideologically constrained invitation for "viewers to fantasize within a serial's given diegetic parameters."[55] The contest continued for all of the subsequent issues. The second episode, in the September 1912 issue, is illustrated with production stills from the movies. That issue's contest announcement asks for "not more than three hundred words."[56] The two-page spread opening the story with the movie images was unique to magazine publishing at the time, and the story's location, pages 12 and 13 with a continuation on page 34, would get readers immersed in the magazine before, during, and after reading the latest episode.

Each film chapter was released nearly simultaneously with the corresponding episode in the magazine. With one story per month, the producers explicitly sought to keep the audience hooked even if they did not end each movie with a cliffhanger. The machinations that created the deal for its staggered release with the films did not involve Brown except as the writer; and, once he realized that his exclusion from that process meant that he lost the rights to the story and, more important, to the movie's and play's profits, he was angered and motivated to become a founding member of the Authors' League of America. The movies and short stories, released in twelve one-reel episodes with one magazine story each month starting in August 1912, were huge box-office and publishing successes, but when Brown gave up the rights to the stories upon selling them to the magazine, he also gave up his rightful place in the history of the movie series' genesis, or, when mentioned in passing, he plays only a cameo role. To this day, writing and writers are too often thought of as freelancers rather than as involved in labor struggles with management. Robert wanted to protect the interests of those who actually produced the creative material.

The magazine promoted the stories with a slick full-color cover with striking drawings. The editors hired Charles Dana Gibson to draw a picture of the heroine in the style of his "Gibson" girls, self-reliant and confident with long hair as a symbol of her emancipation and bold sensuality. The weekly *Home Chat* in Britain would also release the stories in conjunction with the movies, and it marked an entirely new line of publicity tie-ins in the British market.[57] Brown's name appears with all of the stories in the later book collection, but his name did not appear with the stories until the third episode. Those first two stories are left unattributed; perhaps Fred Collins, the owner of *McClure's*, wrote the first stories himself and then hired Brown to write the rest? Or, perhaps the editor and publishers wanted to, at first, stress the reality of the far-fetched stories with the seeming window-on-the-world movie; movies had a more anonymous production process, and only later did the magazine decide to put an author's name on the printed stories and market them as by Robert Carlton Brown (on the covers of all the subsequent issues). Because the only extant copies of three of the movies are from the British market, the credits mention *Home Chat* and Thomas A. Edison Company, but not *Ladies' World*. It's not clear how the negotiations for the U.K. rights to the stories played out, but Brown does not mention the stories appearing there under his name as he does with the Poe stories, and he was rightfully angry over not getting paid for British syndication.

The fast-paced Mary stories follow the life of an heiress, kidnapped as an infant and raised on the fictional location of Moseses Island by the kidnapper until Mary eventually escapes to New York City (as a fourteen-year-old) from the "dull slavery" of her tormentor and lives through a series of melodramatic adventures, mistaken identities, lucky coincidences, and detective work.[58] Although it's unknown to Mary, the reader soon knows that a relative of hers arranged for the kidnapping so that he would be next in line for the large inheritance. The twist is that he has to wait until the date when Mary would turn twenty-one (even though she is assumed dead), as specified in her grandfather's will. Five years after Mary escapes, the relative tracks her down in New York City and incriminates her for a crime she did not commit. At age nineteen, she returns to the island; eventually the entire scheme is uncovered, and Mary gets her inheritance. She makes plans to sail off on new adventures, and in one final twist, Mary uses some of her money to free her relative from prison even after she learns that he was trying to cheat her out of her inheritance and was involved in her kidnapping years before.

After she escapes, Mary's adventure story includes her getting a starring role when a play's star unexpectedly collapses and then receiving rave reviews when the play opens. She works as a secret agent carrying a vital letter to England, attending a party with a princess and other aristocrats in England. She is accused of stealing a valuable necklace and then, cleared of that crime, sets off to solve another crime. She holds the would-be thief under arrest with a revolver, learns she is an heiress, solves a couple more crimes, and leaves behind the stuffy house (but not the fortune) she inherited and a few transatlantic cruises thrown in too. With the island's name, Moseses, suggesting the future role of the orphaned waif, Mary was allegorically leading her people (young, urban, struggling white-collar women) toward a narrative of financial independence (even if the final success was a *deus ex machina* of an inheritance).

Mary, like her readers and her author, dreams of escaping from her provincial surroundings to the big city. She is literally held captive on an island in Chesapeake Bay. Just before she makes her escape, she tells her dream to her only friend and teacher, a salty old sea captain. When "Cap'n Jogifer" tells Mary that she needs more schooling than either he or the local school can provide and that she will "need the schoolin' of life," Mary thrills at the thought of her life away from the island. She says, "I think of railroad trains and big buildings like you've shown me pictures of. I wouldn't like to always live here, see nothing but water, and go to the post office and fill dishes with ice cream."[59] She escapes not into the wild blue yonder but to a working life as a stenographer, with its advantages of consumerism. Her very first adventure after escaping from the island, and waiting for the train to the city, involves buying a hat. The scene reveals the aspirations, and fears, of many young women moving alone to work in offices and fend for themselves in the big city. Like Mary, these young women needed to act with cosmopolitan sophistication, even though they often had migrated from humble beginnings (figurative islands cut off from modern fashions) and they feared having their masquerades exposed as a fraud. The story of a poor waif successfully masquerading as more sophisticated than the small-town shopkeeper and clerks, for a price the poser cannot afford, still functions as a cliché in Hollywood movies. The cliché and morality tale now would have the masquerade lead to many trials and travails and ultimately reward a confession about her true, humble situation. Mary's story has a different message. The accidental lesson teaches Mary to play a role, to have fun, and to overcome her lack of experience as a free agent. Admittedly, Mary learns the pleasure of consumerism and looks like an earlier version of a character in *Sex in the City* buying shoes she can't afford.

> Confused by the array of headgear to select from, she tremblingly picked out a simple Panama and set it jauntily on her bronze coils of hair. The hat transformed her, adding just the needed touch. In that moment the saleswoman was certain of her customer's standing. Changing promptly to a manner almost servile, she asked,
>
> "Are you one of the young ladies from the yacht!"
>
> Mary blushed beneath her tan. It was positively intoxicating to be mistaken for one of the vacation people she sometimes saw sailing in splendid yachts in the bay. She had never realized before what a difference dress made.
>
> "How much is it?" she asked, disregarding the question and turning to select two hatpins from a display.
>
> "Twelve dollars," answered the saleswoman, with pride in the exclusive choice of her customer. The price took Mary's breath away, but she only changed color, and her hands did not tremble as she handed the ten-dollar bill and a five to the woman. Having received her change and purchased the hatpins, Mary started for the door, leaving Mr. Saltman and several clerks in blank surprise, for a twelve dollar hat was seldom sold in Truscott.[60]

As he did in many of his stories, Brown used these adventures to describe the scenes, and allure, of cities he knew well. Mary arrives in Manhattan, and "everything seemed strange, as though she were walking in a dream" and like "Alice in Wonderland, she passed on from one surprising sensation to another. The lights thrilled her, lured her, fascinated her." Mary would "wonder at the up rearing Flatiron Building and gasp at the height of the Metropolitan, with its little lights twinkling from high windows which must house fairies." The street sounds were overwhelming: "[B]ells clanged, teamsters shouted, autos tooted and screamed, newsboys yelled, and all to the rumbling accompaniment of rushing feet."[61]

She soon learns another life lesson and has her purse, containing her remaining money, snatched. A policeman catches the thief, but Mary says the purse is not hers after all and lets the woman thief go. She sees the desperation in the other woman's eyes and thinks of her own desperate situation. She then tries to find the woman to get some of her money back, but the thief disappears. Eventually, Mary gets a job as a typist taking dictation and in one famous scene catches a robber as he prepares to empty the office's safe. The scene's excitement takes for granted the role of the female protagonist overpowering the male criminal. The strong, smart, independent heroine still appears human, overcoming her fears and physical strain and not wanting to shoot the criminal accidentally. A more typical movie solution would have the female protagonist giving up the gun, unable to shoot the man, or having the gun go off accidentally, during a scuffle, killing the criminal. This narrative has a new woman able to fend for herself without stooping to the violent macho level of the criminal.

> Again they stood face to face. This time Dundon huddled against his desk, his teeth chattering, his eyes fixed wide in terror. Mary shifted the revolver to her left hand and opened and closed the fingers of her right in an effort to ease the cramp in them. A moment later she brushed the hand wearily across her face.
>
> Dundon took advantage of the movement. Knocking aside the revolver, he sprang at her. "Keep back!" cried Mary, striking at him with the pistol, and covering the electric button with her shoulders. "I'll shoot!" she screamed an instant later as Dundon's tense fingers bit into her arm. His other hand clutched her left wrist. She sprang to one side, knocking over the screen, and trying to throw Dundon against the porcelain washbasin. Clinging to the revolver, she fought with feline fierceness. Her muscles, hardened by the outdoor life on

> Moseses Island, were more than a match for Dundon's flabby biceps. Neither spoke, but both panted with the violent exertion.
>
> Mary prayed that the revolver would not go off. She clung to it chiefly to keep Dundon from gaining possession of it. Whirling about and straining to evade her frantic lunges, Dundon struggled to wrest the weapon from her.[62]

Brown's novelization, also a first, became a bestseller, but its status in cultural history depends on those serialized stories' serving as the premise for the first serialized movie melodramas with a strong female protagonist. Brown had nothing to do with the movie series or play, but the stories' success as play and movies made him wealthy and famous for a few years and earned him a footnote in film history. Olive Wyndham played the lead in the successful Broadway play, also titled *What Happened to Mary*, and Mary Fuller, who became one of the first matinee idols before she had a nervous breakdown and faded into obscurity, played the lead in the movie version. The movie producers did not like the feminism in the original stories, so the next shorter and less successful series they produced was about *Who Will Mary Marry?*

Although the pulp writing era of Brown's life continued until 1917, his immersion and psychological engagement flourished in the four years from 1910 through 1913. He started to drift away from that life and toward the radical and bohemian world of the artistic and literary vanguard. He had written short and long stories for just about all the contemporary magazines, both pulps and smoothies, and the names of the magazines in which he published suggest the breadth of topics as well as the quantity. He wrote in every genre from adventures for *Nick Carter* and *Diamond Dick* to highbrow verse for the *Century*; short stories and articles for *Everybody's*, *Harper's Weekly*, *Metropolitan*, *Hampton's*, *Broadway Life*, *Judge*, *Bohemian*, *Munsey's*, *Argosy*, *All-Story*, *Cavalier*, *Ocean*, *Scrap Book*, *Peoples*, *Gray Goose*, *Motion Picture Story Magazine*, *Moving Picture Stories*, *Saturday Evening Post*, *Photoplay*, *10 Story Book*, *Black Cat*, and all New York Sunday supplements; *Leslie's Weekly* and *Ladies' World*; and both the American and the British *Pearson's*.

On December 24, 1913, Lillian gave birth to their second child, Robert Carlton Brown III. He would later publish under the name Carlton Brown. With the growing family, Cora's father, Grandfather Brackett, moved in with them in their large house on the New Jersey Palisades in what would later be called the Grantwood Village artists' colony (near Ridgefield). It sat high up on the hills looking across to Grant's Tomb in

Manhattan. Cora continued publishing and was regularly placing stories in girls' magazines. Bob became a contributing editor of the magazine *The Masses* with his friend Max Eastman at the helm.

The multiple enterprises he dabbled in make the extent of Brown's wealth from fiction writing alone a bit of a mystery. On the one hand, Brown claimed to have written at least a thousand stories for fiction magazines, and he, and others who knew him, suggested he made a fortune as a writer—perhaps enough to make him one of the wealthiest writers of the day. On the other hand, his ability to write fiction might have led to exaggerated claims. If we look at the numbers more carefully, then perhaps his wealth and productivity will not seem so fantastic. If we assume that Brown inflated how many stories and articles he published, then we might find only a few hundred rather than a thousand. Keeping in mind that the pulps often paid only one penny for each word (but Brown sometimes got as much as five cents), and, finally, pegging his average words per journal nearer the low end of the range for a short story guideline of the time (i.e., between 9,000 words all the way up to nearly 70,000 words a story), then we can get a more accurate sense of Brown's wealth in the early 1910s. If one does the math, he easily earned a six-figure income over a decade that would average out to tens of thousands of dollars each year. Robert Brown was a very wealthy young man. Although it is likely that Berton Braley grossly exaggerated Brown's yearly income as between $20,000 and $40,000 a year (just under $400,000 to close to $800,000 a year in today's funds), Brown was making a yearly income of at least $200,000 in today's early-twenty-first-century funds, just from fiction writing, and probably three or four times that much. He earned much of the income before the modern federal individual income taxes and 1040 forms appeared in 1914. As a young man in his twenties and early thirties, making more than at least 90 percent of the population, he spent his fortune traveling; living the high life; collecting books and artifacts; renting apartments in Greenwich Village, New Orleans, Spain, and other places, eventually buying houses near and in the Grantwood Village artists' colony; and, after 1914, hiring someone to help him write the stories based on his outlines.

In a poetic description of fellow writers, and himself, working in the 1910s on *Moving Picture Stories* magazine, which published prose story versions of new movies (like soap opera magazines today), he describes how the writers' wives sometimes had to pick up the weekly check when one of the writers was too drunk. These same wives "sometimes substituted at the machine," to type the stories when one of the male writers was "too

H. L. Mencken was a pulp fiction magazine editor decades before he was known for his searing and skeptical journalism.

drunk to tell the typewriter keys apart." Whether this applied to Brown or not, the crucial phrase in his description of the situation was that "Nobody knew the difference. There wasn't any difference."[63] It is not simply that this situation existed, not simply that someone else helped write the stories or articles, not simply that women were doing the wash and writing the stories without credit, but also that Brown states this radical fact of modern writing. If you dig deep enough, then you will find not one author, but who knows how many.

When H. L. Mencken and George Jean Nathan took over *The Smart Set* they "bought as liberally" from Brown as *Top Notch* had, and some of those early issues contained the leading novelette, several stories, articles,

Brown wrote eleven pieces for the first issue of *Smart Set* using different *noms de plume.*

poems, and most of the epigrams—all totaled, eleven by Brown under different *noms de plume.* In 1932, twenty years later, when Nathan invited Brown to contribute to the first issue of *American Spectator,* he said, "Mencken and I depended a lot on your versatility when we had *The Smart Set.* If it hadn't been for your material I don't know how we'd have filled those first issues."[64]

Although *The Smart Set* was founded in 1900 by William d'Alton Mann, it was the years between 1914 and 1923, with Nathan and Mencken at the helm, when it became "a magazine of cleverness" and tried to appeal to a more sophisticated reader. They would later, in 1919, publish F. Scott Fitzgerald's first story. Under their leadership the magazine struggled to make money because "few people actually read the magazine," but that lack of financial success led Mencken and Nathan to cynically start popular pulps, including the seminal *Black Mask*, to fund their real interest.[65] Brown's association with Mencken, which was to last at least until the mid-1930s, led to his realizing the way popular writing could fund other types of writing—political or literary—that might not find a large audience. Mencken, famously contemptuous of genre fiction and popular tastes, was a successful pulp publisher who fed those popular tastes. He helped the young Brown recognize the value of a type of writing that might not sell as well, or at all. Because experimental writers also published in more popular mainstream magazines to make money for their less commercially successful work, Robert began to meet them and learn about this new modern type of writing. Ezra Pound mentions *Smart Set* magazine's call for "top-notch" work and that some issues were filled with "one hell of a lot of muck," in spite of the "muck."[66] Although he continued to publish for the pulps and worked for Mencken and Nathan on getting *The Smart Set* off the ground in 1914, Brown began drifting from the pulp fiction world toward the radical periodicals, bohemian social scene, progressive politics, and the literary experimentation of Greenwich Village. Robert was eager to live the adventures he had written about in the serialized stories.

He hoped that life was one World's Fair after another.

2
A Pulp Nonfiction Adventure Story
Once Upon a Time, 1886–1907

I Buy, Sell & Exchange IDEAS
That's My Business

—*An advertisement placed by the young Robert Carlton Brown*

From early childhood, the life of Robert Carlton Brown II (1886–1959), born on June 14, 1886, in Oak Park, Illinois, a suburb of Chicago, was a self-conscious adventure story of his own invention. At age seven, he began writing his autobiography, "My Life and Times," in a long-since-lost notebook. In the last decade of the nineteenth century, he was just a kid named Robert, the "red-headedest" in a family of redheads. His mother, Cora Louisa Brackett Brown, called him Reddy, and, when she called out his name it sounded like "ready." He was constantly inventing scenarios with his own Robin Hood Club and, in the winter, playing in the snow. He loved the snow, and sometimes, when he slept in his attic bedroom, he would open the windows and let the snow cover his face and body. He wished he had been born during a snowstorm, as that happenstance would have provided a better beginning to his biography than a June birthday.

This comic adventure story of little Reddy-Robert Brown began when he was only six years old. His mother arranged for him to give a short speech at her Women's Club for a Washington's birthday holiday celebration. The assembled ladies must have beamed at the sight of the cute boy about to deliver a serious speech about the country's founding father. The speech began: "George Washington was a great man." Robert then pulled out a cheese grater and waved it in the air as he proclaimed, "but here is one grater, ladies." Perhaps when he heard the peals of laughter with the crowd practically rolling in the aisles, as he later remembered

At age seven, he titled his autobiography, "My Life and Times."

the scene, he knew what he wanted to do with his life: crank out stories, play with words, and write his own visual jokes and poems.

The family lived at what was then 290 Thatcher Avenue, but the addresses changed and the house no longer stands. One can still walk down Thatcher, lined with stately Victorian homes with deep lawns and maples arching over the street. Nearby streets contain more-modern houses designed and built by the young Frank Lloyd Wright when Brown was growing up there. Even though the particular house no longer stands, the neighborhood looks similar now to how it did in the late 1800s with large Victorian-style houses set on a leafy street within walking distance of the Des Plaines River.[1]

His mother called him Reddy.

Next to the Brown house was a vacant lot that became the setting for Robert's scenarios. Even as the neighborhood saw much growth and development, the lot remained vacant his entire childhood. Robert was constantly inventing stories for his friends to enact: He might imagine that one of his friends was kidnapped, and the rest of the gang needed to find her and attempt a daring rescue; or that the gang had stolen a treasure from a corrupt king, and they needed to hide it before they were discovered or before the dinner bell rang, whichever came first. There were paths into the surrounding woods, where he would shoot his BB gun at chipmunks, mistaken for ferocious lions, or a spotted gopher on a hazel bush that might have been a tiger; or he might capture a turtle wandering up from the riverbank. He would play by the water's edge or in the woods. He would stage mock tennis matches on the empty lot and dream up stories about his neighbors.

He saw his neighborhood as filled with a cast of characters. Down the street was a boarding house with a succession of colorful tenants. A Dr. Fawcett and his wife, who looked and acted like a parrot, were particular favorites. The doctor might ask Reddy-Robert, "How's your mother?" The wife, with feathers in her hat, would parrot, "How is your mother?' He would reply politely, imagining the wife morphing into an actual parrot, and walk along, smiling mischievously. A "Jigadier-brindle [Army slang for Brigade Commander] who whistled speech through the Civil War bullet hole in his cheek," as Brown recalled decades later, might pass by, or Bessie Aires, "who was supposed to be a little off, but proved herself not so crazy after all," at least according to Brown's ironic memories. Bessie put "buckets in unexpected places" in hopes that "her ogre-like guardian" would "'kick the bucket' and not bother her anymore." The residents of one house on the street kept their blinds down, raising the suspicions of the imaginative young boy. He would try from a safe distance to see what was going on inside, and he imagined that the two fellows who lived there were thieves hiding out, or undercover Federal agents, and, although he never heard anything, he knew, as a child, that they must be testing their high-powered guns in the woods.

Brown's father had a camera and constantly took photographs of his "showoff" kid camping, skating, picking flowers, and having "the time of our lives." The young Brown thought of life as a photographic scene. One of the key recurring images in Brown's later avant-garde visual poetry and essays depicts eyes on the half-shell. His father would often take photographs of the mugging young Brown. Robert would make "oystering eyes" and also have "wiggling fingers out of my ears." These childhood images stayed with him, and in his autobiographical sketch one sees those wiggling fingers and the oystering eyes on the half-shell. As a teenager, he had taken on a newspaper route for extra money, and one day he found "the most beautiful shell" near Edward C. Waller Gates's Frank Lloyd Wright–designed mansion; Robert added the shell to one of his collections. He polished it until its rainbow colors left him "breathless," and about a year later someone told him it was an oyster shell. Only millionaires, like the man the young Brown called "Mr. Waller," had the means to import oysters to the Midwest in order to serve them on the half-shell and throw the pearly parts in the garbage for, as Robert later wrote, "the likes of me" to find as treasure. Brown took these personally significant images, and, in the late 1920s as a Surrealist, he telescoped them into allegorical significance in his visual poetry and avant-garde projects. These images allude, later, to Brown's interest in the mechanization of reading and writing with eyes floating surreally away from bodies and to the wiggling motion of fingers (on a typewriter) producing letters. From his childhood, Brown borrowed these images, charged with intense personal significance, to help him think poetically about his discoveries, inventions, and innovations.

Although he would spend much of his adult life in subtropical climates, he loved snow and even developed a taste for eating it. He recalls a "Michigan maple wax pulled-candy party" that he helped his mother, Cora, make "by strewing the boiling syrup lightly over pans of snow." It is a pastime that endures, but for Brown it marked the start of his interest in cuisine and eating customs. "Sugar on Snow" parties are usually associated with maple syrup harvest season. If it is handled correctly, heating the maple syrup to 225 degrees Fahrenheit and drizzling it thinly over a pan of snow produces a syrup that becomes a candy-like creation. Warm the syrup too much, and it will melt the snow; fail to warm it enough and it will seep down to the bottom of the pan. Let the syrup get too hot or too cool, and one is left with a watery mess. One must drizzle it in a lace-like pattern or it will form clumps and not set up into a hard candy. Years later Bob and Cora and Rose, Bob's second wife, would write many popular cookbooks, often featuring regional recipes from around the country or world, as much about the folklore of the locale as simply a list of recipes. One of his favorite foods in early childhood was cheese, and this love turned into a lifelong obsession that culminated with the publication of his *Complete Book of Cheese* in 1953.

His father was an "ardent" member of the Methodist Episcopal Church, while his mother remained "devoutly atheist," but neither objected to the other's beliefs or nonbeliefs, and Robert was required to attend Sunday school to please his father. To please his mother, he was required to remember only two words from all of his lessons, "Jesus wept," so that he would not get into trouble when the Sunday school teacher asked for a Biblical quotation. The struggle of the secular modern against

He kept his newspaper route, for ready cash, even after his squibs appeared in that same newspaper.

the stifling Victorianism in his own home was reflected in the larger setting of his youth in and around Chicago.

Brown wrote later in his notes that the two most important years in his early life were those during which he attended the World's Fairs. In 1893, the Chicago World's Fair, also called the World's Columbian Exposition in honor of the 400th anniversary of Columbus's arrival in the New World, made the seven-year-old Brown wish that if he had his way, life would be just one World's Fair after another. In 1904, the St. Louis World's Fair, which celebrated the centennial of the Louisiana Purchase, similarly provoked one visitor to exclaim that her eyes were not big enough to see it all. The Chicago World's Fair inspired Brown's dreams of fantastic adventures awaiting him and especially the possibil-

The two most important years in his early life were those during which he attended the World's Fairs in 1893 in Chicago and in 1904 in St. Louis.

ities of machine-age inventions. Before the Fair, his world revolved around an empty lot, his street, and a riverbank. When he walked through the Fair, its sheer size of 600 acres of fairgrounds, with 200 buildings, must have impressed him. Everything was designed as a county fair scaled up to international proportions. The Fair encouraged the fantasy of living like a leisure-class owner and consumer, rather than as a laborer in the grimy gray environments of industrial production.

Although Robert Brown would later claim to have an affinity for writing about plain folk, he took away from the Fair a desire to write about romance, adventure, travel, celebrities, riches, poverty, struggle, business, art, humor, and poetry. When he later proposed a new version of his autobiography, he called it the "Brown Family Robinson" because his was a life much like that of the fictional family in the late-nineteenth-century English novel. He was inventing, collaborating, traveling, and making do with whatever life tossed his way. The results for both the Browns and the Robinsons were often fantastic and surreal, as they used clever ingenuity to build a life and home wherever they landed and from which they never wanted to be rescued. Brown also shared with the Robinsons a lifelong love of gadgets and inventions. And the Fair fueled and reinforced Brown's interests in media machines, for example in Eadweard Muybridge's demonstrating his zoopraxiscope, the first proto–movie projection system. If the Fair encouraged his wanderlust, his personal life provoked a desperate desire to cram as much adventure and intensity into his life as possible. Although he later criticized the Chicago World's Fair as "insipid" compared with Coney Island's Dreamland, he was fascinated with it. Four years later, Brown's life would change dramatically, further fueling his desire to get as much out of his life as possible.

On a snowy afternoon in 1897, a group of kids were playing around the Browns' stately Victorian house with a wraparound porch. There was a half-built snowman near an igloo-like snow fort. Mittens and wool hats were scattered around, having fallen off in the midst of a play battle. Some of the boys as faux soldiers were using the height of the porch to bombard the fort. Out from the fort popped two redheads shouting a highfalutin-sounding call to arms and a hearty "Huzzah!" There was a lull in the action as one soldier had to answer a real-life mother's call to come home. The two red-headed brothers, Wesley Earl, fourteen, and Robert, now almost eleven, sat on the half-collapsed snow fort and talked about adventure stories. The older brother outlined the plot of their latest adventure story and explained how they would sell their stories to magazines and newspapers, make a fortune, travel the world, and go on exotic adventures together.

One can imagine the little brother's knee-slapping laughs of delight the more the older brother told about their future life together. As they fooled around, intermittently throwing a snowball and then revising a part of their dreamed-up stories, another teenager came by, pulling a sled. He called out to invite Wesley to go sledding on the frozen river. Some of Reddy-Robert's friends wanted to start up a new round of their adventure, so Wesley ran off down toward the wooded land that bordered the river and left his little brother to continue the snowball fight. The afternoon wore on, and near dinnertime, when groups of fathers started walking down the street from the Oak Park train station after working in Chicago, the friend who had earlier fetched Wesley came running out of the woods near the river, screaming and crying. "Wesley fell through the ice! I couldn't get him out!" Some of the fathers heard and ran with the teenager back down to the river's edge, and Robert and his friends ran along, too. Someone pulled Wesley out, and others tried desperately to revive his blue body. When Robert's father heard the news, it was as if someone had taken the air out of his body. He slumped over, shaking his head, crying and moaning. That night Robert took off all of his clothes and slept by an open window, letting the snow fall on him. He dreamed of living as a character in a novel looking for adventures in a utopian world like the Chicago World's Fair.

Although Robert's father tried to compensate for their loss through charity for kids and teenagers, he never completely recovered his joy of life and died, according to Cora, from grief a year later at the age of thirty-five. After his father's funeral, one can imagine that Cora held Reddy tightly to her and looked at him intensely as if to say to the young boy that he had to live and live fully for his brother and father. All of their dreams were now his responsibility to enact. He must have felt shipwrecked and alone early in his life. Two of his siblings, Howard and Helen Maud, had both died as children. His older brother, Wesley Earl Brown, had drowned a year before, and when Robert's father died, he and his mother were the only members of the family left. She never remarried, in spite of the suitors who at first approached her. She spent much of the rest of her life living, traveling, and eventually co-writing cookbooks with her only remaining son. Robert, an atheist even as a young man, did not have hopes of literal eschatological communication, as Alexander Graham Bell had with the telephone. Nevertheless, those early childhood traumas did provoke his desire to communicate through the ether with a past that was gone forever, and many years later, influenced by psychoanalytic discussions among the Surrealists, he tried to reconstruct his earliest memories of sex and sexuality. On a wintry afternoon in 1900, Bob and some other teenage boys were looking at adventure stories and illustrated books. One of his friends, whose father was a doctor, showed the other neighborhood boys a medical book that described male sexuality. They gathered around the book, studying it as if it were a mystical talisman. The doctor's son read a line or two in which the author claimed that the normal male would have 1,000 ejaculations during his lifetime. One boy swallowed deeply, another was nervously adding up numbers with his fingers, and the temperature in the room seemed to rise with anxiety. The boys looked at one another guiltily as they added up in their heads their indiscretions and worried that "we'll have to be more careful, we've used up half of it already." Bob looked out the window at the now-allegorical snow.

Teachers noticed in Robert a profound aptitude for writing in spite of his lack of interest in schoolwork, and they skipped him over the seventh grade; he also skipped that grade's foundational grammar lessons. Missing those lessons, Brown later joked, led to his ready ability to write in a direct prose style. Although giving as little effort as possible to classwork, he was still successful in school. He was the secretary of the Honor Society, and he submitted jokes and short pieces to the school paper, edited by the later famous advertising mogul and conservative pundit and politician Bruce Barton. Barton often rejected Brown's pieces, and Robert would hold a grudge against Barton for the rest of his life as the two went in very different political and cultural directions with their literary talents. His principal wrote on the recommendation form for college: "*Very good* natural ability" but added that until Robert Brown realized he wanted to attend college, he had "very poor habits of study." The high school's administrators "helped out with some mythical credits in Mechanical Drawing, Botany, etc." so he could gain admittance to college, and, as Robert remembered in later notes on his childhood, they urged him to "never show my face there again." He graduated with an A average from Oak Park High and entered the University of Wisconsin, but it was his teenage years in the cultural life of Chicago that had the greater influence on his later life.

By 1902, around age sixteen, he was attending book auctions, building his collection of books and prints as well as continuing his polished-stone and agate collection, inherited from his great-grandfather. He was already trying to write poetry. He attended the grand opera regularly and described himself as a "refined heller in a tuxedo" (*heller* was slang for a noisy and rowdy person, a hellion). He was, at this early age, influenced by a wide array of writers' work, including Stephen Crane's modernist poetics and meaningful graphic design in *The Black Riders and Other Lines*, which addressed "the problem of poetic expression . . . in the age of mechanical reproduction."[2] He read with delight "Mr. [James] Whistler's Ten O' Clock Lecture," which advocates merriment and calls for deflating pompous pretensions among art scholars. He identified with the characters in Samuel Butler's modern semi-autobiographical novel *The Way of All Flesh*, in which one character is coincidentally named Brown and the entire narrative describes the rather miserable time of a teenager at home and school. He thought of Edward Lear's *Nonsense* as a model for his own work. He read Laurence Sterne's *Tristram Shandy*, that modernist eighteenth-century experimental novel that mixes bawdy humor with the impossibility of telling one's own story simply or concisely (if at all). Like many teenagers at the time, he also read Edward Bellamy's *Looking Backward* (1888) and H. G. Wells's *A Modern Utopia* (1905), as well as the many utopian novels that appeared around the turn of the century, for he had a utopian streak and a belief in the liberating possibilities of machines. The chasm between the classics he was reading in school, like

Ivanhoe, Silas Marner, The Ancient Mariner, Idylls of the King, and selections from Milton and Shakespeare, which are all listed in the curriculum for his high school classes, and the modern works he was reading outside school set the stage for his search for a more visceral style of writing, first in popular stories and later in avant-garde visual poetry. Among his reading in high school he was particularly fascinated with Chaucer and Spenser and probably took from them fantastic situations, bawdy humor, and the journey-as-adventure plots rather than the poetic style. He was already a reading machine.

In 1902, he met Chauncey L. Williams, a wealthy book collector and prominent printer who had built his fortune in advertising, who would become his "substitute father for culture." Robert had met Williams while making money as a golf caddy. Williams had co-founded the experimental, high-quality Auvergne Press, with covers by Frank Lloyd Wright, and another prestigious press, Way and Williams, dedicated to producing beautifully printed small editions by authors like Kate Chopin, Dante Gabriel Rossetti, or L. Frank Baum and drawing on artists and designers like Bruce Rogers, Maxfield Parrish, and others associated with the aesthetic decadent style. Now known mostly as one of the first clients to have Wright design his house (and his home was one of the only houses that Wright actually helped build himself), Williams in the 1890s was an important figure in what was called the "Mauve decade" of baroque cultural decadence and refinement. He had started a press famous for quality editions of European works and introduced the young Brown to a small but intense Chicago cultural scene.

Williams lived about eight to ten blocks from the Brown house and introduced Reddy-Robert to how to run a publishing and printing business as well as the ways of advertising. Williams taught Brown hand-press and duplex printing techniques. Some of the terminology, like calling the printing press simply the "machine" or describing the necessity of "make ready" (by testing a print project with extra paper to allow for adjustments like reducing blocks that might be too high or bringing up those too low to create an even uniform printing), would later influence his thinking about his "readies" and "reading machine." He coined those terms as a reference to his years as a printer and publisher starting as a teenager and continuing his entire life. Chauncey took the sixteen-year-old to The Cliff Dwellers Club and introduced the boy to the prominent Chicago wit Opie Read and other authors whom Williams had published. Soon Robert was practically living in the Club, which still exists, an arts club where patrons socialized with writers, artists, and musicians. The Club sought to fill a vacuum left by the closing of important vanguard literary arts publications in Chicago, *The Dial* and *The Chap-Book*, and publishers like Way and Williams.

A favorite haunt of Brown's, the famous bookshop McClurg's, now part of the Newberry Library, kept the budding book collector busy. The tenor of the cultural scene in Chicago was still influenced by aestheticism and proto-modernist sensibilities. Likewise, Brown was reading *Reedy's Paper* (which later became *Reedy's Mirror* magazine) and imbibing the epigrams of Opie Read, like "Art is the old age of trade" and "In nearly all wisdom there is a tincture of cynicism."[3] Although he would later claim to have discovered avant-garde writing and art like a bolt from the blue after the Armory Show of 1912, he was already as a teenager associating with a sophisticated winking vanguard sensibility. Opie Read's epigram about what counts as art seems fitting not just to Brown's work but also to much vanguard art and writing from at least a decade later: "There has never been a great contemporaneous literature, for the narrow lines of the critic run into the past. It takes us almost a generation to discover that a writer is original; at first we call him crude, wanting in art; but afterward we may find that what we took to be a lack of finish is a new art, stronger, bolder than the old art."[4]

He went to hear Theodore Thomas's Chicago Symphony Orchestra, famous for the conductor's virtuosity and for establishing classical music's popularity and importance in America, at the opening of Orchestra Hall. He "often" went to the opera, saw Caruso, and visited him backstage, where, according to Robert, Caruso "gargled spaghetti." He hobnobbed with musicians and artists from the Art Institute and started to build a plan for his own adventure story based on the aesthete's creed: to appreciate the arts as a recipe to make of one's life an art. At the same time that he went to these highbrow venues, he also regularly attended vaudeville shows, and that vaudevillian sensibility appeared in Brown's work later, when he wrote squibs and jokes from 1906 through 1908 and also more generally in the popular pulps, from 1908 to 1917, as well as in avant-garde visual poetry starting in 1913.

Brown learned nonsense songs from Richard Pearce and Chauncey Williams, while they sat around drinking. They'd recite verse by Ogden Nash or Gelett Burgess; the latter had a lasting influence on Brown's work, including Brown's avant-garde poetry and his reading machine. They'd thrill at the then-famous nonsense verse lines of Burgess, like "I never saw a purple cow, I never hope to see one, but I can tell you anyhow, I'd rather see than be one," or, of Nash, "I wish that my room had

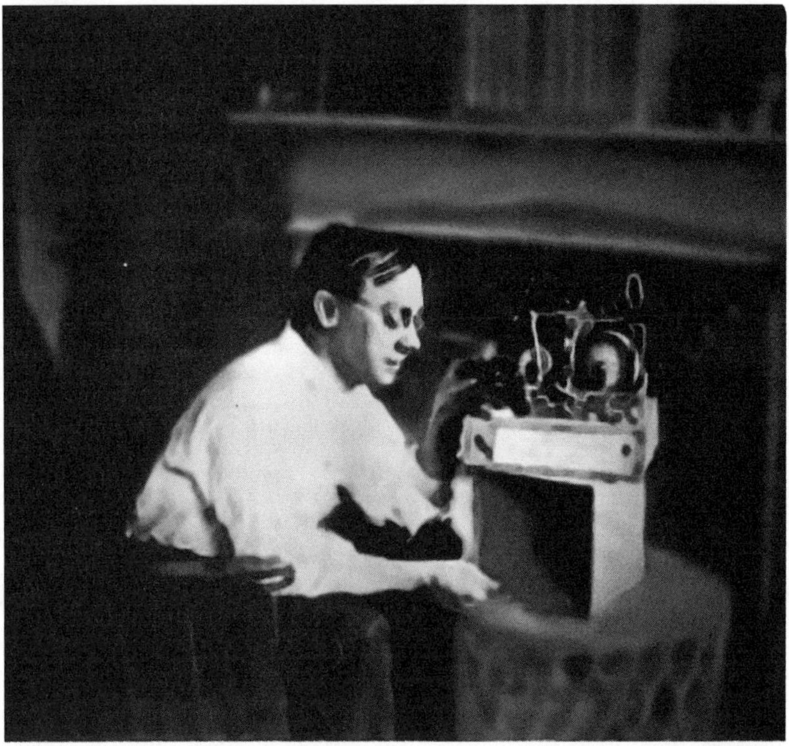

Gelett Burgess and his nonsense machine.

a floor, I don't so much care for a door, but this walking around without touching the ground is getting to be such a bore." Even decades later, Brown would think fondly of these particular lines as the conjured memories of his young life. Johanna Drucker discusses Burgess in terms that could easily apply to the young Brown and his tastes: "spoofing sensibility" and "art for fun's sake." In Burgess's *Lark* magazine, he published his famous "The Purple Cow," and he had a section titled "The Muse in the Machine" that must have also appealed to Brown in which "handwriting and type vie in a contest staged like a dialogue." Much of Brown's own avant-garde work would occupy these same issues, putting him in a lineage with Nash and Burgess. Both Burgess and Brown later wrote mysteries that involved technical gimmicks used by con men, fake spiritualists, and burglars, but Burgess adds a more interesting twist by having these tricksters become his detectives, such as Astro, the phony seer who serves as his detective in *The Master of Mysteries* (collected in 1912). Most important, Burgess would later design a nonsense machine with "ludicrous contraptions with wheels and levers and cams and belts that jerked and jiggered and revolved and wobbled in all directions and at all speeds with no possible sense to any of the activity; hence 'nonsense' machines."[5] Although it's not clear how the machine produced nonsense, Burgess's "No. 2 Machine," with a similar look to Brown's later reading machine and dedicated to similar poetic effects, was a "reciprocal-compound engine for the elimination of thought in all forms."[6] News of Burgess's machine appeared in 1912, and Brown continued to think of Burgess as a seminal influence on his later work and interests.

At the same time Brown met Williams, as a golf caddy he also met Richard Pearce, who lived on Thatcher Avenue. Pearce was, at the time, in charge of figuring out how to supply electricity to the St. Louis World's Fair. Pearce hired Brown as a clerk for the president of the Fair, David R. Francis, who was later famous as the mayor of St. Louis, governor of Missouri, U.S. Secretary of the Interior, and ambassador to Russia during the 1917 revolution. The Pearce family, renting a mansion next to Francis's, gave Robert room and board for $5 a week, taken directly out of his weekly salary of $15. So, Robert did not just visit the Fair; he helped build it, designed the electrification, and ushered in the many celebrities, as many as six an hour, coming to meet the Fair's president. Bob greeted and met every dignitary visiting the Fair. The most memorable visitors included Alberto Santos-Dumont, who, after winning an aerial race and circling the Eiffel Tower in his own dirigible balloon a few years earlier, became one of the most famous people in the world. Brown also remembered, in his notes many decades later, meeting Dr. Mary Walker, the advocate of women's rights and dress reform and a winner of the Congressional Medal of Honor for her work as a surgeon during the Civil War; she wore pants to the meeting, which impressed the young Brown. President Francis would greet his guests, as Brown remembered, by sharing an Old Fashioned with each and every one, except Carrie Nation, the prohibitionist.

One pavilion in particular, dedicated to electricity and machinery, with the De Forest wireless telegraph tower atop the building, sparked Brown's lifelong dream of inventing ways to instantly read a book stored on the other side of the world. This wireless communication device would eliminate geographic distances and create the type of global village found at the Fair, and perhaps it suggested, to the young Robert Brown, that a machine might allow access to all libraries around the world. His later

Chauncey Williams taught Brown the necessity of "make ready" in printing.

fame for inventing a modernist reading machine was sparked by these wonders of the Worlds' Fairs in Chicago and St. Louis. Like the young Brown, everyone saw the potential, and Joseph Pulitzer II, who published the *St. Louis Post-Dispatch*, decided to move the business of newspapers into new forms of media, including radio and later television, after seeing the demonstration. Of course, these ideas of wireless messages seem prosaic now, with wireless web surfing, text messaging, and tweets, but, at the turn of the twentieth century, wireless telegraphy was still just a one-off prototype.

In September 1904, Brown began to attend the University of Wisconsin in Madison, perhaps because of Chauncey Williams's influence. Williams had arranged for Robert to stay with Williams's sister's family, the Fox family, and Brown listed the Foxes' local address on his registration forms. He moved into his (unbeknownst to him at the time) future wife's family home on Henry Street, about four blocks from campus. By the winter he was courting at least one, and probably both, of the two Fox girls. He kept in touch with Cornelia Lillian Fox, the older sister, whom he called Lillian, in the years after he left Madison. Robert's relationship with Lillian, who started attending the University of Wisconsin that same semester and majored in art, was less intense and romantic than his relationship with the younger sister, Katherine Fox, whom Robert liked to call Katrinka or Katrina. When he returned to marry one of the Fox girls (which one was surprisingly not completely clear to the perplexed Robert), he would live to regret the outcome.

He registered for four courses in the fall semester, including the introductory courses in French, German, English Composition, and History (with a focus on medieval history). He muddled through the first semester, with mediocre grades, the highest an 84 percent in English, and later mockingly claimed to have majored in beer drinking. Sometime during the second semester of his first year of college, he stopped attending classes and received incompletes for all of his courses. One of his few vivid memories of his months in Madison was, after a night of drinking, passing out next to an open window as the snow fell and waking happy, if nearly frozen, with the cold snow covering him in the morning. Much of what he learned in Madison consisted of unattributed dirty drinking limericks, and Robert missed the more refined and sophisticated banter of the artists and poets in Chicago; he left Madison and returned to Chicago after less than one year for financial reasons as his mother was struggling to pay his tuition, and he saw little cultural value in college life.

In the same academic year (1904–5) he started attending college, he also wrote and typed out a one-copy edition of a book of love poems, *The House of Content*, made especially for his sixteen-year-old girlfriend, Katrina (Katherine) Fox. In the chapbook itself, Brown describes it as composed in the "contented cow" style of Oliver Wendell Holmes Sr., by which Brown meant that it combined the pastoral with sentiment, but without the cloying sentimentality of most adolescents' poetry and prose. The "contented cows give better milk" trope was the Carnation canned-milk product just starting at the time, and Robert was well aware that his book, consisting of ninety-three pages, resembled the "canned product," as it was "quite guiltless of metre and mighty poor poetry," but it delivered his dream of their (his and Katrina's) "contentment" in the future.[7] Brown had read Holmes's "Ballad of the Oysterman," about two young lovers, one the son of an oysterman and the other a daughter of a fisherman, who conspire to meet secretly at night; he swims across the small bay to avoid his boat's attracting the attention of the parents. They share "kisses sweet as dew, and words as soft as rain," but when they hear the father coming, the young man jumps back into the bay. The father wonders who it is, and after various attempts to pass off the swimmer as the ripples from a pebble the daughter has just thrown, she says it must be a porpoise swimming past. To this answer, the father says for the girl to get his harpoon, and she swoons and never awakes. The young man, taken with a cramp, drowned. The oyster motif, the tragic consequences, and the love story all attracted Brown's attention as he searched for models of writing. Robert's Grandma Brackett, Cora's mother, painstakingly hand-bound the book, using an antique binding, a silk slipcase. Robert padlocked the package with a silver heart and presented it to his sweetheart, Katrina Fox. Although never published, the book gave him the experience of writing a short poetic novel, producing it into a chapbook format and making his later first published stories seem penned by a seasoned writer. Each page of the little chapbook is the size of a 3″ × 5″ index card, typed single-spaced with about eleven lines per page. Bob divided the book into sections representing parts of a married couple's life together along with subsections of specific "dreams" of their charmed life. For example, one chapter in section one is titled "The Seventh Dream. RAIN," and begins as follows.

> ***RAIN.***
> They sat together before the cheery
> fire. All was quiet, in the room.
> Outside, the wind blew and whistled,
> the rain splashed in puddles and beat
> upon the sides and roof of the house,
> THE HOUSE OF CONTENT.
> "Another of Nature's nights, isn't it Katrina," said the man.
> "Oh, it's fine, Bob," came the soft
> answer from the little woman, at his
> side.
> "This is the kind of a night I used to dream about"[8]

In the book, Bob imagines major life events, including marriage, childbirth, fiftieth anniversary, becoming grandparents, old age, and interludes of direct addresses to Katrina about their love for each other and how they will be content. He imagines confessing to Katrina in the distant future that "'now, at seventy, I am more in love with you than ever, but still, in a far different way than I was ten years ago.'"[9] It seems a clear and unambiguous marriage proposal extended into a story.

Robert continued to read and carried on a private parallel education for himself. He carefully studied Stephen Crane's *The Black Riders and Other Lines* (1893). Crane's celebration of newspapers as founts of the wisdom of the day impressed Brown with the idea of a poet in the streets. The young Brown embraced aestheticism but not the poetry of the leisure class, a phrase that Thorstein Veblen, the famously sarcastic University of Chicago professor, introduced in 1899, which described many of the role models of Robert's formative years. Instead, another formative influence on the young Brown's tastes was Paul Laurence Dunbar, whose poems also introduced Brown to a cultural world unfamiliar to refined culture. The poetry and cultural milieu of the famous elevator-operator poet, Dunbar, had a lasting and profound influence on the teenaged writer. Following Dunbar's lead of writing about poor working people, Brown tried in vain to publish stories about the common working man or woman. Robert Carlton Brown didn't try to speak for, or like, the black folk Dunbar wrote about in his autobiographical poems, but Brown recognized in Dunbar his first great literary influence. Dunbar's appeal to a white audience, criticized later as conciliatory or pandering, was popular among black and white audiences alike. Dunbar's *Lyrics of Lowly Life* captured, for Brown, the way poetry could add "zest" to a lowly worker's life; one need not be among the leisure class to write poetry. Dunbar sought to "sing my song," Brown would later recount in his notes, even though "days are never days of ease" and always filled with "labor hard, and toil and sweat."[10] Many years later, the political scientist Emmett Dorsey, associated with Howard University first as a student and later as an instructor and professor, thought Robert Brown remarkably, and even uniquely, knowledgeable about black culture and literary figures for a white person, a fact that Brown credits, in his own notes, to Dunbar's inspiration.[11]

Dunbar wrote poems about poor African American workers trying to find respite in poetic expression after long hours of labor. The poor, often-overgeneralized in literature as pathetic, tortured souls who either find ways out of poverty or find themselves psychologically tormented and grotesquely deformed by it, appeared, in Dunbar, as neither escaping from poverty nor succumbing to its deprivations. The black culture of the time offered to the poor a well of inspiration, something unsurprising now, and even dismissed as another romanticized cliché, but not widely recognized until the Harlem Renaissance twenty years later, in the 1920s. When Frederick Douglass spoke at the Chicago World's Fair as Haiti's delegate, racist hecklers tried to shout him down, but Douglass's eloquence famously quieted the crowd. Douglass's assistant at the time was Paul Laurence Dunbar. Robert Brown often identified with (or maybe even as) a black man, seeing these writers and poets as part of his own lineage.

By 1906 Robert Brown was delivering papers near his old River Forest neighborhood and desperately starting up his career as a writer to make money. He was thrilled to deliver the very newspapers that had his by-line but not quite secure enough in his new career to give up the paper route's more reliable income. He had spent more than $100 in postage before he sold his first story for $1.50. To make money as a writer, he wrote what he called "trick business ideas." His first series was called "Pipe Dreams of a Promoter" for the *Chicago Tribune*'s "Worker's Magazine" with the subtitle "For the Man Who Works with Hand or Brain" (a magazine that continued to publish until the summer of 2009). The series' title seems to summarize Brown's effort to sell even the most unlikely story ideas. Brown's first story for the *Record Herald* newspaper included self-censored dashes in place of anything that anyone might construe as a swear word. For example, the main character was named A— to leave out the suggestion of "damn" in "Adam." The characters would cross the —espont by deleting the "Hell" from the "Hellespont" (the famous river that divides Europe from Asia). His efforts to overcensor alluded to one of the feuding printers, in Edgar Allan Poe's "X-ing a Paragrab" (1850), who, as they run out of type, substitute x's for O's, leading to hilarious results. Robert's efforts also directly relate to his later use of em dashes in *The Readies* for his reading machine and his entire collection of censored poems, in *Gems*, with pornographic suggestiveness where the reader's mind fills in the blanks. He was already setting the stage for his poetic and avant-garde works.

The more regular writing gig began when, in 1907, he placed filler pieces in the popular series "Stories of the Streets and Town" in the *Chicago Record Herald*, the column started by George Ade. When Ade syndicated his popular column and quit the *Record Herald*, the newspaper started hiring young writers to fill in. Because these pieces allowed Brown to make a living at writing, he decided to expand his venues and began sending out work to more newspapers and magazines. He enjoyed writing as much as keeping his many collections of books, prints, and rocks. With his publishing success, editors and publishers began to take note.

The pieces he published in the "Stories of the Streets and Town" series were often jokes about signs one might see on the street, funny ads one might read in the town's paper, or simply comically odd sights in the city. For example, among the archive's scraps of his clippings are these squibs: "an up-and-coming clothes cleaner's sign reads, "We'll dye for you"; "Grinn & Barret, Plumbers"; "Farswego: the name of every streetcar terminal according to the conductor's unintelligible 'Far as we go'"; "Wanted Ad: young doctor in Ill. town, good place to work up practice"; and "Quick—Undertaker. The quick and the dead; and, thousands more." It was that sort of Chicago-based working-man-in-the-street vaudevillesque squibs that characterized Brown's early writing. He also started to place very short stories in the regular column; the stories, later mentioned in Brown's notes, had titles like "The Barbarous Barber," "He Caught the Boy," "The Barkless Dog," and "Foxy Grandma." Like many Chicago writers of the time, Brown started to itch to get to New York City. He had now established himself as successful enough as a writer in Chicago that he wanted to try his luck in the much larger market of New York, where many popular magazines and large newspapers were published. He decided to move east and, as soon as he could afford to, move his mother and his college sweetheart to the city with him.

He started sending his filler pieces and stories to out-of-town magazines and landed a monthly page of "Foolsophy" in *Profitable Advertising* from Boston. Those foolsophy pieces were written in batches, and eventually he produced thousands. They are the sort of ephemeral parodic aphorisms easily digested by a businessman on the way to work: "A man is driven to both drink and suicide—he walks to work" and "A tack in the hand is worth two in the foot." He started placing foolsophy in newspapers and magazines all over the country. He started publishing using *noms de plume* like John S. Brackett, borrowing his mother's maiden name, or inside jokes and word-play names like H. E. Twinells, spelling phonetically HELL or HE linked with twin L's. That last name was later used extensively by at least one other writer. Brown's short stories were soon appearing in *Bohemian*, *Gray Goose*, *All Story*, *Live Wire*, *Black Cat*, and other popular fiction magazines. To supplement his income he also started selling plots, because he simply could not write as many stories as he had ideas, and he even placed an advertisement to sell his ideas to other writers to develop into stories:

I Buy, Sell & Exchange IDEAS
That's My Business

The advertisement drew a reply from an editor, Bob Davis, who had already bought half a dozen stories from him. He told Robert to "come to New York where the money is." Robert Brown was ready to start his adventure story.

The fundraising parties at Webster Hall were staged, prominently advertised, hosted, and emceed by Bob Brown. Brown realized that the bohemians' libertine goals could serve the financial needs of their unprofitable literary and radical publications.

3

Free Love, Free Verse, and Free Radicals in the Avant-Garde, 1913–17

> It was in this period [1913–17] that Greenwich Village . . . assumed a place upon the cultural map . . . which came to be associated with free love, free verse, and all the isms, social and esthetic.
>
> —*Writers' Guild,* New York Panorama, *Federal Writers' Project*[1]

The moment Robert arrived in New York in 1908, he started visiting the art classes and studios flourishing just as the modern Ashcan school and post-impressionists were reinvigorating the art scene. Instead of actually signing up for classes at the Art Students' League, at the center of the excitement, Brown would sit in at the artists' studios to watch, talk, and listen; after class, or during breaks, he would drink with the painters and continue the conversations about art, life, and the bohemian lifestyle emerging around them. George Luks, an influential painter and part of the core group of Ashcan school painters, would often drink with Brown along with two Canadians: Bliss Carman, the transcendentalist poet, literary journalist, and editor, and Peter McArthur, humorist, journalist, and poet. A few years later, one of Brown's favorite studios to visit was that of John Sloan, who would later work with Brown on *The Masses* as part of the dissident artists' group. Brown would visit with Sloan starting in 1912, when they met, and continuing through 1917. Brown was particularly inspired by Sloan's "experimenting in every medium, from oils and murals to egg paints and etching on glass."[2]

The center of the action, and for Brown the greatest influence on his aesthetic perspective, was the studio and classes of Robert Henri, a leader of the Ashcan school of realist painting, which sought to portray the grimy everyday life of poor neighborhoods rather than the pristine studio portraits of the rich. Henri later painted Gertrude Vanderbilt Whitney in pants in a provocative reclining pose as the ideal of the "modern" woman. Whitney's husband was scandalized, and she hung the portrait in her Greenwich Village studio instead of in her mansion. Of course, Whitney went on to found the Whitney Museum of American Art, which has always advocated provocative and political art, as did the Ashcan school in the first decade of the twentieth century. When Brown was visiting the studio, Henri was painting exotic dancers emerging from the dark canvases seductively. Brown felt that Henri was the greatest influence on the young writer's aesthetic sensibility. It was there that Brown first met Stuart Davis, who had become part of a group of artists called the Eight. Also among the young students at the Art Students' League classes from 1908 through 1912, Brown visited Polly Rice's studio, and she in turn visited the Browns in Spain, when they were there in 1913, and where Polly and Lillian both went to study painting. Brown's adventures in studio sitting led William Wallace Cook, Brown's mentor in pulp fiction writing, to think of the young writer as already seduced by bohemian culture in 1908, at least five years before Brown became more closely associated with modernist poetry, radical politics, avant-garde art, and the center of an artists' colony's social scene.

When Brown later wrote about the sea change in his political and aesthetic attitudes and types of publications, from hugely successful and wealthy short-fiction writer to turning life and writing into a series of experiments, he used the metaphor of a stiff collar. "Writing wasn't just Hart, Schaffner, Marx and Arrow collars after all" is what he discovered in 1914 when he read Gertrude Stein's *Tender Buttons*.[3] His friends in the magazine writing business thought of bohemia mostly in terms of a superficially disheveled look (i.e., not wearing a stiff collar), which they took as a sign that Brown had been "doped" and tricked by the radical artists and writers with whom he increasingly worked and caroused. Although Brown suggests that the vanguard life and writing superseded the pulp fiction writing, the two overlapped for at least four years, and arguably from the start of Brown's life as a writer. Still, as his interest in short-fiction writing waned, his fascination with modernism waxed.

Modernism, in the 1910s of Greenwich Village, was inflected with a bohemianism that attracted Brown. Berton Braley, who'd known Robert first as a student in Wisconsin, then as a pulp fiction writer in New York, and later as a bohemian, saw Brown "go hell-bent on his own trail without regard to the consequences."[4] He saw Brown "cavorting about the Greenwich Village pastures with considerable bacchanalian abandon" and said that Robert had started acting like an "undomestic animal."[5] There is a perhaps apocryphal story that epitomizes the Greenwich Village bohemian attitude in the early 1910s, about Jack Reed, the famous radical journalist, asking Lincoln Steffens, the famous muckraking journalist, for money. "Steffens shook his head in bright refusal. 'No regular bills, Jack,' he said. 'I'll never lend you money for that. But whenever you want money for some wasteful, idiotic affair that nobody else would think of, then you can come to me.'"[6] This was the Village setting that Brown entered. Brown, still in Spain in February 1913, missed the scandalous Armory exhibit in which Marcel Duchamp's *Nude Descending a Staircase* scandalized the American press and energized the avant-garde. Before he left New York, Robert had already adopted a similar mocking tone toward polite society.

In a letter to the editor of the *New York Times* late in 1910, Brown humorously explains a solution to church bells' waking his entire neighborhood every Sunday morning. Brown begins by describing the "nice, peaceful little church" and admits that "one could admire a church like that" but then turns his attention to the "brazen bell" that still clangs at 7:30 A.M. on an otherwise quiet peaceful Sunday. Next, he introduces the impact of these bells on the residents (and offers a "conservative estimate, 6,000 private individuals"). After explaining the situation, he turns graciously to the parishioners, who probably do not realize that "times have changed," as they "must have been very busy doing good," and not noticing that they could communicate with the community without ringing the bells. It all sounds reasonable with a building sense of ironic humor. Brown criticizes the parochial prejudice of the church that does not respect the "peace, privacy, and comfort" of "other faiths—Christians, Jews, Christian Scientists, Mohammedans, New Thoughtists, atheists and followers of Swami," and that list makes the parishioners seem arrogant and insensitive. He suggests that the church use "telephones, telegraphs, or some other modern, unobtrusive method to contribute their tenth of the neighborhood's worship to the Lord."[7]

In 1912, after a year living in New Orleans, where he finished the Poe detective stories and culminating in his tour of the Caribbean islands and Mexico, Robert moved back to Greenwich Village. He took a six-room flat, for his growing family, on the top floor of a triangular apartment building at Sheridan Square. (A decade later, in 1924, the Greenwich Village Theater, used by the Provincetown Players, was located at the same address, but not the same building, at what is now a nondescript 75 Christopher Street at Seventh Avenue across from Sheridan Square.)

Alfred Kreymborg, the future editor of *Others*, and also later an experimental playwright with the Provincetown Players, and a few years later a key member of the Grantwood Village artists' colony, lived across the hall. He was at the time an unknown chess player and poet. Kreymborg (sometimes spelled Kreymbourg) shared the apartment with Alanson Hartpence, who at the time was a little-known, if recently published, poet. Hartpence, also later a member of the *Others* group, directed and encouraged the founding of an important gallery of modern art, the Daniel Gallery by Charles Daniel. Daniel was a savvy co-owner of a hotel and saloon, and Hartpence convinced him to parlay his "passion for pictures" into starting the gallery, which would represent many modern artists after the 1913 Armory exhibit. Man Ray sold his first painting to Daniel, and Man Ray's first solo exhibit in 1915 was in the gallery.[8] Brown regularly drank with Hartpence at the saloon, and a few years later, he often visited the gallery. In fact, Hartpence likely introduced Robert to Rose Watson, Brown's future second wife.

Half a block down from Brown's apartment lived Mary Heaton Vorse, a founding member of the Provincetown Players (the first readings were held in her summer rental house in Provincetown), an important feminist and labor activist as well as a journalist, writer, and Art Students' League student. Brown would work with Vorse on *The Masses* in a few years, and Vorse was publishing in the same magazines as the now much-better-known Willa Cather. Also nearby was Theodore Dreiser, one of the greatest realist novelists and also an infamous libertine, who was just starting his writing career full time and becoming part of the Village scene. Characters like the "mayor" of the Village, Jimmy Walker, were already prominent as the Village started to take on a unique identity. Only a few hundred artists, poets, and bohemians were living in that area, and the place had a village feel, not yet inundated with tourists looking to see real bohemian artsy culture. Even the medical clinic, in the still-standing and recently renovated Old Dispensary on Second Avenue near East Eighth Street, had a connection to the emerging cultural scene beyond its free health care for the needy. The brother of the Ashcan school painter George Luk was the attending physician.

In late 1911 and early 1912, when Lillian returned from Holland, Robert met her in Halifax, Nova Scotia, and they stayed for more than a month before traveling back to New York. They moved to an apartment at 210 West 10th Street. Lillian set up a painting studio across the hall from their family's apartment, and Robert had his own writing studio at 45 Washington Square in a recently vacated room in a three-story brownstone, rented to him by Betty Turner, where John Reed and Louise Bryant later lived; when the Browns moved in, Reed lived at 42 Washington Square. That side of the Square was known as "Genius Row" because along that street many famous artists and writers had lived, including Willa Cather, Theodore Dreiser, Stephen Crane, O. Henry (a pseudonym for William Sidney Porter with the O not an initial for any first name and, therefore, never intended to have a period after the initial, but that's how his name now appears; it was the same type of joke pseudonym that Brown was often involved in when he published), and other cultural celebrities. Brown was at the peak of his productivity and success, writing and selling a couple hundred short stories, besides many plots, and he informally taught short-story writing to individual students, including the feminist Rosalind Mae Guggenheim, who published and was widely known under the name Jane Burr.

It was at this time that Eugene O'Neill lived nearby at 53 Washington Square, with a sign on the front door that read: "Eugene O'Neill / Keep Out Dammit." It was put there by the landlady, angry that O'Neill rarely paid his rent; she would lock him out until he paid. When he wasn't at a saloon, like the infamously raucous, bohemian, and always-open Golden Swan, drinking whiskey and reciting his poetry, he would often crash at Brown's studio. During the second decade of the twentieth century, O'Neill was a regular on the Greenwich Village literary scene, where he also befriended many radicals, most notably Communist Party USA founder John Reed. O'Neill had a brief (and now immortalized in the movies) romantic relationship with Reed's wife, writer Louise Bryant. Although his involvement with the Provincetown Players began in mid-1916 when O'Neill is said to have arrived for the summer in Provincetown with "a trunk full of plays," he was already part of the literary scene in the Village when he met Brown. O'Neill would visit Brown's writing studio during the few months before the Browns would leave again on a new adventure, but later in the teens the playwright used Bob's house in Grantwood Village as a rehearsal space for the theater company producing his first plays.

The scenes with O'Neill in the writing studio had clockwork predictability. "Bob, Bob," Gene would weakly intone, "Bob? Bob," a little louder, and Brown would stop typing and glance at the clock, knowing instantly what Gene wanted. If it was 3:00 in the afternoon, then O'Neill, too drunk to do it himself, wanted Bob to pour more whiskey into his glass. With his arm held in a towel tied to the bedpost like a sling, Gene was able to keep the glass, and his grasping hand, from falling to the ground

Eugene O'Neill often got drunk in Bob's writing studio.

no matter how drunk he got. The sling would allow him to swing the next swig of whiskey up to his mouth. He looked up at Bob as the eight ounces of whiskey flowed into the glass. After starting to drink, O'Neill would sing a dirty chantey he'd learned on a ship. Bob looked down and went back to his typewriter. Bob preferred beer to whiskey, comedic adventures to familial tragedies, and the short forms of popular culture he was writing to the long-winded respectability of the nineteenth-century novel. O'Neill was too misogynistic and "elegant" from Brown's populist and progressive perspective, but good company nonetheless.[9]

After Carlton was born, the family moved to a large house in Ridgefield, New Jersey; now, with two children, and Cora, they were a family of five. This was early in 1913, at least two years before the area, about a mile away near Grantwood Village, would become famous as an artists' colony, to which Brown would eventually relocate. Soon after they moved into their house in New Jersey, they planned to travel to Spain. Lillian's interests, in the post-impressionist art that she studied in Holland, would lead her (and this time her entire family) to Spain to study with Joaquín Sorolla y Bastida. One of the most famous painters at the time, Sorolla had won commissions to paint the president of the United States and was attracting students from around the world to Spain; some later art critics would argue that if he had moved to Paris, his later reputation would have eclipsed Picasso's. Sorolla and the other prominent Spanish painter at the time, Ignacio Zuloaga y Zabaleta, both stayed in Spain and are now barely included in art history surveys. Zuloaga, a painter known for naturalism, was also exploring landscape scenes. Lillian was influenced by these painters' visits to the United States. In 1908 and 1909, they had a few important, critically acclaimed exhibits in New York and Chicago, and much like that of the Ashcan school, their work radically changed the focus of art to focus an unsentimental eye on even the most lowly street and market scenes.

Influential art teachers were urging students to get out of the studio to "capture the energy and heroism of modern times" in the streets, mills, foundries, and construction sites.[10] Art students who were friends with Brown, like Polly Rice (later known as Dorothy Rice Sims), also went to Seville, Spain, to study painting, as that was the hot spot for the radical Art Students' League's students. Polly, who also wrote detective stories for the pulps, partied with the Browns in Spain. She went on to become a prominent aviator, memoirist and writer, and a world-famous bridge player. Her humorous memoir, with a smirking Introduction by her friend George S. Kaufman, illuminates the swell optimism of the decades before World War I. Almost as soon as he and his family arrived in Spain, Robert won the state-sponsored lottery (enough so that he didn't need to write or earn money for more than a few months), and while they lived at No. 2 Calle Federico de Castro, Cora wrote and looked after the two children, Lillian studied painting, and Bob made glass bead necklaces and thought he might continue to earn a living just playing the lottery. He started collecting "incunabula and bibelot" and took the very first automobile journey all the way across Spain in a Ford automobile. He published a story in *Ford Times* about the journey with photographs. Later, a whole array of writers and celebrities would publish in *Ford Times*, including Berton Braley, William Faulkner, John Steinbeck, Eleanor Roosevelt, and Ogden Nash. The Browns threw a Thanksgiving dinner for thirteen other Americans in Seville. Sorolla, who famously painted a pile of cow manure with the same intensity usually reserved for a depiction of a genteel setting, had an influence on Robert, as well as on Lillian. For those seeking the cutting edge, they used the impressionist brushstroke style and their emphasis on representing natural light in an oil painting to illuminate the gritty realism of the gutter and street.

When the Brown family returned to New York, the world had changed. World War I began as they crossed the ocean, and another sea change was in process for Robert. Meanwhile, back in New York, the art scene had changed dramatically after the 1913 Armory exhibit. Abstraction in modernism would quickly, and almost completely, obscure the type of post-impressionist painting (e.g., *en plein aire* and Ashcan school) that previously had represented the vanguard of painting. The post-impressionist artists' fascinations with the representation of the light, shade, brilliant colors, and textures of narrative scenes—narratives about common people—produced with vigorous, almost improvisational brushstrokes, were challenged by the modernists' intellectual interest in speed, mass, and abstraction. The concern shifted from capturing the everyday common life out of the studio toward comprehending "the dissolution of matter as a stable form, and the amalgamation of space with time and motion in a four-dimensional continuum."[11] Looking at the scene from a perspective after 1913, it seems difficult to imagine that the Ashcan school of painters advocated the Armory exhibit, as those painters assumed it would demonstrate the global reach of their aesthetic in art and writing.

In 1914, Gertrude Stein was not alone in announcing a new type of poetry: Ezra Pound published an anthology of Imagiste poetry (the "e" later dropped by Amy Lowell and the American Imagist poets); James Joyce published *Dubliners*; Jack Reed published "What About Mexico?" in *The Masses*, about the Mexican revolution; Amy Lowell published *Sword Blades and Poppy Seed*; and small literary magazines, like *Blast*, *Egoist*, and *The Little Review*, started appearing. While Brown was in Spain, he followed the news from New York and sold articles to *Trend*, which would prove to be important as he met that magazine's editor, Allen Norton, when he returned to New York, and they became good friends. Because of those publications, and their friendship, Norton would introduce Brown to Gertrude Stein's writing. Norton later edited *Rogue* for about seven issues in 1915, and that little magazine introduced work by Walter Arensberg, famous as the collector of Marcel Duchamp's work and the sponsor of a few avant-garde publications, including *Others* and *Rogue*. It also had work by Mina Loy, the avant-garde poet and friend of Brown's, and Alfred Kreymborg. Norton had published his own collection of poems with Donald Evans's Claire Marie Press; so, through his connection to Evans, he got one of the early copies of *Tender Buttons*.

Brown had sent a couple of thousand dollars to Max Eastman to pay for half a plot of land in Tenafly, New Jersey, where they planned to start a cooperative colony for writers and artists, mostly consisting of the other *Masses* editors. At first the Browns lived in Max's furnished house in Tenafly until they found a deserted mansion nearby. When Brown discovered that the land where he had invested was swampland, he got his money back from Eastman and invested a thousand dollars of it in Chandler Motor, a company just starting. Brown's initial $1,000 investment was soon worth $14,000. He used that large sum for margin in trading for the next two or three years, and his work trading stocks, and his boredom with the process, led to the emergence of his thinking about machines in terms of poetry: "Stein put an end to my trying to write what other people told me to. I went out to Coney Island and spent the weekend writing free verse in a room of my own in a flea bitten beach hotel."[12]

For Brown, the key issue was that a work of fiction might dispense with plot and character in favor of images and, like pictures, speak for itself. Instead of writing to the editorial tastes of slicks (the high-end literary magazines) and especially not worrying about the magazines' advertising censors, he felt liberated and claimed to have thrown his "typewriter into the air and huzzaed," deciding to write something that superimposed words and experiment. But he did not leave all constraints behind, as some of his friends believed; he simply substituted writing for magazine editors' tastes for the tastes of experimental artists and (visual) poets. Ezra Pound critically told Brown, "Any bloke can experiment!" Brown was clearly hurt and later wrote a poetic note, in the margin of a draft manuscript of Pound's *XXX Cantos*, to Nancy Cunard, the publisher, "What guy can't write a canto, Ez?" In addition to Pound, Brown drew his inspiration from the aesthetic that he used to describe the resemblance between Gertrude Stein's poetry and Stuart Davis's painting: "consistently and consciously sub-conscious expression."[13] He wanted to write an instant poetry of intensities. The connection between Stuart Davis's experiments in painting and Brown's experimental writing continued for more than five decades of friendship and mutual influence.

In 1915, he bought a more modest house in the art and anarchist colony of Grantwood Village, located on the boundaries of Ridgefield and Cliffside Park, New Jersey, on the Palisades above the Hudson River. Imagist poets congregated there during the summers and eventually published *The Others*, and it was where Man Ray began experimenting with new forms of painting. Man Ray already had a reputation as "a daring performer in versatile experiments."[14] In spite of their poverty and the cramped bungalows they filled these tiny spaces in ways that would later, when Man Ray lived in an even more cramped room in a small Paris hotel, inspire Gertrude Stein to note that she had "never seen any space, not even a ship's cabin, with so many things in it and the things so admirably disposed."[15] Similar artists' colonies appeared all around the United States: Carmel, California; Taos, New Mexico; Peterborough, New Hampshire; and Provincetown on Cape Cod in Massachusetts.

The advantage of Ridgefield was its proximity to New York City. The city and the jobs, opportunities, and connections it held was just a walk, trolley ride, and ferry trip away. It was less than an hour commute, making it easy enough for a number of the artists and writers, including Brown, to go back and forth every weekday, and making Ridgefield a convenient place to visit for friends and colleagues from the city. Brown's house in the artists' colony was only a mile away from the house where he had lived before he'd lived for a year in Spain. He fixed up his house by putting on a roof garden and a sleeping porch. All the other writers and artists, who lived in six or seven little frame shacks, thought of Brown's stone house as luxurious compared with their abodes, which were without running water, necessitating carrying heavy buckets from a spring, or adequate heat, and lighting was from kerosene lanterns, when they could afford it.

Manuel Komroff, later well known as a writer, lived nearby and was friends with Man Ray because they both exhibited at the Ferrer Center. Komroff worked for Robert, painting murals on the walls of the Browns' house in exchange for money and access to Robert's car (until Komroff burned out the engine).[16] No illustrations or photographic images exist of the murals, and the vague descriptions give no sense of the palette, aesthetic style, or whether the images were figurative or nonrepresentational designs. According to one source, the murals were intense and "nightmarish."[17] Komroff played the piano and tended to give his paintings names alluding to music, like *Study in the Key of C.* Manuel and Robert talked about "art transfusion," a theory of how "sculpture, painting, and literature were becoming more and more like music."[18]

Man Ray recalled that Brown "associated himself with the Imagist school then forming," and with "a small [amount of] capital he [Brown] made a killing in Wall Street in a couple of weeks." With those funds, Brown was able to buy "one of the larger stone houses in the community."[19] Robert was making money not as a stockbroker, as many of his poet and artist neighbors thought, calling him "Broker Brown," but as what we now call a day trader. He would trade a million dollars a day "on a margin that stayed around thirty thousand," but at the end of each day he would have made or lost only a few hundred dollars. Although his earnings were not anywhere near the sums he traded, his daily take was equivalent to at least $2,000 today, and perhaps triple that amount. This arrangement was not bad for one day but incredibly risky then as now (and with a bust in the market, having potentially dire consequences). He rarely carried any stock from one day to the next, but the style of buying and selling required him to watch the ticker tape very carefully. Because his many trades were making his broker wealthy, the brokerage gave him a private ticker machine in a special room. His sardonic friend H. L. Mencken jokingly told Brown to make sure to leave the broker a commission in his last will and testament.

Robert also returned to buying and selling rare books. He was particularly good at finding a gem in the bookstalls and selling it to a dealer, or at auction, for ten times the price he'd paid. Reading through the books he offered for auction as the Fine Books from the Library of Robert Carlton Brown on March 17, 1915, at the Anderson Auction Company on Madison Avenue suggests another origin for his erudite reading and wide interests. Among the more than one hundred items listed, with each item containing multiple volumes, he was selling six volumes of early British School and Old Masters art and book catalogues, a catalogue of the Rita Lydig collection, illustrated catalogues of the paintings of George Innes, William Vanderbilt's illustrated log of a motor tour of the continent from 1899 to 1908, a *Cursory History of Swearing*, and a dictionary of *Argot and Slang: A New French Dictionary of Cant Words and Quaint Expressions*. He was also selling books on bees and bee-keeping, a number of volumes on bookbinding, a thirty-volume set of boudoir ballads, and four volumes on cannibals and convicts. A list of the topics of the volumes he was buying and selling included volumes on seamanship, U.S. history, costumes in the 1860s, curiosities of bird life, illustrated volumes on dogs, emblems, family crests of Britain and Ireland, plates by William Hogarth, an index to American genealogies and pedigrees, a stamp collector's handbook, charcoal drawings of old New York, and guides to architecture and electrical engineering. Many of the volumes were literary criticism, like *The English Novel in the Time of Shakespeare* or a book about Charles Dickens. There were many first editions by famous authors, from Ralph Waldo Emerson, James Boswell, Robert Browning, Samuel Clemens, Mark Twain (listed separately), Washington Irving, Michel de Montaigne, George Moore, Samuel Pepys, John Ruskin, W. M. Thackeray, Oscar Wilde, and James McNeill Whistler as well as a nineteenth-century edition of William Shakespeare's plays.[20] It was in this context of buying, studying, and auctioning off his large and varied collections, with Brown acting like an information processor or ticker-tape machine in the high-end book dealer's market, that he started to read modernist writing.

Reading Stein in his spare time, and reading ticker tape all day long, he started to read the one in terms of the other. He tried reading the tape backward. This produced a not surprisingly "meaningless jumble of letters and figures," and, although both frontward and backward the tape produced "a dull code compared to that of Stein," the backward version was "different and that in itself was a relief."[21] He would sit there day after day, following the tape toward a financial bonanza and thinking of it in terms of *Tender Buttons*.

> We read the tape. It passed before our eyes jerkily, but in a continuous line. Endlessly, at any speed, jerk, jerk, jerk, when the Market's pulse was fast; click, click when it was slow: BS 1000-608-1/2/500-609-1/8/1/4-200-1/2-500-610 [this is Brown's example of the ticker for a ticker symbol for a stock followed by the shares traded, followed by bids and ask prices] . . .[22]

Brown explicitly compared reading the stock market's ticker tape to reading a crime thriller writer like Richard Horatio Edgar Wallace when the bull market charged ahead predictably or twisted into a bear market decline. "An expert could almost tell how the plot was going to turn out."[23] The Imagist poet Amy Lowell, who was also changing Brown's perception of writing, would more than a half-century later argue that "a poet is something like a radio aërial—he is capable of receiving messages" and "transmuting these messages into those patterns of words we call poems."[24] Lowell is not a Futurist, but her image does get at the sense Robert must have felt as he read the tape as poetry. Sometime in 1915, reading the tape, he started to dream up his reading machine. Imagining an avant-garde machine and working with a socialist publication seems to contradict Brown's reading the ticker tape as a day trader. During the day, Brown was drinking fancy bourbon at lunches of "caviar, *pâté de foie gras*, lobsters, oysters, crabs, thick imported mutton chops, fresh exotic mushrooms, truffles," and other gourmet foods that would not only serve as grist for his career in cookbook writing but also sound like a lunch of an investment banker or titan of capitalism, like an Astor or a Morgan. In the evening, Brown would take the ferry back to the artists' colony near Grantwood.

Because Brown had the only decent house in the colony (the rest were, as noted, shacks), he often hosted the parties. William Carlos Wil-

William Carlos Williams influenced Bob Brown's poetry and wrote Bob prescriptions.

liams would drive over to the colony and years later continued to correspond with Brown not just about poetry but also about Brown's later complaints in the 1920s about various physical and psychosomatic ailments. The lavish parties became "the colony's chief social attraction, and [Brown's] home became a gathering place for the original Provincetown Players acting group."[25] The guests would regularly include Man Ray; his wife, Adon ("Donna") Lacroix; Helen Hartpence; Beatrice Wood; Hippolyte Havel; Orrick Johns; sometimes Marcel Duchamp; Lucien Carey; Mina Loy; Rose Watson; Eugene O'Neill; Louise Bryant; Floyd Dell; Mike Gold; Alfred Kreymborg; Marianne Moore; Peggy and Orrick Johns; Maxwell Bodenheim; Bernard Karfiol; Samuel Halpert; Adolf Wolff; Robert Alden Sanborn; Conrad Potter Aiken; Mary Carolyn Davies; Horace Holley; Floyd Dell; and Skipwith Cannell.

Rolling in "ready" cash, Brown furnished the liquor, beer, and food for a "practically continuous party of startling luxury. Guests could get a kind of vicarious thrill of wealth by digging their hands deep into a garden urn filled with old Roman coins which Brown kept for just that purpose."[26] When the parties were not at Brown's house, he led the revelers to the Old White House Tavern, where the artists regularly awakened the proprietors. Once the last ferry from the city docked on the New Jersey side, the tavern was closed. The owners, Emil and Rosie, would answer the pounding on the door with a yell from upstairs, "Locked since ten." When Emil grudgingly opened the door, the crowd sang and raucously demanded schnapps.

When they visited earlier in the day, Emil refused to serve them anything except beer, but Rosie would regularly feed them lunches, such as her special Swiss cheese salads mixed right at their table, while advising the artists to drink the remaining dressing as a hangover cure. Bob and the artists regularly ate there lunch that consisted of "potatoes and other seasonable vegetables, sometimes homemade noodles," and "often sauerkraut."[27] The meals came with bread, too, and homemade, or locally made, cheese. For dessert, they ate apple strudel.

The weekends would bring workers from the city looking for a place to picnic in the area around the artists' colony. They would leave their broken bottles and litter behind after buying meals and beer from Rosie and Emil. At one picnic for actors from the city, they drank through sixteen kegs of beer; someone took a picture, and later the owners hung the picture in the White House Tavern. The picture is lost to history. Robert would later describe the scene captured in the photograph: "All the actors trying to stand in the spotlight at once, all striking dramatic or comic poses. . . . Chorus girls, dressed up to go back to Nature, sat beating on the drum tops of straw-hats with chicken legs." The artists' colony would hold regular weekday parties in the back room of the tavern and "were quiet compared to the city people. They took out their excitement in talking," but when they knocked over a table, "broke glasses, or threw things around," Emil shook his fist at the long-haired bohemians and called them "loafers, *dummkopfe*."[28]

By 1916, Robert Carlton Brown had become famous enough as a modern poet that Louis Untermeyer parodied Brown's poetry in a volume that also parodied Ezra Pound, Robert Frost, and Amy Lowell. Untermeyer, now most famous for his canonical and foundational anthology of modernist poetry, *Modern American Poetry*, published a volume of parodies of these "*—and Other Poets*." The fake anthology's title poked fun at *Others: A Magazine for the New Verse*. In the parody of Robert Brown's poetry, Untermeyer took aim at Brown's multiple interests, appetites, and world travels when he had his faux "Robert Carlton Brown" write: "My thoughts are little mice./They have a great way of running everywhere,/And a greater hunger./Nothing will satisfy their ferocious appetite—."[29] Untermeyer was a literary celebrity for five decades. He was an essayist, poet, parodist, lover of puns, and TV personality; he was targeted and blacklisted by the House Un-American Activities Commitee and, in the early 1960s, he was named United States Poet Laureate. As an editor he was Robert Frost's "most assiduously cultivated literary operative," and his work did more than any other to define American literary modernism. Untermeyer succinctly captured Brown's manic and inspiring energy as a poet. Precisely because Untermeyer thought to include Brown as a poet worthy of imitation and parody, Untermeyer recognized that Brown had great and lasting significance for cultural history. Untermeyer, years later, considered Brown an experimental writer who later turned to writing cookbooks but does not mention the earlier magazine writing.[30]

When he wasn't throwing lavish parties, making a fortune on Wall Street, or writing and publishing volumes of poetry, Robert served as an owner-editor of the most important socialist magazine of the day. *The Masses* was collaboratively produced and owned, and Robert had a share in the ownership; it was from the start an ownership of the ideas and content, rather than profits or dividends, because the monthly magazine, priced at ten cents an issue (about $2 today), or $1 a year by subscription (or $20 today), with a circulation between 14,000 and 16,000 a month, *intended to lose money* and never pay any dividends. The editors depended, uncomfortably, on the support of wealthy patrons. Only Max Eastman and Floyd Dell, the managing editor, received token pay for their work, and nothing initially, but all of the editors owned shares, even if any future profit would be dedicated to socialist propaganda rather than to enriching the owners. The magazine's format, focus, and especially the generous use of comic illustrations influenced later periodicals, especially *The New Yorker*, which "patterned itself on the early *Masses*."[31] The illustrations also had an impact on the history of art, as "the cartoons full- and double-page drawings, etchings, paintings, and lithographs" are often considered "the most forceful and distinguished ever to appear in an American magazine."[32] It was mostly, but not entirely, a dissident artists' group, including John Sloan and Stuart Davis, both part of the earlier Ashcan artist group called the Eight, who produced these illustrations, and Robert Brown recognized their importance to the entire magazine; he vehemently advocated for the illustrators' "'slapping down pretty art'" in

John Sloan, a leader of *The Masses* dissident artists group.

favor of their "illustrations of the ugly aspects of urban life."[33] The readers' reactions to the artwork were intense, and often intensely negative, especially compared with their reactions to the essays, which were "accepted with little controversy."[34] The magazine included free verse and many discussions of psychoanalytic challenges to bourgeois morality; the line drawings and cartoons scandalized critics who were shocked at the portrayal of downtrodden female figures that did not fit the "Gibson girl" ideal. Even some of the magazine's own editors were unhappy when Stuart Davis's images alienated the magazine's readers and supporters. With no commercial advertising, the editors did not need to worry about a stricter morality, but they could not agree on who would decide what was appropriate to include and what to exclude. The artists objected to

Eastman's adding captions and titles to the artists' works without their permission. Many felt that Eastman's additions were clever and added political meaning to the works, but Davis felt that "having politically oriented captions and titles added [by the editors] to his work" interfered with the magazine's explicit goal to encourage artistic freedom.[35] Davis continued to publish in popular commercial magazines and newspapers, and he thought of *The Masses* as a radical alternative; he saw editorial interference and censorship as essential to avoid. Jack Reed would often sing a jingle that someone had written as a pointed criticism that now shows Reed's own sexism.

> They draw nude women for *The Masses*, Thick, ungainly, ugly lasses.
> How does that help the working classes?[36]

Brown's support of his friend Stuart Davis would eventually lead to a crisis at the magazine. The editors would hold raucous monthly meetings on Thursday evenings that would often involve heated discussions over what they saw as "the question of intelligibility and propaganda versus artistic freedom."[37] The artists' group saw themselves as struggling against a policy that sanctioned editorial meddling (often in favor of bourgeois morality) masquerading as a defense of socialist propaganda. All of the artists involved in the controversy had studied with the founders of the Ashcan school of painting, still closely aligned with both Imagism and the European modernism they advocated. These artists had seen the political potential in the Ashcan approach and sought now to use the style to expose and illuminate the dark corners of modern urban life with all of its ugly, oppressive contradictions. They were not dandies seeking to defend "art-for-art's-sake." Robert Brown's perspective, like much of the modernist vanguard, would find itself framed as art, and artists, opposed to real-world political engagement even though that binary did not correspond to the actual situation. It is Art Young's eloquent summary of the editor's position which unfortunately set up a frame, repeated by all of the later commentary, that saw the struggle as one between decadent artists, enamored of obscure modernist art and apolitical Imagist poetry, and engaged committed socialists.

> They want to run pictures of ash cans and girls hitching up their skirts in Horatio Street—regardless of ideas—and without title. On the other hand, a group of us believe that such pictures belong in exclusive art magazines. Therefore we put an emphasis on the

> value of constructive cartoons . . . to point the way out of a sordid materialistic world. And it looks unreasonable to me for artists who delight in portraying sordid and bourgeois ugliness to object to a "policy."[38]

Eventually, that disagreement would lead to a revolt led by Robert Carlton Brown, Hendrik "Henry" Glintenkamp, Stuart Davis, and Glenn Coleman with John Sloan as their spokesman; Sloan was "an older, more established artist who was also a Socialist party member," but he is now famous as an important painter who captured the characters and scenes of Greenwich Village and also known as one of the group of artists, including Duchamp and Beatrice Wood, who declared Greenwich Village an independent republic in a late-night party atop the Washington Square Arch.[39] Brown's artists' group wanted artistic freedom beyond the arbitrary tastes and morality of Dell and Eastman. The editors sought a policy that would constrain the arbitrary tastes and predilections of the decadent artists. Brown's group suggested they divide the editorial responsibilities, having the writers and artists decide what to include, and eliminating Eastman's "Editor" and Dell's "Managing Editor" positions. Eastman tendered "his resignation with a statement that cooperative editing had proved a sham, that the preparation of a magazine was a task too complex and continuous to be carried on by a large group meeting occasionally."[40] Eastman and Dell postponed the vote on Sloan's proposal, worked hard to get votes against it, and at the next meeting voted it down. Dell then stood up and moved to remove Sloan, Davis, Coleman, Brown, and Glintenkamp from the magazine. Glintenkamp's woodcuts, seen as evidence of an apolitical and detached artistic ideology, would later serve as key evidence of political sedition against the war in a trial to close *The Masses*. Dell's proposal was absurd, but it looked like he might have the votes.

Maurice Becker stood to defend the artists' group and asked that his name be included in the list of those Dell sought to remove from the editorial board and from the production of the magazine. With Becker joining the six who had voted for the proposal to honor the collective editorial organization instead of the two editors making all the final decisions, the Dell proposal to remove the dissenters failed. Quickly the majority instead elected the artists' group to positions running the corporation, but, in spite of the consolation vote in their favor, they all resigned from *The Masses*. The purge of Brown and the others from *The Masses* marked a larger shift that polarized the artistic forces supporting irreverent humor, biting wit, and bohemian mores from the sober revolutionary. The editorial purge marked the start of a larger division between a "broad and inclusive movement devoted, among other things, to creating a better understanding of life under the existing order," and a self-serious humorless correctness.[41] Art, for Robert Carlton Brown, was not an ornament to some higher socialist aims but the lens to clearly focus on current social conditions and emerging liberations. Brown argued that the artistic freedom to visually criticize commercial standards of beauty trumped the editors' socialist perspective.

The magazine, like the surrounding radical politics of the time, sought to include living freely and intensely as part of the magazine's political goals. Led by Emma Goldman's circle, they championed feminism, homosexuality, birth control, free motherhood without husbands, and what would later be called "free love." The magazine also explicitly promised an "arrogant, impertinent" approach, with "no respect for the respectable," but when Stuart Davis repeatedly and insistently delivered just that attitude, the other editors seemed to balk.[42] The artists and illustrators felt that art should "reveal" not "recommend," and Davis's sordid scenes and ugly figures were not easily contained by a caption or title.[43]

Although the magazine limped on and survived the government efforts to shut it down, it never again had much cultural importance. Years later, Eastman, in his *Enjoyment of Laughter* (1936), an enjoyment that he shared with Brown before Eastman's sober, doctrinaire attitude came between them, discussed how he had become an anti-Marxist. He condemned his earlier view as a perverse religion, but, as he looked back on that earlier period, he had a more affirmative view of the bohemianism he'd rejected in the purge of Robert Carlton Brown and the other dissident editors. Perhaps Eastman, a good friend of Brown's, still felt guilty for his actions, as he does not mention *The Masses*, his editorial role, the editors he purged, or any of his earlier socialist activities in his otherwise copious attacks on different approaches to Marxism in his 1940 book.[44] Among the many friends Robert made from his working on *The Masses*, Jimmie Farrell, whom Brown called "young enough and Irish enough to be my son," would later work on preparing a text for Brown's machine in 1931.[45] Farrell claims that his work for the machine led to the abbreviated staccato style in his famous Studs Lonigan series. Years later in the late 1930s, Farrell signed a public call, written by Brown, to start an American Writer's Congress to protect writers' economic rights during the height of the Depression.

Arthur Kreymborg, whom everyone called Krimmie, soon started working on ways to publish the new poetry, established the necessary financial backing from Walter Arensberg, and began organizing a magazine called *Others: A Magazine of the New Verse*. Man Ray's shack became the summer retreat for Kreymborg, who loved the pastoral setting with "the view of the Jersey meadows, striped and streaked with the Passaic and Hackensack rivers, lazily rolling away to the horizon."[46] The members of the core group included Orrick Johns, Mina Loy, Marianne Moore, Maxwell Bodenheim, Robert Alden Sanborn, Conrad Potter Aiken, Mary Carolyn Davies, Horace Holley, William Carlos Williams, and Skipwith Cannell, but Bob Brown is usually not mentioned as part of the core group. The group started communicating with Ezra Pound, Amy Lowell, and others in Europe and America about the Imagist poetry. Kreymborg developed the title for the magazine from his dictum about writing: "The old expressions are with us always, and there are always others."[47] Arensberg wanted the phrase to include a "but" rather than an "and," as he felt the "and" would suggest the magazine's timidity rather than its daring newness.

The English poet Frank Stuart Flint concisely summarized the goals of the new verse in three precepts (later claimed by Ezra Pound as his three principles from 1912): "1) Direct treatment of the 'thing' whether objective or subjective. 2) To use absolutely no word that does not contribute to the presentation. 3) As regarding rhythm: to compose in the sequence of the musical phrase not sequence of a metronome."[48] The second precept would guide Brown's later thoughts on producing texts for his reading machine. In her description of the Imagist poetics, Amy Lowell discusses the "polyphonic prose" or "many-voiced—and the form is so called because it makes use of all the 'voices' of poetry . . . every form of rhythm, even prose rhythm at times, but usually holds no particular one for long."[49] In addition to the polyphonic, the poets omitted capitals at the start of each line and used free verse and cadences instead of rhyme.

The new magazine appeared in July 1915, with Mina Loy's "Love Songs" prominently displayed. Her poems were much talked about in New York's art and literary circles, as she used intimate details and images from her own life; her openness was shocking, and the group hoped that the scandal would put the new poetry and verse on the map in a way that the Armory exhibit had changed the perception of art using scandal strategically—what one might call a scandalography. Krimmie himself was a bit too timid, and Arensberg soon stopped funding the magazine as it was a bit too tame for his tastes. Likewise, Brown, who also published in the magazine, called *Others* "lima beany" in his later notes and recollections (he called it pallid, bland, unexciting, and pasty). He also mocked the Imagists in the poetic dedication of his book of poetry, *My Marjonary*, published the same year *Others* appeared. Brown played a crucial role in the Imagist group, wrote poems in that style, and nevertheless mocked them (and himself). He starts by attacking their amateurish pseudo-erudition, lack of rhythm, and lack of rhyme.

DEDICATION
AUX MES FRERES
You daredevil dilettantes In vers libre
Amazing amateurs!
Why have you burned
Your rhyming dictionaries
Behind you
(The one hope you had)
And gone in for angel treading?
What do you cribbers of the classics
Know
About rag-time

And continues with invented names and inside jokes, like "Amorthorincus (That great Greek goddess / Whose sensitive nose was sprained / By a passing whiff / Of garlic)."[50] The invented name seems to refer to an out-of-joint, or crooked, nose, which fits the parenthetical explanation. As with much of Brown's humor and allusions, the reference is lost. In any case, he seems to have pointed his criticism, in his dedication, at Ezra Pound and the European Imagistes, rather than at the American group. In fact, Brown frequented with Duchamp and William Carlos Williams the African American jazz cabarets in the basement of the Marshall Hotel on West 53rd Street at Sixth Avenue or Barron Wilkin's Little Savoy on West 35th Street; so, in the poetic allusion to the Imagists' lack of knowledge about ragtime, he refers to others besides the Americans who were familiar with jazz cadences.

Others drew more poets to the Village, and Kreymborg saw the gathering of the artists and writers as part of a utopian project of "making an ideal place out of nowhere." The editorial meetings were "loose and informal" outdoor picnics with the "attendance as unpredictable as the agenda."[51] Brown started publishing in *Others* for the second issue, and Kreymborg eventually included five of Robert Carlton Brown's poems in the *Others* anthology of 1916.[52] The magazine was started to allow artists and writers to escape from the grind and "compromise" of the commercial magazines that had defined Brown's career. Krimmie seems to describe Robert's predicament in his anonymous description of these writers and artists:

> That business enterprise should have permeated and directed material America was natural and wholesome, no doubt; but that it should have stolen into spiritual America and contaminated nearly everyone concerned with creative expression—this was loathsome. To his horror [Kreymborg wrote his autobiography in the third person], he had met a number of artists who had been thrust or let themselves fall into the pit of compromise: an unending host, in the course of events, composed of pathetic people the world dubbed hack writers and commercial artists. They were caught in a trap . . . .[53]

In opposition to the commercial magazines that treated the writers and artists like laborers, Kreymborg announced that his magazine would "work on the principle of cooperative, egalitarian editorship."[54] The groups associated with Grantwood Village, like *The Masses*, the Washington Square Players, and the Provincetown Players, proclaimed similar ideals as the *Others*: democratic editorial and creative decision making in pursuit of aesthetic and sociopolitical liberation. In spite of the collegial atmosphere and goals, the *Others* reflected Kreymborg's vision and tastes.

The editor of a collection of William Carlos Williams's letters prefaces one letter from Williams to Bob Brown by calling Brown "the Maecenas of the 'Others Group' in Grantwood."[55] Arensberg was also called the Maecenas of the group, but Brown did supply the lavish parties at Grantwood. In the colony, Robert saw how Man Ray broke with the industrial model of publishing for profit by printing his own newsletters just for his circle of friends and visitors. In the magazine and novel world, publishers were large national and international corporations, but Man Ray demonstrated, as did Guido Bruno in Greenwich Village, a model of publishing that was unconnected to profit, mass organizations, or anything beyond what could be produced in a garret in the city or in a shack in the countryside.

Man Ray's publications included *The Bum* (no copies of the single issue printed exist), *Adonism: Some Poems by Man Ray*, and *The Ridgefield Gazook*, "America's first proto-Dada periodical," with only one issue ever published.[56] Although Man Ray bought a press, it was ruined when the movers accidentally dropped it as they were unloading the truck. *The Gazook,* made from "a single sheet folded to form four pages, was entirely hand-written and drawn by Man Ray, who signed the texts and drawings

Rose influenced Man Ray's experiments in Imagist painting.

with different pseudonyms" that teased his friends in the colony with parodies of their work and names.[57]

The fifteen or so full-time residents, outnumbered two to one by the temporary residents, included Rose Watson and her husband. Rose's husband was a "tall, distinguished-looking man," who wanted to become a writer, "but drank mostly."[58] Rose, well known in bohemian Village circles for her libertine feminism, vivaciousness, and good looks, worked and wrote for Emma Goldman's causes as well as helped sell *The Masses*. On first meeting her, Man Ray's wife thought her a "woman out for trouble," but they soon became friends.[59] Man Ray remembered that Rose and her husband "found a romantic little shack in the woods, covered with bark and the gables ornamental with twisted branches and roots. It was on the property of one of the more substantial stone houses [one of which was Robert's], but quite invisible among the trees and ferns."[60] Robert Brown and Rose Watson started to find each other interesting and attractive when Robert threw an "enormous housewarming party," as Man Ray recounted, "on the roof, which had been converted into a flat terrace."

> About a hundred people came; there was dancing and drinking until early morning, and a few fights. Bob seemed to get along especially well with Rose, but her husband was drunk and too feeble to protest.[61]

When Man Ray's wife suggested he was "too busy with Bob's wife," Lillian, during the party, he denied it.[62] Lillian had already imagined liberation from her marriage and would soon leave Bob for another man; by the mid-1920s, Lillian had already married, and divorced, twice more, but remained on good terms with Bob throughout especially as they had two children together.

> That summer there were other distractions, with visitors, and contacts with some of the literary neighbors. Bob Brown's wife had left him; Rose had left her drinking and unproductive husband. Bob's mother, a grand and vital lady who had helped him with his writing, came down to stay with him and gave the place a more serious look, although we had some gay evenings together.[63]

This was the summer of 1915. Rose's bohemian style, in the fashion of the Greenwich Villagers pre-1917, added a louche quality to her look. She had an intense gaze, which gave her an intelligent air that accurately reflected and reinforced her articulate engagement with politics and the ideas of the day. She often wore her blouse slightly off the shoulder, leaving her long, thin neck exposed. Just as Isadore Duncan's uncorsetted modern dance had loosened the constraints on feminine beauty and movement, Rose's uncorsetted torso showed the contours of her voluptuous body visible under her loose blouse. The blouse was often a loose-fitting, and sometimes brightly colored, smock or Russian embroidered peasant linen shirt. Her hair was long, in the style of the "new woman," but slightly messy, a code for bohemian, instead of in a tight bun.

She wore flat sandals with her heels on the ground rather than pumps with heels. Her skirts just covered her knees at a time when middle-class propriety still encouraged ankle-length dresses; though the bohemian style was cotton stockings, not bare legs, her apparel was still considered suggestive. Because the skinny fashion of the 1920s had not begun, the bohemian women's fashion accentuated a free, loose-fitting spirit and

Rose, the "belle" of the Liberal Club in Greenwich Village.

unconstrained body. Rose would sometimes add a beaded necklace. To outsiders, the cultural code of these outfits expressed a disrespect of Victorian conventions of femininity and a lack of propriety (and even a rejection of the more modern Edwardian images of the "new woman" with long hair). To those who met her, Rose was often mentioned as beautiful, good-looking, seductive, or the "belle" of the Liberal Club in Greenwich Village, where ragtime music would play on the phonograph and the writers, radicals, and artists would lubricate their discussions.[64] She was also a regular at Romany Marie's restaurant, which fed the Greenwich Villagers. From the moment they met, Bob's story became Rose's story too, and he would later call her his "Rose-rib," heretically alluding to Eve's physical connection to Adam. They were joined intensely and erotically—as Bob would often say, they were "free mating"—but attracted to each other's revolutionary spirit to see the (entire) world (literally and figuratively) as if through new eyes. She soon took the name Brown as her own, and records indicate a civil union; they traveled, and lived, as Mr. and Mrs., but were certainly not married in a church.

The crucial events involving Rose in the history of art, specifically for Man Ray's development as a modernist artist, would occur not too long after she had moved to the Village. Alanson Hartpence suggested a group go on a "camping tour for a few days into the wild country up the Hudson" to paint landscapes and commune with nature. "Rose and her [first] husband liked the outdoors and asked to go along. We were three couples, each one with a blanket rolled around the shoulder and knapsacks with provisions."[65] After a tense false start to the trip, with Man Ray's wife upset with the supposed flirtation between Man Ray and Rose, they eventually arrived at a campsite on Bear Mountain on the west side of the Hudson River; the mountain area was a couple of years before it was opened as a New York State Park, and campers were beginning to find the area a pleasant respite from urban life. At the campsite, Man Ray vividly remembered the scene.

> Rose [Watson] and Helen [Hartpence] went down to the brook and bathed; Donna joined them a few minutes later. We watched the nude figures moving about through the branches; I thought of Cézanne's paintings, and made a mental note of the treatment of figures in a natural setting, for future works.[66]

He saw Rose running and swimming naked; the image stuck in his head, and he began to think about painting immediate impressions and snapshot images. The scene led Man Ray to embrace a kind of Imagist painting technique in which one paints from memory. This was a radical break from the realist painters and increasingly led Man Ray to art that involved internal memories and motivations. The epiphany that provoked Man Ray to change his process of art making, and the first step to embracing an internally motivated Surrealism, involved this scene with Rose. Painting and art were traditionally produced by reference to the external world; even cubism referenced an abstracted reality. Man Ray's turn to painting from internal memories was a radical break difficult to imagine now as unusual, as it was part of reorienting modern art and literature based on memories, dreams, ideas, and internal realities. That the event involved Rose seems fitting in this book's *Zelig*-like comedy about a biography that places the protagonists in the background of scenes involving so many luminaries of artistic and literary innovation. One can imagine captioning the scene as if it were a Man Ray photograph: "Here's Man Ray having his Eureka moment, and there's Rose in the scene provoking his epiphany." Although Man Ray was already considering having the subject directly in front of the painter as a hindrance to creativity, the memories of the charged scene gave him the push he needed. Not only did memories become available for art, but also words on the page became visual possibilities, not just a transparent means of description.

It seems fitting that Rose would appear in this crucial scene of Man Ray's development of a new aesthetic; she, like Robert Brown, popped up in many crucial scenes, but in the background or, in this case, "through the branches." Rose had already worked as a writer and editor with vanguard efforts. From these formative years in New York, and especially Grantwood, her family became the always dispersing and displaced avant-garde she first found in the Village rather than any relatives she'd left behind in the Ohio of her youth. Rose's father, Robert Johnston, had died while she was still a young girl; during the winters her mother, Sally Rosa Johnston, sent her to Winter Park, Florida, to protect Rose's own delicate health. Soon after Rose left for college, Sally developed what would likely today be diagnosed as Alzheimer's disease, and there was little reason for Rose to return home ever again. Although her ancestors had come to America on the *Mayflower*, she adopted the avant-garde as her diasporic home as she traveled the world.

Rose was part of the emerging feminism with its "increasing emphasis on the question of combining career and marriage among a small but articulate and visible segment of urban women." This emphasis "marked a new phase in the development of the women's movement. And sometime around 1909 or so a new word appeared to describe this new departure: 'feminism.'"[67] Even the popular magazines, like the ones Robert had written for, sought to appeal to the emancipated woman likely working in urban offices. The more radical feminists gravitated to Greenwich Village, "characterized by an unprecedented easy mixing of the sexes"; and men, like Brown and his new friends, became vocal advocates of feminism, which they saw in terms of their own collective liberation from a traditionally dependent and passive femininity.[68] In general, the sexual liberation and feminism of the times was a self-conscious political protest against the dehumanizing demands of modern capitalism. At the same time, an emerging marketing machine channeled this resistant and bohemian ferment in the Village in order to turn the "new woman" into "the new consumer." Robert Brown and the majority involved in the charged political resistance were also writing for popular women's magazines, working in advertising, writing and performing in popular plays, and making movies.

When Sigmund Freud visited Clark University and Coney Island in 1909, the conversation among the radicals turned to sexual liberation, and when Emma Goldman's followers distributed pamphlets on explicit information about contraceptives in 1910, the conversation turned to how to liberate women from respectability and from the burdens of what polite, oppressive society thought. Other prominent labor organizers like Margaret Sanger were prominent birth control advocates. It was in this context that Rose moved to Grantwood Village and decided to reinvent her life as an equal partner in work and life—she just needed to find the right partner. And, Bob was going through a similar liberation in both his life and writing as he embraced a type of Imagism that later came to be known as visual poetry but at the time was simply called poem-painting by Man Ray. Sexual liberation, control over one's own body and desires, and, in particular, birth control brought to the fore how the personal is political. The vanguard poets, writers, and artists produced their works and thought of their everyday lives in this context. Then, as now, the forces of repression saw art, culture, and education as fundamentally aligned with people's rights and autonomous desires against corporate capitalism. The members of the Grantwood Village group saw their experiments in poetry in the context of searching for a new language.

Conversations and projects at Grantwood often involved the notion of a visual poetry, and Man Ray produced a visual poem-painting, *Man Ray 1914*, that resembles a landscape but on closer inspection is simply the letters of his name. The letters of his name become the artwork: Letters and words become visual images. His poetry also is about the visual design of the page, and one can imagine his poem "Hieroglyphics," about words on the page, being of great interest and inspiration to Brown.[69] Words as images were also becoming legitimate images for art and, more important, demonstrated the poets' and artists' interest in the poetics of visual design and layout. In the fall of 1915, Duchamp met Man Ray and Bob Brown, and Bob produced a visual poem for Marcel Duchamp's *The Blindman* (sometimes published as *The Blind Man*), "Eyes on the Halfshell," that later was reproduced in a collection of handwritten visual poetry. Brown's poetry and publications started to reflect his personal transformation as well as his experimentation with free prose verse and visual poetry. He published *Tahiti*, an allusion to Gauguin's evocation of an aesthetic and personal freedom radically different from the work-a-day world of the laboring, paid-per-word, magazine fiction writer or the stock speculator alike. He embraced the radical perspective not as an opposition to earning more money than one needs to survive but as advocating the expansion of those fundamental needs and rights to include an un-alienated connection to one's work and emotional well-being.

In 1916, Brown published two volumes of poetry, one with Guido Bruno, the "Barnum of Bohemia." Bruno represented a model of independent publishing that fascinated Brown. Bruno produced a long list of publications all with his name in the title: *Bruno's Bohemia*; *Bruno's Review of Life, Love, and Literature*; *Bruno's Weekly*; *Bruno's Review of Two Worlds*; *Bruno's Scrap Book*; and *Bruno's Chap Books*. The publisher was often listed as "Guido Bruno In His Garret," and Bruno published Brown as well as Alfred Kreymborg, Djuna Barnes, letters of Oscar Wilde, and others in the Bruno Chap Books series. The "bewildering succession of little magazines" put Bruno on the map and made him the best-known venue for bohemian Greenwich Village poetry and perspectives.[70] In an article in the *Times* describing an exhibit at Bruno's garret the year before Brown published in the Chap Books series, the third subheading shouted in all capitals: "PURPLE HAIR ON ONE GIRL" with the opening sentence concluding "art still rules in Greenwich Village."[71] Regardless of the mainstream culture's view of the apparently scandalous goings-on at Bruno's, his weekly mixed local Village news with reports on the national and international literary and artistic world with especially useful coverage of small literary magazines around the country.[72] The title poem in the *Tahiti* collection (written after he was separated from Lillian and practically living with Rose) gives a sense of the new morality and Brown's romantic exoticism. Compare that poem with another one written around the same time that again portrays Brown's romantic exoticism.

> She said, "Will you come with me to Tahiti?"
> Yes, I will go.
> Leaving my babies to be spoilt by another parent,
> Leaving my wife shift for herself.
> All the way I will go
> With her.
> Because in Tahiti there are soft skies that will be
>   strange and new to us:
> Flowers, birds and beauty of a fresh and wond-
>   rous kind;
> Curious customs, quaint houses, new names, a-
>   waiting us.

I will go as lightly as I came into the world,
Knowing that where happiness is
I must be.
Lured by romance,
Carried there by something whose name is not
  known.
Yes, I will go with you to Tahiti.[73]

Brown published a second collection of poetry, *My Marjonary,* in 1916. He had the publisher send free copies to writers whom he thought highly of as people, poets, and writers: Carl Sandburg, Susan Glaspell, Edna St. Vincent Millay, Fred Ellis, Carl Van Vechten, and others. The title prose poem of the collection tells the story of an allegorical donkey, Marjonary, whom the narrator feeds with four-leaf clover he has planted in a back room of his store. Brown thought of his writing and life in terms of poetic luck that one, nevertheless, had to cultivate. As an indication of his fascination with exoticism and his identification with the Other, rather than the tourist on a visit, one poem has a unique take on a love poem as a condemnation of white imperialism and a celebration of gruesome hilarity. In this poem, neither the narrator nor his lover identifies with the "White man whose bones they happily gnaw." The poem's deconstruction of love poems also illuminates the new morality of the time that did not reject passion, love, or even sentimentality but disoriented the notions of beauty, appropriateness, and legitimacy. One wonders how many love poems celebrate happy cannibals eating a white man's bones and compare it to the pallid existence of the poet.

My Love
My love is a tidy cannibal girl
Far off on a pink coral isle.
When I am pleased with her
I crack cocoanuts with my strong white teeth
And drop them bit by bit into her smiling mouth.
Together we gnaw the bones of
White men
Ship-wrecked on our coral isle.
And we laugh while we eat.
Our digestion is robust
We never take pink pills
To condition our conscience.
And when I am tired of my

Wholesome love
I ship back here in my submarine
And write poems in this dull little room,
Love poems to my dainty Duckewawa,
Far off on our cannibal isle of coral.[74]

The collection was, according to Brown in later notes, adopted as a text for English classes at New York University and other colleges. The challenge to both modern marketing that sought to cure any intellectual indigestion with a "pink pill" as well as polite society was also a call for a different sort of transcendence, respite, and relief from a "dull" existence.

Rose and Bob moved back into the city in 1916. Rose ran a colorful hand-weaving shop, Flambeau Weavers, just off Fifth Avenue near East 39th Street, behind the Union League Club's previous location on Fifth Avenue. Rose decorated the apartment in an eclectic mix of styles that made the place seem like an art installation. They bought ultra-modern furniture, and Rose decorated the bedroom with Japanese gold paper, with a large Ben Franklin stove, a life-size Belgian rooster in gleaming white porcelain, and a Dutch brass coal scuttle bucket. Beatrice Wood, the Dada artist and intimate friend of Marcel Duchamp's, would go to the roof of the building with Rose to batik fabric. Perhaps the eccentricity of the apartment's interior design attracted the burglar-neighbors, who would regularly steal something every time the couple went out. Instead of outrage, Bob greeted the regular thefts with resignation, and he soon left notes for the burglars, asking politely that they leave this or that, and the burglar-neighbors obliged and made their thefts tidy and respectful of Bob's requests.

He continued to regularly visit Coney Island, which he thought of as the embodiment of popular culture, populist aspirations, and experimental poetry. Brown's new style of experimental writing, a comical Imagistic listing of which now seems like a precursor to George Perec's list-like poems from his work with the experimental poetry group, known by the acronym of the group's full name in French, OULIPO (*Ouvroir de littérature potentielle*; translated as laboratory or workshop of potential literature). The list form was perfectly suited to Brown's "oystering eyes" that took in all the thrills at Coney Island. Brown would write down each of the images that stuck in his mind and poetically connect each of the items in an associative link that allowed one to get a sense of the scene and the sensibility of the place. Brown would also narrate the scenes as if he were one of the performers—as if he had joined the permanent fair and side-shows. One could travel the world. His journeys would regularly begin with a trip to "pasteboard Alps, and waiters with comic conic felt caps at Feltman's" helping blonde beer hall Fräuleins serve "blonde beer.'"

> The balloonists, and lady cyclists in ballooning bloomers, and Dr May Walker in pants; Dame [Eden] Musée's, flea circuses, bullfights, cockfights, cattle fairs, in a lot of lands. All I had to have was a world's fair every day and here in Coney I reviewed it in miniature, shooting the chutes and white tin birdies in the rifle galleries, pumping up my lungs and muscles and getting a forbidden eyeful in the penny arcades, getting seasick on the sea-saw [misspelling—a pun—in original], short-changed a whole dollar on every two dollar bill, imagining myself a cane-twirling bawling barker, flirting with the Fat Girl, the Tattooed Lady, the Circassian Beauty, the Pinhead Girl—oh, I would marry a midget, we'd have plates of cherrystone clams gargled down with the beer and soft shell crabs, and have the time of our lives![75]

Instead of publishing an extended poetic meditation on Coney Island, he published a *Comic Map of Coney Island* in the summer of 1916. The entire project took a month to complete. He arranged for a meeting with the freakish "odd assortment" of the Coney Island Chamber of Commerce and "sold them a couple thousand dollars' worth of advertising on the funny map."[76] Brown hired an unnamed "artist friend" to draw the actual map and had 10,000 maps printed on spec—gambling that he would sell out quickly. He hired newsboys to hawk the maps at the entrances and charged ten cents for each map. He waited for the customers and expected an avalanche.

> The avalanche came, but with millions of non-buyers rushing out of the ferries, buses, subways streets cars to get at the babes sweating on the beach, and at bumpers of beer sweating on the bars. They actually knocked down my dozen kids and stepped all over their new nifty [newsboy-style] caps embroidered [with the title] *Comic Map of Coney* . . . Rose, and I, had had made for them.[77]

Their partner in the project, Allen Norton, had made sure the hats were on the kids' heads "at the proper jaunty angle, when he drilled them in selling our product."[78] The maps were one of the few failures in a string of business ventures, but rather than slouching away in defeat, Brown planned his next stunt to raise money, while promoting fun.

He invested another couple thousand dollars in a restaurant on 57th

Street, which Cora ran for about a year, and she selected the day's menu; twenty-five years later she would use those recipes and menus for their cookbooks. Robert's friend B. Russell Herts had started the restaurant and designed its interior in order to popularize his interior decorating business next door. Although Brown did not see any profit from his investment, his owning a share of the restaurant meant that he could use the basement space for special events. He threw the "Censorship Ball in honor of Anthony Comstock" in 1916 and later described the party in poetic terms: The "clandestine bar maids bit clandestine bishops on their necks and me on my bare behind, for I came as Cupid."[79] Some of these balls became emblematic of the decadent bohemian excitement especially in Greenwich Village. Unlike some of his businesses, the balls were profitable, and the artists' fun became legendary.

In search of funding, the *Masses* editors decided to hold a costume party or ball. Culturally, this might have been the most important contribution of *The Masses* to Village life in the 1910s. Once again, Robert Carlton Brown played an important role in the staging of that party. They decided on Webster Hall, on Eleventh Street close to Third Avenue, for the fundraiser. In a probably apocryphal story, the group approached the owner, who also owned the saloon next door. When they asked how much the hall would cost to rent, the gruff question came back: "'Is yours a drinking crowd?' the owner demanded. 'Hell, yes,' the poetic-looking [Floyd] Dell replied. 'All right, you can have it for nothing,' the owner said."[80]

After the success of the *Masses* party, many others followed, including one to raise money for Duchamp's *The Blind Man*. At the Blind Man's Ball in 1917, Duchamp swung from the chandelier, and Joseph Stella challenged a man to a mock duel over the supposed stealing of Beatrice Wood's virginity. Soon Brown had started a business staging these costume dances. Bob rented Webster Hall, which became synonymous with these costume parties. The very notion of the wild-partying bohemian artists and poets began there—began with Brown and others in his crowd realizing that one could combine the needs of their unprofitable publications with their libertine goals. Among the Webster Hall gatherings, beyond the fundraisers, there was The Pagan Rout, The September Morn Ball, the Bal Primitive, and The Falling Leaf Eve Revel—all staged, prominently advertised, hosted, and emceed by Bob Brown. That Revel was announced by a drawing, on gold paper, of a post-impressionistic Eve both before and after the leaf had fallen.

For the Bal Primitive announcement, Brown drew an Adam and Eve together on the fig-leaf ticket. "The uptowners flocked down and tossed

Bob used Webster Hall for many elaborate costume parties.

dollar bills in at the ticket window until our cashier actually had to push them off onto the floor of this little box and tamp them down."[81] He sublimated all of his remaining literary ambitions into the copy and illustrations for the announcements for those balls, and "Don Marquis called them 'flitterature' in his *Sun* column and Allen Norton and I opened an office as dance promoters after the success of *Rogue*'s Funeral Ball—'Come in a Taxi, go home in a Hearse.'" Not everyone was pleased. The official report of the Committee of Fourteen, the city government's investigators of vice, named Bobby Edwards and "Bobby" Brown as the organizers and insinuated that the government would have to stop these notorious troublemakers.

Brown began to grow dissatisfied with the imaginary travel at Coney Island, so in his characteristic response, in 1917 he took a White Fleet tour down through the Caribbean to Colombia and back. He took along a friend, Roger Babson, and got a suite on the deck. He would cable his buy and sell orders back to his broker and kept "two secretaries busy so they didn't even see that hot, *alligatory* bit of the world through the port hole."[82] Unfortunately, when he arrived back in New York the bull mar-

The flyer for Bob Brown's Paris and the Golden Apple party.

ket had busted, and Brown lost everything. He was forced to freelance and started working for Tousey's *Photoplay*, a motion picture fan magazine, where Brown rewrote movie scenarios into prose.

After those "lush living years" all Brown had left, after the now-forgotten market fall of 1917, was his house in Ridgefield, a "couple of used-up cars," and his "dwindling stake in the 57th Street restaurant."[83] Cora continued to manage the restaurant, and Robert knew he could always eat there for free, "together with the elite, Teddy Roosevelt's young, who liked the 75 cent Southern chicken dumpling dinner, Theater Guilders, and members of Mrs. Stuyvesant Fish's Club de Vingt that used the floor above." Instead, Robert and Rose would go to the downtown Automat with only a dime between them. There they would share "one beef pie browned in a tiny porcelain bird bath and, with a fork apiece, be-

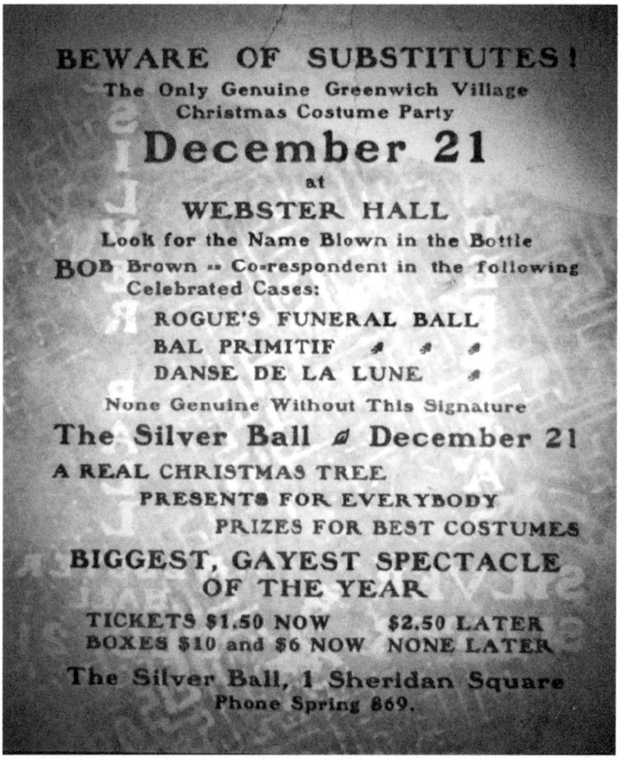

The flyer for the Webster Hall Silver Ball.

gan gobbling it up from opposite ends."[84] He was, at thirty-one years old in 1917, starting over again with little money, a new wife, and increasing political tensions making life difficult. He loved the mechanized restaurant not only because of the prices but also because of the efficiency and utopian possibilities of mechanizing everyday life.

He once again returned to his profitable hobby of buying and selling rare books. Rather than try to build a collection, he thought of himself as a "'sharp-shooter' like [the famous book collectors and dealers of the time] Harry Stone, Dr. [Abraham Simon Wolf] Rosenbach, Gabriel Wells, [Samuel G.] Drake, Jake Schmartz, any bibliophile who can unerringly pick a plum out of a five and ten cent, three-for-a-quarter bin, enjoy it for a while and then sell for anywhere from a hundred to a thousand, maybe a million, times what he paid for it." He thought of himself as "a

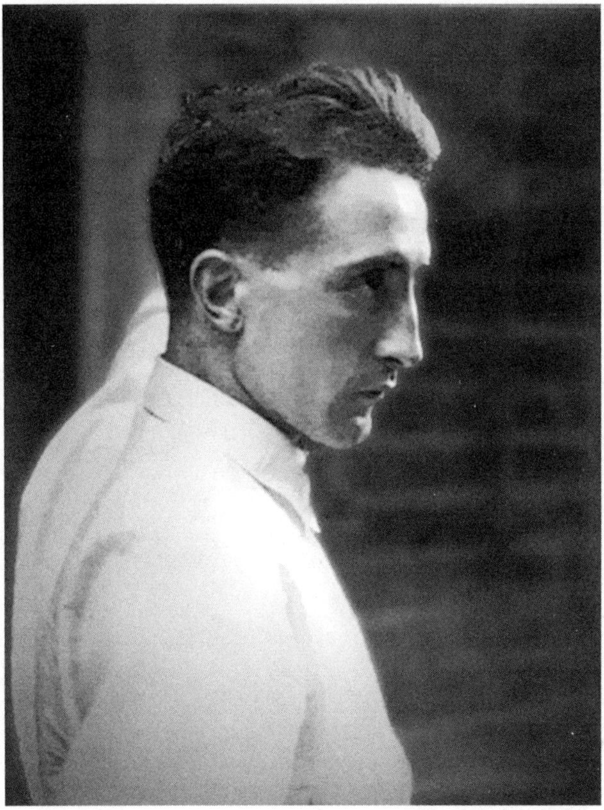

Two of Brown's poems appeared in Duchamp's *The Blind Man*.

cut below the ones who made a business of it," for Brown had no regular customers.

> The best I could do when I picked [up lucky finds was] Thoreau's school books, with his own and his father's name scrawled in the white spaces, and his presentation copy of *Walden* or something to "the only woman he ever loved," with a tiny eagle feather thrust through the page with his poem to an eagle.[85]

Once Robert grabbed a find like that he would pass it on to a dealer for "ten dollars apiece for the dime" he had paid. In turn, "the dealer would write up the find for *Harper's* or some other highbrow magazine and then maybe sell them [*sic*] to the Mr. Morgan for his library at a

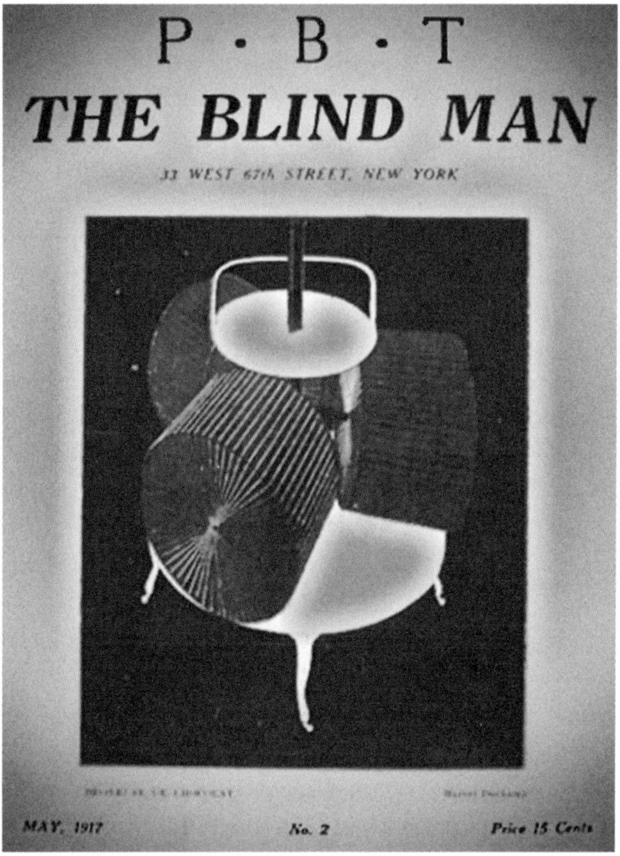

The Blind Man.

similar rate of profit for his invested sawbuck."[86] He had auctioned many volumes of rare books at least since 1915 as a mostly unprofitable hobby, but now, in 1917, he needed the money. He became so involved with looking for the lucky find that he "holed up in the rickety Roland Hotel just across the street from the book bins I shook down every day" around West 59th Street near the corner of Fifth Avenue over to the corner of Park and East 59th where butlers and servants were discarding their employers' old books. He would again return to bookselling in New York, but not for another thirty-five or forty years. His itch for the great find and his collecting bug, however, would become a lifelong obsession.

In spite of his economic difficulties, Robert was now at the center of the emergence of American Dada publications. He had two poems in the May 1917 issue of *Blind Man*, and he had one in *Rongwrong* in July 1917. The war had brought some of the European Dadaists to America, and with Man Ray, this group of artists unofficially founded what came to be known as New York Dada. Francis Picabia produced three issues of *391* in the summer of 1917, and although Brown did not contribute, he began to also to have proto-Futurist discussions about machine art. In 1915, Picabia had proclaimed, "The machine has become more than a mere adjunct of life. It is really part of human life, perhaps the very soul." In that same year, he exhibited a series of 'object portraits,' reminiscent for Brown of William Wallace Cook's "I am poems," in which Picabia's drawings of machines were portraits of specific people, like his "Here is Stieglitz" (1915). A couple of years later Man Ray built a sculpture, *New York* (1917), from a bundle of chrome strips held together with C-clamps. Brown started thinking about a portrait of a reading machine as early as 1915, not for the first time in 1929 when he announced his plans for the machine to the expatriate avant-garde in France.

There was another machine threatening Brown: the war machine. In the 1910s, as the ferocity against progressive social causes increased and war hysteria intensified, many sought at least temporary refuge outside the Village, which previously was a haven for bohemians, experimental modernist writers, and radical political organizers. President Woodrow Wilson's decision to enter World War I in 1917, the Russian revolution, and the ferocity of the debate on whether to enter the war or not made even the Village a tense and contentious scene. The government shut down *The Masses*, deported Emma Goldman and Alexander Berkman, and the "disputatious seminar of all brands of radicalism" had no place in the tense partisan atmosphere.[87] The Conscription and Espionage Acts of 1917 were directed at the publication of "false" information that might incite desertion, mutiny, obstructing conscription, or more broadly fueling opposition to the war.

The government used these laws to go after political opponents, especially the socialists, anarchists, and bohemians. State-supported vigilante groups began parading even in Greenwich Village looking to forcibly compel young men to register. Brown was already a bit old, but certainly he felt the political pressure to leave as others involved in *The Masses* were indicted and his name appeared on blacklists. None of the poets and activists could imagine the dangers, tragedies, and adventures that awaited them.

At each train stop, soldiers searched the train looking for spies or Yaqui soldiers masquerading as sick patients under the smallpox sheets. As the soldiers neared Battery J, Bob and Rose held their breath in fear.

4

Exile, Escape, Empire, and World Travels, 1917–28

—Where was Battery J during Your Great War?—Why, Battery J was in hell catching red-hot rivets . . . bare red-handed without a bucket.

—*Bob Brown describing in "readies" style his group's experiences as exiles during World War I,* You Gotta Live[1]

Refugees expelled from one country to the next represent the avant-garde of their people.

—*Hannah Arendt*[2]

In literary histories of modernism, the word *expatriate* has, until recently, referred to a group of American writers and artists living in Paris and the Côte d'Azur in the 1920s.[3] Ernest Hemingway immortalized this supposedly high-living crowd in his novel *A Moveable Feast* (1964), as did Gertrude Stein and F. Scott Fitzgerald, but counter to those decadent and politically detached expatriates, a number of these same expatriates, including Rose and Bob Brown, began by fleeing, penniless, through Mexico and into Latin America in 1917 (often to avoid jail for sedition or draft dodging). In their actions, they broadened the definition of *expatriates* and stressed the literary and artistic vanguardists' connections to loss, exile, violence, and narrow escapes. These were not just themes in later avant-garde art; these were the lived experience of a generation, where a poverty-induced make-do resourcefulness reinforced collages of found, often discarded, objects; where exile led to a fascination with otherness and displacement; where disgust with the xenophobia sweeping the United States and Europe in the late teens and early 1920s led to flaunting diversity, difference, internationalism, and otherness; and where the necessity to avoid arrest fueled an interest in masquerade, coded allusions, and inside jokes. The colorful cast of writers and artists struggled, fled, and tried to live, often literally struggling to stay alive, in spite of the hardships in Mexico. They included the Dada artists Mina Loy and her lover Arthur Cravan, who also boxed as a prizefighter both as a Dadaist stunt and to make money. Bob's good friend Allen Norton, editor of the important literary journal *Rogue*, which first promoted Gertrude Stein's poetry, fled with Bob and Rose. Henry Glintenkamp, one of *The Masses'* illustrators and political cartoonists, whose images of war and poverty had provoked the government to indict him, fled on the expectation of certain conviction and a long prison sentence. The government also used his illustrations, etched cartoons of the degradations of war and poverty, as evidence to seek to but unsuccessfully shut the magazine down. The sedition clauses in the new laws trumped any rights to free speech at least temporarily. More than a decade later, in the early 1930s, Bob wrote a fictionalized account of their adventures in Mexico and Latin America called *You Gotta Live*, written almost entirely in a proletarian realist style. The title summarizes the liberationist attitude and pragmatic concerns in escaping from constant threats of the groups of refugees called "slackers"; American congressmen used the term *slackers* to describe war resisters and conscientious objectors, who were seen to be slacking in their military duties. The anti-war radicals soon adopted the word to describe their own oppositional stance to the military-industrial war machine. *The Masses'* managing editor, Floyd Dell, summarized the radical "slacker" attitude by explaining that "Idleness is not doing *nothing*. Idleness is being free to do anything." In this context, slackers stood at the ready to resist an imperialist war machine. As a badge of honor and bravery, Bob, in his fictionalized account, described himself and his fellow exiles as "valiant slackers." One U.S. senator claimed that 30,000 slackers were hiding out in Mexico, and others had similar estimates. Many of the slackers were writers, editors, poets, and artists aligned with the then-powerful and popular socialist anti-war agenda. They were under particular threat from the Espionage Act, which curtailed freedom of speech if any illustration, essay, or editorial opinion was seen as not supporting the war effort.[4]

In the spring of 1917, shortly after the United States entered World War I, and shortly before Congress passed the Espionage Act in June, tens of thousands of war resisters, draft dodgers, and deserters fled to Mexico. The tide of exiles increased with the Sedition Act of 1918, which was not actually an Act but just a set of amendments to the Espionage Act. J. Edgar Hoover, the special assistant to the Attorney General at the time,

Bob later novelized their life in exile.

championed the strict enforcement of these stricter rules. These new rules also forced the arrest and eventual deportations of prominent activists who were involved in protesting against the Espionage Act. They chose Mexico as their destination because boarding ships to unaligned countries was impossible without papers, and Canada was about to enter the war. Once the critical mass of fellow travelers sent word back that Mexico offered a relatively safe haven, many more followed. Bob's former colleagues at *The Masses*, including John Reed, Max Eastman, Henry Glintenkamp, and Josephine Bell, were indicted. Emma Goldman was already in jail, awaiting deportation. The Espionage Act would also allow the government to arrest Eugene V. Debs for speaking against the war as a candidate for president. While in jail, Debs received nearly a million votes for president—not enough to win, of course, but three times as large a percentage as more recent third-party candidates, like Ralph Nader, received, but he was not released from prison until a general pardon of all peace activists released him. In his five presidential campaigns, Debs received as much as 5 percent of the total. Even with that level of support, the government decided to jail any, and all, opponents of World War I.

The deportations grounded the apparent decadence of radicals in hardship and loss.[5] The growing Prohibition movement and social gospel also concerned Bob; these Prohibition groups often had direct, and indirect, ties to xenophobic groups, like the Ku Klux Klan, even as the women's suffrage movement advocated Prohibition too. The anti-immigrant groups saw the German brewers, Jewish distillers, Irish and Italian drinkers, and the "irresponsible" African American voter (with a ballot in one hand and booze in the other) as a vast threat to WASP puritanism. The purge of the liberationist left from the United States was necessary as their perspective joined the suffrage and feminist movement with an array of other groups and issues that Prohibition would drive apart as a wedge issue.[6] In arguing for moderation toward pre–World War I Germany, they included many urban labor-organizing and entrepreneurial German American Jews in their anti-imperialist pacifism. Their numbers were full of the powerful voting blocs of other immigrant groups, especially in major urban areas as well as black laborers in the progressive South. But, in the real world, political positions had other, more mundane consequences; Bob Brown's love of German pilsners, and the suspicions this provoked, became symptomatic of the larger threat to his freedom in the United States; so, although he was never indicted for sedition, nor drafted, and therefore not a resister, his asking for drafts of pilsners kept him under surveillance.

Among this group was a self-proclaimed faux army unit "Battery J," consisting of Rose, Bob, and Allen Norton, three close friends who decided over beers at the Sailors' Snug Harbor saloon, on the corner of 8th Street and Sixth Avenue, to get out before they found themselves on Creel's blacklist (the Committee on Public Information [CPI], led by George Creel and often referred to as Creel's Committee). Allen was also worried about being drafted, and Rose and Bob were worried about being served sedition papers in a climate where Bob couldn't get a bartender to serve a German pilsner instead of an English Bass ale. This saloon was kitty-corner from "The Working Girls' Home," where a poet laureate of England from 1930 until 1967, John Masefield, had decades before, in the 1890s, worked sweeping floors and doing other odd jobs to avert destitution and homelessness. Another saloon they frequented in the neighborhood, The Working Girls' Home, was sarcastically named after the "working girls' homes," which were charitable organizations set up to inexpensively house single women on the Lower East Side; although the "homes" were intended as a refuge from the gritty realities of the city and the steep rents often charged, they were often in worse condition and more restrictive than the alternatives. After Prohibition laws eventually closed the Hell Hole saloon, the more famous of Eugene O'Neill's Provincetown Players' haunts, The Working Girls' Home saloon became a favorite hangout for them. There were many bars in the Village whose names reflected the "grin and bear it" attitude of those struggling to find refuge.

War hysteria was in the air, and even Greenwich Village bars were filled with tension and suspicion. According to Bob's later notes and his fictionalized account, spying eyes were peeking over newspapers, necks were craned to eavesdrop, regular patrons were looking over their shoulders, and everyone pretended to talk about trivialities, while under their breath in whispers and codes they spoke of who had already been arrested, had been drafted, or had escaped to Mexico. In real immediate danger, Rose was rumored to soon be on the blacklist for her work with Emma Goldman's group, and Allen Norton's in-laws were pressuring him to enlist, or they would turn him in to the authorities, as Norton's wife came from a long line of military officers. Bob did not appear to feel any direct threat to his freedom, even though he knew he was already blacklisted, but he could still publish using pseudonyms. He was annoyed about not being able to choose only German beers, and he was concerned that he could not speak openly about his opposition to the war; he feared that government agents were surreptitiously watching Rose. Every aspect of life seemed infected with war hysteria. At one matinee, the show was canceled. Instead, the ushers took "a collection for the Knights of Columbus war-work, Eva Tanguay, the very famous vaudevillian singer and publicity hound, sold Liberty bonds from a box and gave away a two-cent postage stamp kiss with every one." Bob found the scene "disgusting" when a comic skit had a maid kick "a comedian with a German flag sewed in the seat of his pants" and the crowd, playing Romans at the circus, repeatedly gave "thumbs down and bellowed for more blood." In real life, the situation was similar as the Justice Department arrested union organizers associated with the International Workers of the World, known as Wobblies, as well as socialists or dissenters against the war.[7]

Not surprisingly, Bob and Rose started to plan their escape. They met Allen Norton in the back room of the Sailors' Snug Harbor saloon, where writers and artists often met to talk; officially the saloon reserved the room for "ladies and their escorts" (a way to keep prostitutes separate from other women customers). Bob had just come from talking to publishers about a how-to manuscript he was preparing on the formulaic guidelines for writing popular fiction. The bar was ornately decorated with extra-large mirrors surrounded by large frames with intricate scrollwork. From his notes and his fictionalized account, as Bob entered, looking for his group, he heard talk at the bar: "We'll give the Heines [a derogatory term for Germans, especially German soldiers, that refers to the slang word for buttocks] hell now [that] we're in!" "Make the world safe for democracy!" "Make the Huns swallow their own dum-dum bullets or shove 'em way up their ——" (elided in Bob's description). The raucous talk made him uncomfortable. Bob, now in his early thirties, had a stocky physique with a big head of reddish-brown hair; his look was a mix of the characteristics of the bohemians, a little unkempt without a stiff collar, but also the jacket and shoes of a businessman, so that he could easily cross among the worlds of finance, popular fiction magazines, and the avant-garde bohemian scene. The only clue to his actual profession and avocation was his forefinger, pounded square from typing.

When Bob sat down at the table, he held Rose's hand under the table as they always did. In spite of their troubles, Rose had a serene, smiling countenance. She had short, smoothed-back hair and wore a fedora that Bob described, in his later notes, as "femininely mannish." Allen explained that he had received his draft card; he needed to leave before the government caught up with him. In the midst of their plans to leave, Bob was working himself sick to finish yet another serialized story for money. Rose had started sewing a money-belt and planned to withdraw from the bank all the money they could get. The three discreetly looked around for any undercover police agents. They talked in hushed tones about how others had crossed the border over a river at El Paso by wading across at night. Bob explained, hopefully, that he could, as he described in his fictionalized version, "finish the serial by next Saturday," and "maybe they'll pay me for it in time to get away the week after." He was not eager to flee, and, as he recalled years later in his notes, he had wanted to spend the next year finishing his first serious novel, conceived eight years before. He had filled a series of bulky envelopes with material for it and currently had a large manuscript that he would need to keep with him during his travels. He hoped that the publication of this novel would lift his reputation, allowing him to leave behind the life of the plodding pulp writer. Bob was exhausted from leaving Lillian and finalizing the divorce, and he was already suffering from an internal struggle between making a living by selling commercially viable popular feuilleton, and writing artistically viable works. He could not bear another war (after he visited Mexico during the early years of the Mexican revolution) and just wanted to run away with Rose. He was determined not to abandon his novel.

"I'm going to take the manuscript along, that's certain," he said loudly enough for a stranger to peek over his newspaper. Bob talked animatedly about how there was no choice about whether to stay. He started to list others who would probably end up in jail.

"You, too, Bob, if anybody hears you," Rose cautioned.

They quieted down, and Allen argued that he needed to flee quickly. He was being pursued for draft dodging, and his in-laws, determined to make him a war martyr, had given the federal agents leads as to Allen's regular haunts and possible hideouts. He was living in a ramshackle and decrepit apartment on Jane Street in Greenwich Village.

They listed everyone who had been indicted, preparing to flee, or had already gone. Henry Glintenkamp had already "skipped out after he was indicted because of his cartoons," and he was lonely and missing his wife. He had sent word back that the Mexicans hated Americans. They talked about Arthur Cravan, who had recently been blacklisted after a provocative lecture he delivered on art at the Armory. Cravan planned to flee north to Canada, but they all agreed that Canada was not a safe haven as it would enter the war and likely arrest those fleeing from the States. It would have to be Mexico, and it would have to be soon. Michael Gold, the radical writer, activist, and associate of the Provincetown Players, had fled too, and he had sent back advice and news about crossing the border into Mexico. Battery J, the name Allen, Bob, and Rose gave to their small group, learned that if they encountered any problems with Mexican authorities, they should use the Spanish word for "German," *Alemán*; that word would also serve as the password to get help from other American slackers.

They went to their apartments and started packing. Bob and Rose went to their Village apartment, where Rose had hung a few batiks from Java and a Japanese print to make the place look less austere. On the mantelpiece, Bob had put a Belgian porcelain rooster. Bob started packing hurriedly. His major concern was stuffing the last envelopes full of writing material into his briefcase, which he had to sit on to get it to close and lock. He fastened the tiny key to his watch chain. He knew he would not be able to write until he was safely settled. In the meantime, which might last indefinitely, they would suffer through an "enforced leisure." Rose stashed a stack of the gold coins from Bob's urn (filled with coins at his lavish Grantwood Village parties) in her money belt. Bob left his children with his mother, Cora. Allen, Rose, and Bob hopped a train south to eventually find their way to the Texas border with Mexico.[8] None of them could imagine the dangers, tragedies, and adventures that awaited them. It was like an escape movie with the characters avoiding bullets, soldiers, Secret Service agents, and their own fears on both sides of the border. Rose transformed her style from louche bohemian to a more respectable look simply by wearing her Buster Brown collar a little more neatly and wearing matronly pumps instead of sandals. Still, Bob was able to use her easygoing attitude and good looks at a key moment as Battery J sought repeatedly to cross the border without getting shot.[9]

In the prefatory chapter to the novelization about their journey, *You Gotta Live* (1932), Bob wrote in the "readies" style, with em-dashes (—) suggesting the flickering of a movie projector and the excision of the many unnecessary words he eliminated. The resulting cinematic, imagistic description lasts only a few paragraphs in a short preface but captures something of the spirit of Battery J and the Slackers Hotel.

> —Quartered at the Slackers Hotel rationed on flabby damp tortillas—playing poker and pinochle—restless coin-sweaters fidgeting their few pesos back and forth at the Guatemalan border—sleeping in stifling city caves—carrying their own toilet paper—lounging in frowsy frontier hotels with loud-mouthed, lousy dicks—shooting craps—catching crabs—hiding under beds—buying boot-leg liquor from one-eyed hyenas, one-armed, one-legged, one-idead buzzards, nickel-starred bastards, moving picture sheriffs. [One-idead, a word coined by E. A. Poe as a possessive for someone having one idea, and in this context allowing Bob's use of the possessive form of one-idea to rhyme with one-legged and one-armed as well the dead creating a link to buzzards; it simply means a desperate buzzard-like person with one pathetic idea—to just survive and live.][10]

Bob wanted to write the great American novel even on the run. He picked up his portable typewriter, much heavier and less portable than later writing machines, and tucked his fat manuscript case under his arm. He exclaimed to Rose, "These are my weapons." They took a train to St. Louis, and then another south through Texas to the Mexican border. The trip to St. Louis was uneventful. Bob wrote more of his novel. Unfortunately, on the trip south the train was too hot for him to concentrate, and when he started to open a window, pages of the manuscript started blowing around. He put the manuscript away. When the train pulled into El Paso, they saw a big celebration; always up for a party, they collected their few belongings, bounded out of the train, and asked a reveler what they were celebrating. The drunken reveler explained that today the whole state of Texas was going dry, a few years before all of America. Everyone was buying up what they could. Battery J bought the last bottle of Chateau d'Yquem, a highly-rated Bordeaux, in Texas.

They started talking to the locals, and one fellow, fictionalized by Bob as a redneck Texan, told them that the Secret Service had deputized him and his buddies so that they could shoot the slackers trying to cross the border. Bob and Allen laughed at the Texan's stories, trying to cover their fear and anxiety. They thought he would be shooting at them in a few days, but at least they knew what they were up against. Back on the train, Allen decided to get off halfway to Brownsville in Laredo, Texas, to attempt to cross the border there. Rose and Bob continued on to Brownsville. As soon as they got off the train, a tall man wearing a Stetson, and with the air of a Secret Service deputy, started following them around. After a few hours, they went to the telegram counter at the train station to see if Allen had sent them any news of his luck crossing the border. They read the telegram described later in both Bob's notes and in the fictionalized account.

> Auntie, very ill think she'll get better in Nogales meet me there
> Union Hotel (signed) San Alain

This was just the first of many messages they were compelled to write in code. This was a code different from the stock ticker tape that Bob had seen as an analogy for modernist writing, but both codes were sent through a machine. When they arrived in Nogales, Arizona, they went directly to the Union Hotel. Allen greeted them with frowns and whispers in a somber tone in part to pretend that the invented Auntie was sick or had passed away, but also because he genuinely worried that they faced arrest or death at the border. They remembered that vigilantes and government agents alike used illegal border crossers as target practice. They started walking toward the border in Nogales. Obviously aware of the dicey situation, they spotted a bunch of young recruits or vigilantes aiming their guns through the bushes ready to shoot anyone trying to cross.

They left Nogales and went northwest to Ajo, Arizona. As they unpacked in Ajo, they decided to meet the locals to learn about the place and to figure out how to cross the border there. They met a captain in the U.S. Army, whom they called Cap to add a familiarity, who had little to do while he waited for the military to call him up for duty in Europe. He drove them around the town as an informal tour guide and got them bootlegged liquor from the sheriff, who, as in most rural towns, controlled the illegal trade as he could stifle the competition by arresting them. Cap talked to them about Ajo, flirted with Rose, and laughed at, and sometimes with, the city slickers Bob and Allen. Rose charmed him into taking a trip to a beautiful oasis he had described to her, across the border; she planned a picnic, and Cap arranged for a driver to take them. Cap seemed eager to please, and, as an extra treat, he suggested that they first meet his friend who worked at the border patrol. He was "an artist at shooting those trying to cross, and he adds more bullet holes in a pattern on the corpse," Cap, in the fictionalized account, happily explained to his new artsy friends. Rose agreed to the trip, but first, she explained, they needed to pull together the picnic supplies. They got back to the hotel and started frantically preparing. Although Bob desperately wanted to take his typewriter, he realized that it might arouse suspicions; no one takes a typewriter on a picnic. They quietly conspired to send for their baggage when in Mexico and to pay the bill by mail. They would simply explain in a letter that they'd been detained unexpectedly and wouldn't be able to return to Ajo. They left as if they planned to return later that day, talking loudly about the fun they had planned in Ajo for the next day so that the hotel staff and guests would overhear their conversation.

Cap picked them up, and his hired Mexican driver started off. The driver had agreed to a flat rate of fifteen cents a mile, and Bob was happy to pay for the chance to see, he told Cap, the oasis. They talked and joked, and Cap told them more about the oasis in Mexico, and the group let him convince them to cross over to have a little party there. Everyone had a few more drinks as they drove south; they sang, "Pack up your troubles in your old kit-bag and smile, smile, smile." Everyone was relaxed as they went by Cap's friend at the border, who waved hello instead of shooting patterns of holes in their bodies, but, when they had safely crossed the border into Mexico, Allen's excitement made Cap suspicious. Rose calmed him down, and he confessed that the "New Yorkers were too crazy for him; they laughed too much and said silly things." She agreed, and they arrived at the oasis for their picnic.

As they talked, Rose asked Cap and his driver to take them to Nuevo Sanchez because she'd never seen a real Mexican village. They rolled their eyes at her girlish excitement to see something so mundane and uninteresting. The driver agreed because he would make more money for more miles. It meant that they would have to spend the night in the village and return later the next day after some sightseeing. When they reached Nuevo Sanchez it was twilight.

They went to a restaurant and ordered beers. The driver sat at a separate table and flirted with the waitress, drank beer, and ate his dinner alone. Cap sat there thinking he was already in France, with city slicker intellectuals-turned-faux-soldiers from New York City. He imagined himself in a fast-paced action adventure movie, while the others appreciated the romance of sleepy old Mexico.

In the morning they planned to explore the town, but, as they tried to drive around town, they had to stop frequently to push the car out of ruts and arroyos where there was a semblance of a road, and they had to drive places where there was no road at all, until the car was caked in dust and dirt. They were all exhausted and decided to stay there another night, then drive to Hermosillo in a day or two. They slept well until, in Bob's fictionalized account, a loud parrot woke them. Allen slept on the porch near the parrot's cage and had to listen to the bird's telling the same news of the town over and over again. The parrot said, "Honk, honk, honk, Juanita . . . hahahahahaha . . . honk honk honk Juanita . . . hahaha." Over breakfast, they learned that there was only one car in the town, and that the owner drove around and called out a girl's name to take a ride, but the car holds only a few at a time, so the girls all mill around pretending not to notice the car. Then he calls their names: Juanita, Maria, Carmencita, and Cepcion. The hotel's server explained, in the fictionalized account, that that's what the parrot is calling, "the sound of the car, and the girl's name, and the laughter." While they now understood the parrot, their understanding didn't make its morning call any less annoying. They drank strong coffee with goat's milk and lazed around all day. They were well into Mexico now. They relaxed and stayed another night. The next morning, the bird again woke Allen with a similar sound, "Honk! Honk! Honk! Chug-chug-chuuuuggg! Camencita! Caramba! Carrrrrrr-ra-a-amba! Honk! Honk! Ladrones!" Allen had had enough. He convinced them all to move on to Hermosillo, as Bob's later notes explained their route. As they left Nuevo Sanchez, Allen stood up and waved, calling, "Viva Mexico! Honk! Honk! Hurrah! Honk!"

In Hermosillo, Battery J left Cap with little drama even though he had driven them nearly 200 miles from the border. They claimed that they wanted to keep exploring Mexico, and, in Bob's later fictionalized account, they explained that they could get the train to Mexico City from this point. Cap urged them to return with him mostly for their own safety. They said they would soon return, and they gave the Mexican driver a bonus for not driving them back. They waved goodbye to Cap. He drove off with a skeptical look on his face as he began to realize that they were at least scofflaws if not fugitives and war-resisting slackers. As soon as Cap drove off, they hurried to the train station only to learn that no trains were running. The Yaquis were having a small rebellion and blowing up track, shutting down trains all around the country. The rebellion eventually spread to Nogales, Arizona, where the U.S. military engaged the Yaqui trying to get supplies and their own troops to Mexico. Corpses were filling the town, rumors of murders by the Yaquis or government agents, soldiers were everywhere, and an outbreak of smallpox was killing those not murdered. The Yaquis still used bows and arrows, but with the efficiency of machine guns. Rose bemoaned the dismal situation.

"I thought we came here to avoid war," she said.

Bob was unhappy too, while Allen spent his time drinking tequila and watching the local war unfold as if it were a movie. They finally found a heavily armored train to the coastal town of Guaymas, south of Hermosillo, where they had to wait for days for the track to be repaired. To kill time, they went deep-sea fishing for 300- or 400-pound sea bass that were caught with raw meat on large hooks. Rose caught half a dozen fish, to Bob's and Allen's empty hooks. She gave away her catch to the poor on the docks. In amazement at Rose's ability to hook fish, Bob half-jokingly argued that they "ought to settle down here and start a fish-canning works." Rose noted more pragmatically and realistically that with the Mexican revolution unfolding around them, they wouldn't be able to get the product out. They could catch them and can them, but they would spoil waiting for a train.

The three blacklisted refugees, Allen Norton and Rose and Bob Brown, stood on the train platform at Hermosillo, already 175 miles, and two days' driving, from the U.S. border, which they had crossed illegally. They eagerly awaited the train to the coastal town of Mazatlán. The delay had lasted for nearly a week, caused by the Mexican government's war with the Yaqui tribe, and the town now had serious shortages of supplies and a surplus of corpses from the surrounding battles and the smallpox epidemic. When the train arrived, the scene was horrific. Instead of gathering suitcases and baggage, porters and soldiers unloaded wrapped-up dead bodies, and the living passengers staggered out in single file taking deep, relieved breaths. They had all traveled packed so tightly that everyone had to stand and could barely breathe. The armored cars, filled with soldiers to protect the passengers, unintentionally provoked more anxieties by making the dangers involved in train travel more extreme. The three exiles considered their options—to wait in the town, to look for a car, to set out on foot, or to take the train; with no other reasonable choices, they reluctantly decided to take the train.

They packed themselves in with the locals. Bob clutched his manuscript case in which he had his first serious novel. He hugged the case tightly to his chest, desperately trying to keep it off the filth of the boxcar floor as the contents of the case held his greatest achievement. The finished novel would combine elements of modernist poetry, pulp fiction, and allusions to, and pastiches of, other forms of popular culture that he had been involved with, like advertising, amusement parks, and tourist maps. In his experimental novel he planned to embed stories and allegories within stories to create a "hall of mirrors" effect.

While they traveled, and in order to amuse his two comrades in Battery J in light of the dire situation, Bob told Rose and Allen the story of the Persian prince's gardener:

> Well, the gardener of the Persian Prince met Death walking in his garden one morning and he was scared out of his wits by the dirty look she gave him; he ran to his master and told him he must have horses at once and get away to Teheran.
>
> "But why?" the Prince asked him.
>
> "I just met Death in the garden and she gave me such a strange look. She terrified me. I must fly to Teheran at once. Give me your fastest horses."
>
> The Prince gave him fast horses and he galloped off in a lather. A little while later the Prince was walking in his garden and he, too, came upon Death. "Why the devil did you scare my gardener just now?" he asked.
>
> "I? Scare him?" Death looked puzzled. "Well, I certainly didn't mean to do that. I was only surprised to see him here in your garden so late this morning when he has to meet me in Teheran early this evening."

"God, what a story!" Allen laughed morosely.

"What a horrible story!" Rose protested. Gesturing across at a group of smallpox patients squatting on the floor, she added darkly, "Do we get to Teheran early this evening?" At each stop, Bob noticed peasant women gathering to fill clay pots with sanitized steamed water being released from the train (and not meant for drinking). The conductor, trying in vain to stop them or perhaps just for his sadistic thrills, would shoot hot, scalding steam at them, laughing as the women howled in pain, rolling in the sand to keep their skin from burning. Then they got up and tried to get more water in spite of the conductor's attacks, because the women needed the boiling water so desperately. It was a cruel allegorical slapstick comedy played out over and over again with its tragedy building through accretion. After each stop, soldiers searched the train looking for spies who may have snuck on at the last stop or been Yaqui soldiers masquerading as sick patients under the smallpox sheets. The searches took time as the soldiers looked in every car. As the soldiers neared Battery J, Bob and Rose held each other so tightly their hands hurt. Allen's face, white with fear, with sweat beading on his forehead, betrayed all that he had already lost, especially his recent life as an important modernist publisher in New York—a life and focus that seemed like a dream now. In their train car, soldiers grabbed one peasant and threw him off the train to a throng of waiting soldiers who dragged him away. Bob could feel his heart pounding, his throat tightening with fear, and his tight grip on Rose wet with sweat. Finally, the inspector came upon Battery J: "*A donde van ustedes? "Americanos! Americanos! Ustedes son burros! Burros Americanos. No pueden hablar*?" he shouted both directly at them and to proudly alert his soldiers to his potential capture of spies. To the inspector's angry questions about where they were going and his accusations that they were smugglers, "*Burros Americanos*," American mules or donkeys, they could not speak out of fear. Petrified, as they realized that the soldiers might kill, torture, or jail them, they stared stupidly ahead imagining their arrival "in Teheran." The soldiers grew more insistent; one pushed a Colt revolver into Allen's stomach, and the inspector answered his own questions by telling Battery J in English, "You are American, that is certain." Allen, starting to remember how he was instructed to react to claims that he was a hated American, answered, "No Señor. *Alemán*." When the gun was pressed tighter against his abdomen, he insisted in a staccato voice rising in volume and pitch with each repetition,

"*Alemán*! *Alemán*! *Alemán*!"

Rose shaking off her fear and realizing what was happening, chimed in: "*Alemán*!"

"Si, Señores, somos todos *Alemán*!" Bob said, hearing himself as if in a dream, remembering his lessons about the code to tell anyone who accused them of being Americans. It was the same code word to tell fellow war resisters when, or if, they ever arrived in Mexico City. The soldiers grumbled in disappointment, as they could not torture these apparently German foreigners. Even if their accents when speaking Spanish were not German, their pronunciations were foreign and imperfect; the soldiers had no time to interrogate them further. The inspector and his soldiers went on to search the next car, and Rose, Bob, and Allen slowly started breathing again, relieved that their facility with codes and languages had saved them at least temporarily.

In Mazatlán they met three former Columbia University students who had stood trial for distributing anti-conscription pamphlets like "Will You Be Drafted?," for publishing the magazines *Challenge* and a bit later *War?* (an avowedly anti-war newsletter, based on the *Masses* format), and for activities in the Anti-Militarism League and Socialist Party. Although they faced up to two years in federal prison, a steep fine, and loss of all citizenship rights, their trial ended with the acquittal of Eleanor Wilson Parker and the conviction of her fellow publishers, Owen Cattell and Parker's fiancé, Charles F. Phillips. The jury gave them light sentences (five days for Phillips and time served for Cattell) explicitly because the pamphlets were distributed before passage of the Espionage Act of 1917, which forbade interference with the draft, but informally because the three looked like nice innocent kids in college and from "good families." Phillips later published his memoirs under the name Charles Shipman as he had a wide array of careers and political avocations after his student years as a war resister, including serving as a delegate to the Moscow Comintern congress under the name Gomez, an underground organizer, a railroad executive, and an investment columnist for *The Wall Street Journal*. In any case, after being forced to enlist, suffering as a conscientious objector, and being let out with a dishonorable discharge, Phillips soon learned he was to be drafted again by order of the Secretary of War. He and Eleanor, more jailbird comrades with a shared verve and vision than romantic lovebirds, fled to Mexico.

As Bob and Allen were walking into a cantina in Mazatlán, Charles and Eleanor, who had just left the same cantina, noticed them and went back inside. Without fanfare or surprise at why they were all so far from home, the group sat down together. Charles and Allen had met before, and Charles and Eleanor knew of Bob's activities with *The Masses* and of Bob's work as an impresario of the wild fundraising parties and balls at Webster Hall. As the night wore on, they shared the stories of their travels, and the young couple had similar tales to Battery J's. They had stopped in San Antonio, gotten advice about crossing the border, moved on to El Paso, used assumed names, pretended to sightsee near the border, and gotten arrested for accidentally crossing into the United States (not knowing that they had crossed the border into Mexico). They booked a train to Los Angeles, and then, at a stop along the route, they pretended to miss the train as they ran to catch it with their luggage checked through to Los Angeles. They feigned frustration, hired a driver supposedly to pass the time, scouted the routine of the border guards, and eventually crossed the border at night. They eventually made it to Agua Prieto, Mexico, dirty and without any other clothes, but free.

Eleanor had the classic American good looks, with reddish-brown hair like Bob's, that made her seem, at least to her new husband, as if she could have posed for a Norman Rockwell *Saturday Evening Post* cover illustration as the stereotypical image of "exuberant girlhood," save for her spirited socialist activities. Bob liked the couple and flirted with Eleanor, who in her deep, sexy, sonorous voice made it clear that she was liberated and available; it's unclear if and unlikely that they acted on their attraction. Bob found them a room in the *pension* where Battery J was staying, but he did not see them again because Battery J left the next morning. At the end of the week, the young couple was forced to leave their room and slept and lived on the beach, as they could not pay even the small amount they owed. Bathing naked, collecting coconuts and handouts from the shrimp fishermen, they lived an existence common to the slackers. Eventually, they too would catch the boat to Manzanillo and eventually meet Bob and Rose in Mexico City.

Battery J boarded a steamer to Manzanillo, which was farther down the coast and west of Mexico City. At first they were thrilled to be traveling by boat instead of the suffocating train, as they enjoyed the fresh turtle soup made by the crew, who would hunt sea turtles and fish during the day. The boat trip, however, was equally fraught with anxiety as each night the searchlights kept them nervously awake. After four days, they drowsily got off the steamboat. From this coastal town, they took the train inland from the coast, and finally, after an eventful journey up to this point, they actually slept on the train. When they arrived in Guadalajara, they found the charm of old Mexico in the architecture and a strolling *mariachi* band. The *mariachi* style and tradition had begun in the area only a few years before, but it was already associated with older authentic traditions of Mexico. The city was relatively wealthy and tranquil compared with the troublesome poverty, treacherous war, and endless searches they had witnessed traveling south. Eventually, they boarded one more train to Mexico City.

Bob now had the romantic look of a lean rebel on the run, complete with mustache, soul patch, and brooding eyes.

When they arrived in the city, they knew to visit the *poste restante* (a part of post offices that holds mail for people who "call for" or pick up the messages or packages) to get any messages or make necessary connections. There were no messages, but as they were leaving, an American, seeing them looking around wondering which way to go, approached them and asked if he could help them find their way. Rose showed him the address they were looking for, The Villa Rubin at 16 Calle Flores, and Bob made clear to the stranger that they were not Americans by interjecting, "*Alemán*." The stranger smiled broadly and introduced himself, in Bob's fictionalized account, as "Red" Winchester. He told them that that address was that of the Slackers Hotel, and because he was their informal welcoming committee, he'd take them there. As they walked along, Red told them the news: Max Eastman would be along soon, but he was holding out, before fleeing the United States for as long as he could; a few folks at the Slackers Hotel they already knew, like the cartoonist with the German name Hendrik "Henry" Glintenkamp, who had skipped his bail and fled.

At the Slackers Hotel, Red started cooking, and they saw both the conditions they would have to deal with and the make-do attitude of everyone involved. Red cooked on a kerosene camp stove, and there was no running water, but he was able to cook hamburger meat with onions and *shish kebabs* with tomatoes and tartar steak cubes. As the smell of the food wafted around, a half-dozen other slackers showed up, a few whom they knew from New York, but the rest new faces. They ate and partied past midnight, recounting their escape adventure stories converted to the style of Hollywood comedies in Bob's hands with interjections from Rose and Allen. They recounted how the inspector had stuck a gun in Allen's gut, and everyone laughed. They told the story about the parrot, and, one imagines, the group kept laughing. They settled down only enough for one of the slackers to advise the three to move on to Vera Cruz very soon in order to avoid the impending roundup of slackers. The character named Red scoffed at the suggestion, but others worried that the authorities would want to make a very public example of these slackers so that the illegal immigrants would stop flooding over the border into Mexico.

Everyone shoveled the food into their mouths, and someone exclaimed that they all "ate like capitalist pigs gorging," but Red laughed and said, "Well, you gotta live," and the party continued. They sang songs, including the labor IWW (Wobbly) songs; they sang "All American Mothers I want to say to you!," and songs to soothe the disillusioned, embittered, and homesick. There was plenty of woe in this group because of the lack of open communication with those they had left behind. They knew that censors read letters going both ways across the border; they knew that anything really interesting or informative would arrive redacted. They knew that they could not tell anything personal or revealing as that might threaten to divulge their situation or location or provoke the authorities into intimidating their loved ones back home. They knew that they must avoid public independent expression of their opinions, as that would draw the atttention of the authorities. They knew they had to either not work or work only illicitly and under assumed names, to avoid capture. Some received money from home, some did work or one-off gigs (like boxing), and some withered under the enforced slacking. They knew that the secret police and censors were their nemesis; anxious evasion and codework, their hope, and poverty, their fate.

Soon, Hendrik "Henry" Glintenkamp, often called Glint, as his apt name highlighted his passionate and mischievous look, and Charles Phillips started a newsletter at the hotel. They also placed articles, with radical perspectives, in a local paper, *El Heraldo de Mexico*. Eleanor had gone ahead from Guadalajara to find work in Mexico City. When Phillips arrived (at a time before cell phones or easy communication), he found a fleabag hotel and sought out Glintenkamp, who had done cover illustrations for Phillip's *Challenge*, but when he arrived at Glint's room, he was surprised, but not shocked, to find his wife, Eleanor. She was heedless of protocol, often showing up unannounced at friends' just to visit, and Glint was their old friend. Phillips still felt jealous, but the couple fetched his suitcase and moved into her furnished room above a Chinese restaurant. Charles and Eleanor started publishing their radical newsletter for the slackers, and Glintenkamp supplied the illustrations. Soon Eleanor moved in with Glintenkamp, and although Phillips was upset, he continued to publish the newsletter with his rearranged team. The three worked together until Phillips, now called Gomez, left Mexico for meetings in the Soviet Union, and Eleanor and Glintenkamp circuitously made their way back to the United States, where they were married, and later divorced. Bob saw the newsletter as a model for starting his own press and publishing a newsletter. He wanted to find a stable and secure location to launch his next career as a publisher, but first he simply needed to survive.

Thirty-five years later, after Rose died in the early 1950s and when Bob returned to New York City, Eleanor would console, comfort, and eventually marry Bob. She helped him restart his publishing and bookselling businesses as a way to put food on the table. Perhaps if there was any mutual attraction, it was inconvenient in 1918, or if Eleanor's deep, smooth, sexy voice stayed with Bob, or if it was, in the 1950s, a comradely marriage between two survivors of the Slackers Hotel. Who else could understand their lives in art, politics, publishing, and privation? The "comradely marriage" option seems most likely.

Back in Mexico City, nearly 7,300 feet above sea level where they lived, the low end of high altitude, Rose complained of altitude sickness, and they decided to move on to a lower elevation, perhaps to Cuernavaca, 50 miles southwest of the city and more than 5,000 feet lower in altitude, or another southern location on their way to South America. Rose found the yellow-green *maguey* worms, *chinicuiles* sautéed with cilantro and chilis, at one restaurant serving the native cuisine, nauseating on top of her altitude sickness. As Bob was eating, and Rose not eating, the *chinicuiles*, they read a story about a prizefighter on his way to Mexico City after some successes. It was their good friend, and they decided to wait

Mina Loy, Dada poet.

for Arthur Cravan, the Dadaist provocateur and prizefighter, whom they had known in New York.

They joked that after Arthur's scandalous lecture at a gallery talk, they were surprised it had taken him so long to flee. Cravan, educated in Europe and England, spoke English, French, German, Italian, and Spanish fluently. His own pronouncements, and faked passports, made his nationality difficult to pin down, and his profession, as a publisher-poet and what we would now call a performance artist, made his prizefighter's physique of muscular arms and a 6′4″ frame seem like part of a Surrealist stunt; some even considered all of his fights as Dadaist performance even if he, at least sometimes, sought the prizes because he desperately needed the money. For two years before leaving New York, Cravan was involved in an intense, and now famous, love affair with Mina Loy, also a Dadaist in the Arensberg circle. Bob, in his personal notes, later described Cravan

Arthur Cravan, Dada boxer-poet.

as putting "every fraction of his feet and inches into loving" Mina, but leaving her as he fled, first north to Canada and then south to Mexico, and had her chase after him.

Like Duchamp, Man Ray, Kreymborg, and Stieglitz, Cravan was also an arts magazine publisher, of *Maintenant!* (*Now!*), and it was as a publisher that he was invited, while still in New York City, to deliver a lecture on modern art at the Grand Central Gallery. Given the context of years of scandals around modern art exhibits and bohemian fundraising balls for their magazines and groups, the audience included many dowagers, as if straight out of Central Casting as clichés of the easily scandalized bourgeois matrons, supposedly looking for aesthetic enlightenment but probably unconsciously desiring a thrill with a built-in excuse of social respectability. The rest of the audience, dressed respectably, had close connections to the radical art and culture scene, including Bob and Rose Brown. Cravan showed up an hour late, drunk and swaying, and stumbled up to the lectern. The organizers had already alerted the police as part of their effort to assure a scandalous reaction. He took off his jacket and began his lecture. No one could understand him as he feigned efforts to get organized. He muttered under his breath. A few of the shills shouted heckles. Cravan answered with insults and angry gestures. He then proceeded to remove his pants, and the police rushed the stage as the crowd reacted in real and faux outrage. It was great fun if too short a spectacle, but it marked Cravan as a dangerous radical for the authorities. Some in the Imagist poetry circles, like William Carlos Williams, thought Cravan acted brutishly, and he (Williams) reacted dismissively, if perhaps jealously (as Loy had had a fleeting affair with Williams), when Mina Loy fell in with Cravan. Bob and Rose found Mina, who "radioed rhythm" from "her free-verse eyes," an irresistible friend, and they were upset that Cravan treated her badly when she finally arrived in Mexico. Cravan was drunk and partying when Mina arrived, living up to his boorish reputation, and rather than interrupt his fun, he quietly complained to Mina that she should have telegrammed in advance and asked her to stay in Allen Norton's room for the night. Bob apologized to Mina for Cravan's behavior, but soon Mina and Cravan were almost happily living together as husband and wife after a wedding party thrown by Rose and Bob. Mina embraced the slackers' endless work life in their pathetic squalid living conditions. The Browns often supplied meals and supplies to Mina and Arthur as the couple suffered from depravations and poverty, verging on starvation, in spite of Mina's inheritance and Arthur's intermittent winnings from fights. Mina threw herself into the Sisyphean chores even though she had never cooked or cleaned before: cooking soggy tortillas; cleaning dust off of mud walls and dirt floors; trying to eradicate bedbugs, lice, and cockroaches; scrubbing laundry outside without running water; and nursing Arthur, either recovering from a fight or from frequent illness that the Browns thought related to food-borne dysentery. Bob started to plan the next leg of their escape, with Mina and Arthur, when fellow slackers explained that Cravan's papers were not in order, and he could risk neither leaving nor being discovered by the local officials. Arthur confessed to Bob that he needed to earn more money before he could leave, but he didn't want anyone, especially Mina, who was now pregnant, to help him. So, he decided to crank up his boxing career.

With Bob's urging, Arthur agreed, in the fictionalized account, to let Red become his manager, especially when it became increasingly clear that Arthur's glory days of fights with greats like Jack Johnson were behind him. In his first fight arranged by Red, Arthur lasted ten rounds with the Mexican champion, Honorato Castro, but the fight money allowed Mina to buy some necessities. In the next fight, Red, noticing Arthur's worsening health, got the opponent to agree to get KO'd in the third, and even though Arthur knew nothing of the scheme, he seemed to his potential opponents too dangerous; after that, no one would agree to fight him. So, Arthur eventually took a fall, and Red was able to arrange more fights. Meanwhile, Arthur tried to convince Mina, who could leave, that she should leave Mexico City with the Browns. He would stay behind until his papers were in order and he had enough money to join them. The creation of the Arthur Cravan myth was already brewing, but Bob's fictionalization of his friendship with Arthur and Mina, clarified the episode (Parmar, 2009). In mid-September 1918, Arthur had a prize fight in the Mexico City bull ring against the American Jim "Black Diamond" Smith, and although Cravan was able to knock out Smith, Smith landed some pounding blows to Cravan's head. Bob, Rose, and Allen had just left Mexico City nd prepared to meet Mina and Arthur in the coastal town of Salina Cruz. While Arthur was resting and trying to recover from his wounds, Red and Mina saw Battery J off at the train station.

Bob took his manuscript case with his now-completed experimental novel, the American take on Joyce's *Ulysses*. They also had Allen's shoebox, which they used for toothbrushes, soap, collars, playing cards, combs, buttons, hairpins, pencils, notebooks, and notable knickknacks. Rose had a wicker basket with sandwiches, and a handbag, obtained in Ajo, for a first-aid kit. They had little else. Red said he would eventually come along, too; he had planned a rigged fight wherein a boxer would fall down in the third, and he was planning to skip out as soon as he won the bets. On the way to Salina Cruz, they might stop over for some more fights in Oaxaca.

The Browns and Allen Norton headed for Salina Cruz, where they could get boats to South America, Tahiti, or wherever they decided to go. They focused on the border of the Panama Canal, as, psychologically, that was the dividing line where they would have more freedom from U.S. government agents working in Mexico to round up suspected war resisters. When they arrived in Salina Cruz, they took a swim in the Pacific Ocean and thought of it as a political baptism washing away the past struggles of life on the run and in expectation that they might soon find themselves free. Soon Red and Arthur and Mina showed up; Mina was now showing in her pregnancy with Arthur's baby, and this impending birth weighed on Arthur as he could barely feed himself, let alone a new baby. Red and Arthur bought a very cheap rickety old boat, planning to sail it to Chile, and they set out to make it sea-worthy. They worked on it, and finally Arthur decided to take it out for a test. He hopped into the boat, sailed over the horizon, and was never seen again. That began the myth of Arthur Cravan, as through the years rumors circulated that he was alive and had lived out a new life in America, or that he had fled from Mina and the new responsibilities of fatherhood, or that his sailing away was yet another Dadaist stunt. Mina waited. The others did not try to convince her to leave. They knew she would not. The Browns and Allen Norton decided not to catch a boat after all because of the trauma of Arthur's disappearance; they boarded a train toward the border between Mexico and Guatemala and started traveling south.

The lists of Cravan's occupations seem in line with, if not identical to, Brown's own myriad careers and adventures: "poet, professor, boxer, dandy, flâneur, forger, critic, sailor, prospector, card sharper, lumberjack, bricoleur, thief, editor [and] chauffeur."[11] The long list suggests a certain trait of modernity in which a "'plurality' wilfully annihilated any fixable identity."[12] In fact, without a single identity, with all the circumscribed facts of his life and death in place, "Rumors that he had staged his death and produced forgeries, paintings, and poetry under various pseudonyms persist today."[13] Brown, Cravan, and many others in the vanguard did *not* draw tidy, if inaccurate, boundaries around their oeuvres or lives; they did not distinguish between dilettantism and focus because they actively thought of plurality as the focused goal, and they thought of their new forced, and often nightmarish, exile as part of their avant-garde endeavors. Cravan's was just one in a long string of disappearances and loss that Bob would experience among his closest friends.

On the train again, Allen Norton worried glumly about their fate. The surreality of the aisles, littered with bundles, bunches of bananas, flower caskets, babies, shivering hairless dogs, and *pulque* pots, was matched by the scene unfolding in the flickering of the jungle zipping by as if in a movie.

"It's a green paradise," Rose said.

"Purgatory! you mean. The natives call it the Green Hell," Allen explained ruefully.

Bob, also skeptical about their chances in crossing more treacherous borders, started to imagine a descent into this hellish jungle as an allegory for their own future.

The jungle reached out fronds for fingers, snatched at the passing train; vines knotted into elbows and kneecaps snapped against the car sides to try their reflexes; the jungle was a peevish old witch, plucking, rapping, pinching, snatching at everything that passed. One in a while a monkey chattered, showed its angry red gums in a treetop and leaped farther away, a dizzy acrobat getting frantically far from the puffing, smoke-belching dragon twisting through its back yard. Green brilliant snakes resented the invasion, too, and crawled deep into the twining underbrush tangle away from their favorite sunning Edens beside the shining rails. Sometimes the snakes were stuffed with rabbits, gorged with birds, lying in languid digestion draped over the tracks. Those snakes woke up in hell with Dante. Parrots screamed; the engine screamed, played crack-the-whip with the coaches around unexpected corners, came to crashing stops for herds of goats to get off the tracks. Rather than reinforce their fear, the image delighted Bob and spurred his futurist imagination, as he imagined that "If they had a ride like this in Coney Island it would make a billion."[14] Of course, the mechanized automatronic jungle cruise idea, set in a World's Fair or Coney Island–like setting, would later make Walt Disney billions, but back in 1918, the Browns were suffering inside a ride through hell, not charging admission.

When they arrived in San José, Glintenkamp was at the station. Rose brought honey for Glint; Glintenkamp loved honey, and, in the fictionalized account years later, Bob described Glint as a "sensitive artist honey-bear . . . his clumsy paw gripping drawing paper, putting himself on paper with a pencil." Because Rose had correctly destroyed all of Bob's papers and passports just before they illegally crossed the U.S. border, they now needed to get him a new set. This was obviously before the days of electronically, instantly accessible, massive networks of information for border and passport controls. Still, as late as 1999, one could obtain a new U.S. passport immediately at any U.S. embassy or consulate in the world, but now, in the twenty-first century, instant access to information translates into increased delays, not instant service, because of multiple levels of security checks. Rapid access often means slower service and output rather than the opposite. Rose, in early 1919, walked into the American consulate in San José, Guatemala, showed her papers, vouched that Bob was a childhood friend, an American; he, then, showed his photos and filed paperwork about his birthdate and place, his parents' names, and his citizenship. The fellow in charge was a lowly assistant, young and inexperienced; the boss was out of the office. This was his first official act, and he drew up an emergency passport.

As soon as they had Bob's new passport, they boarded a tramp steamer to Panama City, while Allen stayed behind with old friends from New York and promised to meet up with the Browns later. As they traveled farther south, the trips were getting less eventful, but they knew that they were not home-free yet. In Panama City, they went to the wire service and received money addressed from someone pretending to be Allen's mother (Allen himself) and sent to Rose; the accompanying note said to rendezvous on the *Asia*, a boat to Ecuador. From Ecuador they made their way to Chile, but they did not rendezvous with Allen, and they began to hear rumors that their good friend had decided to return to the States. Of their original belongings they had little left, but Bob still had his now-finished manuscript in its own leather case. They eventually arrived at Valparaíso de Chile after a long voyage, they and their baggage smelling from disinfectants like *eau de Javel* (a weak bleach solution), often used in third-class steerage or public toilets. They felt safer here, but also exhausted and despairing. Bob said of his manuscript, "It [the manuscript] was all the hope [Bob] had left."

They met up with an old friend whom they knew from the Slackers Hotel, who filled them in on the underground news, and they learned when to expect their own belongings. On the steamer, the friend made a wisecrack to Rose and Bob about Arthur that he had "made his getaway good this time," afraid of family responsibilities with a slacker's salary of little to nothing. Or, maybe he'd stolen Mina's money belt and fled with "more than a thousand dollars on him," but Rose protested and thought it unlikely that he would have abandoned Mina, and he certainly had no money. There was no sign of Allen, and the feds had arrested more of their colleagues in the States and they received stiff sentences (at one point Eugene V. Debs was arrested and sentenced to a long term). Bob and Rose decided to catch the train inland from the coastal town of Valparaíso to the city of Santiago, Chile, where they could find work. It was an uneventful, if long and uphill, trip, except that a porter convinced Bob to stow his manuscript case; so, Bob worried about it a bit on the trip.

When they got off the train at Santiago, there was no sign of the manuscript case. Bob frantically looked around, asking everyone, grabbing a shrugging porter, calling out to Rose to ask everyone, and searching in the stacked luggage of other passengers. Eventually, he stumbled morosely around the slowly emptying platform and resigned himself to the fact that more than eight years of work were lost just for the value of the manuscript case. He imagined the worthless manuscript paper, likely immediately discarded by the thief, fluttering away in the wind. Bob even scanned the sky, according to his notes about the loss, and looked through discarded litter on the streets for pages from the manuscript; perhaps they could follow a loose page, like a rainbow, back to a more complete pile of pages. The thief was likely just a kid, who might have paused momentarily as he dumped the pages only to realize that the pages were not money, not written in Spanish, and just weighed down the manuscript case. Perhaps the thief used the pages to write a diary on the blank side of the pages, used them to cover a hole in a wall, or simply wrapped up fish. The case was never found, the manuscript lost forever. Bob would not write another creative work for another decade. The loss was devastating. He had kept the manuscript with him for 5,100 miles only to lose it in the last 75 miles from Valparaíso to Santiago: eight years, more than 5,000 miles, and nothing to show for it. His friends were disappearing and the culmination of his creative life had been lost. Bob Brown was forced to reinvent himself to live.

Through a connection that Rose made, Bob landed a job in the U.S. Office of Communication and Publication, known as Compub, in Santiago. The office, charged with manipulating news and spreading anti-German propaganda, needed writers to prepare stories, manipulate photographs, and place stories with the local press. The brand-new office of Compub functioned, according to Bob, by Washington's wire-pulling direction of a leaping little acrobatic puppet publicist. When the publicist hired Rose for an elaborate interior decoration, she included Bob in the package. Soon he was enjoying the regular salary even if he peddled faked news produced by the same group that had one year earlier blacklisted him and Rose for publishing seditious anti-war materials. Rose set to work on her interior decorations. She bought thick wool rugs, large mahogany desks, "pictures for tired businessmen to moon at," upholstered chairs, and beveled mirrors set in wood frames. In this stuffy, if extravagant, office, looking very much like a nineteenth-century setting, the demands of modern communications, publicity, and networked propaganda made the furniture and decoration seem anachronistic. Dictating machines, telephones, built-in push buttons to summon this assistant or that one, a modern swivel chair, and other equipment made the whole scene look ridiculous, reflecting the publicist's inflated sense of his importance in directing what he thought of as a crucial aspect of the entire war effort. On the director's door was stenciled in gold lettering, "Private." The publicist at first hired Bob to deliver "blood-curdling shiny Solio prints of photographs freshly faked every day," as Bob remembered later in his notes, of German atrocities and war scenes to the local newspapers. Eastman Kodak's Solio paper, widely used for three decades from the 1880s, produces a high sheen and rich color tints of a reddish-brown on heavyweight paper now associated with old photographs; after this treatment, they looked real and official. The United States, working though publicity agencies in every neutral country, realized the power of media manipulation as a crucial weapon in the war effort. Perhaps this recognition also fueled the effort to control, censor, and ultimately punish, with twenty-year jail sentences, any so-called seditious illustrations.

The Browns had landed here, in a foreign capital, and in the belly of the propaganda machine, precisely because of the government's realization of media's importance as a weapon. The apt symmetry, or unwitting irony, was that they had hired experts at pacifist sedition and propaganda. Most important, Rose and Bob translated and expanded the super-condensed telegraphese cabled from the Creel Bureau, the same government agency that had blacklisted them as seditious, into news stories. Although they knew that the stories and pictures were "manufactured in wily Washington by a murky staff of truth-clouders" and that they were "peddling lies, giving new lies for old, keeping the pot of Hun-hatred boiling, and offering a war to end war," they nevertheless saw their work as the only way to survive and would repeat their mantra: "You gotta eat! You gotta live!"[15] They tried to save enough money, from their dirty work and gambling on the horse races, to escape next to Buenos Aires. Suddenly, Washington closed their office but paid Bob a severance, and the embassy hired the Americans in the office for a few months rather than simply leave them hanging without jobs.

After Arthur's disappearance, Mina would soon have a new baby, and the Browns became the baby's godparents. Mina had more complicated feelings toward the Browns; they were, at once, the practical grounding force she needed (who else but Rose would later travel to the coast to meet her at the train station and escort her back to Santiago?), but they were also a constant reminder of Arthur's tragic disappearance at Salina Cruz. Mina had waited for Arthur to return, but to no avail; perhaps he had drifted so far south that he had been forced to dock at another location and was now traveling south as they had intended. If he was lost at sea, then there was no point in waiting for his return. Mina boarded a tramp steamer from Salina Cruz to Chile. Later, Mina wired Rose to ask her to meet Mina's boat at Valparaíso. Bob took Rose to the station, and she took the long train trip down from the highlands to the coast, and, with a depressed and frazzled Mina in tow, they took the train ride back up to Santiago, Chile, where the Browns would soon live. Rose had tried to protect Mina from the slackers' gossip in Santiago: They speculated that Arthur had fled purposefully from Mina, and that talk led eventually to the worldwide myth of Arthur's living on for decades in the United States under various aliases. Mina thought Buenos Aires would help her escape from the slacker-vibe that made her think of Arthur. Bob, Rose, and Allen decided to take the train to San José, Guatemala.

It was about this time that Rose and Bob started to think of themselves as one unit, growing out of their group identity in Battery J and the valiant slackers, and they often began referring to themselves as RoseBob, even signing letters (and, later, co-written manuscripts) with that combined name. Bob had long before bought shares in a mining company operated in Peru by an old friend from Wisconsin—a friend who a few years later would marry Lucia Fox, Lillian's youngest sister. The mine never paid Bob a substantial dividend, but it served an extremely useful purpose for Robert C. Brown, who had no U.S. passport papers; he could honestly claim that his occupation was as a "miner" instead of a seditious radical writer. He applied for a new passport in July 1918 but claimed to have last lived in the United States only until 1915. Setting his emigration date before the Sedition Acts would mean he had spent the years from 1915 until 1918, when he actually worked for *The Masses* and staged decadent fundraisers at Webster Hall, supposedly setting up mines in Mexico and South America. The rest of the information was correct: two children, with correct birthdates, divorced from Cornelia Fox (Lillian), deceased father, lived in Ridgefield, New Jersey, was now staying at the Hotel Suize in Valparaíso. There was no mention of Rose. The application was approved. With the U.S. passport, Bob could now apply for jobs with the U.S. government outposts—consulates, propaganda offices, and embassies.

Rose got Bob a job creating a flood of propaganda, coding neutral images from or about Germany as sinister and drowning out any pro-German sentiments in the local newspapers. Their work sought to get the then-neutral Chile to side with the Allies against Germany. Bob positioned his embassy desk next to a window on the first floor in case he needed to jump out and flee if any of the half-dozen Secret Service attachés ever tapped him significantly on the shoulder and asked about his past as a war-resisting seditious socialist writer. He was characteristically amused by his bittersweet luck in landing a job editing, translating codes, and writing, but a job where every day could be his last—not his last day at the job, but his last before the firing squad. He was equally bemused by the carelessness of the spies. They left secret codes lying around, and when he asked a Secret Service agent, "Shouldn't the codes be locked in a safe at night?" the agent laughed off the idea: "No," and winked in explanation, "if there are any German spies around, then they don't need to steal any of these," and went on to brag, "I've seen Blue Codes on sale in second-hand stores in Berlin as cheap as fifteen marks, even before we went into the war." Even though the spies had a nonchalant attitude, as soon as Rose and Mina returned from Valparaíso, Bob thought that they should flee sooner rather than later across the border to Buenos Aires. The

Browns traveled to Buenos Aires by train, where they picked up Marcel Duchamp, who was flying in for a visit.

It was now May 1919. Duchamp mentioned in a letter to a friend, Ettie Stettheimer, his having met Robert in Buenos Aires: "I met here a certain Robert C. Brown whom you probably know by name, Ettie: He belonged to the Max Eastman Gang and used to write at one time. We chat about New York. In short, nothing entertaining to tell you."[16] In spite of his nonchalance about the meeting, Duchamp carved a chess set for the Browns, which they later gave away as a prize to one of the contributing editors at *Brazilian American*. The Browns soon traveled on to Brazil, and eventually to Saõ Paulo. The year of living dangerously was closing. Bob summarized the struggles in his readies style more than a decade later:

> —living out Nick Carter novels luridly—escaping revolutionary bombs that sprawled long, living, flaming passenger trains down bare, bouldery mountain slides in Tehauntepec, leaving eye-scars, smoking skeletons of writing fire-frozen iron.—Where was Battery J during the Great War?—Battery J was detailed to border duty—Bathing stark-naked in the warm blueing waters of Salina Cruz—discussing forged passports with the Ways and Means Committee—flopping into trouble—flopping out of it—all over Amerique Latine chasing and being chased by mental and physical devils with acrid shooting irons and irritating lightning forks—Where was Battery J during Your Great War?—Why, Battery J was in hell catching red-hot rivets with General Sherman, bare red-handed without a bucket.[17]

The deep bitterness and biting irony quickly faded in Brazil out of necessity. Bob and Rose once again started looking for ways to make a living ("You gotta live") by writing, editing, and publishing. They took their skills with entrepreneurial organizing (called harebrained scheming when it fails and prescient brilliance when it succeeds) to meetings with American expatriate businessmen. Counter to the few citations of Brown's publication in Brazil as a "literary journal," the publication was a business newsletter *with absolutely no literary or artistic content*. Instead, he was using his skills from Compub, when he approached American businessmen and described the possibility of publishing an English-language news source as a clearinghouse for all the most mundane business news, from which ships had docked, what cargo was unloaded, and who worked for which companies. It most closely resembled the present-day Bloomberg model of news, relatively quickly delivered English-language informa-

The *Brazilian American* news office fed the need for English-language business information.

tion with very little analysis and no cultural stories; Brown's company soon also resembled Bloomberg, Inc., in its scope and financial success. In fact, Brown would later in the 1930s joke that he represented the printers at one of his printing presses in Brazil, helping to organize them into a union; how else to justify and explain to his comrades in the Left Front his international success at running a business? He soon had spread a similar model of English-language business news magazines to Mexico City, London, and throughout Latin America. He first pitched the idea in São Paulo, the business capital, but, to his surprise, he found more interest and investors in Rio de Janeiro.

His *Brazilian American*, founded in Rio, quickly became an empire. With their newfound wealth, Bob and Rose raised orchids at their plantation and collected Braziliana, antiques, rose diamond rings, stones, and much more. Lillian sent the children down to Brazil and later sent large parcels of both children's books and books for Bob too; although she admitted to missing them immensely, she thought it best that the children stay there if at all possible because she was going through another divorce and could not care for the children. Her sister Lucia had joined her new husband in Peru, and a family trip was planned to visit her. In 1924, Rose and Bob started the *Mexican American* in Mexico City and appointed Cora as the editor of that newsletter. Two years later, they founded the *British American* in London but continued to print and publish all three in Brazil, while traveling constantly between the three countries. They were making more than $50,000 a year (equivalent to nearly $700,000 in the present day). In 1925, they started the Associated Latin American Magazines with offices in New York and every South American capital. All of this success was based on the Browns' organizational skills, familiarity with printing and publishing, expertise in financial deals and business information, and interest in international networks of readers. Once again, these new Browns seemed almost like different people from the bohemians of Grantwood Village, magazine fiction writers, day-trading stock speculators, or war-resisting exiles. They became bourgeois businesspeople. Contemporary literary scholarship has no place for the business newsletter genre; outside academia's narrow constraints and disciplinary boundaries, the business newsletter was an important part of Brown's disjunctive life story and part of a history of writing.

The Browns turned down many offers to sell the business, including a deal that would have earned them a million dollars' backing (in mid-1920s dollars) to put thirty similar magazine/newsletters in the leading world capitals. They regretted not selling sooner, but they still sold in time to spend two years of world travels; during their travels, they collected art, artifacts, rare books, and jade jewelry; at each stop they learned about national cuisines and local culinary traditions. When they sold their empire, they made enough to fund lavish living for six years, including the two years of travel with extended stops at many foreign cities; Bob's son, Carlton, even enrolled in school during a particularly long stay in Shanghai, China.

Much of this chapter in the Browns' life seemed tied up with political persecution, exile, and poverty as they suffered through the disappearance, and probable death, of friends, and the loss of Bob's greatest creative achievement, a culmination of eight years of work. The persecution was mostly in 1917, and the decade from the fall of 1918 to the winter of 1928, the year they arrived in France, was filled with lavish living and capitalist success. The twelve months of loss and trauma in Mexico were enough for a lifetime, and the success at business a footnote in their own conceptions of the significant events of their lives. Their perspective on

Bob and Rose now played the roles of plump international business owners and publishers.

their own situation might not have corresponded with reality for most of the decade, but their internationalism now looks like the vanguard for multicultural practices.

If the business empire was a reinvention of their personae, then their world travels were an even more powerful sea change. After building a publishing empire in Brazil, they decided to sell the international business newsletter business, keep one of their plantations in Petropolis, and travel the world. They traveled around South America and toward Asia. Around the Far East, they took the *Kamkura Maru*, a commercial shipping vessel with limited space for passengers; the *Kamkura Maru* crew was buying up metal scrap at each port to sell to the Japanese war machine. The Browns stayed in China long enough that Carlton, who'd decided to travel with them, was enrolled in a local American school. During their time in Shanghai, Bob started to feel vertigo every time he spent a night

Bob morphed into a plump, cheery, bourgeois owner of an international empire.

out on the town, which was frequently; he wrote to his doctor, William Carlos Williams, who is much more famous as a poet but often gave his avant-garde pal medical advice about Brown's afflictions, which started to include agoraphobia, which was a cruel phobia for someone who lived to go to crowded restaurants and raucous bars. The reply from Williams has since been lost, but eventually Bob, perhaps on the advice of Williams, visited a health spa in Germany, and, two decades later, he stopped drinking entirely.

After China, they traveled to Singapore, Yokahama, and Kobe. In Nagasaki, they stayed at Rivermouth's Hotel. They ate lobster in Hiroshima, a cultural center before its annihilation during World War II, and sampled food and liquor from every place they lived in their journeys. They were keenly aware of the political situations they saw as well. For example, Bob saw soldiers in Japan learning to bayonet much taller men using dummies dressed like U.S. soldiers; they were obviously preparing to fight American invaders just as the United States, in the mid-1920s, was trying to contain the Japanese empire-building in China and a destabilized Russia. Although Cora carried a spoon with her wherever they went, so she wouldn't have to use chopsticks, she was busy writing down each and every recipe for the cornucopia of exotic dishes and drinks. They traveled to Malaysia, and for more than a month they lived on the *Lahn*, a ship collecting, and trading, for exotic animals at Belawan, Sumatra. The wild animals, being sold to zoos around the world, were caged on the deck with claws grabbing at passersby. They traveled to Colombo, Ceylon (present-day Sri Lanka). And then they traveled to the African continent. They collected gems and other artifacts. With less modern ports, Rose went ashore climbing down a taut rope from the deck, hand-over-hand, into a dinghy that they would row ashore. They stayed in Cape Town, Durban, and Zululand. They traveled north to Europe, cruised by the coasts of Sardinia and Corsica, and eventually landed in Marseilles on March 31, 1928. When the Browns finally arrived in France, they had forty trunks filled with artifacts from Shanghai's Jade Bazaar. The customs agent in Marseilles, not wanting to be late for his dinner, let everything pass through without opening any of the containers. Marcel Duchamp helped the Browns sell most of their artifacts, and jade jewelry collection, at auction for what Bob described decades later in his personal notes as "only slightly *less* than what they paid for them." They stayed in a hotel for a few days, and Bob was drinking "recklessly," "out buying books," and eating great meals of bouillabaisse, according to Cora's diary entries, even though he was suffering from various psychological and physical ailments. They arrived in Paris on April 6.

Soon after arriving in Europe, Brown started Roving Eye Press to join and collaborate with the lively avant-garde publishing scene, including Nancy Cunard's Hours Press, Harry and Caresse Crosby's Black Sun Press, and Eugene Jolas's *transition* magazine. Soon Gertrude Stein and others would celebrate Brown's plans for the reading machine.

5
Expatriate Avant-Garde in the South of France, 1928–32

> I'm not really interested in writing either prose or poetry. All I want is words. Words with the punch of hieroglyphics, words with the sweep and color of a painter's lines . . . . Words with optical interest whenever possible.
>
> —*Bob Brown*[1]

> The reader slips it smoothly into its slot in the machine, sets the speed regulator, turns on the electric current and the whole 100,000, 200,000, 300,000 or million words spill out before his eyes . . . in one continuous line of type.
>
> —*Bob Brown*[2]

After traveling around the world for nearly two years, including a long stay in China, the Browns arrived in France in time to attend Eugene Jolas's New Year's Day celebration. (Jolas was the experimental writer and co-founder and editor of the influential avant-garde *transition* literary journal in Paris.) There they met Kay Boyle, who had just five days earlier given birth to her daughter Apple, and as Bob would later recount in unpublished notes, Kay was "always about babies, but mostly about work." Around that intense work ethic, they built a lifelong relationship of mutual admiration, respect, and love.

Boyle and Brown became fast friends. Many of their old friends were also expatriates in France, and Bob immediately fell back in with his now-extended group from the artists' colony, including Man Ray and Marcel Duchamp; at the party he met James T. Farrell, who was, unbeknownst to the partiers, living in dire poverty. People talked about the expatriate scene, including stories about Josephine Baker, E. E. Cummings, Aaron Copland, F. Scott Fitzgerald, George Gershwin, Ernest Hemingway, Archibald MacLeish, Dorothy Parker, Cole Porter, John Dos Passos, Janet Flanner, Sylvia Beach, Ezra Pound, Nancy Cunard, and Gertrude Stein. In Paris, Bob drank regularly with Stuart Davis at the Brasserie Lipp on Boulevard St. Germaine. Davis, his pal from *The Masses*, was developing a style that twenty years later he described as the "euphoric method," which fit Brown's style as well. They would visit the Brasserie at least three or four times a day, often with the many poets and artists who frequented the bars near that corner; it was during those many chats together that Stuart started to formulate his euphoric type of jazzy pop abstract painting. In honor of his productive friendship with Bob, Stuart dedicated a 1959 painting to him; it was a reworking of *Rue Lippe*, and now named *The Paris Bit*. Also in the late 1920s, Davis was working on the highly abstract still-lifes, including *Egg Beater, No. 1* (1927), copied by Sherrie Levine in her *After Stuart Davis* (1984). Sadly, Stuart's name later appeared in the news again around 2007 as his son Earl Davis was defrauded out of many of his father's paintings by the prestigious art dealer and gallery director Larry Salandar, who had claimed to Earl Davis that the pictures were out on consignment to museums; instead, Salandar had sold many of the paintings for millions of dollars but never compensated the Davis family. Salandar eventually pleaded guilty; it seems apt, if infuriating, that a corrupt art dealer and business owner stole the monetary value of the paintings.

Drinking up the expatriate scene, Bob started talking about the experimental writing of the time in relation to his own form of automatism, related to the Surrealist projects. Brown sought to connect the automatic writing and séance-like automatism of the Surrealists, Duchamp's ready-mades and automatic-conceptual art, the experiments with grammar from the *transition* crowd and Gertrude Stein and his own plans for processing texts for his reading machine. Kay Boyle, a key force in the expatriate avant-garde and the *transition* literary journal's circle, started to talk with Bob about how to write in popular forms, and later she won critical acclaim and financial success from her popular writing. Kay, in turn, got Bob up to speed with the advances in the avant-garde since 1919. The efforts to adjust to a world in transition depended on experiments and experiences that uncovered an alternative reality haunting the mundane reality of everyday life. The artists and writers added the prefix "sur" in describing this other reality that was a heightened, stressed, dialectical, doubled, and echoing multiple reality. This surreality was present all along, but unnoticed. The use of multiple perspectives or, in Brown's phrase, "a roving eye," instead of a single and singular perspective appeared

Bob refined his plans for the machine during convivial conversations with Stuart Davis at the Brasserie Lipp.

in cubism, Surrealism, Dada collages, and in other experimental types of writing. In *transition*, Robert Desnos, James Joyce, Peter Neagoe, Philippe Soupault, Max Ernst, Juan Gris, and Pablo Picasso were all involved in employing this style (portmanteau words, not quite recognizable allusive images, multiple perspectives, etc.).

Others appearing in *transition* were using this pared-down writing style most closely associated with Gertrude Stein, who was at first closely aligned with the magazine but also associated with a future mechanized writing. Léon-Paul Fargue, Konstantin Fedin, and Murray Goodwin wrote about "A Day in the Life of a Robot," and there was among the avant-garde an interest in imagining the everyday activities from the fantastic perspective of a machine or robot. Franz Kafka, Samuel Beckett, Hemingway, and others were working, in the 1920s, with a prose style that moved writing toward a cinematic style simply by eliminating the "unnecessary" literary conventions (conjunctions, prepositions, and other short words). This left a slightly more disjunctive style: clear, crisp, almost flickering, with the stress on nouns and verbs—things in action. Many of the others publishing in *transition* were part of the Imagist group from Grantwood Village, including William Carlos Williams. Many saw the new experiments as growing out of that earlier work. The art and writing were part of a dreamed-for revolutionary transition to a liberated wor(l) d, and soon Boyle, and others, would publish a *transition* manifesto to that effect. Bob soon saw this new condensed and abbreviated form as a new take on his same fascinations with reading, machines, and visual poetry. He set to work in yet another genre: the manifesto.

In Paris, Bob began drinking in the avant-garde experiments in performance, music, radio, writing, and manifestos. The *transition* crowd inspired the Browns; the magazine was advocating a revolution of the word in the literary arts. Among that group Kay Boyle in particular led Brown to think of a literal type of revolution of the word: words spinning by the eyes. He often talked with George Antheil, the expatriate American musical performance artist, whose loud sound machines and performances led Brown to think about analogous performances with his own avocations: publishing and reading. Of course, Bob read the Surrealist manifestos for clues to applications and experiments. He thought of himself as affiliated with the Surrealists and a few years later published in a Surrealist anthology. He began writing his own proclamation, and, much like the avant-garde manifestos of the time, Brown wrote with enthusiastic hyperbole about his planned-for reading machine's breathtaking potential to change how we read and learn. In 1930, beaming out printed text over radio waves or in televised images had a science fiction quality or, for the avant-garde, a fanciful art-stunt feel. Today, Brown's research on reading seems remarkably prescient in light of text messaging (with its abbreviated language), electronic text readers, and e-books. Brown's proposal for a modernist style of reading, with speed, movement, and an odd clarity, needed a machine. So, he started making plans for his reading machine, descriptions of its implications for reading; and the abbreviated style of the processed texts (what he called "readies") had practical implications for libraries and reading in the future. To disrupt the charms of reading would outrage the middle-class public just as avant-garde music, literature, and performances sought to disrupt pleasantness.

Rose designed their apartment on Boulevard Montparnasse in Paris. She used the modern eclectic style popular among the vanguard and drawing on the Browns' collections. They hung Japanese prints illustrating Commodore Matthew C. Perry's coming into Yokohama harbor. Drinking up the Surrealist cubo-futurist buzz in the air and suffering from dysentery picked up in his world travels, Bob soon found himself in need of a rest cure. He decamped to Bad Ems, a Bavarian, German spa town, famous for its medicinal springs. He had earlier complained in letters to his informal physician, William Carlos Williams, about various ailments that had first appeared in the Far East and that continued in Paris. In a particularly cruel and ironic symmetry, Bob seemed to have developed a case of agoraphobia by the time he arrived in Paris. If he went out on the town (which was a daily event), he would soon develop sweaty and vertiginous panic attacks. These psychological disturbances were on top of his suffering from tropical dysentery. The cure consisted of a garlic flush in which everyone taking the cure would drink large quantities of garlic juice.

As he was recovering in Bad Ems, he threw himself enthusiastically into publishing, collaborating, and starting his own mobile Roving Eye Press; his press's first publication was a pamphlet-length manifesto he composed and produced while going through the garlic flushes. In the midst of the rest cure, and ongoing afterward, he tried other cures, too: the punch cure, the grape cure, and ultimately, his favorite, the beer-cure. Only these three seemed to have had a lasting, positive impression on Brown. A few years later, the Browns published the bestselling *Wine Cookbook*, while Bob published *Let There Be Beer!* The thriving community of avant-garde publishers, including Contact Editions, Beaumont Press, Ovid Press, Nonesuch Press, Fanfrolico, Seizin, Sylvia Beach's Shakespeare & Company, Black Sun Press, Black Manikin Press, and Bob Brown's own Roving Eye Press, became an opportunity for Bob to collaborate with other publishers.

In 1929, just before Brown's rest-cure vacation in Bavaria, Harry and Caresse Crosby's Black Sun Press, in Paris, published a book of hand-drawn visual poetry, *1450–1930*; no copies appear to exist, but the collection was republished in 1959. Perhaps this biography will provoke someone to announce that a copy does exist. The 1959 edition was titled *1450–1950*, and the references here are to that edition.[3] The Crosbys published Harry's poetry and experimental writings alongside works by Joyce, Jolas, Hemingway, D. H. Lawrence, Boyle, and other modernists as well as an illustrated ancient erotic Hindu book. All of the books from Black Sun were famously beautifully produced and with transgressive themes and approaches. In a scandalous demonic act that was planned and composed like fiction, Harry Crosby committed suicide with one of his mistresses after his wife, Caresse, wanted to wait to fulfill their own suicide pact. Caresse carried on the press's work, and it continued for a few more years as a venue for Surrealist and modern writing, but history dismissed the Crosbys, until recently, much like Bob Brown, as dilettantes in the avant-garde in part because they thrived for only a few years in the late 1920s and early '30s. The collection that Bob Brown published with them is never mentioned among lists of their important publications.

One of the most famous poems in Brown's collection, "Eyes on the Half-Shell," was published in Marcel Duchamp's *Blindman* in 1917. This collection of hand-drawn visual poems was partially influenced by Apollinaire's "Calligrammes" experiments (published in 1918, a year *after* Bob published the first visual poem in the modernist era); so, more than influence, all of the visual-poetry experiments going on in Paris created a context for Bob's earlier work. In describing this volume, Bob punned on "Apollinaris" mineral water, bottled eighty kilometers upriver from Bad Ems: He claimed to bathe in Apollinaire as part of the cure for what literature had become, and released what it could become. More than half a century after Brown first published a visual poem, and nearly three decades after publishing this chapbook, the publisher-poet Jonathan Williams's Jargon Society Press reissued Brown's collection to an American audience in 1959.

Another poem in *1450–1950* offers in a *mise-en-abyme* another context in which to read this entire collection of poems and all of Brown's life and career; Bob Brown's own self-portrait as visual poem functions as a schematic map to reading this volume. The handwritten captions on different parts of his stick figure include references to poems in this volume, like "My Skeleton Both Articulates and Gesticulates," and, again, in *mise-en-abyme* fashion, half of this book's title appears in the upper left hand corner, "1450," and the other half appears in the lower right corner, "1950." One handwritten tag, "my art," is scribbled over his heart; and that heart is a dingbat-like visual design he used as the logo for this collection of visual poetry. Next to the logo-heart is "My Rose Rib," an allusion to Adam's rib and to Brown's partner and wife, Rose. In this same self-poem, or what we now might call a conceptual poem-selfie, he includes a miniature of his entire "Eyes on the Half Shell" that shows the influence of Marcel Duchamp. Brown turns his autobiographical sketch into one of his characteristic comic visual poems that make the abstracted shape an essential element of the meaning and self-conception.

The optical aspect of these poems is of course crucial. When one talks about modernist visual poetry, one starts with Apollinaire's calligrams and Cummings's manupictograms and typograms wherein the poet imbricates writing and illustration inextricably together.

Of *1450–1950* Brown explains,

> I try to express myself through optical poems, as Apollinaire and cummings try, as I already tried in "Eyes on the Half Shell" in 1917, excited by the first "Armory Show" and by the *Tender Buttons* of Gertrude Stein, excited by the combining of drawings and words. I don't believe that words by themselves are worth anything anymore, except when manipulated by artists (cummings and Boyle for example). I think that Coolidge (today: add Eisenhower) and Will Rogers exhausted them to the point that they were left without meaning, so pale and dirty as the cents that Rockefeller and Woolworth rub among themselves. I think we need words in motion, to be read by the reading machine, I think we need to recapture something of the healthy hieroglyphic writing, now that oratory is dead and the rest of poetry that is still read aloud is vociferated at us by *electronicsniks*.[4]

The text is handwritten through most of the book, including its dedication to an eccentric list of writers, artists, printers, whole categories of artists and artisans, and even a fictional murderous clown from the opera *Pagliacci*; Brown includes "MYSELF." He stresses in the visual form of the all-caps-handwritten list, and in the wacky allusions, his own mix of visual and clowning elements that this collection embodies: Brown invents a type of slapstick poetic burlesque. Calling it visual poetry is too staid and decorous; scratch and scrawl would illuminate its spirit better. If sonnets have a singular form and unvarying constraints for each and every instantiation, then scratch and scrawl depends on the absolutely particular trace, passions, and imperfection of the handwriting. The play between words and images shifts from a poetic tension to a conceptual game in which hand-drawn scribbles and pictures—blurring the boundaries between literal scribbles and conceptual poetry—it is difficult to describe them as one would a single medium like painting or film. Instead, the process of reading *1450–1950* follows an intimate discovery of a literally marginalized poetry (since the invention of the printing press). Brown's collection is an extension of Gutenberg's creative legacy from 1450 and, at the same time, a resistance to the standardized lines of type set. The handwriting reinforces these poems' improvisatory mood. The brevity of the poems, never exceeding one page (and sometimes seemingly two or three in one), add to the immediacy and intimacy; they feel like snapshot poems. The readers feel as if Bob is sitting next to them at the bar, while drinking beers, as he draws these poems on a napkin as he did in a bar with Duchamp. There is a subfield of poetics focused on visual poetry, but little of it studies the literary meaning of handwriting. It is difficult to talk in general terms about something so specific, something literally (and figuratively) not of "type," and something that is rarely reproduced outside of the documentation of an author's original notes. Although there is a rich semantic play in these poems, there is no versifying formalism, no sign of any verse, not even free or Imagist verse.

Now in Bad Ems, Bob worked on another major project. He described plans for a reading machine that depended on his "readies." Bob wanted to conjure a machine that would not be out of place in a popular science fiction story in a pulp magazine. To add to the realism, he included exhaustive descriptions of the reading machine's operations. The details seem at once quaint and futuristic. To the contemporary ear, they sound like a description of an e-reader:

> Extracting the dainty reading roll from its pill box container the reader slips it smoothly into its slot in the machine, sets the speed regulator, turns on the electric current and the whole 100,000, 200,000, 300,000 or million words spill out before his eyes . . . in one continuous line of type . . . My machine is equipped with controls so the reading record can be turned back or shot ahead . . . magnifying glass . . . moved nearer or farther from the type, so the reader may browse in 6 point, 8, 10, 12, 16 or any size that suits him.[5]

Bob considered the prepared texts as a genre of writing and a brand (like Google today), and he often capitalized the word "Readies" in his manifesto; he thought that one day Readies could become readies, with a lowercase "r," the way "Escalator," a brand of the Otis Company, became "escalator," a moving stairs machine; if that acceptance had occurred, one would think of readies as superseding the book as Bob intended. It would be a machine for the new wor(l)d that the avant-garde was preparing. Only now does the machine seem outdated with the advent of e-readers, e-books, and cloud-based digital repositories. In 1930, the machine, and the possibility of the universal adoption of Bob's machine, elicited laughter at its marvelous absurdity suggesting a possible future and parallel universe. Much like Duchamp's claim to speak to an audience fifty years in the future, the manifesto contained language that seems encrypted for

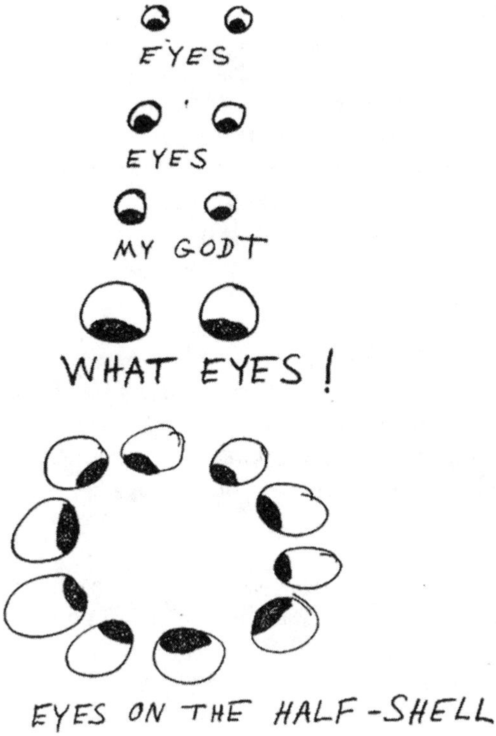

Brown's most famous visual poem, "Eyes on the Half-Shell."

a future audience to more fully understand. Bob's manifesto, in keeping with the conversations, experiments, and proclamations that everyone was talking about, was written for an audience fifty years in the future. Some of these guesses about the future seem quaint now, but others are spot-on. For example, the reading machine was designed to unroll a "televistic readie" for the general public to use in their homes, but television was only a limited experiment at the time. Gertrude Stein understood that Brown's machine, as well as his processed texts for it, suggested a shift toward a different way to comprehend texts, and in a note to him she expressed her delight with his plans. That is, the mechanism of this book, a type of book explicitly built to resemble reading mechanisms like ticker-tape machines rather than a codex, or bound book form, produced, at least for Stein, specific changes in reading practices. In Brown's readies, punctuation marks become visual analogies. For movement we see em dashes (—) that also, by definition, indicate that the sentence was interrupted or truncated. These created a "cinemovietone" shorthand system. The old uses of punctuation, such as employment of periods to mark the end of a sentence, disappear. Reading machine-mediated text becomes more like watching a continuous series of flickering frames projected as an old flickering, but continuous, movie. From page 37 of *Readies*, Bob's transcription of a readie (without the machine), suggests the speed of the mechanism.

Recognizing punctuation marks as analogies for cinematographic zooms, close-ups, and special effects makes reading into a new, unfamiliar process; using punctuation as hieroglyphic analogies for visual and emotional meanings might seem obvious today when we create emoji and emoticons by using punctuation marks in precisely this way. Using punctuation for visual rather than reading cues makes reading into a dramatic scene, or an allegory about the process of reading as the words run on "before the eye continuously." The machine demonstrates reading in the age of machines, but, as in much modernist art, one also becomes aware of the general processes. *Readies* sought to illuminate the form of a process rather than the form of a medium. Mechanical poetics (like Duchamp's descriptions of an impossible fourth dimension) magnify reading as a cultural and technological medium without a single essential form. Using punctuation in this way, as a visual score rather than as cues for reading aloud, and creating an endless array of portmanteau words (the most obvious and important of these was combining "ready," "read," and "talkies" into "readies"), as Brown so enthusiastically does, makes literary interpretation problematic but places the project within other Surrealist efforts to change everyday life. Precisely because punctuation marks usually function to guide the voice to read prosody, the use of punctuation as analogies for motion and other optical effects moves reading from interpreting words in connection with an author's voice to emphasizing design, visual aesthetics, and movement. Readies do not efface expressivity, but they put the tone of voice in doubt. A line functioned as a dash, a mark of redaction, and/or a speed mark (perhaps telling a future machine operator when to press down to increase the speed). That kind of visual logic, in which a simple line took on many meanings, was common at the time in works by such artists as Duchamp and the Surrealists.

After Bad Ems, Cora, Rose, and Bob along with Carlton moved to

Gertrude Stein was delighted by Bob's manifesto for the readies.

81 Montée Bourgade, Cagnes-sur-Mer, halfway between Antibes and Nice, France, to live in Le Manoir, the manor house atop the hill in the village. Cagnes-sur-Mer had already become a satellite community of the expatriate avant-garde in much the way that the artists' colony near Grantwood Village was a satellite of, and respite from, the Greenwich Village scene in the 1910s. Bob made oceans of punch in the bathtub (a Bishop of Toulouse's hip bath, a double-ended bateau bath with tinned copper walls first seen in the 1860s) for parties. The romantic poet Richard le Galliene occupied the manor house before the Browns moved in. The rumor, fueled by Bob, was that le Galliene lived, and worked, in the attic studio as that was the most fitting setting for a satirical cliché of a romantic-decadent poet. As an interlude from their home in Cagnes-sur-Mer, the Browns also decamped to Villefranche-sur-Mer to be near Kay Boyle. It was in Villefranche that they met Charlie Chaplin, Jack Dempsey, and many other visiting celebrities, as well as their old friends, now in exile and residing in Nice, Emma Goldman, Frank Harris, and Alexander Berkman. Kay Boyle "preferred having cocktails with their neighbor Frank Scully, joining the Browns and Mary Reynolds and Mar-

cel Duchamp, visiting with Emma Goldman and Alexander Berkman or having dinner in Nice and the evening in the cafés . . . [and it was at those gatherings] when Kay and [Bob] would exchange stories or sections of novels."[6] Although Bob published his manifesto, first in Bad Ems as a pamphlet, then in *transition*, and finally in various versions from Cagnes-sur-Mer, he continued to develop the idea and plans in these iterations and in the conversations the machine provoked. Chaplin saw the potential humor in these avant-garde critical machines as he was starting to develop his plans for *Modern Times* (1936).

Duchamp, a formative influence on Brown's experimental and visual poetry since 1913, had already designed, built, and found readymade machines. Brown saw those as models for his own "ready" reader, and he started to use that pun in his thinking about what he would invent. Raymond Roussell built his own Surrealist reading machine relatively soon after the *Readies* manifesto appeared. It seems fitting that Brown would call the processed texts "readies"—explicitly alluding to talkies and movies and implicitly, as an inside joke, to readymade works as well as alluding to "ready writers," the phrase used to describe a writer who was ready to write words (in any genre) to fill a space in a magazine. In light of his own claims in *The Readies* to do for reading what Pablo Picasso did for painting, or what Joyce, Stein, and Cummings had done for writing, one might call Bob Brown the Marcel Duchamp of reading.

The fascination with machine aesthetics was very much of the moment in June 1930. In the June issue of the modernist magazine *transition*, in which Brown announced his machine, the magazine's editor, Eugene Jolas, declared,

> The mechanical surrounds us like a flood. The machine and its relations to man is doubtless one of the major problems of the age. Ever more accelerated becomes the tempo, ever more whirling are the pistons, ever more violent is the influence of this titanic instrument upon the thoughts and acts of man.[7]

Bob Brown sent a copy of the *Readies* manifesto to Gertrude Stein, and she loved his invention and laughed aloud at his playful presentation of plans and ideas. She answered his plan with an essay celebrating "Absolutely Bob Brown, or Bobbed Brown," alluding to Brown's call to process all texts in a telegraphic cut-up style that eliminates all unnecessary words. With Stein's poetic allusion in mind, the readies' writers and editors bobbed sentences as flappers bobbed (cut short) their hair. Stein had cut her hair in a bob a few years before and saw the bobbed style, and Bobbed Brown, as quintessentially modern.

The expatriate modernists in Paris embraced Brown's readies project. Section number 12 of the "revolution of the word" manifesto by the *transition* editorial collective almost seemed to introduce Brown's efforts and many of the poetic experiments of the time ("THE PLAIN READER BE DAMNED").[8] Any plain reader would quickly grow fatigued by the new poetry as well as by Brown's machine, but these readers would find no sympathy, or consolation, in *transition*'s dismissal of those bland readers. Instead of their publishing empire of business newsletters and their world travels' dulling the Browns' sensibility, their lives between 1919 and 1928 had heightened their interest in what the Surrealists were calling the marvelous and uncanny.

Bob Brown's uncannily prophetic manifesto on a possible future of reading, using his machine and prepared texts, readies, speaks not only to students of modernism but also to a wider audience interested in media technologies' possible impacts on a process we take for granted: reading. A hundred years later, his machine looks like a precursor to the electronic reading machines, and he was celebrated in a 2010 *New York Times* article as the "godfather of the e-reader."[9] Brown's important manifesto, on a par with André Breton's Surrealist manifestos or Tristan Tzara's Dadaist declarations, includes plans for an electric reading machine and strategies for preparing the eye for mechanized reading. There are instructions for preparing texts as "readies" and detailed quantitative explanations about the invention and mechanisms involved in this peculiar machine. Brown published his announcement of the machine in three versions: *The Readies* (1930/2014); a condensed version in *transition* (1930); and a follow-up version as an appendix in *Readies for Bob Brown's Machine* (1931). He included in these works examples of the specially prepared texts for his machine, and in another volume, *Words* (1931/2014), he included a different approach to the prepared texts for the machine: miniaturization to less than 2-point font size requiring magnification to read. In a later novel, *You Gotta Live* (1932), he wrote the preface in the readies style.[10] After those publications, the machine's influence and significance lay dormant until the twenty-first century.

As an example of Brown's speaking a then-unknown language of the future, the use of the word "browse," in reference to a graphical interface device (rather than perusal in a bookshop or library) did not appear again until the late 1980s, with the advent of database browsers. And, a couple of decades before the general public had access to television on a wide scale, Brown promised that his reading machine would "unroll a televistic readie film."[11] The idea of miniaturizing reading material data to fit into a pillbox and connecting it to the reader in a slot was completely unfamiliar to readers until at least half a century later. Today, that description seems like a pitch for a new wireless miniature e-reader complete with slots for expansion.

Brown's electrically powered machine, initially planned to be the size of a typewriter, unrolled "one moving line of type before the eye, not blurred by the presence of lines above and below."[12] This type of procedure, with the user controlling and increasing the speed of the words either moving linearly or one word at a time, closely resembles speed-reading machines introduced in the 1960s and online versions available today. Brown planned to print the type "microscopically by the new photographic process on a transparent tough tissue roll," and this roll, "no bigger than a typewriter ribbon," would unroll "beneath a narrow strip of strong magnifying glass." It resembled a microfilm reader (at least in one iteration) for which Brown started to apply for a patent, and it was intended specifically to "rid" the reader "at last of the cumbersome book, the inconvenience of holding its bulk, turning its pages, keeping them clean."[13]

Bradley A. Fiske had already held a patent (Patent 1,411, 008) for a "reading machine" since March 28, 1922, about a decade before Bob's prototype, and many versions had existed since the late nineteenth century. Fiske's device became the model for the microfiche and microfilm machines that were widely adopted by libraries and archives after World War II, when engineers connected printers to the readers. Bob corresponded with Fiske with enthusiasm for helping develop the machine and consulted with engineers to develop his own machine. The differences in their approaches to reading had to do with Bob's emphasis on also processing the texts into readies for the machine, while Fiske produced photographic facsimiles that miniaturized the documents. Under the influence of the modernist's call to radically change the word and writing, Bob's approach to reading depended on the readies aspect that made the social technical apparatuses of reading more explicit. Fiske sought to make reading processes more efficient and transparent.

Eventually, in Brown's plans, one would be able to "radio" readies as easily "as it is today to [produce] newsies on shipboard and words perhaps eventually will be recorded directly on the palpitating ether."[14] In this sense, Brown conceived of the future of the machine as something like a telegram but more closely resembling the shorthand languages emerging now around new media technologies (e.g., instant messages, text messages), but the name's allusion to talkies and sending the texts through the airwaves explicitly tied it to film, an imagined television, and at the time, an unimagined Internet.

The material conditions of type were also something he knew well, for he owned presses, including "a monotype" from which he "watched molten letters pour through it into an endless stream of words."[15] He was regularly talking to the expatriate publishers in Paris, especially Harry and Caresse Crosby. These publishers were not simply supplementing or promoting the poetry, visual art, and other modernist experiments but were an integral part of the expatriate modernist project: designing, printing, publishing, and distributing books and magazines as a kind of truly modern poetry. Photographic composition and the use of new machines like the August-Hunter Camera Composing Machine, which Brown had used for his business newsletters, would allow for "a multitude of words" to be "printed in a minimum of space and yet [be] readable to the naked eye."[16]

On a warm May afternoon in Cagnes-sur-Mer in 1931, a group of expatriate avant-garde artists and writers gathered at Le Manoir to witness the unveiling of a newborn reading machine. (The house still stands and is now a restaurant.) Many among the avant-garde avoided the town because American tourists had poured into the quaint village to take in scenic views and the charming architecture, but the breakaway colony of expatriate vanguardists held out against the tour guides and their flocks. The village's scenes and sunshine had attracted artists for decades since the painter Pierre Auguste Renoir settled there in 1908, and the modernist avant-garde artists began moving to the villages around the Côte d'Azur in the 1920s, at least for the summer season. The frivolous party time in the south of France was nearing its end, as the worsening economic depression, and rise of fascist states in Europe, would soon push all of the tourists, and many of the expatriate artists, to leave. The assembled group that day likely included Kay Boyle and Laurence Vail, George Antheil, Hilaire Hiler, Abraham "Linc" Gillespie, Peter Neagoe, and Ross Saunders. Later Marcel Duchamp might have stopped by to see the amusing machine. Gertrude Stein had sent congratulations to the inventor and had written an essay prepared for the machine. Her note, about how she greeted the plans for the machine with "giggles," might have been passed around. From notes about visitors, it is likely that Charlie Chaplin, Emma Goldman and Alexander Berkman, and other celebrities would

Bob Brown's reading machine was constructed by Ross Saunders with help from Hilaire Hiler.

learn of the machine during a night out with Brown, now known as the Surrealist-inventor, in nearby Villefranche-sur-Mer.

The assembled group would have had expectations that the machine would be part of a revolutionary transition to a liberated wor(l)d or, at least, great fun and frivolity. They might have sampled Hilaire Hiler's fruit soup, a favorite of the Browns'; the soup included a quart of claret mixed with cooked and sweetened berries, and a tiny bit of pearl Sago, what we now call tapioca pearls, to thicken it into the consistency of a thick cream. It would be served ice cold, on a warm day, and poured over a few small macaroons. Visitors usually started with champagne cider and eating Cannes canapés (canapés made with smoked salmon, black caviar,

Without any whirr or splutter writing is read- able at thc speed of thc day — 1930 — not 1450, without being broken by conventional columns confined to pages and pickled in books, a READIE runs on bcforc thc eye continuously — on forever in-a-singk-line-I-see-1450-invention-movable-type-Gutcnberg-Wynkyn-dc-Worde-Jimmy-the-Ink- -- Caxton-though-Chinese-centuries-before-printed - thousand-page-books-on-silk-leaves-furnished-by- - local-silk-worms-no-two-leavcs-tinted-alike - - - - printing-from-dainty-porcelain-type-same-stuff- -

Making words move at the speed of the day with readies' hermaphroditic hypodermic hyphens.

and capers arrayed on thin triangular toasts) prepared by their hosts, who included the machine's inventor. Later in the early evening, their hosts would likely serve a French peasant soup with a recipe from Bordeaux. It was a type of soup that Gertrude Stein would describe as "the standard of comparison with all the other soups in the world. Sometimes some approach it, a very few have equaled it but none have surpassed it."[17]

They might have mingled around a metal contraption constructed from a breadbox with spools and wires and other mechanisms inside. There was laughter and delight as their host showed them the prototype of the reading machine. Everyone would tip their glasses in appreciation, and would agree that this box was the future of reading and the readies' future! His toast was greeted with cheers and more tipped glasses. The party would have happened toward the end of the two years the Browns had spent in the south of France. In total they lived among the expatriate avant-garde for less than four years.

Reproduced here is a photograph of the prototype of the reading machine constructed by Ross Saunders, with help from Hilaire Hiler, built between late 1930 and early 1931, according to Bob Brown's instructions. The photograph was glued on a flyleaf at the front of each of the 150 copies of in the *Readies for Bob Brown's Machine* (1931). Judging by this photograph, the prototype's construction resembles a film-editing viewer stuck on a wooden cold frame, but what Brown intended was a small, fabricated metal, mass-produced mechanism: more e-reader than printing press.

Brown saw Kay Boyle as an important inspiration and guide to avant-garde publishing—so much so that when he described his first experiences with experimental art and writing, when he first read *Tender Buttons*, he explained in *The Readies* that "there was nothing else in America to read. No *transition* back in 1914, no Joyce, no Cummings, no Kay Boyle, just a peep of Sandburg, no tricky little playful magazines of word experiment."[18] That Brown puts Boyle in the same category as Joyce, Cummings, and Sandburg gives a sense of the importance Brown saw in Boyle's guidance and avant-garde work. She would write two readies for the famous anthology of modernist writers who produced texts for Brown's reading machine: "Change of Life" and "Landscape for Wyn Hendeson." From Boyle's perspective, she found in Brown a connection to the popular writing world that would fund her interest in experimental writing. She trusted him for his honest advice as she transitioned from an experimental writer to a storyteller concerned with characters and plots rather than the free play of words. She, for example, wrote a note to Bob about a story she was working on: "Bob, don't show this story to anyone. It's rotten. I thought you would tell me how bad it is and then I won't write anymore like it," but soon she was advising Brown on his popular writing projects and wrote to him, "From the point of view of great popularity, you might have to change the personal side of the story."[19] Brown had already written a bestselling novel, published 1,000 stories in pulp and high-end popular magazines in New York, and knew many publishers and editors in the States. His advice and connections would continue to guide Boyle through the rest of her career, and the two remained close friends until Brown's death in 1959; he visited Boyle at her Connecticut home a few weeks before he passed away. Instead of thinking of Brown as a footnote, Boyle, in the late 1920s and early '30s, and others in their circle of expatriate writers and publishers already thought of Brown, now in his early forties, as a seasoned professional writer and publisher, and many thought of him as an important modernist writer. His stature was great enough that an issue of *Contempo*, an important modernist journal, was focused on him (as was done with William Faulkner and Hart Crane). Boyle had written an article on Brown in the "writers to watch" section of *Contempo* and, in that same year, wrote a type of Irish folk ballad, called a *comeallyee*, dedicated to Bob Brown if not didactically about him. For Boyle at least, Brown was a guiding light, not a dilettante on the periphery.

Bob Brown, in this context of the publisher-as-poet, was one the most important (if now, almost, forgotten) avant-garde artists among the expa-

Nancy Cunard had an intense connection to her work.

triate group. During the time he was among the expatriate avant-garde, Brown published approximately eight volumes of experimental poetry, mostly with his own Roving Eye Press, from 1929 until 1931, five in 1931 alone, including four volumes in which the visual design played crucial roles in the meaning of the texts. He published volumes with the other two key modernist publishers, Harry Crosby's Black Sun Press and Nancy Cunard's Hours Press, and in the *transition* magazine. After he left the expatriate scene in France, he continued to publish avant-garde works, advocated Surrealist writing, and published many volumes in popular genres throughout the 1930s. It was within the context of all this other work, going back to his work with Chauncey Williams's Auvergne Press as a teenager and churning out pulp fiction in his twenties, that Brown produced his manifesto. He wrote it and revised it as if in an ongoing conversation first in Paris, over drinks with Stuart Davis at the Brasserie Lipp, and then talking to others going through the garlic cure (and wishing it were a beer cure) in Italy, and then at Bad Ems Bavarian spa, and finally in the south of France among yet another artists' and poets' colony. In his ongoing conversation, begun in 1906 or before, he thought of the visual qualities of reading and writing and dedicated the manifesto to "all eye-writers" and "readers who want an eyeful," alluding to a recurring motif in his other work of the "celerity of the eye" (versus the "clumsy hand" turning pages), especially in visual poetry. In the late 1920s, Stuart Davis started painting abstractions of mundane realist scenes. While in close conversations with Bob, Stuart started developing a new style that looked at street scenes and still-life objects in an increasingly lively abstract way. Davis was productive and was finding great success among collectors like Gertrude Vanderbilt Whitney. In some ways this style was a constant theme in the work that most interested Bob and his contemporaries, works that looked at the most banal aspects of everyday life as the subject of art challenged the grand and exalted narratives and themes of previous art and literature. Bob and his contemporaries (not just in the late 1920s, but also starting in the first decade of the twentieth century) sought to twist the smudged, mundane, and profane into the sublime or surreal. It was the milieu that Brown was working within when he started his experiments in the mechanical act of reading.

In the manifesto's Chapter I, "An Eyeful," Bob illuminates that literary context all the way back to his reading Stephen Crane's *The Black Riders and Other Lines* as a youth in Oak Park, Illinois, before the turn of the twentieth century, and through the socio-technological changes he had, since that time, witnessed that necessitated a more fitting way to read: "[W]e have the talkies, but as yet no Readies."[20] The introductory chapter of his manifesto, written with a playful but passionate tone, demonstrates and explains the readies' style, filled with what he calls "smashum" words, including a type of condensed anagram or portmanteau word, and a visual design in which a "hermaphroditic hypodermic hyphen" replaces unnecessary words and chops up long words; he presents this new grammar in a series of parodies and experimental writing. Toward the end of the chapter, after singing the praises of Joyce and Stein, he hints at the larger goal: "I know words can do anything, become anything, all I hold out for is more and better reading of the words we've got . . . reading will have to be done by machine; microscopic type on a movable tape running beneath a slot equipped with a magnifying glass and brought up to life size before the reader's birdlike eye, saving white space, making words more moving," using Brown's machine and his processed texts.[21]

In the context of the intimate relations, in the twenty-first century, between smartphones and their owners, Brown's intense, almost erotic relationship, in the early 1930s, with his machine might seem mundane. One aspect of the modernist avant-garde often overlooked is this infusing erotic passion into the media technologies of the time: movies, printing, publishing, and distributing. Because one can't easily collect, or profit from, the poetics of distribution, Brown and the other expatriate publishers found themselves footnotes to the painters and poets. Just as artists in the second half of the twentieth century and early in the twenty-first century made music by sampling, processing, and remixing using machines, Brown wanted to think of reading as a mediated process that might involve processing and riffing on the original texts. Brown and his vanguardist friends realized that what some took as a natural fact, reading and literacy, was in fact a mediated process that one could manipulate and compose instead of attempting to invisibly represent, by reading aloud, a given reality of spaces, figures, or emotions set down by an author.

"A Two-Way Fish," the title to Chapter II of the manifesto, alludes to a prop in a carnival game that allows a grifter to surreptitiously change a winner into a loser after the player-as-sucker picks a fish with a winning number (the shills win a few when the operator switches in the losing number for a winning number). Brown, like his friends, thought of themselves as shills, working at a Coney Island of their imaginations, involved in *epater les bourgeois*, or *tromper les bourgeois*. The pointed inside jokes in their films, paintings, and poems would also find a place in Brown's distribution mechanisms. The chapter begins with a series of notes before an extended two-column experimental essay that seeks to challenge the for-or-against binaries usually found in critical essays and manifestos.

The numbered entries in the two columns telescope autobiographical details into poetic allusions and dissect neologistic portmanteau words. The dramatization of the struggle to avoid critical judgment, with the two columns perhaps serving as visual and soundtracks, or two voices of dialogue, ends with the phrase "apple sauce," at the bottom of one column, and "applause" at the bottom of the other. "Applause" is a visual pun, a condensed anagram or smashum of "applesauce." The chapter reads like

I AM A TWO — WAY FISH

YEZNO	NOYEZ
For	**Against**
(Notes)	(Text)
A 2-way Fish is a Coney Island contraption used in a Prize Fish Pond; on one side it bears a winning number and on the other side a losing number, each concealed by a sliding tin tag painted fish color. The player of course is as unconscious of this as is the modern reader of other things.	A twiceweighed twofister tooarmlong twotooto and lovetoyou, two-toothy two trouty underoverishway Fish.

"A Two-Way Fish" alludes to a prop in a carnival game that allows a grifter to surreptitiously swap a winning number to a losing number.

an absurdist play, with soundtrack and visual track in two columns, about modern reading. One might see Brown's manifesto as a script for a Surrealist film made by his old friend Man Ray, or like Ferdinand Léger's *Ballet Mécanique* (1924) with a George Antheil score.

Bob would publish the third chapter of the manifesto, "My Reading Machine," in *transition* in the June 1930 issue as "The Readies." Here he returns to an explanatory mode to suggest that the machine substitutes for the book as a distribution mechanism, and that the machine will shift reading away from cognition toward optics. He also returns to building a context for the machine in modernist culture, where "only the reading half of Literature lags behind, stays old-fashioned . . . cumbersome . . . bottled up . . ."[22] The chapter focuses on specific technical details and quantitative comparative analysis of reading and its mechanisms both in Brown's time and in his imagined future. The Steampunk aesthetic, which imagines alternate histories of design as if contemporary technologies had been invented in an earlier Victorian or Edwardian era when steam was a dominant or prevalent energy source, would today embrace Brown's clunky futuristic machines, perhaps with the slightly modified name MachinePunk, reveling in cogs, gears, magnifiers, and spools running on a whirring electric motor. An alternate or counterfactual history of the reading machine's significance would describe the machine's moving beyond a single primitive prototype with a small audience of modernist poets to have mass appeal and use. That alternate history of the machine highlights the aesthetic dimension and appeals to designers and artists outside of literary history. If we remember Bob Brown as a poet only, then we completely miss his art of publishing; and, in conversations with Harry Crosby and later, with Nancy Cunard, he thought of their art as doing to reading and publishing what Marcel Duchamp had done to painting or Gertrude Stein had done to writing. His idea was flamboyant, and outrageous, but could be appreciated and read only from the context of the distant future. Only from the perspective of smartphones and e-readers, which seamlessly mix visual-sonic-textual sources into an interactive stew, can one now see what those avant-gardists, especially Bob Brown, were up to in the late 1920s and early '30s. It was about changing the way we received and read e-books (before we even had e-books).

In the fourth chapter of the manifesto, "Eye-Lingo," Brown goes on to describe his "inkless" revolution, which seems prescient now, in the age of the Kindle, online texts, and ubiquitous handheld texting devices. Brown explained that his reading machine made "a need for new words" to work with the speed of the machine; those new types of words would resemble portmanteau words in what Brown called a smashum style. The examples of these new smashum words that Bob used included "nowtime" and "machinewise." The necessary new style had no need for conjunctions, articles, prefixes, quotation marks, grammatical marks, and other "bulky residue" of traditional prose. Although Brown insisted that he was not inventing a new style of writing but simply wanted to prepare for the modernization of reading "at the speed of the day," the context of his own tastes and writings made it easy for even the best critics, and sometimes Brown himself, to think of the project only in terms of the modernist revolution of the word and a "stab in the dark at writing modernly." Instead, the readies function as a printed analogy for what reading will feel and look like "spinning past the eye out of a word-machine." He admits in this chapter that it is a "crude" attempt to simulate motion. Bob Brown was watching Chaplin comedies, early talkies, thinking about his own *What Happened to Mary* serial, seeing Surrealist experiments, and talking with painters and poets attempting to put that motion into their works, while he wrote about how the movies would change reading itself. He saw how Man Ray and Marcel Duchamp had reinvented themselves from Imagist painters to filmmakers dealing with new ways to think about cinema as a toy-like mechanism. The final chapter of the manifesto, "A Story to Be Read on the Reading Machine," offers an extended example of a readie that converts an otherwise unremarkable story into a cinematic Imagist scene. Again, Brown's explicit goal is not to offer a new literary style but rather to suggest "the abbreviated dispatches sent by foreign newspaper correspondents to cut down cable expense," as if one applied the technologies of the day to reading all texts, literary and practical.[23]

One year after publishing his manifesto, Brown published an anthology of texts especially prepared for the machine and titled descriptively as *Readies for Bob Brown's Machine*. The later anthology included works from forty of his friends and fellow avant-gardists, with contributions by Stein, Boyle, and F. W. Marinetti. The anthology also included works of such Imagist poets as William Carlos Williams, with whom Brown had worked in the Grantwood Village art colony in 1916–17, and a sane Ezra Pound (Pound was institutionalized from 1946 to 1958 after pleading insanity to charges in 1945 of treason in supporting the fascists). Pound had corresponded with Brown and the writers associated with *Others: A Magazine of New Verse* in those earlier years. The anthology's contributions, of uneven quality, have a giddy, clubhouse feel and lack the coherent focus and serious intent of Brown's manifesto. Without any explicit editorial interference and Brown's contributing only an appendix (a condensed selection from the *Readies* manifesto), some texts seem more explicitly written, and prepared, expressly for the machine while others, like Marinetti's, seem to ignore or loosely interpret Brown's constraints. Some of the contributions, especially those not associated with modernist poetry, wallow in adolescent humor, as if baiting a fantasized censor with sexually explicit and racist language. (One, in fact, was literally adolescent in perspective; written by Brown's teenage son, it describes his unpleasant first sexual encounter a year or two before, while they were living in Brazil.)

Many involved in the project were important players in the expatriate avant-garde and radical scene in France. Peter Neagoe, who edited *American Abroad: An Anthology* (1932), which included a chapter by Bob, was at the time of the readies experiment already established as an important editor and writer among the expatriate Surrealists (born in Romania, he later moved to the United States and became a citizen there).

Neagoe's novel *Storm* (1932) was banned for its mildly erotic content, and in that way, Neagoe was part of the same mixing of libertine sexual politics, Surrealist aesthetics, and a type of literary documentary realism that played a larger role in the sur-*realism* that connected many of the readies for Bob Brown's machine. Jay du von, an editor of *Contempo*, *The New Quarterly*, and other important Surrealist collections and newsletters contributed; *Contempo* also had a "Bob Brown" issue. Norman Macleod, also associated with the Imagist poets and an important journal publisher and poet throughout the twentieth century and friends with William Carlos Williams, was connected to the readies project through Williams. Poems by Macleod and Brown appeared together in experimental and radical journals in the 1930s. Others like John Banting are better known as painters and artists; Banting, a close friend of Nancy Cunard's, vehemently opposed racism and was an editor for the Communist *Our Time* monthly. B. C. Hagglund, best known for his later pro-labor and Communist essays and poetry and his work as the founding editor of *The Anvil*, which published Langston Hughes, James Farrell, William Carlos Williams, and others in Brown's circle, saw in the readies a potentially democratizing force.

James T. Farrell, publishing one of his first stories in the anthology, later discussed how the readies' constraints led to his staccato, short-sentence prose style in *Studs Lonigan*. Rather than employ a nonrepresentational style, Farrell (and others, including Boyle) had found in Brown's constraints a foundation for a politically engaged writing of the street. Likewise, Brown had championed the work of Farrell and other politically engaged writers as part of the revolution of the word but later thought of Farrell as having "sold out" to the demands of publishers. Brown saw his machine as a democratizing tool, with the style of the readies bringing literature to a wider audience by virtue of its resemblance to styles of popular writing generally regarded as beneath even lowbrow genre pulp fiction: linear single-line ticker-tape news reports, secret codes, cartoon visual poems, advertisements, and telegraphic communications. Brown's appendix for the anthology includes the third chapter from the manifesto, along with other autobiographical materials, explicitly setting the context of the machine in relation to his work in publishing and printing magazines, reading the ticker tape as a stock trader, writing for pulps, book dealing, and advertising.

Eventually, one would be able to radio readies "as easily as it is today to [produce] *newsies* on shipboard and words perhaps eventually will be recorded directly on the palpitating ether."[24] In this sense, Brown's work directly alluded to telegrams but also meant to suggest a future lineage to the smartphones and shorthand languages of instant messages, emoticons, and other abbreviated systems. He was, with the other vanguardists, living in an imagined future of fifty to a hundred years ahead of their time. The fascination with machines as alternatives to codex and other traditional forms of representation was not new to the avant-garde poets and artists of that era. In the early 1920s, the Dadaist Tristan Tzara wanted to know if he "could transcribe at top speed everything that fell, rolled, opened, flew, and continued" within his head.[25] In Cagnes-sur-Mer, Brown started talking with expatriate writers and artists like George Antheil and the eccentric Abraham "Link" Gillespie. All three shared an interest in building "critical machines"—critical of the complacent, invisibly efficient, and quiet machines of modern culture. Antheil, self-proclaimed "Futurist-terrible," provoked audiences to riot during his machine concerts by using his wind machine to produce cacophonous soundsin his musical composition *Mechanism* (1923). With the help of his friends, as shills in the audience, including Jean Cocteau, Man Ray, Francis Picabia, Pablo Picasso, Ezra Pound, Fernand Léger, James Joyce, and Eric Satie, Antheil attracted large, raucous crowds to his performances. He also composed the music for Léger's *Ballet Mécanique*, which found beauty, similar to the beauty in Gertrude Stein's poetry, in the mechanical and artificial rather than in the naturalized.[26] Bob wanted to build a similar machine combining elements from Gillett Burgess's "nonsense machine, No. 2" and George's sound machine. Another contributor of a readie, Abraham Lincoln Gillespie Jr. Gillespie Jr., nicknamed "Linky" or "Link," was influenced, like Bob, by Antheil's antics and musical experiments. Gillespie was already experimenting with supercondensed styles of writing and saw Bob's machine and readies as the perfect vehicle for his own visio-musical writing experiments. Gillespie, a frequent contributor to *transition*, was particularly flamboyant and eccentric even among the vanguard circles. He championed Antheil's polyphonic music and sought to find a corollary in writing by ignoring conventional grammatical rules, creating neologisms, and omitting unnecessary words and adding purely visual effects.

The contributors were not just the modernist writers one would expect; they included writers that were in exile, but not just to be with a moveable feast with other avant-garde artists and writers. These non-modernist contributors were, in some cases, poorer and more politically engaged than the now well-known expatriate modernists. For example, other expatriate writers who contributed readies for Bob Brown's machine included Axton Clark, a Harvard University philosophy professor (known there as Donald Clark), who lost his job there in the 1920s when the administration determined he was a homosexual; he then moved to Mills College and in 1927 started one of the first departments of Cultural Studies. Clark was in exile. Brown's acceptance and celebration of Clark, and Brown's admiration and inclusion of the openly gay Charles Henri Ford in the anthology, led to rumors about Brown's own sexuality. Ford, who was writing with Parker Tyler what would later be considered the first gay novel, was already talking about homosexuality in terms of poetic practice, and Brown's championing of what he called "hermaphroditic hypodermic hyphen" as central to the readies style also seemed to suggest a strategy from the twenty-first century: queering or transgendering the reading process. Like much else, this fascinating choice of words and strategy would remain latent and not come out for at least another eighty years. From Bob's own unpublished notes he was aware of the rumors, but he claimed to have eyes only for Rose. What he noticed, which is somewhat more scandalous, was a machine's gender*less* situation as something more and different: the potential of a robot sexuality. In machine reading, Brown discovered a possibility of a reading beyond binaries (male/female) with what he called a *hermaphrologics*, in which the hyphen visually opened a space by occupying the blanks. In the twenty-first century, readers will now take heightened notice of the term used to describe these em dashes, "hermaphroditic"; many of those readers will have also considered the erotic intimate life of the cyborg. In the interim, between Brown's em dashes and now, the hermaphrologics was there all along, missing from the conversation, in plain sight, like Bob Brown himself.

Charles Henri Ford, who subtitled his first publication at the age of sixteen "A Bisexual Bimonthly," would soon leave for Morocco with Paul Bowles, who had also contributed a readie, and the next year Ford published his novel *The Young and Evil* (1933) with Obelisk Press. The novel portrayed the fictionalized lives of these queer poets and their sex lives. Later William Carlos Williams wrote the Introduction to Ford's collection of poems *The Garden of Disorder* (1938). Ford and his partner Pavel Tchelitchew sought to find new audiences for Surrealism in their art journal, *View*; they also published premiere monographs on Marcel Duchamp's works and André Breton's poems. Ford's influence on art and poetry was profound and prolific from the mid-1930s until his death in 2002; when the readies appeared, he was just a nineteen-year-old poet full of potential.

Another contributor included Brown's colleague and friend who worked on the *Brazilian American*, George Kent, who continued to run the magazine even after Brown sold the network of newsletters. Kent contributed three pieces (one of which has four parts) to the *Readies* anthology. He had begun his writing career as a United Press stringer, worked with the Browns starting in 1919, and later became an editor of *Reader's Digest*. His pragmatic interest in the machine and the readies style, as potential tools for journalists, had absolutely nothing to do with the modernists' interest in the art-stunt disruptive power of the readies. Kent believed that the machine was the future of a super-efficient type of journalism. In that he was more in line with Farrell's understanding of the project as pragmatic and efficient. The machine, for Kent at least, was not a Surrealist disruption but a realistic boon to broadcast media.

Charles Beadle, whom Bob had known as a pulp fiction adventure writer, had moved to Paris and was famously experimenting with hashish; Beadle's readies reflect the record of those experiments, and the readies style helped illuminate the flowing sense of time and space Beadle sought to chronicle. Once again, the connection between popular culture and the bohemian avant-garde was not just suggested or a matter of interpretation; the very same person, Beadle, lived and worked successfully in both worlds.

The shift, from considering *Readies* as another attempt at experimental writing, an aesthetic experiment, to an epistemological alternative sought to expand the possibilities of the lyric expressivity to include new forms of media technologies and machines: an expressive poetry of media distribution or publishing. Eighty years later, it was common to see publishers and reading-machine makers, like Steve Jobs, described as creative geniuses or artists. The different reading technologies and practices that informed Brown's shorthand included a wide array of systems: reading and writing technologies ranging from wartime code machines to cookbooks or party guides, from Hollywood movies to a wide spectrum of magazines. These were not simply the commercial foil that professional writers like Brown reacted against in fleeing toward experimentation. Rather, Brown's work demonstrates a much more nuanced connection between the cultural milieu and a type of reading practice peculiar to the twentieth century. The machine highlighted the ways of reading abbreviated code systems: Readers have to change their pace and focus. We find this abbreviated language in stock market ticker tape, shorthand, technical manuals, recipes, and specialized actuarial and accounting codes that came into widespread use in the first quarter of the twentieth century, during an era when "streamlined" equaled "modernity." The connection to the movies and talkies may have been direct not just in Brown's case, but in that of other readies authors.

The three readies by one Donal MacKenzie, who was likely the same Donal MacKenzie who was the director and co-director of some of the *Perils of Pauline* serialized movies, have a cinematic feel to them. Although there is very little biographical details about the author of the MacKenzie readies or the director of the silent films, Brown would have known MacKenzie, the film director, and thought of him in terms of making reading cinematic, but, like the name Bob Brown, Donal/Donald MacKenzie is not an uncommon Scottish name, and, in fact, Ezra Pound was using the work of a famous folklorist by that same name.

In that sense of Brown's manifesto's referencing an entire history of the machine's relation to reading, the details and wordplay suggest that the project is about layout, graphic design, and printing books as much as reading. Much of the wordplay involves well-known modernist writers, for example Proustly (for Marcel Proust) or Gert (for Gertrude Stein) on page 1 or Whitmanized (for Walt Whitman) on page 2. Brown claims to have gotten the idea for his visual poetry from the blank page in *Tristam Shandy* [*sic*] on page 2.[27] The visual poem below that citation uses blank space as a poetic element. The kerning of individual words (the space each character takes) may have some significance beyond simply trying to make the line justified. Some of Brown's many typos seem intentional either as part of a portmanteau word or, in at least one case ("adriot" [*sic*]), a meta-commentary on an editor's adroit proofreading (and the tendency of some readers to read significance into typos). On page 13 and elsewhere, Brown directly addresses editors and proofreaders, but it is unclear whether he intends that the proofing will be "well looked to" or whether one should regard the apparent typos as part of the meta-commentary. Normally, one would not mention these trivialities, but because Brown's work explicitly and forcefully addresses printers, proofreaders, and book designers as much as readers, authors, and literary scholars, what Brown calls, capitalized as if the title of an essay, the "Optical Art of Writing" becomes significant.[28] Brown mentions that the spools of reading materials will be available like safety razors in stores and even in telephone booths.[29] Although cell phones have made phone booths obsolete, in the twenty-first century those phones' ability to download reading fits perfectly with the vision of a future wherein texts are "tele-vistically" delivered over the airwaves.

Brown lists many authors, to the point that the extended essay reads like a catalogue of authors in relation to printing and literary design. He includes representatives from three groups: modernist artists and writers and other innovative writers; the authors of canonical literary works; and printers and designers important to the history of the book. He singles out Anthony Trollope (1815–82) for ridicule.[30] Trollope, one of the most respected and admired Victorian novelists, was often disparaged for his long-winded prose and prolific output. Brown takes aim at Trollope to suggest that modernity's demands, and the efficiencies of reading machines, will make novels in the future much more condensed than Trollope's. On page 37, Brown mentions William Caxton in a list of authors and printers involved in inventing the traditional notion of the book. Caxton, the first English printer, lived in the early and mid–fifteenth century and began printing in England in 1476, after a long career as a merchant, trading wool, luxury goods, and illuminated manuscripts. Typically stationers were early printers, and Caxton fit that mold, but he began his second career as translator and printer late in life. The first book printed in English by Caxton was the *History of Troy* (c. 1473) and the second was *Game and Play of the Chess* (1475). By the first decade of the twentieth century, Caxton had become a trope of bibliophiles as his image had appeared, in 1902, in Howard Pyle's cover illustration of Francis Frognall Dibden's *The Bibliomania, Vol. 1,* published in Boston by the Bibliophile Society, and this was a book that Bob Brown very likely collected. In the same list of early printers and canonical authors, Brown mentions Jimmy-the-Ink. Brown referred to his friend and fellow pulp writer in the first decade of the twentieth century, William Wallace Cook, as a "modern day Jimmy-the-Ink." It seems likely that, here, however, Brown uses the phrase to refer to a fifteenth-century type-founder and printer like James Grover, or a generic early English printer. But the placement of the pseudonym next to the names of other founding printers and authors suggests a different allusion: Jimmy-the-Ink was also the pseudonym used by the author/illustrator James Daugherty, who was famous as a modernist painter and was a *New Yorker* magazine cover and cartoon illustrator. His illustrations in the 1920s often have elements of movement. While he was already considered a canonical illustrator and children's book author, an important figure in the definition of the modern book, and later won both Caldecott and Newberry awards, he was not an early printer. Bruce Rogers (1870–1957), mentioned on page 40 of the manifesto, was one of the most important American typographers of the twentieth century. Known mostly for his use of typography in book design rather than for typeface design, he designed more than 400 books. Brown strategically places himself with the Gutenberg, Caxton, and Rogers lineage in the development of the book, and beyond. On page 32, "Chiswick Preß" includes the German character eszett (ß), that usually replaces the letters "ss," and, in this case, the word is read as "Press." The Chiswick Press, publisher of William Morris and influential in English printing and typography, was part of the lineage of literary meaning by typographic design that Brown constructs in *The Readies*.

Unlike some of the expatriates who worked with him and who were practically starving while they honed their craft, like Farrell, Brown had already made and spent three fortunes as a popular writer and successful publisher. Brown's work also illuminates works in popular venues by writers like Joyce or Pound, who are usually studied in terms of experimental writing, and writers crucial to avant-garde publications, like Boyle or Farrell, who are usually associated with popular and politically engaged work. The reading machine has aspects of both parodic performance-art stunts, in the style of Tzara, Duchamp, and Antheil, and a practical tool or product ready to serve a mass market. It is a truism of literary and art studies that the avant-garde opposes, by definition, mass-marketed products, and even the expatriate vanguardists saw themselves in this romantic light, but, in fact, the publishers, like Brown; the artists, like Marcel Duchamp; and the writers, like Gertude Stein, saw themselves as in direct contact with the market as part of their work. Can a parodic art-stunt also function as a practical tool? In theoretical terms, can an attack on reading practices and the book's form serve an audience of book readers, or library users, looking to read mysteries or adventure stories? Does Brown's project present an intentionally paradoxical formation or does it represent an unresolved contradiction in his project and career? While *The Readies* did not initiate an avant-garde group or movement, like Dadaism or Surrealism, dedicated to mechanical forms of reading and processed texts, Brown's manifesto now describes implications of the digital revolution in reading and publishing.

Although *The Readies* created a sensation among the avant-garde and expatriates and was greeted with the kind of enthusiastic praise that other, more immediately influential manifestos garnered, the limited run of 150 copies, with no subsequent editions until now, assured that it would pass into obscurity. The two other strikes against Brown—his huge success in popular genres of writing and the great variability in the types of his writing—have made it challenging for scholars to find a place for him in either modernist avant-garde circles or in popular culture studies of pulps, movies, and cookbooks. Brown's work as both popular writer and avant-garde innovator makes those genre lines, generally used to divide publishers' lists of books as well as scholars' areas of study (e.g., modernism, popular culture, media, digital media, conceptual art, cookbooks), an irrelevancy. With its publication in a new edition by Roving Eye Press in 2014, with my new Introduction to that new edition (as well as Introductions to three other new Roving Eye Press editions of books by Bob Brown) and with the electronic version accessible to a wide audience, *The Readies*' significance in literary and artistic history and technology's impact on reading might become more apparent. The manifesto presents a clear and concise statement about the avant-garde's interest in preparing for changes in the sensorium and especially their fascination with the eye's importance in reading relative to the perceived dominance of aurality and interpretation. It also presents the practical side of the avant-garde's desire to intervene in the machinations of everyday life. What if a machine illuminated the visuality of reading hiding in plain sight? Bob Brown's manifesto asks that question and demonstrates its potential.

The radical criticism of the avant-garde applies particularly well to Bob Brown's machine; and Michael Gold, who would later publish a book with Brown's Roving Eye Press in 1960 (after Bob had died in 1959, but the press continued to publish), wrote an essay in 1930 condemning Proust and the avant-garde in terms seemingly directed at Brown's project. Although he does not mention Brown's reading machine, his criticism of the avant-garde that produces "merely a new *frisson*" or his opposition to any avant-garde "machine" that "produces nothing" and functions "only as an adult toy" seems to target Brown. Although he explicitly condemns Marcel Proust as the "master-masturbator of the bourgeois literature," and also the "intellectuals" who are trying to make literature into a mere "confectionery," Gold advocated "a cinema in words" that sought to use the fewest words possible, and in that he seems again to highlight unwittingly the productive contradiction in Brown's machine's promise.[31]

In January 1931, Bob started working with Nancy Cunard's Hours Press to publish *Words*, two sets of poems printed in a single volume. Cunard had heard of Brown's innovative writing and publishing and wanted to publish one of his projects. She suspected that Brown was an important figure among the expatriate avant-garde, and, after working on the book with him, she was convinced that it was an important event in the history not just of layout and design but also in the history of publishing and reading. The book was subtitled "I but bend my finger in a beckon and words, birds of words, hop on it, chirping." One set of poems was printed in 16-point Caslon Old Face, a classic font style used in all Hours

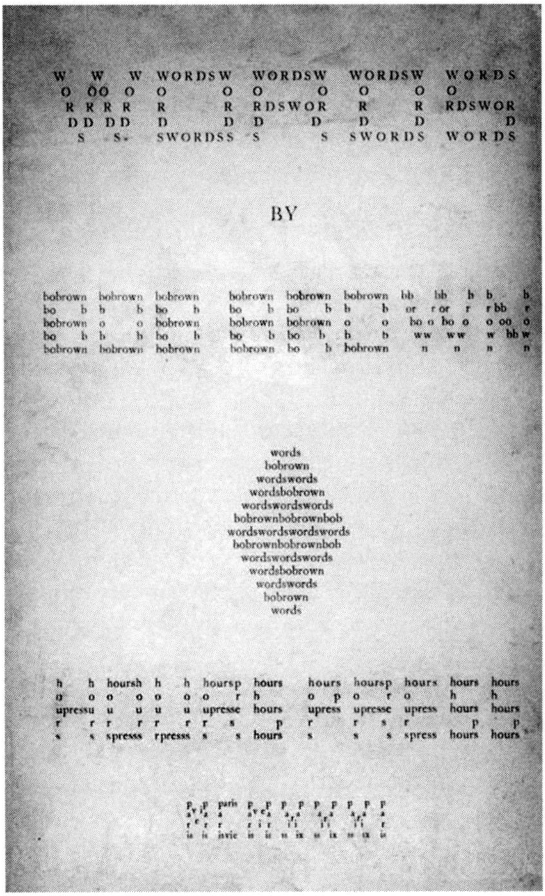

Words' cover design, by John Sibthorpe, resembles a typewriter poem from the 1960s.

Press publications. The other was relief-printed from engraved plates at less than 3-point size (perhaps, according to Cunard, less than 1-point). Because the subtitle was also printed in the microscopic text, archives, libraries, and bibliographies often mistakenly omit it.

Although Brown was, for Cunard, "at the very center of his time, a zeitgeist in himself," Hours Press printed only 150 copies, and the book passed into relative obscurity until it was reprinted in 2014.[32] It is generally mentioned only as a footnote in discussions of Cunard's life; or, it is mentioned in reference to Brown's better-known anthology of experimental texts by modernist writers, including Cunard herself, titled *Readies for Bob Brown's Machine*. One can place *Words* at the intersection of three lineages. Nancy Cunard wanted to produce elegant modernist works in the fine-press artists' book tradition that Hours Press helped initiate: "to achieve impeccably clean things with fingers grease-laden."[33] Brown wanted to demonstrate how microscopic texts for his reading machine might appear if printed next to poems set in 16-point type. A reading of the book from the perspective of an avant-garde audience places it in the tradition of art stunts. (In this regard, Brown's friends George Antheil and Marcel Duchamp influenced his interest in art stunts involving machines and mechanisms.) As a performance of reading strategies, *Words*, with its magnifying glasses and hidden clues, alludes to detective stories or to the paranoid's micrographia and art brut.

Nancy Cunard, famous for her iconic, glamorous fashion with African bangles and bobbed hairstyle, was a key part of the thriving group of small-press publishers in the 1920s. She announced *Words* in a December 1929 edition of *transition* and had already started talking about the possibility of the project after Brown had sent her a copy of his "beautifully produced" book *1450–1950*. The title refers to the evolution of printing from early presses into a then-imagined future, and the meaning was immediately clear to Cunard, a printer; but the poet William Carlos Williams wrote to Brown, wondering what the "numerals meant."[34]

Cunard saw in Brown's work "another new slant" in the ongoing experiments in reshaping writing by the Surrealists, Dadaists, and others.[35] The design and craft involved in its production make Cunard and her printers more collaborators than simply invisible technicians. Clearly, Cunard embraced the "pristine joie-de-vivre" of the "persistent experimenter" looking for "felicitous discoveries." She and Brown both were "intoxicated by words" and yet, rather than its being a completely chaotic process, they also knew "how to bring them to heel."[36] Both shared passions for ethnography, collecting, and most of all work. Their intense productivity, with Brown publishing five of his books and Cunard's press producing ten books in 1930 alone, speaks to an atmosphere of excitement for writing, printing, and publishing.

The story of Brown's collaboration with Cunard is, to borrow Hugh Ford's phrases, the "story of how books were made, of how ideas became the words on a printed page," and of how "author and publisher conferred during each step of the production of the book." The lesson that this edition of *Words* should teach us is that small presses "could and did cultivate an intimacy between authors and publishers as well as a creative

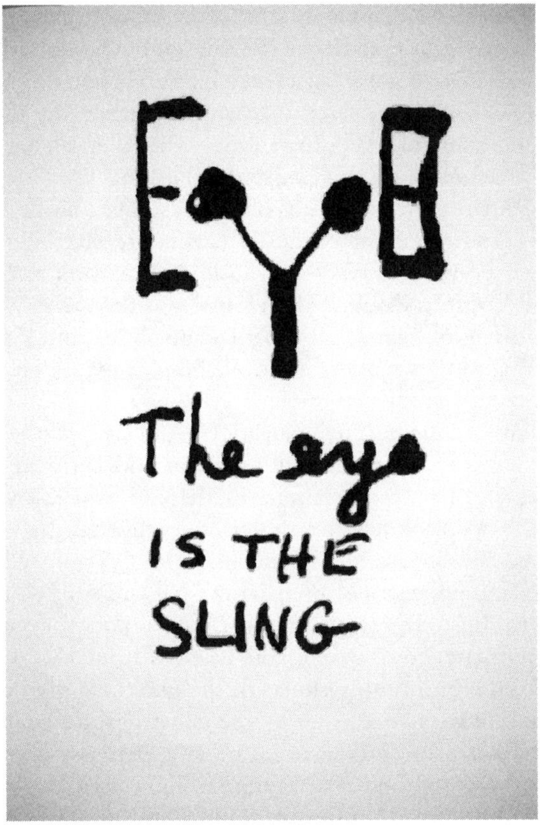

"The Eye Is the Sling" in rapid reading.

atmosphere that large commercial publishing houses, now as well as then, nearly always lack."[37] In working with Cunard on *Words*, Brown described the situation in an untitled poem:

> But for years I have
> Peered through venetian blinds
> At poets
> Without yet catching a glimpse of
> One at work.[38]

We might know more about what he drank (Brown, for example: beer and wine, not whiskey), and whom they had affairs with during the late 1920s and early 1930s (Cunard, with an array of artists: from the co-founder of Surrealism, Louis Aragon; to the co-founder of Dada, Tristan Tzara; to the African American jazz musician Henry Crowder; but, not with George Moore, the influential poet and novelist, who repeatedly asked Cunard to let him see "[her] naked"), than about what they accomplished, and their erotic attachment to printing and publishing: the "love of printed letters."[39] Both Brown and Cunard had intense, even erotic, connections to their work, and an exposé of those affairs has received less attention.

Cunard named Hours Press as an allusion to the work and work habits of her friend Virginia Woolf. "The Hours" was the name Woolf gave to the draft of the book manuscript that eventually became *Mrs. Dalloway*. That manuscript was a modernist novel about the work and scheduling for the systematic preparations for a party; the novel's embracing modernist style, feminism, and libertine sexuality, Cunard saw, was the perfect emblem of her new press. Virginia, with her husband, Leonard, gave Nancy advice about, and hands-on training in, the endeavor she was about to undertake; the Woolfs knew from their Hogarth Press that "Your hands will always be covered in ink."[40] And, like *Mrs. Dalloway*, which focuses on the mundane processes of preparation, Cunard wanted to make the process of printing and writing, rarely motifs in poetry or art, as part of her design aesthetic. For Cunard, "the smell of printer's ink pleased me greatly, as did the beautiful freshness of the glistening pigment. There is no other black or red like it. After a rinse in petrol and a good scrub with soap and hot water, my fingers again became perfectly presentable; the right thumb, however, began to acquire a slight ingrain of gray, due to the leaden composition."[41] They were "looking at possibilities, at possibilities[,] say, of bringing innovations up against some of the consecrated rules of layout," which for Brown and Cunard alike had become a kind of prohibition and self-censorship.[42] The story of Bob Brown's life is an erotic love affair with the reading/writing machines we take for granted and repeatedly forget as the physical choreography of fingers, ink, metal, hand and eye coordinating in a poetic dance and bodily pleasure bound up and folded with bonefolders (the tool used to fold pages in handmade books), for, as Bob Brown thought, "words and I are one." The two set out on a love affair with serifs and inks that would soon involve a small group at the Hours Press in a challenging project.

Cunard always printed in the serif Caslon Old Face type on the heavy Vergé de Rives paper, both of which she acquired in "generous amount" when she purchased a 200-year-old hand-press from Bill Bird, whose Three Mountain Press had already published modernist poets Ezra Pound,

Ernest Hemingway, William Carlos Williams, and others.[43] With her press, inks, paper, and type, Cunard quickly established a look for all of the books she published, and she also commissioned covers by Louis Aragon, Paul Eluard, Georges Sadoul, Man Ray, Yves Tanguy, Elliott Seabrooke, and the animator Len Lye. Brown's project would throw a wrench into that tidy process and house style. Although Cunard had hoped to design the binding for *Words* as "a reproduction of a large slab of old ivory, the veining standing out dark on the printed surface, this turned out to be too difficult; the reproduction would not have been sharp enough. So the covers are cream paper boards with a red leather spine."[44] The cover design, by John Sibthorpe, perhaps the only element that went off as planned, resembles a typewriter poem from the 1950s and 1960s rather than a modernist printing exercise. No one involved in the project ever thought to give the book's miniature font a name, because it was a one-off, not produced as moveable type and never used again. The microscopic text might be categorized as an illustration of printed letters or a visual poem about microscopic printing rather than a traditional font or typeface.

The microscopic text, "too small to be read without a magnifying glass" or without using a variant of Brown's proposed reading machine, "strained the ingenuity and perseverance" of the press's management when they sought type small enough for the micrographic poems.[45] The "only solution, a costly one, was to print the miniature poems from specially engraved plates, the whole to measure not more than one-eighth of an inch when completed."[46] For Cunard, the project served as "an excellent example of what one plans to do and how circumstances can alter the idea. Many attempts were made to get really microscopic type."[47] The originally planned heavy paper stock would not work with the microscopic text that tended to blur as it imprinted in the rougher paper; they substituted a different, smoother, paper stock called Canson-Montgolfier to get a crisp, rather than luxurious, print. The efforts to engrave the copper plates and relief-print the text produced mixed results, with many letters appearing even with magnification as dots, smudges, or typed over.

As part of their collaboration, Nancy Cunard contributed her own readies contribution, referring to its style as "condensed," and Brown certainly thought much about mass-produced condensed food products' entering the popular imagination because he would, in the 1930s and 1940s, co-write many cookbooks.[48] In *Words*, the type is cut short in an entirely different way: instead of with dashes as in *The Readies*, it is reduced with microscopic scale. In reference to this cutting-short process, Brown writes in the opening poem, "Operating on words—gilding and gelding them / In a rather special laboratory equipped with / Micro and with scope."[49] Both sets of poems, 16-point and micro, perform a semi-autobiographical illumination of the literary and cultural meanings of printing in both form and content. For Cunard, the poems express the "Bob Brown spirit" and dynamism: "Everything about him had zest."[50] The content of the poems often employs an Imagist style to telescope concrete luminous details, like the image of hollow dice, into abstractions about (in the case of the dice) the lessons of Pandora's box and, in general, about art, printing, reading, and life.

The experience of reading *Words* resembles reading the miniaturized secret messages used by spies (at least in movies and pulp fiction stories). A century after *Words*, the U.S. government defends against counterfeiters' efforts by using micro-printing techniques to produce micrographic lettering; it's the same strategy Brown used for poetic ends. Common in actual espionage and military intelligence, the trope of secret messages was a staple of Brown's pulp stories and part of his job working for a U.S. propaganda unit in South America about a decade earlier. *What Happened to Mary*, his bestselling series of 1912, included episodes with secret messages, intercepted letters, and interpretations of message fragments. During the early months of World War I, Allen Norton, one of Brown's closest friends especially during their escape and exile from the United States in 1917, was arrested in Liverpool in 1914 with a bundle of experimental poems and writings because the authorities thought he was carrying dangerous messages that were clearly written in code.[51] The arrest had a lasting impact on Brown. And, Brown's first vague inklings of building a reading machine, also in 1914, took the code machines of the time as a type of readymade (the name Marcel Duchamp gave to a series of his found, and sometimes remixed or manipulated, works) and as a way to avoid censorship even as the microscopic or processed readies would inevitably attract the censors' bemused attention.

The effort to conceive and print *Words* produced poetry demanding a technological solution just to read it: For readers to see the smudge at the bottom corner of the page as a microscopic poem, they need an external apparatus (a machine either as simple as a magnifying glass or as complicated as a microfiche lens or a computer). The human eye has no zoom function. Where *The Readies* emphasized the linear motion on the x-axis, *Words* focuses on the z-axis. Imagine a machine that supersedes the unaided human eye with scanning and magnification in constant change and motion; this volume presents a print-version simulation, where you toggle between large and small texts.

Reference to the history of micrographic writing, neither explicit nor exact in *Words*, begins at least by the time of Cicero, who reportedly saw an example of it. By the seventeenth century, it had been used in printing. In terms of using microscopic text to avoid censors, *Micrographia* discusses miniature writing and its possible utility in sending secret messages.[52] Microfilm was used in libraries before the turn of the twentieth century. The Surrealists' interest in miniature writing arose with reference to Jean-Martin Charcot, an influence on Freud, discussing micrographia as a symptom of neurological disorders at the close of the nineteenth century. Miniature books and book collecting were popular around the turn of the century as well. And, the Surrealists became fascinated with producing their own micrographic miniature books to tap into Charcot's unconscious zone of (paranoid) connections and (overly) imaginative inventiveness. In banking and business, microfilm became more than a novelty or secret in the late 1920s. All those uses inspired Brown. His microscopic print alludes as much to condensed foods, paranoid's micrographia, and business records as to the precise history of graphic design. His conception of the history of microscopic printing and writing was filtered through his own adventure-story imagination rather than through a scholar's erudition; so, he meant to relay these allusions through layout and design rather than through didactic lessons.

The microscopic poems in *Words*, initially planned as smaller versions of the otherwise identical larger poems, became separate works for technical reasons (the publisher could not fit the longer poems in the small space even using the smallest type size possible). So instead of the reader's choosing whether to read the same poem in different sizes and making the actual reading of the miniature poems a merely imaginative activity, the technical problems led to a different experience in which the poems seem to comment on one another. For example, the poem "TO A WILD MONTANA MARE" portrays a sex scene in 16-point font for all to read. On the same page, hiding in what looks like a thumbprint or smudge, is a miniature poem about the narrator's lack of Romantic awe when visiting cultural icons like the Sphinx. Printing the sex scene in 16-point type next to the poem about a great cultural wonder of the world in microscopic type pokes fun at censors' arbitrary choices: Why not censor a poem about the lack of appropriate passion and excitement during pilgrimages to the Sphinx or Leonardo's *Mona Lisa*? Brown uses the unique design (the combination of microscopic and 16-point fonts on the same page), and the anticipation of a reader's reactions, for poetic effect.

The short squib form of the micro-poems was not new to Brown, who plundered his own popular-culture past to produce an avant-garde literature, a kind of pop-vanguard. It was essentially a genre of the squib that had launched his career more than two decades earlier. His first series of publications in 1907 consisted entirely of squibs, similar to the found-joke-like mistakes from other publications placed at the bottom of a column in *The New Yorker*. In one of his newspaper columns, he published jokes about signs one might see on the street, funny ads one might read in the town's paper, or simply comically odd sights in the city: "an up-and-coming clothes cleaner's sign reads, 'We'll dye for you'"; others that caught his eye (or ear) included "Grinn & Barret, Plumbers" and "Farswego: the name of every streetcar terminal according to the conductor's unintelligible, 'Far as we go.'" His column, which promoted "Foolsophy," also used this short form in parodic aphorisms: "A man is driven to both drink and suicide—he walks to work"; "A tack in the hand is worth two in the foot." One can read visual-social-semantic poetics, or what I call elsewhere sociopoetics, in the micrographic poems. In one such poem, titled "Zany Zed's Inarticulate Skeleton," the alliterative play, the repetition of letters, the capitalization of the alliterating letters, and the allusion to articulated skeletons poetically hint that the visual form and layout (or articulated skeletons) remain mute except in this zany comic bit.

In another (untitled) micro-poem (the micro-poems often have no space for a title), the wordplay involves Louis XV's using the bilingual visual pun on Louis quinze (fifteen) as Louis quince (which works as a visual, but not homophonic, pun). One squib pokes fun at British food. Another describes red type on white paper. One describes the natural cynicism of a newspaperman when dealing with words, much like a baker's distrusting a pie or a butcher's looking at tripe. (Brown saw himself as a newspaper publisher who needed to fill column space with squibs and who distrusted writing with an editor's eye.) Another micro-poem wonders about the relation of thought to type on the page, and yet another complains comically about writing with a fountain pen (using the image as a way to consider the larger issue of writing technologies). The mini-poem "Death of Words" suggests a textual script for a comic book or movie treatment by using all capitals to indicate loud sounds and em dashes to suggest a shorthand system much like the system used in the readies anthology, with its cinemovietone quality. The condensed poems, packed in a small space like the condensed soups that soared in popularity in the 1920s, provide an analogy for the post–book-reading experience, with variable magnifications and focus.

In the condensed poem "New York 1930," Brown again illustrates the analogous relationships with other technologies, like cranking Ford cars (a favorite theme of Gertrude Stein's), talkies, telephones, vending machines, audio plugs, phonographs, and the experience of watching a movie of a rhino braying when someone twists its tail and cranks the camera (perhaps an allusion to *Simba*, released in 1928, one of the first nature documentaries). The poem uses a staccato style suggesting a series of similar images (wires, cranks) and activities (jiggling, twisting, turning) to produce a new type of cinemovietone poetry.

Changing the focus (literally) to the larger poems, one sees the same satirical intent and a similar focus on printing, reading, and writing through titles like "Lament of an Etcher," "A Grace Before Writing," "Writing," "Sonnet (count the lines)," "I But Bend My Finger in a Beckon and Words Birds of Words Hop on It Chirping" (the poem's title as well as the subtitle of the collection), and an homage to Harry Crosby, the poet-printer-publisher; Bob had just published *1450–1950* with Caresse and Harry Crosby's Black Sun Press. Brown later proposed using the image of the bent finger as part of an animated introduction to his plans for a "poetry TV" series, which was rejected by his agent and never proposed to any network or production company. In his proposal, the finger would bend and the animated words would jump on it and hop around like birds chirping.[53] Although Bob had not seen American TV while living in Brazil and did not know the conventions of TV at the time, he once again imagined (correctly) a future children's television with color animated letters, words, and cartoons unavailable and unimagined until *Sesame Street*, *The Electric Company*, and more recent computer games. Also, commercial TV was not as open to experiments. There is a multicultural perspective throughout these poems. One poem, republished in his aptly named *Nomadness* (1931), portrays Nirganth, a Persian style of meditation (an ancient form of spirituality that later developed into Hindu practices), that has as its goal a detachment from everyday worries. Brown also makes fun of European national figures, customs, and mores, as in a poem about street dogs in the upscale spa town of Royat, in France. One untitled poem expresses a goal of the volume:

In the reading-machine future
Say by 1950
All magnum opuses
Will be etched on the
Heads of pins

Not retched into
Three volume classics
By pin heads.[54]

The opening poem of the collection, about birds of words, is a poetic explication of the process of deflating the long-winded into congealed, condensed constructions.

Rose was equally active as a writer in 1931. She was collaborating with Cora and Bob on magazine articles about food that would soon lead to the start of their cookbook-writing empire, but her own publications were often more obviously politically engaged. Her mentor Emma Goldman visited with them, and, in general, the conversations and the scene in the south of France were not merely about drunken decadence but often soberly focused on social, economic, and humanitarian crises. Rose wrote about the now almost entirely forgotten famine in Niger, for example. As a poorly administered French colony, Niger had no planning or adequate response to the locust swarms that swept through west Africa and that precipitated the 1931 famine, killing or displacing a third of the colony's entire population. After 15,000 had already died, the French delivered food shipments that were too little, too late. To make matters worse, the French sought to help solve their economic depression by continuing to raise taxes on the west African colonies they controlled, such that demand for payments forced more of the land into cash-crop production; at the same time, the French charged the west Africans more for manufactured goods from Europe but paid the west Africans less for the raw materials and agricultural products from Niger. As the famine unfolded, Rose wrote a nonfiction story explicitly about farming in the context of the famine in Niger for the American *All-Story* magazine. It was a time in the United States when the magazine industry was consolidating and major publishers were merging, but Rose and Bob still had many connections to all of these publishers and magazines. Rose wrote nonfiction stories, cooking-advice articles, and stories all the while entertaining many visitors, and her publications made politics and humanitarian issues into stories; she also helped with a lawsuit concerning property and payments back in Brazil in which they recovered about $4,000 out of a possible $32,000. They increasingly needed to publish popular works to make ends meet. Adding to Rose's struggles, Bob was often drunk. In an unpublished (and unarchived) diary entry, Rose worried about Bob's acting "crazy" during his late-night drunken parties or card games, and in one entry she sadly states to herself, "Hopeless about Bob."

In *Gems*, Brown took more explicit aim at the censors. This time he also spoofed the purported goal of protecting school-age children from less exalted literary works (like limericks, which seem especially suited to recitation and rote memorization). Before the school reform movement of the 1920s, school primers focused on small literary gems for recitation.[55] He printed and published *Gems* in the same year as *Words* and dedicated it to Cunard in the hope that she would find in it a "lifelong fountain of innocent and exalted pleasure."[56] He also begins that collection of found poems with a detailed discussion of Havelock Ellis, whom Cunard also published and whose books on sexuality were banned, denounced, and burned in England. With this ongoing prohibition in mind, Brown thought of his use of micrographic texts in *Words*, and the em dashes in *Readies*, strategically, not ornamentally or neutrally. With his one-man Roving Eye Press, he published *Gems* in 1931 shortly after Cunard's press finished an edition of Ellis's *Revaluation of Obscenity*, a surprisingly unsexy history of obscenity's definitions (or lack thereof), etymologies, prohibitions in history, and legal cases that advocated for a moral re-valuing of obscenity. In his studies, Ellis specifically alluded to the poems in Victorian literature and how those previously considered gems now seemed dated, leaving him, and most other contemporary readers, reading those gems only from an irreverent perspective.

> In my independent irreverence towards the idols of Victorian literature and art, I scarcely deigned to read their poems or look at their pictures, while I eagerly searched for the things that pleased myself, things, some of them, which afterwards also pleased other people, so much so that they have since left me tired. . . . the perpetual slight change which taste is always undergoing.[57]

Ellis, in the volume published by Hours Press, argued that "the legal conception of obscenity has been carried to such dizzy heights of absurdity that it is toppling over into laughter."[58] And, in that line, Brown found an opening for his ready-made conceptual commentary on the absurdity of censorship that ultimately topples "over into laughter."[59] Brown wanted to produce an irreverent volume that would use visual design to expose the logic of censorship, by redacting words and phrases using the ■■■■, or ■■■■ boxes because he typeset the marks individually. Reading a censored document produces a material and poetic situation that differs from reading the same text without any censored lines. The demonstration makes all of the classic poems, or the gems of the literary canon, seem obscene.

Craig Dworkin describes how the found (and then processed) "gems" demonstrate censorship's ability to create the circumstance for obscenity rather than obscenity's creating a need for censorship.[60] The anthology of gems makes visible, by covering and obscuring the expressive text, the usually invisible social situation of a censor's decisions. Reading these poems again, now censored into suggestiveness, writes a social poem about the cultural practice of reading socially acceptable anthologies of great poems in the canon of literature. Precisely because the visual poetry of the censored lines uses a social cultural convention of a widespread reading practice, the poems ironically de-familiarize that reading practice as well as highlight the usually invisible censored texts in literary anthologies. It also suggests how a social technology (i.e., the censors' ability to black out passages, or in radio or TV, bleep the offending █████. Brown sees himself as a satirist parodying the censors' titillating art of redaction. He talks of "book-legging" as analogous to bootlegging, in terms of an interesting and profitable career, as if he were trying to convince the young to take up the trade. Much like George Carlin and the seven dirty words that censors did not permit on radio or TV, Brown seeks to spoof the concern with the inappropriate. He demonstrates in the readies and the salacious-ized gems how the visual design (e.g., blacking out words or adding lots of punctuation) can both defeat a censor looking for specific words and amuse the audience (of Surrealists, Dadaists, and other vanguadists) who were struggling to avoid the censors. The visual poetry did not seek to limit, restrict, or efface cultural meanings. Each of these poems, easily recognized as polite classics including children's poems, takes on sinister meanings simply by censoring.

The Surrealists were particularly sensitive to censorship in the early 1930s. With only 150 copies of *Words*, and fewer than twice as many copies of the *Readies* anthology or *Gems*, these works sought to speak to a specific group of readers (i.e., avant-garde writers and artists trying to avoid the censors' bars). Man Ray had produced a completely censored poem in 1924, and the immediate joke of his poem is slightly different from the meaning of the poems in *Gems*; in Man Ray's poem (the title is also censored), the reader does not cognitively fill in the blanks but simply immediately notices the complete censorship of it. Brown decided to embrace censorship, to borrow or steal its logic and visual poetics, in order to write a poetics/poetry of censorship. Brown's efforts, like the Surrealists, sought to illuminate the sociopolitical dimensions of what censorship and obscenity laws seek to confine to the private and personal. Sex scandals uncover the connection between the private and public. Havelock Ellis discusses these connections in terms of an early case in the eighteenth century involving Sir Charles Sedley, who, "in a drunken freak," stripped naked on the balcony of the Cock Tavern in Bow Street, Covent Garden, and gave a mock sermon, in imitation of an itinerant quack. The situation quickly degenerated into Sedley, a notorious libertine and member of the group of courtiers sometimes known as the Merry Ballers, emptying beer bottles containing urine onto the crowd below. The ensuing court case, about the riot that Sedley provoked, was one of the first cases to deal with the high politician debased in a public display, but then, as now, it is difficult to define obscenity or to prohibit it legally. Instead, the censors' work puts a "premium . . . on things that are dirty and worthless," and "it is law alone which makes pornography both attractive and profitable."[61]

Gems is also likely the first and most important literary ready-made because Brown copied the "gems" from Palgrave's *The Golden Treasury*, a classic anthology of poetry and drama popular from the late nineteenth century through 1914 (that was published in at least nine printings). The editor of later editions, Edward Hutton, explained, "[N]o one has been able to make an anthology that has been so generally received by Englishmen as in itself almost a work of art, as really fulfilling precisely its promise to be the golden treasury of the best songs and lyrical poems in the English language."[62] Bob then took the poems, the gems of English poetry, and strategically redacted, using the censors' black bars, specific words. Redaction, sometimes called, suggestively, "sanitization," blacks out words in often "inappropriate," or secret, texts. A censor redacts a text in order to make it unreadable by those not given permission to see the hidden words. The censors' bars open texts to meanings outside the author's intended meaning much as photomontage, ready-mades, collages, cut-ups, Surrealist games, and even literary theory seek to produce. By spoofing the supposed sanitization of these poems, Bob hid the apparently obscene reading lurking in the readers' mind if not in the originally intended meanings.

Conceptual art works, like Ben Rubin's *Dark Source* (2005) and Jenny Holzer's *Redaction Paintings* (2006) open a new genre of art that Bob Brown's *Gems* initiated about seventy-five years earlier. Ed Halter, in an essay, "Erase You" (2008), describes this genre as "one in which numerous and varied artists have attempted to wrest information from the powers that be, not so much to share the data, but to bear witness to the nature of its obfuscation."[63] The condensation of the themes and passions explored in a lifetime of writing, both chronologically before and after the years they spent mostly in France, would lie dormant until a new audience in the twenty-first century rediscovered the significance of Brown's work. They had thrown countless parties, made bathtubs full of punch, and cooked marvelous meals. Their hedonistic decadence, of a moveable feast of sodden fleshpots and naïveté, suggests an irresponsible ignoring of real political dangers, threats, and prejudices. Instead, the stories of the revelry have now effaced, rather than reinforced, the actual project of the avant-garde; their goals were much more serious and engaged precisely because they saw libertine means as a crucial part of reaching toward the goal of liberty and the pursuit of happiness for everyone.

Soon after *Gems* appeared, the Browns were on their way to London. In 1932, the world economic crisis had worsened. The Browns were forced to leave, and they could not even afford passage all the way to the States. Once again, they were broke, having lost the entire fortune from their publishing empire begun in 1919. As they prepared to leave for London, Rose, Cora, and Bob sat surrounded by trunks, boxes, and crates in their south of France manor house. Books, papers, and artifacts sat scattered about, and some objects looked as if they waited in queues in front of their soon-to-be shipping containers. Shipping, unlike passage for themselves, was still relatively inexpensive, but they could not send their belongings ahead to the United States alone. They would have to station themselves in London until they could afford to pay their ship fares. They could not even afford to bring Carlton with them, so they bought him a one-way ticket to Paris and suggested he visit a girlfriend there for a month or two until they could send the fare for travel to London and, they hoped, soon to the States. Bob assured Carlton that they would send for him as soon as they could and laughed off Carlton's befuddled look. Years later, Carlton would remember his feelings of abandonment as helping to set the stage for his later mental illness. Although many of their friends were fleeing fascism and the worsening economic crisis in Europe, there would also be continuity among this group of radicals. Kay Boyle and Bob continued to correspond, depending on each other for constructive criticism over and support for their respective writing projects. According to Brown, Boyle wrote around 150 letters to him and, likewise, he wrote to her regularly. Letter writing was a major part of their lives, corresponding with many writers, publishers, and friends; in one letter Boyles mentions that she had written 45 letters that day, and she needed to get back to writing fiction. A few years later, in 1936, after two additional careers for Bob Brown, Boyle included a short story by Brown in her anthology *365 Days* with a 300-word story for each day of a year.

Bob Brown and every savvy investor thought they had dodged a bullet back in 1929 with the infamous "crash" of the stock market in the United States. They even profited when the market, and the Dow index, recovered completely by April 1930. Now, in the summer of 1932, the market lost 85 percent of its value, and, unlike in 1929, it did not bounce back. Bob had, like many others, reinvested in 1929, and now there was nothing left except the traces of the amazing few years they'd spent in Europe. They sat sorting and deciding whether to discard or keep each item, like a somber auction. Cora would hold up a large stack of index cards, for example, filled with recipes and tidbits on cuisine and customs in Shanghai; they'd motion it as a keeper as they were beginning to think of publications that could make them money, and those cards could come in handy. The papers and objects reminded them of the marvels they'd experienced in a few short years. They remembered those two years of globe-trotting, much of it in China and Japan, and then continuing in Europe for the next three-and-a-half years: a German spa town, an Alpine village on the border between Italy and France, and two charming Côte d'Azur villages near where Marcel Duchamp, Kay Boyle, and other artists and writers lived. The condensation of time and geography, the folds and overlaps in simple chronologies, and the revolutionary poetic intensity gave those few years the feel of a jazzy cubist painting by their good friend Stuart Davis, a Surrealist story told from multiple perspectives and mixes of genres. It was as if Mrs. Dalloway, the eponymous character from Virginia Woolf's novel, preparing for her party, stopped off to visit a print shop that telescoped into a Surrealist game: an automatic reading spun out by a machine, one that responded to others in the avant-garde circles, including Duchamp's machines and ready-mades, Stein's abbreviated writing style, Marinetti's machinaphilic poetry, Tzara's transcriptions, Léger's film about machines, Antheil's music by machines, and the entire *transition* group's call for a revolution of the wor(l)d. Like much else in Bob Brown's life, the reading machine prototype was lost, and never seen again.

The exclamation point in the title *Let There Be Beer!* was Bob's toast to the repeal of Prohibition. It also celebrated the Browns' embrace of the struggles against austerity and for the common wealth of the people, especially during the economic crisis. The Browns' politics did not diminish their enthusiasm for international customs, cuisines, and fermented drinks.

6
Let There Be Beer, Wine, Snacks, and Radical Social Change, 1932–40

Cook-books have always intrigued and seduced me. When I was still a dilettante in the kitchen they held my attention, even the dull ones, from cover to cover, the way crime and murder stories did Gertrude Stein.

—*Alice B. Toklas,* Alice B. Toklas Cookbook, *1984*

. . . the expression "It's gravy," for something extra . . . any juicy reward obtained without effort.

—*Cora, Rose, and Bob Brown, 1939*

. . . years of tossing up snacks and tossing down drinks in cafés and home kitchens of all foreign capitals . . .

—*Bob Brown, 1937*

. . . one of the most unusual museums in the United States.

—*News report on "The Museum of Social Change," curated and organized by Bob Brown, 1935*

In 1932, the party continued in London. Sergei Eisenstein had recently published an essay that mentioned the earliest serialized movie, *What Happened to Mary*, and Bob's avant-garde friends learned of his connection to the films. They celebrated by parading from pub to pub, hoisting Bob up on their shoulders as their temporary hero. Bob continued to see himself as part of the expatriate avant-garde scene but, at the same time, felt forced to publish in a more marketable genre than modernist poetry. In London, Bob wrote fictionalized accounts of his life at the

Slackers Hotel with Mina Loy and Arthur Cravan, in *You Gotta Live*, and an extended encomium on beer, *Let There Be Beer!* The exclamation point seemed fitting for Bob, as his enthusiasm only increased, in spite of the economic woes. The books sold well and allowed Cora, Rose, and Bob to live in London and eventually buy passage back to the States. It was in London that Bob began to realize he could mine his own life story for fiction and nonfiction that appealed to a popular audience. He had done this before in finding realistic settings for his Christopher Poe stories, but now the plots and characters would also follow his own adventures.

You Gotta Live built on his recollections for a novelized version of his life in Mexico in 1917 and focused on Mina Loy and Arthur Cravan. On the boat back to the United States after a twenty-year hiatus, the Browns began to think of ways to turn every aspect of their lives into moneymaking publications. As Bob wrote and drank, the Browns asked themselves how they might read their own lives differently, not just for the exotic settings (as Bob had done in the pulp fiction) or characters in the avant-garde (as Bob had done in *You Gotta Live*) but in a way that would illuminate what Ernest Hemingway famously called the moveable feast. They began to realize that the visceral, gustatory, and inebriated pleasures they had known for decades were something that even a middle-American audience, with the end of Prohibition, could embrace. Instead of the literary genres that employed abstract conceptual art practices or hermetic modernist styles, they needed a genre much more familiar; they needed a genre that would be welcomed into every home in America. They started to write cookbooks filled with generous helpings of anecdotes and what we now call the cultural history of beer, wine, and exotic cuisines.

Bob converted decades of pub-crawling into his popular book about beer, *Let There Be Beer!* He described all the many places he had drunk beer, from his college years in Wisconsin to his life in the artists' colony near Grantwood Village to European pubs. The reader feels as if he or she is sitting next to Bob as he describes all the aspects of beer (from an informed personal perspective), from brewing traditions, the pubs where it is served, national drinking customs, and the taste, texture, look, and smell of different beers. One review at the time compared the book's style to "the vigor of a glass of good beer."[1] *Let There Be Beer!* served, at the time, as a celebration of the repeal of Prohibition, the exclamation point suggesting a toast to the return of legal beer drinking in the States. The title was literally drawn from a quote from "King" Gambrinus, probably the name given to a fourteenth- and early-fifteenth-century Duke who was an innovator and champion of beer brewing. The book's title page has an epigram, "Gambrinus said: 'Let there be Beer!—and there was Beer,'" that suggests the elevation of Gambrinus to a heathen king and beyond to the patron saint of beer like a modern Bacchus. Bob regularly saw the iconic image of the "King of Beer," Gambrinus, in Milwaukee, where he often visited as a teenager, and at the Falstaff Brewing Company's New Orleans headquarters, close to where he lived in 1911.

Brown dedicated the beer book to H. L. Mencken, who had edited the fiction magazines where Bob had placed so many stories. Mencken had since risen to a more respected political and social platform for his ideas in *The American Mercury*, which he edited; and the general public respected him as a leading public intellectual and social critic. Mencken also championed beer. Brown uses the opening quote and dedication to position the book as a serious advocacy of beer drinking. He starts the book with a self-help–like description of a "beer cure" and ends the book with a series of charts outlining his own schedule of his beer cure in detail, including what brand, how much, what he ate with the beer, where he drank the beer (the beer hall's name, festival, etc.), the cost of the beer, and even the amount of the tip. Some reviewers found his condescending and "sarcastically smiling tone in extolling the benefits of beer-drinking, pub-crawling, free-lunches and old-time saloons" cloying pap.[2] The schedules list what appears to be Bob's own pub-crawling from beer hall to beer garden stand. He lists every detail: the time he arrived and the place names, like Schottenhamel or Austiner. He lists every detail in a chart: the time he arrived, like 11:00 A.M.; the place names, like Schottenhamel or Austiner Halle; the brand of beer he drank, like Pschorr Marzen or Thomasbrau Light; the container he drank from, like glass or krug; the quantity he drank, usually a liter; the food he ate with the beer; like Weisswurst with wild deer or a whole broiled chicken or turtle soup; the price of the food and beer. He even calculated the amount of the tip in absurd specificity to the penny. The list goes through seven systematic days using a ledger-like listing of details that illuminates Brown's poetic fascination with lists, details, and ephemera. Beer becomes a cure-all tonic, a stimulant, and an essential component to a healthy diet. Thinking about how machines and inventions might play a role in this beer cure regimen, Brown argues, "Some gadget should be invented for the absent-minded drinker to accurately register his daily beer-fall. A drink meter of some sort, on the plan of the cash register, speedometer, adding machine or pedometer . . . . A gauge like a barometer, a beerometer perhaps."[3]

Much like his work on the reading machine, the tone of discussion of the beerometer (and the entire chapter advocating the reader to "Take the Beer Cure!") makes the reader laugh at the obvious parody and yet appreciate the earnest attempt to win over converts. Brown's convivial tone—the modern tone—once again makes it a challenge to pin him down and makes readers appreciate the possibility of a convivial rhetoric and the usually effaced importance of encomium. We certainly do not teach students how to write encomium, the delivery of a tribute, extended toast or panegyric celebration, even as we bemoan the lack of civility and appreciation in public discourse.

One could read each chapter as a series of toasts or encomium on people, things, places, and customs related to the chapter's beer-related topic. For example, at the same time that Christopher Columbus discovered America, in 1492, Christian Mumme discovered a brewing process in Braunschweig, Germany, that made it last even on long sea voyages (i.e., high alcohol and sugar content) and thus became the first "exportbier." Brown recounts this by quoting the last lines of Tiede's "long paean in his [Mumme's] praise, and then explains, "Simple sincere rhymes go as well as piquant pickled onions with the drink of substance foster-fathered by Mumme. The poem points out with spirit that anyone too silly to praise Mumme is nothing but a great big dummy."[4] Bob found piquant poetry a pressing part of partying rather than mere ornamentation for sanctimonious sober-sided prigs. In his poetic imagination, Prohibition challenged not just beer drinking but also his living life as a passionate poetic celebration. And, in his typical poetic-political fashion, Brown mentions a statue of Mumme "with a glass held high in his hand. A statue more inspiring today than the Statue of Liberty with her hollow torch."[5] The full glass of beer, for Bob Brown contemplating his return from a decade of exile from the States, rings truer than the hypocritical hollow promises made toward immigrants and citizens yearning to be free.

Building on his self-awareness of his working in every form of writing, he uses, in the beer book, multiple genres, including a full play script called "Resurrection Day," in which all U.S. post offices are remodeled to "include federal bar-rooms" serving beer and where postmen double as police busting gangsters' speakeasies. Other forms of writing include supposedly real memos in German beer halls from professors announcing lectures and meetings (which were supposedly posted in a university town's beer hall) and transcriptions of pranks and joking schtick like the following bit.

> Students preparing for life, students cutting up, acting natural, calling out to newcomers: "Herr Schmaltz, you're wanted on the telephone!" "Fräulein Arzt! Hello! Have you read Hare on the Abdomen?"[6]

In a book about beer, not completely legalized in the United States when Brown finished writing, it is surprising how much of it deals with teenage drinking as an important right of passage. The puns, pranks, and beer in a school setting portray drinking as frivolous, not physically and morally dangerous. In another section, Bob describes a scene, likely loosely drawn from his own childhood, wherein "the drug store served instead of the saloon . . . where adolescents too short in inches and years to be allowed in saloons first learned all about the sex-life of the bees and flowers."[7] The drugstore, where "the sexes could mingle freely and drink together without undue gossip or scandal," was a place of experimentation overseen by soda clerks mixing lemonade and tutti-frutti with imported red wine claret. At forty-six years old and the father of a twenty-one-year-old son and a teenage daughter, Bob remembered learning about sex and drinking in the back room of the drugstore where "all shameful, hidden things came to life . . . shrieked with laughter, shuddered with Freudian hair-raisers."[8] Novelty gimmicks have long since passed from saloon culture, but Bob remembered this goofy tomfoolery from his childhood and teenage years in Chicago and the Midwest, from bars like the humorously named Heine Gabubler's, Hinky Dink's, or Luke McGluke's. These bars were for the tourists and country cousins, not for locals, and thrived on tricks involving singing beer mugs, drinking games that involved the proprietors' names, dice without dots, trick mirrors that seemed to put a red nose on customers, trick shelves with paste-board bottles falling on unsuspecting customers, Calico snakes, exploding boxes of soot, rubber toads, and sinister bat wings. What Brown describes as an annoying "comic hell" that nevertheless did appeal to visitors to the big city was part of a culture of fun, frivolity, and everyday life outside laboring.

Promoting this usually effaced cultural history of the nonserious, Bob continued to see this aspect of life and history as essential to modern life and culture: Beer-drinking rituals may help define a diverse culture outside of the soberly efficient modern workplace. That said, he would soon embrace physical farm labor in a communal setting as the foundation of freedom, but first he'd toast to beer and "free lunch" (the faintest resemblance of that surviving only in mixed nuts or popcorn at a happy hour). To Bob, "free lunch" was "America's one outstanding achievement. Its chief claim to international fame."[9] Although he recognized that this tradition had faded, he saw in it a small, unrecognized liberating achievement and connected its loss to other culinary changes like the shift from small entrepreneurs selling hard cider being pushed into unemployment by the apple trust that preferred selling raw, unfermented apples as is still the custom and business practice today. He closes his encomium to beer with a discussion of cultivating the American taste buds for "good beer" rather than the "pyrotechnical displays of firewaters, bursting bouquets of booze flames," and, counterintuitively, "some temperance work will have to be done on them before they will accept the genuine joy of natural drinks."[10]

The book now serves as a reminder of a less homogeneous brew than the product sold in supermarkets. It also illuminates Bob's style and attitude, which like the brew he celebrated was neither amateurish nor homogeneous. This now-extinct type of book was more like a long blog post than a history or coffee-table book (with no illustrations or photographs at all). Now, well-illustrated books on beer would have either more practical advice about beer brewing or literal images of beer and people drinking beer. Bob disliked home-brew and argued that if Prohibition did eliminate beer drinking, then "amateur home-brewing may yet finish it off."[11] He thought of beer brewing like a high art cultivated over centuries: a genre of drinkable art. When done well, beer brewing conjured rich and complicated cultural histories. Bob read these stories by drinking the beer, and he shared these stories in his book. He intended his book to inspire someone to publish a weekly publication, much like the content of the beer book, "full of hearty, healthy drink jokes, with a few beer truths shining out between the lines. Drinking history, toasts, recipes, famous beer bouts, feats of sudsy skill, booze battles and doughty drinking chronicles of days gone by, but sure to come again."[12] Bob's beer book, implicitly an autobiography including scenes from his life as well as his tastes and sensibilities, implied that he thought of himself as a professional trying to navigate between prohibitions, including those issued by censors and commercial editors, and amateurish dabbling. One might accuse Bob of exemplifying both, rather than neither, of those failings. He wrote commercially popular publications for fifty years, and he wrote in enough genres that "dilettante" seems particularly suited to describe him. In 1932, Bob began to see his hodge-podge of experiences as a composition or portrait: a coherent whole. In his imagination, it was the story of a writing family—one he called the Brown Family Robinsons (alluding to the inventive and self-reliant Swiss Family Robinsons). It was also the story of how something as frivolous as beer drinking might fit into his self-portrayal. When he invented the reading machine, he thought of it as a Surrealist self-portrait, and now he thought of himself as a beer connoisseur or beer-drinking artiste (with the half-joking and self-mocking tone). In a more specific sense, the Browns learned from the list of ingredients in Bob's expository style, in the beer book, how they might write a series of cookbooks that combined recipes with cultural history and personal anecdotes from their many adventures.

Of course, cookbooks represented, even epitomized, the bourgeois values that the Browns had spent three decades attacking and running from and presented the same dilemma of embracing/rejecting aspects of their talents and identity, but cuisine, cooking, and cookbooks were always part of the avant-garde they knew well. In fact, avant-garde artists, poets, and groups, most infamously the Futurists, had produced anti-traditional cuisine cookbooks.[13] Although it would take the Browns another four or five years before they more fully realized the cookbook form as a vehicle to insinuate a radical perspective and agenda, their first cookbook was part of their liberationist politics. They decided that with the repeal of Prohibition, cooking with wine would quickly become a way to allow alcohol back into the American home. The beer book was more encomium than domestic advice, but the wine book would make alcohol safe for the home. After Prohibition's repeal, sales of beer went up, while most wine sales went down, but cooking wine did find a place in the kitchen and was more widely accepted by women. So, although wine production fell after repeal, and its reputation sank considerably as it became associated with "winos" and cheap products, its presence in desserts and as a way to spike the meal increased. The Browns rode that wave.

When they arrived in the States, they lived for less than a year in the wealthy beach town of Atlantic Highlands, New Jersey, near enough to New York City to meet with colleagues and publishers. A steamer and train trip would allow the Browns to easily get to the city but still live in a location not too dissimilar, in the summer months, to the south of France's seaside climate and mood. As soon as they started to publish popular cookbooks, many of their previous friends in avant-garde circles, to Bob's dismay, thought of the cookbooks as a sign of their disappearance from the literary and artistic scene. He seemed to have shut up the avant-garde shop. He did not publish any poetry with his Roving Eye Press until the 1950s, and he seemed to temporarily shift his energies from a revolution of words toward revolutionary and radical politics. Under the radar, he continued to publish more poetry as well as recollections of his cultural adventures from pulp fiction writing to the expatriate avant-garde. In fact, he was even a more productive poet and essayist in the four years after he returned to the States than in the four years in Europe publishing volumes of avant-garde poetry and experiments. He published short pieces in anthologies of Surrealist work in *Americans Abroad* (1932). In 1933, he published essays and poems in *American Mercury*, *American Spectator*, *Americana*, *Panorama*, and other magazines. He also published two booklets, *Houdini*, an extended poem, and more of his poetry in the Modern Poets Series. The work on Houdini consists of a series of scenes of how the magician created his own identity and the significance of his work.

> shouldering loads of
> second hand rusty locks
> from the town dump
> lugging them home to practice on
> picking them as a maestro plucks strings
> making them a vibrant part of you," or working "alongside
>   museum freaks
> fraternizing with the Dog-faced Boy
> studying art in the gallery
> on the Tattooed Lady's thighs.[14]

These biographical details about Houdini also implicitly hint at Bob's own sense of his adventures as a magic act:

> At the age of eight
> already a circus in yourself
> I see you always swinging in three three-rings
> ablaze from the parlor chandelier
> winking up peeks of strewn needles
> in the miraculous twitch of an eye.[15]

Around this time, the Browns got an advance from Little, Brown for a cookbook on using wine in recipes. Because they had already collected recipes during their stay in Europe, it was simply a matter of compiling the recipes and adding a smattering of discussion about national customs or combining foods. While in Atlantic Highlands, the Browns wrote that first and most successful cookbook on cooking with wine, which in hindsight seems like a sure-fire commercial success. The success of that cookbook also indicated the Browns' return to writing for a large audience.

Throughout the 1930s the cookbooks sold well, and a few became bestsellers for many years, establishing the Browns in yet another genre of writing and publishing. Skimming over the recipes, one finds champagne and caviar, gobs of butter and cream, exotic and extravagant recipes for everything from calves' brains cooked in a black butter wine sauce to detailed advice about buying authentic champagne by timing the effervescence, humorous anecdotes, and ingenious, if often impractical and surreal, solutions to a cook's every economic or culinary dilemma. For example, to save money they recommend, in *Most for Your Money Cookbook* (1938), using "freshly fallen snow" as a substitute for "two eggs" in a pudding. In the *European Cookbook* of 1936, they describe how in Lusitania, a statue of Saint Anthony sits in the kitchen; if a dish burns or displeases the cook, she takes the Saint out to the "well and hangs him head down in it, in dire disgrace—for the fault is obviously his and never hers."[16]

The recipes in *The Wine Cookbook*, later reissued as *Cooking with Wine*, also subtly refer to their life among the expatriate avant-garde. For example, one of the recipes, titled Hilaire Hiler's Fruit Soup, and the popular cookbooks were not a rejection of their previous lives but another perspective with similar goals: to change (or brighten) everyday life with diversity and to infuse labor (cooking, writing, publishing, making books and machines, etc.) with pleasure. Besides the obvious and topical inclusion of alcoholic wine as the key aspect of the recipes, the cookbook did not have any prose sections for cultural contexts or sociopolitical perspectives.

After the success of the wine cookbook, the Browns did not write another cookbook for a few years until after returning from teaching at Commonwealth College and traveling to the Soviet Union. At that time, in the late 1930s, they added an essayistic component to the recipes, and the prose gave them more opportunity for placing cooking and cuisine in context and framing the recipes in their social and political perspectives. As soon as they finished the wine recipes cookbook, the Browns left Atlantic Highlands to begin another adventure in changing everyday life, starting with their own, that would seem to many of their friends as a radical departure from their lives so far.

Even though they were able to sell books, and get advances on future books, the early spring of 1933 was the depth of the Great Depression, and the Browns' sympathies, and their actual economic struggles, continued to align them with progressive socialist agendas. Unemployment rates of a quarter of the work force meant that the entire country was receptive to at least talking seriously about communal and socialist solutions. Bob began contemplating how he could surround himself with what many thought of as the new vanguard (thinking of writers as laborers and part of a national, especially southern and rural, effort). He got an advance from Farrar and Rhinehart for a book about living on a commune that eventually appeared with the commune's own publishing arm as *Toward a Bloodless Revolution.* That book about communal living must have seemed like a lark to their friends and publishers, considering their backgrounds as gourmands writing about cooking with wine or drinking beer, but it made complete sense in terms of Rose's work with Emma Goldman and Bob's work on *The Masses*, and in the context of their fleeing the United States with the war resisters from World War I. They saw the new approach in continuity with their liberationist politics. They set out to the commune to write more as journalists and with the advance contract from Farrar and Rhinehart, but soon the Browns recognized that they had found their niche.

Although one might imagine that the economic crisis would drag the Browns' spirits down, they reinvented themselves once again to embrace the struggles of poverty without diminishing their enthusiasm for exotic cuisines. Instead of a contradiction, the cookbooks fit neatly with the politics because all their activities in the mid- to late '30s suggested to their audiences a do-it-yourself–reliance attitude that embraced intuitive frivolity as well as the seriousness of a shared vision and consciousness in what communes now call an intentional community.

Although it seemed as if the Browns changed from the avant-garde liberationists of the 1910s and '20s to adopt a dour soberness during the Great Depression, they still thought of themselves as involved in publishing and networking as part of a revolution of the word. In the Introduction to his Communist tract, *Toward a Bloodless Revolution*, Bob confessed that his friends thought it wildly out of character for him to work as a laborer on a commune, which he did in 1934, as they thought he wouldn't last a day without cocktail hour, lavish meals, and urban, avant-garde culture. The Browns did live that hardscrabble life, first in New Llano, Louisiana, on the commune for a few months, and then in Mena, Arkansas, at Commonwealth College where both Rose and Bob were on the faculty. Bob bookended the experience with another tract called *Can We Co-operate?* that he published in 1940 with his own Roving Eye Press, then relocated to his home on Staten Island.[17] Before moving to the commune Bob wanted to stop for a few weeks in New Orleans, where he and Cora had lived for about a year in 1911 and where he had visited in 1917 as he and Rose moved to Mexico.

On this trip, Bob visited with Bruce Manning and Gwen Bristow, novelists and later important Hollywood screenwriters. Manning became the producer of the movie star Deanna Durbin's films. Manning and Bristow would sell their first script to Universal, based on their 1930 mystery thriller *The Invisible Host* (later reissued with the movie title as *The Ninth Guest*), a few months after the Browns visited. They ate a stew of black-eyed peas and set in motion Bob's later efforts, in 1940, at selling story ideas in Hollywood. They also visited Roark Bradford, the writer known for his southern dialect writing in plays and stories about folk characters like John Henry. Roark was, at the time, most famous for his collection of stories *Ol' Man Adam an' His Chillun* (1928), which was later made into a Pulitzer Prize–winning play and Hollywood movie. Roark set the stories in in the Depression-era South and New Orleans with a young African American girl who interprets *The Bible* with the scenes and characters in her life and neighborhood. The Browns talked with Roark about their plans to work at New Llano and to write about life there. Another old friend, Lyle Saxon, the respected journalist and friend of many southern writers from William Faulkner to Roark, entertained the Browns. Saxon influenced the Browns with his bestselling "Gumbo Ya-Ya" (1929), a compilation of native folk stories from Louisiana, which the Browns referenced later in their cookbooks and recollections. When he became the W.P.A. Writer's Project director for Louisiana, Saxon gave the Browns guidance about their projects.

Giving up the decadent lifestyle, they moved to the New Llano commune and started to work on the farm. Bob later claimed that a group in the New Llano community had driven them out after a resident had given Bob a manuscript on spiritualism, and Bob had dutifully sent it to Theodore Dreiser's agent, asking if the agent might find a publisher. Dreiser, the famous novelist, who was well known for his critically acclaimed naturalistic novels, did have an interest in spiritualism, so Brown thought he might persuade a publisher of the worthiness of the New Llano resident's manuscript. Six months later, and soon after the agent returned it, Dreiser published an essay in a magazine that, according to Brown's account, supposedly plagiarized most of the resident's manuscript. At the time, Dreiser had become extremely well respected with a reputation for personal integrity and sense of fairness, so there was little recourse for the actual author because no one would believe him over Dreiser, the paragon of virtue. Bob remembered the scene like a comedy with the farmers chasing Rose and him as they drove away, but it seems more like a melodramatic twist to the story of why they left the commune. The actual, if more mundane, reason they left, that Commonwealth College needed

Bob Brown, proletariat writer, organizer, teacher, and tour guide to the Soviet Union, supposedly was born into humble working-class beginnings.

their skill set and that they were a better fit there than at the farm, does not have the thrill to it. In any case, they left Louisiana and moved to Arkansas.

They took unpaid faculty positions at Commonwealth College, a center of communitarian farm and labor efforts, where students were trained as farm and labor organizers. To encourage self-reliance and democratic forms, students used first names when talking with faculty or administrators. The Commonwealth faculty and administration, with connections to the New York City Theater League and to progressive publications like *The Masses*, knew of the Browns and their importance

COMMONWEALTH COLLEGE FORTNIGHTLY

VOL. X., Nos. 21-22 MENA, ARKANSAS, NOVEMBER 15, 1934 $1.00 A YEAR

FAMILY OF WRITERS JOINS COLLEGE STAFF

Bob, Rose and Cora Brown To Gather Material For Book

A family of authors has joined the permanent staff at Commonwealth.

Bob Brown is author of "You Gotta Live", "Nomadness", and a dozen other books, some of which are known all over the world. He has written a thousand short stories, most of them in the old days under the name of Robert Cariton Brown. Bob is the American representative of *Preslit*, Soviet Russia's foreign press and literary service.

Rose Brown, his wife, has edited several magazines and has worked on newspapers. For ten years she was co-editor of the *Brazilian American*. She has collaborated with Bob in many literary jobs.

Cora Brown, Bob's mother, is author of the "Wine Cook Book," a recipe book that is in millions of homes. She was on the editorial board of the *Brazilian American* and many other South American magazines.

Bob and Rose were members of the editorial board of *The Masses*, forerunner of *The New Masses*, along with Jack Reed, Art Young, Max Eastman, Mary Heaton Vorse, Howard Brubaker and others. Rose sold the first issue of *The Masses* on the streets of New York.

The Browns will gather material and write a book on Commonwealth.

"When a Man's Hungry," a four-act play by Agnes Cunningham portraying the need for organization among the farmers, was the main feature of the November 7 program at Commonwealth.

William Cunningham, acting director, spoke on "Why We Celebrate November 7." The program included also songs and dances, etc. Several hundred farm people were present.

Many Respond To Commonwealth's Appeal For Immediate Financial Aid

Little Mag, What Now?

Since Commonwealth took over publication of the WINDSOR QUARTERLY we have not only become little-magazine conscious, but little-magazine disturbed. Fred Maxham and Irene Merrill have us all excited by saying their next issue will present the best collection of proletarian stories ever put to paper. Bob Brown, new to the campus but a veteran contributor to the little mags, says this would make a swell center for the revolution of letters. We have with us already, Clay Fulks, Bill Cunningham, Bob Reed, and there is even talk of Jay du Von moving down here with his *New Quarterly*, or Ruth Widen and Lew Ney with their *Latin Quarter-ly*.

This fugitive field has grown to perhaps two hundred monthlies, bi-monthlies and quarterlies, mimeographed on butcher paper or embossed like the slicks. But no matter how arty or pink some of them started all are now engaged in a left wheel manoeuver along a United Red Front stretching from Brooklyn Heights to Beverly Hills. Yet they come out at such long and erratic intervals that a clearing house of information concerning them is badly needed. So the FORTNIGHTLY will start a regular column in its next issue, entitled "Little Mag, What Now?" Here we will record still-births, births, deaths and near-deaths of these Vol. I. No. 1's, together with highspots in their careers and spot news of them and their contributors. We are open to all news bulletins from little mag publishers and writers. Address them to Bob Brown, Commonwealth College, Mena, Arkansas.

The demand for the fall number of the WINDSOR QUARTERLY will exceed the supply, the editors report.

School Expects To Do More Efficient Work Than Ever Before

One hundred and thirty-two persons have donated $603.50 since Commonwealth announced its desperate financial plight in the last issue of the FORTNIGHTLY, according to Charlotte Moskowitz, treasurer. Money is still coming in and it is estimated that enough will come in to buy food and other necessities until the first of the year.

Because winter clothes, bedding, etc. have not been purchased, for several weeks the expense of running the community will be slightly higher than usual, despite rigid economy. Donations of clothing, bedding and dishes for the kitchen would be acceptable, the treasurer says.

Donations range from $200 down, most of them being under $6. The list of donors is too long to publish in this issue of the FORTNIGHTLY.

The largest gift was from A. E. O. Munsell, who stipulated that a few dollars of the $200 he sent be spent on a "big feed" for the group. The feed was held on Hallowe'en night, in banquet style, with a toast on "the new spirit at Commonwealth," and a song composed especially for the occasion.

There is no danger of the school being forced to close, since teachers and maintenance members are determined to keep it operating. Student prospects for next quarter are good and it is generally predicted that the school will operate more efficiently this winter, despite its financial handicap, than ever before.

Commonwealth's maintenance staff is the best the school has ever had, says William Cunningham, acting director.

The newspaper announced Cora, Rose, and Bob's arriving on Commonwealth College's campus.

to literary innovation and progressive politics. In the perfect summary of the literary avant-garde's style and aspirations, the Browns thought "Commonwealth would make a swell center for the revolution of letters." Mixing the language of fun, "swell," with literary experimentation and revolutionary politics characterized much of their work, travel, and goals at least in the years between the wars. Soon after arriving at Commonwealth in 1935, the Browns founded the Museum of Social Change and the Associated Little Magazines, a coordinating agency and clearinghouse for more than one hundred small labor and radical newsletters and magazines throughout the country.

While Bob began teaching creative writing and started thinking about organizing an exhibit with the students, Rose taught effective writing (a more basic writing course that proved the most popular among the students). There were no grades or diplomas. The small group of students, never more than fifty-five total, took courses in small six-to-a-class courses. The students would take three classes a quarter, and the classes often consisted of discussions and debates. Classes began at 7:30 A.M., and afternoons were spent working to maintain the campus—growing and preparing food, and other labor. Rose became the faculty advisor for the newsletter, the Commonwealth College *Fortnightly*. She revamped the newsletter to promote the Browns' effort to help form an Associated Little Magazines group. Through the newsletter, the many small-run magazines, focused on labor issues and/or literary innovation, would learn of one another's magazines and together promote themselves to a wider audience. It was the same collective ideal that the Browns' had found in their work with avant-garde groups and publications: collective promotion *and* protection of individual creativity and freedom. Alone, none of the little magazines would survive (and, in any case, most did not), and the Associated Little Magazines helped singular, if all progressive or radical, voices find an audience. A student was elected secretary of the magazine and wrote a regular column on the news of the magazines for Commonwealth's school newspaper; sometimes Bob wrote these columns. The college also started publishing the militantly pro-labor *Windsor Quarterly*, and the Browns took an interest in that publication as well. Drawing upon his contacts with all the little magazines, Bob published essays in many of these magazines about his life's adventures and experimental poetry.

With the Browns' leadership, Commonwealth became a coordinating agency and clearinghouse for more than one hundred small labor and radical newsletters and magazines throughout the country with titles like *The Left, Blue Pencil, The Anvil, Hinterland, Kosmos, Dubuque Dial, Pen and Fist, Latin Quarterly, Manuscript, Medallion, Trend, Windsor Quarterly, Poetry World, Smoke, Space, Spinners, Plowshare, The Magazine, The Rocking Horse*, Commonwealth College's *Fortnightly, The Grape-Vine Telegram*, and *The Social Frontier* (to name just a few). Each of these publications had a small, narrowly defined audience, but the Browns and their colleagues felt that an organized effort would increase the impact of these tiny publications.

Many of these small press publications did not even know of the existence of the others. As with the later assemblings, 'zines, and blogs, the magazine editors sought a way to communicate among themselves, collectively increase their potential audience, prevent overlap, and primarily to appeal to advertisers by promoting their combined circulation of 22,000.[18] The college formed the Associated Little Magazines in April 1935. Each member of the association received a subscription to the *Fortnightly* that increased its "circulation to approximately 6,000 copies every two weeks." Each issue included a regular column about the "Little Mags, What Now?" This important aspect of small, fine, or little press publications usually remains separate from discussions of similar efforts in the literary avant-garde to publish poetry and art, but many of these magazines explored literary innovations and experimentation. *Manuscript* published Bob's visual poems, and that year it also published Tennessee Williams; the next year it published Eudora Welty. Just before *The Left* closed its doors, it prepared an issue with poems by Bob Brown and Ezra Pound (in his lesser-known progressive Communist phase). These little magazines saw themselves as the life-blood of the arts and letters in a culture suffering through an economic crisis and struggling through a transition to greater democracy and much wider participation in, and appreciation of, the pleasures of cultural pursuits. The Browns heralded those pleasures: Diverse and different cuisines, art, and writing (published in little magazines, not mass media), no longer for the avant-garde, or rich, alone, found an audience all over the United States. The Browns were the direct link to the earlier "modernist little magazines" of the first twenty-five years of the twentieth century.[19]

In the December 1, 1934, issue of the *Fortnightly* (Vol. 10, No. 23), Bob asked for students to name their museum with the headline exhorting "WORKERS, NAME YOUR MUSEUM" and offering a stipend to cover tuition, room, and board for one term of work-study for the winner (and transferable to another student at the winner's discretion). In the New Year's Day issue of 1935 (Vol. 11, No. 1), he announced the name, The Museum of Social Change. Some of the other titles suggested included "Museum of Capitalistic Decay; Class Conscious Museum; Museum of the Forgotten Man; The Collapse of Capitalistic Culture; Museum of Decadence; and, The Class Struggle Museum."[20] The runners-up in the contest for the new name included "Masses Museum, Fetters to Freedom, Museum of Class Struggle, Morgue, and Museum of Unnatural History." The last one, on Unnatural History, was suggested by at least "four contestants from widely separated parts of the country."[21] A few years later, Michael Gold, in his book *Change the World!*, had a different title in his mind when he wondered whether the "Museum of Capitalist Decadence is still functioning at Commonwealth College in Arkansas" and made a suggestion to include an editorial that correctly identified J. P. Morgan's interests as a crucial component in getting the United States to enter the First World War.[22] Gold was probably contacted, either directly or through the *Fortnightly*, to contribute something, and Bob wrote to his many contacts to help supply the museum with exhibits. The list of contributors read like an "intellectual *Who's Who*, headed by Einstein, H. L. Mencken, Charles Angoff, editor of *The American Mercury*, Erskine Caldwell, Harvey O'Connor (*Mellon's Millions*), Art Young, M. C. Phillips, author of *Skin Deep*, and Ezra Pound."[23] Reports began appearing about the museum, and it was mentioned widely as one of the most unusual museums in the United States.

The general goal of the museum was to illustrate "the entire history of the working class . . . And for contrast, the decadence of capitalism will be shown in sharp relief."[24] The museum's plan resembled a conceptual art installation using montage, found objects, and images and organized to suggest a complicated history and idea. It is now a museum missing from all art and cultural histories, as of yet, in part because it was staged outside the art world and used avant-garde and agitprop strategies not widely recognized as legitimate; but at the time, it created a stir among public intellectuals in the United States, Europe, and the U.S.S.R. and shocked conservative politicians. News reports at the time recognized that it was "one of the most unusual museums in the United States," and these reports would sometimes close with the suggestion that "More articles are sought. Anything that contrasts the affluence of the rich and the plight of the poor is subject matter for the museum."[25] In hindsight, the museum might represent the first example of conceptual installation art in the United States. With Bob Brown as the link between the museum and the European avant-garde, the museum's first and only exhibit fit neatly in the tradition of the political experimental arts or with an alternative version of labor history not opposed to experiments in presentation. The museum was also carefully linked to the curriculum at the college, but its form was montage and mixed media rather than heroic Soviet (or Hollywood) realism.

Instead of a folk museum of labor or of craft production, the museum was radical in form and content. Instead of reinforcing the idea of a labor museum with old-timey quaint things and images, rural ("hillbilly") culture of Arkansas, or the enduring myth of the transcendent folk culture of the common man, the museum's exhibits had a more aggressive and interventionist approach. It sought to expose cultural contradictions and mythologies using the avant-garde strategy of creating new contexts by placing lynch ropes, for example, next to photographs of the idle rich at Atlantic City, or strike relics next to luxurious Episcopalian collection plates (promised by H. L. Mencken). Although it is a simple idea, there is little (if anything) like a museum of cultural contradictions and de-mythologies today, almost a century later. In the art world, many artists have staged installations and photomontages that are similar to the type of work that Bob and his students presented in their museum, and the works of Hans Haacke and Barbara Kruger come to mind, as do Andrea Fraser's faux art catalogues and museum docent tours and magazines like *Art Threat*, but political art practically defined much of contemporary art especially in the late twentieth century. Still, no museum dedicated to exposing cultural contradictions existed before or since Bob opened the one at Commonwealth. The goals of the museum seem contemporary to our current concerns with wealth inequality and xenophobia as Brown's museum sought to expose the "greater and greater concentration of wealth in the hands of a few coupon-clippers who seek escape in Europe in summer and Florida in winter. Increase in armaments and armored trucks. The rapid growth of fascism. Jingoism. Chauvinism. Regimentation in CCC camps. In a word, a cross section of national and international breakdown."

Here is a list of some of the items Brown requested (and the contrasting images and items they are paired with), selected from the same *Fortnightly* article in which Brown exhorted the "Workers" to "Name Your Museum":

actual harnesses made for human beings used as draft animals (pictures of Teddy Roosevelt in a sedan chair carried by Brazilian tribes people;
an American missionary in a Chinese rickshaw;
college students pushing frat boys in strollers at the Century of Progress exhibition);
samples of scrip made of tin, wood, and leather (images of art collections of first editions, postage stamps, coins, medals, trophies, etc.);
a photographic history of the Calumet-Hecla strike in the copper region of Michigan in 1913;
images of flop-houses and breadlines would be next to items like silver corn-on-the-cob holders;

pictures of slums, sharecropper shacks, souvenirs and flags from Hoovervilles (pictures or models of yachts, luxury autos with owner's coat-of-arms, pent-houses);
clothing including used tires made into shoes, flour-bag lingerie, and press clippings of children not attending school for lack of shoes or clothing

Set among these artifacts would be "quotes and statistics on death and worry among the poor and unemployed including the increase in suicides and misery indexes, and other indications of a lack of value in their lives" all set against images of opulent wealth. The museum would includes images of "Barbara Hutton's $10,000 birthday party, society column on Doris Duke. Revival of fox-hunting on private estates, [and] polo" playing. And, these images would appear with literal signs: "Keep Out" and "Keep off the Grass."[26]

Brown included his own cookbook, and examples of his own collection of first editions, in the exhibit on the bourgeoisie's excesses (excesses at the expense of the laboring poor).[27] It was this sort of decision that illuminates how Bob both recognized his own conflicted position and the evolution of his thinking. After the year at Commonwealth College, Rose, Cora, and Bob would return to writing cookbooks, and really start cranking them out, but instead of recipes alone, the next set of cookbooks would insinuate a cultural critique in subtle and not-so-subtle ways. Although at first glance, Bob Brown's story looks like a lifetime of decadence and frivolity, he was, instead, constantly struggling to write, and live, something meaningful: not simply taking what the world offers, not settling (down), not laboring for a wage or hoarding surplus value, not living the appropriate buttoned-down middle-class life. He did not see himself as always on the right side of history, but as always trying to get out from under its weight: not escaping, but not surrendering.

The museum exhibit would include editorials "illustrating the "kept press" by Bruce Barton, who co-founded one of the most successful advertising agencies (that later became BBDO) and wrote religiously oriented pro–free-market self-help books. Brown still held a grudge against Barton, the editor of their Oak Park high school newspaper who often rejected Brown's jokes and catchphrases. The section on the press would also include examples of how the big syndicates control what the public reads, and how advertisers manipulate the messages we hear on the radio or read in the newspapers. The exhibits would also include police torture devices (rubber hose and blackjacks), chains used in chain gangs, photos of injuries inflicted during torture, and images of cops beating strikers and using tear gas. These images and objects would be matched with the tools and artifacts of strikes and picketing. One section called "increase in terrorism" would include items from lynchings (rope, images, descriptions), Ku Klux Klan cross-burnings, billboards advertising the American Legion, images of strike-breakers, and a series of items about sound and terror from factory and police car sirens and alarm clocks. Loaded dice and images of gangsters were matched with Wall Street manipulation and tricks. Another section would examine how prices were dependent on manipulating consumer psychology rather than connected to cost of the items. The exhibit would include sermons and memorabilia from megachurches and quack preachers, like Billy Sunday or Aimee McPherson, priestly vestments, and collection plates (both silver platters and a purple plush bag on a mahogany fish pole). There were planned sections on the appeal to the "artificial" and commercialization of sex, insanity, drug consumption, medical frauds like magnetic belts, New Thought booklets, fraudulent mail-order diplomas, commercialization of sport, dancing, amusement, and every aspect of life.

After the museum opened, it received national and international attention. Walter Winchell mentioned it in his column of jokey squibs by noting snidely that the museum included in "its exhibits silk underwear discarded by members of the New York Athletic Club. (Come the revolution!)"[28] The First Baptist Church built a concrete Ebenezer stone in 1936, referencing the Bible story in which a stone celebrates God's intervention on the side of the Israelites in a battle with the Philistines, to match the museum's concrete illustration of organized religion's complicity in the poverty of labor in capitalism. In July, James T. Farrell, who had participated in the *Readies* project and had since found fame from his Studs Lonigan trilogy, visited Commonwealth. Bob had invited Farrell, who was young enough to be Bob's son, but nevertheless best of friends since they both worked on *The Masses* in the 1910s and later in Paris in the late 1920s. Many other visitors and tourists visited the campus to see for themselves it and the museum; some would stay a few days, others a few hours. Some were appalled, others inspired.

The threat from reactionary forces made letter writing and protest campaigns constant. Students, trained to work as community and labor organizers, often found themselves in trouble soon after leaving. For example, the U.S. government threatened a former Commoner (what the students were called), Alfred Miller, with deportation to Germany, where the Nazis planned to send Miller to a concentration camp. Miller's crime was publishing the "Producer's News, a militant farm paper in eastern Montana. In this capacity he has carried on a good fight against foreclosures and local relief administration practices."[29]

Another typical protest involved the Commonwealth College Experimental Theater's asking for help to "fight theatre censorship" and demand "prosecution of the kidnappers of Will Ghere, whose production, *Till the Day I Die*, offended California fascists."[30] Kidnapping, deportation, arrests, and suspicion from allies and enemies alike raised the stakes on the lessons learned at Commonwealth. The influence the college had on progressive folk music, experimental theater, community art, and social networking of the time (with print publications, letter writing, phone calls, and meetings used to support causes and fundraising) was enormous. The college's director, Lucien Koch, called the emphasis on art, music, writing, and drama "cultural sprouting" and everyone saw it as central to labor and community organizing.[31] Among the prominent artists at the school, Joe Jones, the major midwestern regionalist painter, painted a large mural covering nearly an entire wall in the center of campus. Lee Elhardt Hays, who taught at Commonwealth, went on to form the Almanac Singers with Pete Seeger and Woody Guthrie, and he later helped form the Weavers (made famous for their renditions of "If I Had a Hammer," "Kisses Sweeter Than Wine," and "Goodnight Irene"). Agnes Cunningham, a student at the college, started the Red Dust Players in Oklahoma and also joined the Almanac Singers; she later wrote songs later covered by the New Lost City Ramblers, Ry Cooder, Pete Seeger, and Bruce Springsteen. She is now most famous for publishing a little magazine, *Broadside*, which printed the words and music to folk songs by Bob Dylan, Malvina Reynolds, Phil Ochs, Janis Ian, Tom Paxton, Buffy Sainte-Marie, and many others. The most famous student was the future Arkansas governor Orval Faubus. A number of faculty members had connections to the New Theatre League of New York City, and the League played an increasingly influential role at Commonwealth.

The school allowed such shocking practices as female students' wearing pants, students' making administrative decisions, and supposedly allowing someone to paint the hammer and sickle icon on a cement walkway. Some unsubstantiated rumors suggested that co-eds went skinny-dipping and a local neighbor may have seen a few of them naked. These scurrilous rumors made their way to the offices of conservative legislators, but for the most part the local farm workers supported the school's efforts (especially as the students helped organize support to stop the wholesale unlawful eviction of sharecroppers and tenant farmers). Provoked by the college's activism, a committee from the Arkansas legislature visited the school in 1935 and proposed shutting it down as a "Communist training camp" that taught "un-American doctrines"; on their investigative visit, they singled out the museum as proof of the dangerous work of the college.

On January 26, 1935, the Arkansas House of Representatives passed a sedition act (H.B. 211), called the Gooch Bill, after its sponsor, Representative Samuel A. Gooch. The bill made sedition a felony and defined it as importing into the state and publishing, printing, or circulating any writing suggesting the propriety of using crime, violence, militancy, or terrorism as a means of political reform or change in government. The college put out a call for letters and telegrams protesting the legislation. The legislature's effort failed, and the plans to close the college were shelved after intense pressure and hundreds of letters and telegrams from prominent writers; congressmen; union leaders; labor lawyers; progressive groups; many college administrators; religious social services leaders; newspaper editors; neighbors of the college; former students; even a telegram from Paris, France, with nearly a thousand signatures; and many of Bob Brown's friends and contacts. Many of those who wrote were subscribers and readers of the Commonwealth College's newsletter, the *Fortnightly*. Among those who protested, H. L. Mencken also suggested that the the college move to his hometown of Baltimore, Maryland.

In 1940, after breaking its connections to the Southern Tenants Farmers' Union and failing to merge, or form an alliance with, the Highlander Folk School in Tennessee, the college faced a new funding crisis and sought the sponsorship of the radical New Theatre League. The college prepared to function as an Arkansas outpost and performance center of the League, but that new affiliation propelled the local Polk County government to levy fines against the college for failing to fly the American flag and other crimes; the college could not pay the $5,000 in total fines, and all of the property and name were sold, and the college was closed by the end of 1940. Its cultural significance had ended years before, and the locus of radical farm and labor organizing in the southern United States, Arkansas in particular, has faded from memory. The Browns did not return to the school after their first summer abroad program in the U.S.S.R. in 1935, but they ran a second summer Soviet Union program the next summer.

In the fall of 1936, internal dissension among the school's administrators led to ceasing publication of the *Windsor Quarterly* and the "little magazines" newsletter; much of the creative ferment fizzled in the late

'30s, and when the legislature forced the college to close, none of the prominent voices (many of whom were friends and associates of Bob's) protested. Its artistic influence, especially in the countercultural folk music scene, flourished, and its potential bloomed from the "cultural sprouting" the college cultivated. The Highlander Folk School, which had looked at Commonwealth as a model in the mid-1930s, still continues the efforts to encourage grassroots organizing and movement building. In this way, Commonwealth's mission and goals continue. The Browns brought their experience of the avant-garde to the experiments in democracy at the college, and those experiments sought to prepare people for participation in and leadership of a more democratic society by demonstrating the potential power of collective organizations, like the Associated Little Magazines or the museum's requests for donations. The experience there and in the U.S.S.R. provoked Bob to think of ways to spread the message into the homes of every American.

On the way to the summer program in the Soviet Union in 1935, the Browns stopped in New York to attend a conference of radical writers, and on the boat trip they spent time with Eleanor Glintenkamp, whom the Browns had known from their exile in Mexico. Eleanor was, at that time, the ex-wife of Charles Phillips and later Henry Glintenkamp. They visited friends in Paris and London, including meetings about Surrealist anthologies to which Bob and Rose had contributed; and, finally, they went on to tour the Soviet Union's showcase factories, farms, and food markets. Bob and Rose published short pieces in Kay Boyle's *365 Days* (1936), consisting of page-length stories by various writers from Langston Hughes to Henry Miller, and Bob published in John Lehmann's book-periodical *New Writing* (1936). On these journeys to Moscow, the Browns met with friends including Nancy Cunard; Fred Ellis, radical editor and cartoonist for the *Daily Worker*; and Oakley Johnson, who lost his teaching position at CCNY (City College of New York) for his Communist sympathies in 1932, which had provoked large student protests, and later wrote about Ellis's cartoons. The students in the Browns' group included schoolteachers and unpublished writers looking for inspiration.

When they returned from the Soviet Union, they also returned to writing cookbooks. The Browns settled at 97 Bloomingdale Road in the village of Pleasant Plains, Staten Island, for three years in what they called a "farm retreat in New York City." They had "six acres with peach trees, pheasants (that the City cop shot), herb garden and all."[32] Once again, similar to their Atlantic Highlands, New Jersey, home, the relative isolation and open space of their Pleasant Plains farm had a location close enough

The critics raved about the cookbooks: "mouth-watering and entertaining" and "discriminating eaters will rise up and bless these Browns."

to the city to meet regularly with literary agents and publishers and old friends like William Carlos Williams (who advised Bob on both poetic and medical concerns). Together the Browns would write at least nine cookbooks in the next three years, and the wine cookbook, with the subtitle "Being a selection of Incomparable Recipes from France, from the Far East, from the South and Elsewhere, all of which owe their Final Excellence to skillful use of Wine in their preparations," had already become a bestseller with new editions continuing to appear for decades. The publications not already mentioned included *The European Cookbook* and *The*

Four-in-One Book of Continental Cookery, Italy, Spain, Portugal, France, both in 1936; *The Country Cookbook: Cooking, Canning and Preserving Victuals for Country Home, Farm, Camp & Trailer, with Notes on Rustic Hospitality*, 1937; *10,000 Snacks: a cookbook of canapés, savories, relishes, hors d'oeuvres, sandwiches, and appetizers for before, after, and between meals*, 1937; *Homemade Hilarity: Country Drinks both Hard and Soft*, 1937 (by Bob alone); *Most for Your Money Cookbook*, 1938; *The South American Cook Book including Central America, Mexico and the West Indies*, 1939; *Soups, Sauces and Gravies*, 1939; *The Vegetable Cook Book, from Trowel to Table*, 1939; *Fish and Seafood Cook Book*, 1940 (the last book that the team published; it appeared in print after Cora had died); *Look Before You Cook, A Consumer's Kitchen Guide*, 1941 (Cora had died, and this one is written by Bob and Rose alone); and *The Complete Book of Cheese*, 1953 (by Bob Brown alone).

Cora had earlier written stories for the pulps and had coached Bob in how to crank out the word counts. By the time they published the important cookbook on the then-heterogeneity of American cuisine in 1940, they were able to claim that they'd "put in twenty years of culinary adventuring in as many countries and wrote a dozen books about it . . . ."[33] Bob, Rose, and Cora thought of themselves as reading and writing machines: collecting, collating, and processing. He wrote so many cookbooks with Cora and Rose that they eventually signed their dedications CoRoBo (for Cora, Rose, Bob as one entity), and one publisher, the prestigious J. B. Lippincott & Co., marketed the books as written by "The Browns." The cookbooks received critical as well as popular success and earned the Browns a place in culinary histories. *The Wine Cookbook*, in particular, had lasting appeal over multiple editions and attracted much critical acclaim.

The *New York Times Book Review* raved that it "will delight the epicure and the connoisseur of food and drinks." Burton Rascoe, the editor and literary critic, wrote in *Esquire* that it was "the most mouth-watering and entertaining of all cook books." A book review in the *New York Herald Tribune* "Books" section announced, "discriminating eaters will rise up and bless these Browns." The *Chicago Tribune* called it "A glorious collection of inspirations." It was not just critics who endorsed the Browns' cookbooks; one prominent restaurateur declared, "It is a rare thing that I ask the Chef of the Mayflower to even look at a cook book prepared for the lay readers but he was enthusiastic over many of the suggestions contained in this totally different volume."[34] Simultaneous to this surge in productivity, and connected to their *Most for Your Money Cookbook* (1938); *The Vegetable Cook Book, From Trowel to Table* (1939); and *The Country Cookbook:*

Cooking, Canning and Preserving Victuals for Country Home, Farm, Camp & Trailer (1937), they drew on their experience with communal living, do-it-yourself radical social change, and visits to the Soviet Union.

Around this time, Brown corresponded with a vast array of radical writers from Langston Hughes to James T. Farrell. In those three years, the publications bring into focus the Brown's worldview and do-it-yourself politics reflected in the title of one of their books, *Homemade Hilarity* (1937). If the scene suggested an abandonment of avant-garde interests, then the actual publications demonstrated a continuing interest in Surrealist and Imagist poetry as well as politically engaged perspectives insinuated into the most widely accepted and, by definition, domestic genre. Nearly a quarter-century later, in a short film on self- and familial discovery, Bob's great-granddaughter Phoebe Brown portrays them through their recipes as gritty eccentrics cooking up a storm of odd combinations and exotic choices. Phoebe then folds the Browns' history into her own story; in her childhood, parents and other adult relatives avoided questions about her great-grandfather and her grandfather, which only added to the mysterious appeal of learning more about the Browns when she became an adult.

Back in the late 1930s, the Browns drew together their ethnographic research and their continuing interest in letting juxtaposed items tell the story to write *10,000 Snacks*. For example, they asked "three American girls of exactly the same age, eighteen, living not ten miles apart, in uptown New York City," about what they ate for snacks, and then they "let the extensive and radically different lists speak for themselves." They listed the many snacks of a Detroit debutante attending the exclusive and expensive Sarah Lawrence College—for example:

> Potato chips with Avocado paste—Toast, caviar, raw onions, hard-boiled egg—Chocolate ice cream in beer (a Surrealist shock reminiscent of the midnight dill pickle and icecream of our mothers' boarding school days)—Waffles with icecream and butterscotch sauce next to an equally long list supplied by a girl who polled her friends in the Public School of Harlem that includes for example Shrimp and ham with rice—Barbequed spareribs—Pineapple rice pudding . . . Southern stewed tripe—Western cheese fondue—Jamaican hot patty—Johnnycake with plenty of butter and Georgia cane syrup—Hog maw (Southern style)—West Indian pepper pot—Butterscotch benny (candy)—Hopping John (peas and rice, Southern style with pork; or West Indian, cooked with coconut).[35]

The listing continues:

> The third poll was among office workers, chiefly stenographers including vanilla and lime cokes with the inevitable cigarette. (This last snack, fruit-flavored Coca-Cola and a cigarette is also called "reducer's lunch"; it reminds us of a coffee sandwich which was Floyd Dell's pet snack in Greenwich Village days: a cup of coffee sandwiched between 2 cigarettes, or a 3-decker, of 2 cups, with a third cigarette smuggled in between).[36]

These lists illuminate Bob's poetic sensibility, Rose's interest in ethnographic and historical detail, and Cora's love of recipes. There is a delightful heterogeneity and anachronistic peculiarity in conjuring specific cultural milieus and the often hilarious images of peculiar snack habits they evoke. For Bob, the form of the list without the flow of prose, missing what Brown refers to in the *Readies* as the "unimportant words," like conjunctions and prepositions, makes the lists poetic, allusive, staccato—something to be skimmed over—picking out a line or two from a long list almost flowing by, but still alluding the way a poem does to a larger image—not quite a narrative, but suggestive of one. Here is an example of "skewers of all sorts, sizes, and materials." These lines read like Imagist poetry:

> Wooden ones for pinning meats together and brochetting fish, since fish should never be broiled on a metal skewer. Strong steel or silver for other brochettes such as kidneys, giblets and game, to be forked right off the skewer into the mouth.[37]

Or the surreal juxtapositions of cultures, tastes, images as in "for the tongue a sauce of horseradish with whipped cream sweetened with watermelon pickle."[38] The lists appear throughout the cookbooks; for example, in a discussion of apples the Browns list "the most popular kinds and the seasons when they're cheapest. The Consumers Union's Buying Guide has summed up the apple situation for us," in this way:

> Favorite cooking apples are those having a slightly tart taste (Wealthy, Jonathan, Willow Twig, and Rome Beauty). Grimes Golden, Delicious, and Stayman Winesap are excellent dessert apples—but let us add that the Macintosh is best of all.[39]

Two months from the list give a sense of the diversity of apples available at the time.

> December—Jonathan, Spitzenberg, Stayman Winesap, Delicious, Northern Spy, Rome Beauty.
>
> February—Baldwin, Rhode Island Greening, Yellow Newton, Stayman Winesap March—Yellow Newton, Stayman Winesap, Willow Twig.[40]

If Bob Brown wanted his machine to recover some of the physical intensity of reading without slogging through its polite pleasures, and to separate reading from the detached and isolated myth of a natural reading practice, then his cookbooks and Dionysian lifestyle presented models not just for his own work but for the modernist avant-garde in general. Many have noted the importance of the café and the aperitif Dubonnet for early modernist Parisian painters, but fewer have connected the avant-garde's strategies to cookbooks' odd mix of genealogical cultural analyses, visual design and fragmented style, collective—even networked—source and production, and their explicit—if sometimes unnoticed—efforts to modify any habituated, homogeneous, and parochial quotidian events (obviously starting with eating, drinking, and partying). The modernist effort to de-familiarize thinking and desire had turned to more mundane activities like eating, cooking, or reading. Sigmund Freud begins one discussion, on the sources and stimuli of dreams, with a citation to a popular saying, "Dreams come from indigestion." Although he goes on to mention many other sensory stimuli that may provoke, and become grist for, dreams (like strong smells, a chill, movements, gnat sting, thunder, crowing cock, straw between the toes, hot-water bottle, damp night shirt, tickled by a feather, alarm-clock dreams, diseased internal organs, and many more), he never specifically returns to an example of indigestion—like dreams of the rarebit fiend—to explain the cause of dreams.[41] Of course, he ultimately focused his attention on psychical tensions as the stimuli for dreams and dream content, but he does not attempt to disentangle the long tradition of connecting what one ate to what one dreamed. The poetic lists in the cookbooks fit the Imagist-Surrealist form (mundane topics, simple descriptions of things and facts, and letting the lists and nouns alone create the mood) to the surreal perspective (the accretion of the simple description opening onto a dream logic and overwhelming sublimity).

The cookbook's list becomes the perfect vehicle for this poetic strategy. The surreality appears in lists like these of Italian specialties served at a meal:

> Italian specialties . . . succulent sausages, salami of Verona, mortadella of Bologna (now exported in cans); ravioli in every imaginable style; chicken livers genovese; corpretto (kid); the maremma, tortoise and wild boar of Tuscany; the fish grills of Genoa; Umbrian baked pudding of rice and chopped pigeon; festive fish, eels, frogs' legs, swordfish, tuna, mussels, Roman red mullet (truglia), frutti di mare, octopus; endless rice dishes (risoto); corn meal mush (polenta); eggs in unbelievable array; bistecca (beef steak); exceptional raw hams; osso buco (marrow bones); animelle (sweetbreads); artichokes and cardoons, pungent squashes; frittata; almonds and walnuts eaten green, chestnuts roasted. Ices, Neapolitan and tutti-frutti ice creams. Zabaglione. Distinctive wines and cheeses from every province: pale mahogany Marsala and heady Corvo from Sicily; Chianti, Capri; Parmesan cheese, Bel Paese, Stracchino, Bra and Southern Caccio Carvallo. A full rainbow of figs, a cornucopia of fruits. Watermelons red as lipsticks.[42]

The Futurists—Alice B. Toklas and The Browns—all wanted to rescue and celebrate everyday life outside the Puritanical work ethic. Even though the Browns knew that the problem with that rejection was that it appeared to advocate a sloppily unconcerned *joie du vivre* in the late 1930s reminiscent of the later fictional Finzi Contini family, who in Vittorio de Sica's film *Il Giardino Dei Finzi Contini* (1970) play tennis and throw parties even as anti-Semitism and fascism rise around them, and even as Bob included the *Wine Cookbook* in his museum exhibit as an example of surplus value's relation to oppression, the Browns still seemed overly optimistic about the threat of fascism in Europe and about the power of their cookbooks to spur progressive political change. Given this optimistic sense that innovation in the kitchen (and the arts) would lead to a liberation of everyday life, the Browns unsurprisingly began one cookbook with the saying "*Non in solo pane vivit homo*" (Man does not live by bread alone).[43] They describe foods as scared manna when, for example, they quote the Bible, Numbers XI, 4–8: "the manna was as coriander seed . . . and the people went about, and baked it in pans, and made cakes of it; and the taste of it was as the taste of fresh oil."[44] They also make sodden pronouncements like "if anyone wishes to indulge that artistic streak inherent in most of us, the cocktail hour is the time for it."[45] One wonders if Bob Brown finally sublimated his artistic drive, evident in his visual poetry and reading machine, and implicit anti-Fascist politics into the cocktail hour. If nothing else, the Browns mock Mussolini's dictate (and the Futurists' central claim against pasta) that "too much starch must not be consumed, for fear of ruining the race through indigestion" by noting that "spaghetti, macaroni, vermicelli, ribboned fettucini (noodlelike), or some other of the score of succulent pastas, spiced with garlic and with Parmesan strewed over it, is almost sure to appear at the noon meal."[46] Besides their cookbooks' obvious political decadence (perhaps shared by the experimental poetries), they sought a poetic style appropriate to their goals, and the cookbook form was, unwittingly perhaps, a way to popularize the visual and poetic style with which Brown had continued to experiment in his more explicit championing of Surrealist poetry and a do-it-yourself attitude. Here is a list of items to barter at a swap meet: "no limit to things in the vegetable, animal and beverage kingdoms that are eminently swappable, so don't hesitate to offer your excess herbs, pedigree pups, baby chicks, gold fish, silk worms, homemade wines and applejack."[47] Once again the mundane and pragmatic list of stuff you can barter at a swap meet sounds like a surreal juxtaposition.

One does not read a cookbook from beginning to end. Even when one follows the recipe carefully, the results have different smells, looks, and, most important, personal connotations for each reader/cook. The lists, instructions, anecdotes, and instructions also teach about cuisine. For example, a simple list of cities also explains in condensed fashion how French cuisine is not limited to Paris: "Epicurean tradition rates the province of Burgundy, together with Alsace, Perigord and Dauphiny, as the chief runner-up to Languedoc and Provençe, and thus adds the city of Dijon to Paris, Lyons, Marseilles, Nice and Strausbourg."[48] Some of the lists seem innocent enough; for example, a list of ingredients: "Prepare stuffing as follows: take strips of both fat and lean salt pork, some ham, morsels of cold roast veal, a slice of dry bread, parsley, two small onions, salt and pepper, put through grinder."[49] The image conjured by this list suggests an excessive dream or, as they say in this citation, "a ten-course dinner in miniature."

> [in France] . . . chitterlings and anchovies to tiny portions of melon and salted tarts of chicken blood. The best butters of each Province are served as hors d'oeuvres, often in a garnished block weighing from ten to fifty pounds. Other standbys are mussels, sardines, anchovies, oursins, cockkles, pickled cock's combs, roe, tunny, olives all colors, radishes, salads of everything, hard-boiled eggs, sausages all sorts, hams cooked and raw, pickled mushrooms, peppers, artichokes, smoked meats, blood puddings, brains, sweet-breads, cucumbers,

> shrimps, galantines, oysters, tongue, onions, panisses, little pâtés of liver and almost anything else, the raw sausages of Arles, pain Daussé, rillettes and rillons of pork, onions, [wild] game patties fried in pig's blood, tapenade, terrines, prunes in vinegar, saveloys, celery and celeriac, in fact, anything and everything tasty, but chiefly local salads, sausages, pickles and garnishings, in fact, a ten-course dinner in miniature, generously descriptive of the great dishes to follow it.[50]

The Browns include an etymological digression, in their fantastic lists of snacks, tracing the word "snack" from a "share of something divided" and also from the German "to snatch." As the Browns explain, snacks are the opposite of appetizers,

> consisting as they do of every kind of informal piecing together provided by hostesses, tea shoppes, coffee pots, bars with beer and free lunch, soda fountains, clam and oyster push carts, lunch wagons, nut stores, hamburger and popcorn stands, street vendors of hot dogs, whistling peanuts and salted pistachios.[51]

By the time the Browns published their volume on snacks they were already well-known cookbook writers, and they still remain important in the modern history of the genre, but it is unlikely that cookbook collectors would ever compare notes with and scholars of avant-garde poetries let alone make connections between experiments in reading and the Browns' cookbooks. To read cookbooks as experimental poetry, or as literature at all, is usually reserved for cultural histories of cuisine or of a particularly enchanting substance like chocolate or beer.[52] To read the two together, like having T. S. Eliot propose starting a Foundation for the Preservation of Ancient Cheeses (Brown makes that connection; see below), looks like a Surrealist reading and research method. Without the Browns' openness to mixing cheese with war histories, how else could one find out that "well aged, let us say up to a century" Parmesan becomes the "Rock of Gibraltar of cheeses," or that the "so-called" "Spanish cheese" was used as "a barricade by Americans in Nicaragua almost a century ago."[53]

Brown's world traveling, publishing, rare book and bibelot collecting, food-loving adventurism does not suggest that the literary and avant-garde activities were necessarily dilettantish or unrelated domains. The cookbooks discuss literary sources (from the Romans Cratinus and Apicius to Milton to Lewis Carroll to Jack London), allude to avant-garde movements and artists (including Constantin Brancusi), and track arcane etymology and allusions through what would now be called a cultural study or genealogy (e.g., that Thomas Jefferson brought the first macaroni machine into America). More important, the tradition of cookbooks, among the avant-garde of the time, was not peripheral—consider for example the cookbooks from Brown's friend Alice B. Toklas or *The Futurist Cookbook*. The Browns' cookbooks may have received less attention than its due because of a certain logic prevalent in art, literary, and visual studies that sees the cookbook, recipe, and party throwing as marginal feminine forms versus the serious works of an artist.

Recent scholarship has resurrected the importance of cooking in the avant-garde from the Futurists to the Eat Art Movement (co-founded by Daniel Spoeri and Antoni Miralda in the early 1960s to create a synergy between art and food, and soon after joined by Dorothée Selz), but that scholarship does not mention the Browns.[54] Against this trend to keep the palate and palette separate, even as they homophonically commingle on the plate, the Browns mention that Lewis Carroll was "a gallant thrower of tea parties and indefatigable *snacker* who sang chiefly of turtle soup, lobster quadrilles, and walruses ganging up with carpenters to gorge on helpless oysters."[55] They go on to press the point more firmly by concluding that, "[J]udging from the feverish way Surrealist surprises are sprung on us at ritzy hostess tray parties, where snacks now come not singly but in courses, astride toothpicks, wrapped in blankets, and on horseback, we're beginning to doubt that there's a Boojum of difference between a Snark and a Snack."[56] They include a version of Carroll's "Hunting of the Snark" with the word "snack" substituted for "snark" (a Surrealist strategy of composition) to surprisingly convincing results that conclude the poem with the following lines:

> You boil it in sawdust; you salt it in glue:
> You condense it with locusts and tape:
> Still keeping one principal object in view-
> To preserve its symmetrical shape.[57]

It parodies catering guides and instructions explaining how to produce symmetrical *hors d'oeuvres* and alludes to a Surrealist scene and reading strategy via substitution.

The *bon vivant*'s literary lifestyle, during the first two-thirds of the twentieth century, saw rich foods and decadent cookbooks as part of the scene. For example, it was appropriate for Bob Brown's last food book,

The Complete Book of Cheese (1955), to include an Introduction by a literary jack-of-all-trades, Clifton Fadiman (poet, scholar, storyteller, reporter, quiz-show host, Introduction writer to myriad books, and more). Fadiman, a longtime friend of the now-infamous quiz-show cheat Charles Van Doren (who collaborated with Fadiman on a poetry anthology), was one of the best-known public intellectuals in the 1950s. Fadiman saw highbrow literary pursuits on the same continuum with appearing on television and being a being a turophile (i.e., a lover of cheese). Fadiman confesses, in the opening of his Introduction to Brown's book on cheese, that he too collected notes on around 500 varieties of cheese, including Chinese soybean cheese, *hoi poi.*

He begins his Introduction with a piece of music including the lyrics to Heigh-O the der-ry O: "The cheese stands a-lone, The cheese stands a-lone, Heigh-O the derry-O! The cheese stands a-lone." The Browns saw themselves as connoisseurs of all fine things that "stand alone," "gifts of God which have filled [them] with most joy," from food and wine to literature and cutting-edge art.[58] The Browns wrote essays about qualities, using many literary citations and historical or mythological allusions (e.g., they cite James Fenimore Cooper on the Otsego fish, Izaak Walton's *Compleat Angler* on cooking pike, and Jack London's recipe for *slumgullion*), rather than something that would resemble scholarship as later specialists who generally use quantitative evidence (e.g., economic data, statistics, biology, chemistry, etc.) and definitive historical documentation (e.g., archival proof, social contexts).[59] Natural histories and cultural studies usually expressly avoid literary allusions (unless as pretty ornamentation or to dismiss them as mythologies or incorrect). Looking for the viand, a particularly tasty dish, may have faded with Brown's generation and appeared to a later vanguard in the late 1960s and '70s, as merely a decadent bourgeois pastime. Because Bob had already drawn an analogy between politics and beer drinking, the Browns now wanted to make the case that preparing a delicious meal, a passion for food and cooking, the poetic reveries a viand might inspire, and an interest in social history of what we ate were political.

The Browns saw themselves in line with writers about food who did not avoid classification or clarity but used analogies and allusions as part of the argument. They used poetic prose, analogies, and metaphoric descriptions—not simply as ornamentation but to express their absurd personal joys. They wrote like readers showing their path of discovery rather than obscuring it in scientific justification. Here, for example, are Fadiman's suggestions for classification.

> The eye of the turophile may consider the eighteen basic varieties of cheese or the thousand variations on those varieties. In either case, he tries to classify. He may arrange them according to their resistance to life's onslaught: yielding, such as the chaste cream, the mold-maturing Camembert, the bacteria-ripened Roquefort; firm, such as Gorgonzola or Münster; obdurate, such as Parmesan. Or, with André Simon [the nineteenth-century author of the book *Food*], he may grade them by the degree of their aggressiveness: the gentle Petit Suisse, the strong Roquefort, the brutal Limburger or Marolles. Or he may borrow the late Edward Bunyard's [writer, epicurean, and rose garden expert] division, based on their poetical style: the romantic cheese, the Brie, given to excess, evento tears; the classic cheese, such as Stilton, growing like Nestor nobler as it ages.[60]

Bob quotes Robert Benchley, who talks of "literary and munching circles in London," proposing a memorial to Stilton cheese, and how "T. S. Eliot does not think that anyone would look at a monument, but wants to establish a Foundation for the Preservation of Ancient Cheeses."[61] This seems funny, in part, because cheese seems to have an ironic air attached to it as in cheesy, or cloying over-the-top sentimentality, but also a triviality inappropriate for monuments or foundations. Skeptics referred to the boat the *Monitor* as "a cheese box on a raft."[62] The smell of cheese can stir a riot as some "early Wisconsiners" staged a "Limburger Rebellion in Green County, when people rose in protest against the Limburger caravan that was accustomed to park in the little town of Monroe . . . They threatened to stage a modern Boston Tea Party and dump the odiferous bricks in the river" because "five or six wagonloads were left ripening in the sun" in the middle of the town. Soon, the Limburger was stored underground.[63] Yet, connecting it to an endless web of literary, historical, and cultural allusions, Bob Brown's encyclopedic Surrealism—as if he had cross-referenced a giant library's sources—makes cheese a hero and an analogy for political and cultural change. Livarot is described as "decadent" and "the very Verlaine of them all," and Brown quotes his "free translations" of a Victor Meussy poem in which "Livarot gesticulates / Or Weeps like a child."[64] Brown himself often cannot quite believe the glorification of cheese, and some of the citations seem even more anachronistic more than half a century after Brown quoted a review from *The New Yorker* of May 6, 1950. The reporter, Sheila Hibben, wrote about the arrival of a Swedish cheese with a French name, Crème Chantilly, as "enthusiastically as Brillat-Savarin would have greeted a new dish, or the

Planetarium a new star"; she called it a "historic event" and approvingly quoted the maker's own slogan, "a very special product that has never been made on this earth before."[65]

Just as the Surrealists spoke of recovering the uncanny in the everyday, rather than inventing a fairy tale Brown presents the evidence in a way that combines sober objectivity—"Napoleon is said to have named [Camembert]" in honor of the tiny town where he first tasted it—with possibly apocryphal highlights (e.g., Napoleon "kissed the waitress who first served it to him") and something mistaken for fantasy if not actually true (e.g., "a statue stands today in the market place to honor Marie Harel who made the first Camembert"). He then uses poetic coincidence "Camembert rhymes with beware" as a helpful way to remember "if you can't get the *veritable* don't fall for domestic imitation or any West German abomination such as one dressed like a valentine in a heart shaped box" for these are "tasteless, chalky with youth, or choking with *ammoniacal* gas when old and decrepit."[66] This essayistic style is still common in cookbooks, perhaps lacking only the richness of allusions and playfulness. The popular how-to genre, including cookbooks, demands bite-sized lists, advice or rules of thumb, and surprising combinations. This kind of art-of or how-to book, championed by Michel de Certeau decades later as a model of social science, fascinated Bob and explains his interest in machines, directions, and recipes.

The Browns often use a poetic list in the context of iterations, substitutions, and misunderstandings. Once again, it is, in one context, simple, clear language about a mundane fact of how to spell the name of an Italian dessert, and the ingredients of that dessert. What it becomes is a kind of visual incantation (because it is not clear that the different spellings would produce different pronunciations).

> This is the classic Zabaglione we Browns learned to make (and to spell, as well) in a small Gardonne inn of sublime cookery, nearly twenty years ago. But there are many versions, including a similar fluffy cream used as a pudding sauce, with half Madeira and half rum in place of the Marsala, or with a mixture of vanilla and sherry. And the difficult name in its travels has been Americanized to Sabayon, defined variously as a "custard," "a kind of egg punch," "a Russian wine sauce," and with the sugar left out, a "savory sauce." Everything in the butler's pantry has gone into it—French cognac with sauterne, up to white wine flavored with kirsh. And it is still spelled any old way—Zabilione, Saboyant, Zabajone, Zabione and

> Sabiagone. But however you misspell it, the Americanized Sabayon Sauce ingredients have been standardized to: 2 egg yolks, 2 tablespoons sugar, 1/2 cups white wine and 4 tablespoons Marsala, Malaga or Madeira.[67]

And, then the Browns follow up that discussion with a few recipes including "Pierre's Frozen Zabaglione."

At least one critic saw the frivolity and often "very entertaining reading" in the Browns' cookbooks as an insidious masquerade for their Communist propaganda.[68] M. C. Phillips, the co-editor of the *Consumers' Digest*, wrote an exposé of one of their more consumer-oriented work, *Most for Your Money Cookbook*, in which she respected the Browns' worldwide search for good food but warned readers of their dangerous advice and propaganda. The consumer magazine began as a progressive organization testing and rating products as well as lobbying for more consumer protections and publishing bestselling and influential exposés on the way—for example, corporations used consumers as guinea pigs, especially in the early 1930s. Big business and advertisers took aim at the consumer movement, and soon it was difficult to place advertising in magazines. Anti-consumer groups started a campaign in books, articles, and advertisements to make fun of Consumers' Research and to accuse them of being Communists.

In 1935, the Consumers' Research group split over a strike and formation of a union among the workers, and the now-better-known Consumers Union formed from the disaffected striking union members (the group that currently publishes *Consumer (Union) Reports*); the new group dropped the possessive apostrophe from *Consumers'* when they split. The group that remained with *Consumers' Digest* quickly reframed their politics as rightwing. M. C. Phillips and her co-editor husband, Frederick Schlink, felt that Communists orchestrated the strike in an effort to take over their organization. The acrimony and lasting grudge against the Consumers Union tainted all of the subsequent work by Phillips and Schlink, who had founded Consumers' Research. The product research necessitated an independent laboratory to test products outside of corporate control and influence, and up until the split the Consumers' Research lab were being accused of being poison pen Communists themselves because of their efforts to conduct objective product research. After the split, they immediately sought to expose Communist evil and to become apologists for corporate neglect. To this day the *Consumers' Digest* has a cozier relationship with the corporations whose products it tests, by getting com-

M. C. Phillips saw the frivolity and often "very entertaining reading" in the Browns' *Most for Your Money Cookbook* as an insidious masquerade for their Communist propaganda.

panies to donate products, than *Consumer Reports*, that dropped both the plural form and the possessive apostrophe, which buys the products like a regular consumer. In any case, *Consumers' Digest* became a forum for Phillips and Schlink to expose Communists and Communist propaganda especially if their targets were associated with the Consumers Union organization (made up of their former employees, testers, and engineers). Because of Schlink and Phillips's efforts, the House Committee on Un-American Activities initially had C.U. on its list, but in the early 1950s it removed them. It was in that context, in 1940, that Phillips belatedly exposed the Browns' book *Most for Your Money Cookbook*, published in 1938. The Browns published that book with the Communist-sympathetic

Modern Age Books, but the later *Look Before You Cook* (1940) was published by the Consumers Union and must have caught Phillips's eye, as it would once again confirm her paranoid suspicions that C.U. was filled with Communists.

Phillips began her review by describing her sleuthing to find out more about the Browns and their book. First, she heard a speech by the advertising manager of the *Christian Science Monitor* that described the book as "bald Communistic propaganda," but because the speaker did not mention any names, she had to keep searching. She found a brief mention of the book as pro-Soviet and anti-capitalist in the then–right-leaning *American Mercury*, where Bob Brown had published earlier in the 1930s when H. L. Mencken and George Nathan were still editing the magazine. Phillips also explained how she figured out which company (still in business), specializing in cleaners and polishes, had given away the book as a premium, raising her suspicions that Communists were in the advertising business too. Turning to the book itself, she found a "decided bias" of the "'proletarian' ideals of the U.S.S.R."[69] She seemed particularly upset that the Browns thought the pure juice fruit drinks in the Soviet Union were the "best in the world," because the bottler whom the Browns meet in the U.S.S.R. tells them that when he worked for Tsarist-era companies before the revolution, he used to water down the juices, but now the "proletarian" bottling system served the proletariat pure fruit juice. In contemporary culture, U.S. consumers, not Communists, advocate for high standards for fruit drinks; businesses respond in advertisements for "100% pure fruit juice." In the mid-1930s there were many American apologists for Stalinist purges and deniers of famines, most prominently Walter Duranty, and one might argue that the Browns fit that mold, but they focus on fruit juices and haggling with a vegetable seller, not show trials.

Phillips collected a series of similar quotes to build her convincing case. She turned to a discussion of berries in which the Browns discuss how they "always ask the seller to turn them out in his cupped hands or pour them into another box to show you that the bottom ones are fair-sized, sound and dry, not mildewed, unpalatable runts. Naturally, you'll have to allow a little for those packed far down out of sight, since *cheating has become an accepted practice in our competitive society*."[70] Phillips then pointed out, ironically, that "The Russians, one assumes, never cheat, never take over smaller countries by force of arms or shotgun elections where one votes 'yes'—or else."[71] The logical fallacy that equates warning buyers beware when buying raspberries with totalitarian Stalinist politics and imperialism seems like a stretch; the Browns were blindly sympathetic to the

Soviet system during the era of the worst atrocities, but this quotation from the cookbook simply suggests consumer consciousness. Phillips then turned to another quotation that had also raised the hackles of the speaker from the *Christian Science Monitor* in which the Browns appeared to offer a direct comparison between the economic systems of the Soviets and the Americans. "By way of contrast, when we lived in Moscow, grocery clerks who had nothing to fear would give us exact weight, cutting a last snip of bread to balance the scale precisely at 1 kilo. With nothing to gain or lose in non-profit commerce, we got full value—to a kopek."[72]

For Phillips, the quote she selected proved that the Browns thought the Soviet Union was, in their words, "a place where the prevailing customs in buying and selling are immeasurably superior to those in the United States," but the passage appeared in a paragraph on haggling with sellers in New York City. The Browns explained that they entered into bargaining by being informed about common practices and by kidding with the produce dealers they knew. The dealers then explained that they could not make a profit because of the competition in the market, where customers won't buy without a low price, so they skimmed off, in one case, an eighth of a pound of mushrooms from a one-pound purchase. To prove their good will, the dealers then threw in a "a couple of tiny button mushrooms to show their hearts were in the right place" even if they never actually sold a full pound even with the additions.[73] The conclusion of these anecdotes is not to once again celebrate the Soviet system but to advise the reader that now the Browns, "by way of self protection, keep a reliable spring scale in the kitchen drawer and it's paid for its cost over and over. And the best part of it is, our local dealers know that the scale is there and that's a healthy threat that pays dividends in more food for our money."[74]

The Browns were painfully aware that, in the mid-1930s, "a third of the average family income goes for food," and another 40 percent went toward shoes and clothing, unlike contemporary American budgets in which food accounts for less than 10 percent of the average family income (and nearly half of that percentage is spent at restaurants) and food and clothing account for around 6 percent.[75] Of course even now, the poorest families spend a far greater percentage of their income on food, around 25 percent. Part of the reason for these large percentages in the midst of the Great Depression was that the average family was not consuming and desperately struggling to avoid repossession of appliances and houses bought on credit with draconian terms, so the percentage for food and clothing was high, and other expenses and commodities are now relatively expensive (e.g., oil, gas, cars, medicine, etc.), especially compared with food and clothing. Household debt, few consumer protections, and the lack of government jobs and health programs made the situation even worse. The Browns advocated for the luxuriant "most" with less.

The Browns, in their cosmopolitanism, discussed where to get the best quality and value by advocating many national market customs, not just the Soviet customs. For example, in another cookbook, the Browns advised their readers to shop for olive oil at the Italian markets because "Italo-Americans refuse to be swindled with the cheap substitute."[76] Even when they recommended Soviet-style food, they usually described the national custom and often focused on what Phillips would, most likely, have considered bourgeois tastes.

> Open-faced red caviar sandwiches or canapés, Soviet style, are just the thing to sell at a money-raising organizational party, for they cost but a cent apiece and keep everybody happy and coming back for more, not minding a bit that the appetizing saltiness creates a thirst that keeps the bartender busy. Buy whole loaves of Russian black bread and cut it as thin as you can, for thus it goes best with caviar. Be careful not to break the orange-colored salmon eggs, but preserve them intact by using a little wooden spoon or paddle to transfer them from package and strew them over the bread. Open sandwiches covered with minced hard-cooked egg white and minced onion, with a sprinkling of the egg yolk pressed over through a sieve, will disappear too, but only because the taste of these combines so well with the caviar.[77]

The Browns' perspective on including caviar in their recipes had to do with their primary concern, to demonstrate that luxurious cuisine had a place in every kitchen, not just the kitchens of the rich:

> The fact that the rich will pay up to fifteen dollars a pound for the fanciest of caviar does not keep New York's East Side from enjoying just as much festivity on the toothsome red variety which comes out of an open can for thirty cents a pound. The very same anchovies that keep company with orchids and diamonds find their way to every Italian worker's table, but they are bought by weight out of barrels and twenty-pound tins, at a reasonable cost. These three gourmet treats can be enjoyed by all who will take the trouble to shop for them in the groceries, delicatessen and fancy food shops which abound in modest foreign neighborhoods.[78]

Once again, the Browns wanted to challenge a "false notion of elegance" that focused more on

> special forks for salad, bread and butter knives and tiny ice cream shovels, just one silly tool after another with which to toy with miniature "courses." So nowadays people who can least afford it will start a dinner, especially if there's company, with half a pound of assorted synthetic sausage from the delicatessen, followed by a thin soup, maybe more costly because it's out of cans, then an entree before the regular meat dish, and always a characterless salad with a dab of bottled mayonnaise, probably made of cottonseed oil, and finally a fancy dessert and coffee.[79]

Phillips missed this distinction between advocating for the best quality regardless of national origin and dispensing with formalities that have nothing to do with the quality or value of the food. The Browns had a more nuanced notion of economics in their recipes to "stretch the food dollar by countless culinary tricks, all of which are appetizing, healthful and interesting."[80]

Phillips then turned her investigation to the Browns' biographies and their previous, noncookbook publications, with Bob "the militant" of this "pro-Soviet family."[81] She ran off the list of evidence: Bob's work on the editorial board of *The Masses*, representative of *Preslit* (the literary service of the Soviets), living at "the very left" Commonwealth College, radical poet and manifesto writer. She identified "well-known communist writers" signing Bob's call for resisting "the influence of bourgeois ideas in American literature and against the imprisonment of revolutionary writers and artists."[82] The fact of Bob's Communist sympathies does not necessarily support Phillips's major claim that the "ideology of Communism rears its head frequently in the *Most for Your Money Cookbook*," in part because Phillips cherry-picked all of the citations to the Soviet system of government and ignored the larger issues that fit neatly within her own pro-consumer perspective. Further, she dismissed the Browns' apparent product placement in their recommendations as puffery "just like any writer hired by a 'capitalistic' magazine." She correctly noted: "When this sort of thing appears in a promotional book or publicity release for a big commercial company, there is likely to be considerable hullabaloo in the left-wing press about the wickedness of commercial propagandists working on concealed subsidies."[83] Given how she began her exposé by mentioning that a company selling cleaners and polishes sent the book to customers as a premium, one might assume that the Browns were as much, if not more, commercial propagandists and advocates of "exotic and sophisticated dishes" as Communists.[84] Phillips did highlight the key aspect of Bob's contradictory life as she scoffed at the Browns' misguided sophistication (e.g., including tarragon and shallots in a recipe when the average American wage-earning worker would not have access to these spices) with the overriding advocacy of a multicultural cosmopolitanism that promoted some excellent Soviet products (e.g., red caviar) alongside their promoting Mazola Oil, Herb Ox, and George Washington Aces coffee in American markets. Phillips correctly noted that their recipes were often exotic, but she seemed condescending toward the potential readers who would have more plain tastes and reject the "foreign" tastes in the book. Phillips's overdetermined criticism had no effect on the Browns' ability to sell cookbooks, nor on the topics they chose to write about. By the time the review and exposé appeared, Rose and Bob were floating down the Amazon, and Cora had died.

The Browns' major concerns had much less to do with traditional politics than with the quality of food available in markets. For example, they wrote, "Parsley is popular only because the green grocers always have it. Chervil is better, especially in cream soups."[85] And, they noted, "Commercial noodles, unless purchased at a specialty shop where they are supplied fresh every day, are usually too dry for the discriminating noodle eater."[86] They did try to encourage class, or at least economic, consciousness, but much more often, and more intensely, they wanted to encourage food consciousness and an awareness of the social and aesthetic aspects of eating and drinking. The food consciousness included discussions of "the ghastly exposé of certain commercial ice creams and similar frozen products," which led the Browns to argue that "such foods should be under the same control as our milk supply, since they are subject to the same adulterations, and are carriers of typhoid and other dangerous disease germs." From this situation, they concluded that the "legal standards for the manufacturers are undoubtedly too low and inspection to enforce existing laws has proved inadequate"; it sounds more like Michael Pollan, the food critic, than Joseph Stalin.[87]

In a later cookbook published in 1940, the Browns explained the key context to the processed food problem by referencing the publisher of that cookbook, the Consumers Union, and referencing the "tests of over forty bulk and packaged frozen creams and milks, made in New York City and probably typical of most cities," rather than revolutionary politics. The tests "revealed that many of the well known makers are guilty of slick practices to defraud the public and of permitting unwholesome conditions of manufacture. In the case of bulk ice creams, the chance of un-cleanliness of the distributor doubles the health risk."[88] Because "some canned foods are simply terrible" compared with what anyone can cook from scratch "simply and cheaply," the Browns advised their readers to "be as canny as the canners themselves."[89] There is a politics here, one that might in contemporary times be called DIY, Buy Local, or Slow Foods. They wanted to appeal to a wide swath of consumers, from the "can opener cook" to "one who makes an exciting artistic enterprise," and often praised government efforts, like those of the U.S. Department of Agriculture.[90] They narrated their own "buy local" efforts as their personal history of buying bread:

> When we lived in Manhattan we could always find a neighborhood baker whose foreign trade demanded honest, flavorsome loaves made of proper hard-wheat flour. . . . When we moved to Staten Island a few years ago and found no neighborhood baker, we were served by five big commercial bread manufacturers, in succession . . . . a procession of sellers of inferior baked goods . . . we tried a glut of chain store "breads" . . . our bakers have been carried so far by their greed that they have almost destroyed our normal appetite for bread.[91]

Given this lack of bakers, they also decided to bake their own bread as they continued to worry about the "hurried city workers" who grabbed what we now call fast food or a "lousy ham sandwich . . . with just a trace of ham paste blown on, and then a watery drink for a dime."[92] To contemporary ears, the Browns sound like Slow Food advocates, arguing against "foodless food" and for supporting "immigrant truck farmers, especially Italians, [who] have enriched our fresh vegetable scope enormously with such things as anise, artichokes, spaghetti, squash and broccoli. And the Chinese have given us bean sprouts, easy to grow in a big flat pan in the kitchen, and Chinese cabbage. Such domesticated importations, added to our own indigenous potatoes, tomatoes, and pumpkins, grown from coast to coast and climate to climate[,] give us a swell assortment at what should be fair prices the year around."[93] They repeatedly made the connection that consumer apprehension about advertising and the shoppers' pursuit of fair value led to more resources for extravagant fun (for the gravy of life) that might include "more food, or the theater, parties, tropical fish, flowers—any hobby out of which we get real refreshment."[94] To get to the gravy, they warned their readers to treat "the seductive voices of food advertisers" like that of the Biblical serpent, and to head the advice of the Consumers Union.[95]

In all of these supposedly radical cookbooks, the Browns continued to push for a do-it-yourself approach to food; specifically, they championed the idea that self-reliant, make-do personalities need not live ascetics' lives. M. C. Phillips was particularly worried about this perspective because it led to what Phillips considered dangerous advice to, for example, learn as much as possible about mushrooms so that one could find them on trips to the country: advice that can prove fatal. Counter to Phillips's simplistic and dull-witted reading of the cookbook's politics, the Browns succinctly summarized their politics and ideas about value by explaining that "Much of the value of food is lost by serving it dully."[96] In fact, contemporary audiences will find the cookbooks' suggestions and recipes decadent and crude (sometimes verging on the cannibalistic) rather than inspired by a Communist ideology. The Browns introduced a recipe to cook monkey meat by explaining that there is "no reason why [monkeys] should be spared from our carnivorous appetites."[97] They recognized that eating exotic birds, like parrots, macaws, and parakeets, might appear "strange" to outsiders, but they also seemed immune to that skepticism. On the one hand, they explained matter-of-factly that "if old and talkative, as parrots usually are since some species live as long and get as garrulous as human beings, it sometimes takes as long as five hours to cook them tender."[98] On the other hand, every time their Brazilian cook had served a well-dressed camouflaged bird of unknown origin, they would check with concern the old parrot's cage to make sure the bird was still there.

Bob's exotic adventures included eating cactus sandwiches during the Mexican Revolution and horsemeat sandwiches in France, but never anything he could pet, including goats, even though goat meat makes "the most popular sandwich in all Mexico."[99] The Browns also made regular American fare more interesting by, for example, dressing "a hot dog Panhandle style by splitting it open and pouring red hot chili the full length, to make a real smoldering Chili Con Carne Sandwich" or eating the then-exotic to some in the northern United States "tamales and enchiladas wrapped in crisp tortillas to take the place of sandwiches."[100]

The Browns saw themselves as emulating

> a life-loving genius [as Constantin] Brancusi gets as much kudos in Paris for his creative cooking as for his modern sculpture. He assembles whatever he has in the cupboard when guests arrive, and

> beginning with a deftness worthy of a *cordon bleu* molds and slaps the ingredients together into an original dish which is said never to be a duplicate of any other he has made. He, like so many other artists, is a one-dish-is-a-meal cook, and, when that dish is done, everyone eats of it ecstatically. And because of such creative achievements, cooking in France has been officially recognized as the eighth art.[101]

Whether one agrees with their politics or not, the Browns, with Bob leading the charge, thought of themselves as championing life-loving art of everyday life wherever in the world they found it, ate it, and drank it. In terms of the politics and poetics of the cookbooks, this passage from one of the cookbooks is telling:

> Last Thanksgiving the whole Brown family sat down to a turkey dinner with all the fixings—the most modest of which was a tureen of buttered string beans—and everything was enjoyed unto the third and fourth generations and helpings thereof. Sylvie, Cora's great-granddaughter, aged four, watched as her plate was carefully prepared with juicy bits of drum stick, some mashed yam sluiced with rich giblet gravy, a dab of every vegetable, and appetizing bits besides including spiced pear and cranberry jelly. She possessed herself in patience until the napkin was knotted in place and the plate set before her. Surveying the many good things, she made a quick choice, jabbed her fork into the beans with a forthright gesture, appraised the mouthful, wiped a buttery trickle from her chin, beamed around at everybody and gave a little squeal of delight—"Oh, I just love string beans, don't you, Bob?"[102]

The Browns lived for those fleeting moments of delight created, in this example, by a four-year-old speaking like a sophisticated gourmand. In the midst of their cosmopolitan adventures and Soviet sympathies, the Browns celebrated the commoner's rural life far from the maddening crowd. Drawing on Bob's earlier popular folksy short stories about rural life, they encouraged a DIY sensibility that is as American as apple mash. Bob described "the homemade hilarity that surrounds the little brown jug and the old cider barrel" that seems far from their life among the expatriate avant-garde or their world travels.[103] Bob's Introduction to a collection of homebrew recipes recounted a memory from his teenage years which insinuated that Bob had grown up in a folksy rural setting:

> The tinkle of drinks in mulberry tinted old glass amid the twittering of Kentucky cardinals and Colonels, the snap of champagne cider

> out of the cellar barrel, hiss of wine in the making and promise of cozy winter nights when you're snowed in and chuckling over that boyhood trip to town on the broad back of the plow-horse for a thrilling Cincinnati, half beer and half pop. And the ladies, God bless 'em, and their hooked rugs and quilting bees; no alewives they, but dainty makers of dandelion wine from blossoms gathered in the wane of the April moon and sippers, too, of all sorts of homemade berry and fruit cordials, with juicy slabs of plum cake and careful jockeying for one another's treasured recipes. So here are some high spots in homemade hilarity—the kind that made Great Aunt Agatha dance on the table and kick the lamp over—about the time of the Chicago fire.[104]

The homemade hilarity and rich foods were catching up to Bob, and William Carlos Williams, acting as his doctor, not as a poet, and Cora, his mother, encouraged him to slow down and dry out; so, by the time he traveled down the Amazon in the early 1940s, he was on the wagon, but still eating the most exotic foods he could find. Williams found a surgeon at New York Hospital, and Brown's ulcer was treated.

The years they spent on the small farm on Staten Island were due in part to Bob's health problems and the long time it took for him to recover from them. Cora was also in the last few years of her life and could not easily travel. Through it all, they continued to publish, travel, and taste. In New York, they had reunions with Orrick Johns, Allen Norton, Peggy Baird Cowley (the ex-wife of the chronicler of the expatriate writers, Malcolm Cowley), Tom Bevan, and Djuna Barnes (who returned to the States just before the Browns left for Brazil again). Bob and Djuna had written for the *New York Telegraph* years before when the rate was $7 a column; now she was making $7,000 for one short story. Bob also continued his work for the Writers' Union and League of American Writers, which he had helped found, and he had tried to get funds from Gelett Burgess for the fledgling union (Gelett had already lost all his life savings in a co-op building for the earlier Authors' League of America). He worked with Parker Tyler, a writer who had collaborated with Charles Henri Ford, on building the Writers' Union. When Cora died in 1939, Rose and Bob decided to travel again, this time to the Amazon, and to write about food, customs, fauna, and flora in a genre that they had not yet explored: the travel memoir.

Brazilians call the effort to assuage an indefinable longing *matar saudades*—literally, to kill the longings. To assuage their *saudade*, the Browns ate with the enjoyment of learning a new name, a new word, a new pleasure, a delicacy one longs to taste again. They funded their travels by selling story treatments in Hollywood.

7

Saudade and Going Home Again

The Amazon, Hollywood, Brazil, and Manhattan, 1941–59

The only things in life I am not sure of
Are established names, Recognized words . . . .

—*Bob Brown, from "A Soft Sweet Name" (poem),* Tahiti, *1915*

In 1942, with Carmen Miranda's *The Gang's All Here* in production and promising to be a big hit, Hollywood producers, eager to make more movies with Brazilian characters or settings, decided to send Bob and Rose Brown down the Amazon to generate ideas for movies. Producers knew Bob from the pulp fiction writing heydays, and they also knew of his connections to Brazil. As Cora had passed away a few years earlier, the couple was eager to return to Brazil, where they had lived from 1919 to 1927, to find new adventures. They arranged to travel along the Amazon River in a deal with movie studios and as "good neighbor ambassadors" for the U.S. government, resulting in the publication of *Amazing Amazon* in 1942.[1] They funded their travels down the Amazon, in part, with an advance on the eventual book and with Bob's profits from an uncredited Hollywood movie treatment for the comedy *Nobody's Baby* (1937). That story, made into the movie produced by the Hal Roach production team, illuminated aspects of the Browns' lives, some tragic and some comedic. With no money, the main characters try to make ends meet by hawking their creative talents; they shuttle babies and children among parents and guardians and assume multiple identities. The comedic discombobulations were partially drawn from Bob's life, although his creative contribution was likely limited to only a plotline; it was a plot that many other studio hacks turned into the eventual movie. For Rose and Bob, it was a paycheck and a ticket to the Amazon.

The Browns left the States as self-described "defunct rebels." During their research for the Amazon trip, the Browns discovered that Brazil had been a destination for emigrants, in the late nineteenth century, from a less civilized country: the United States. The defeated Confederate rebels fled to Brazil in the tens of thousands after the Civil War, not to create a new Confederacy but to flee for their lives (displaced people in a diaspora that complicates the term); Union soldiers also went to Brazil. Zora Neal Hurston recounts, in her autobiography *Dust Tracks on a Road* (1942), how "three white men" who had initially fled to Brazil, only to return a few years later, founded her hometown, Eatonville, Florida.[2] The Browns adopted a poem written by one of these "defunct rebels" as their theme song for their trip through the Amazonian region, and described themselves, in their book on the Amazon, as the new "defunct rebels."[3] While it is common to think of the Amazon as untouched by travelers from the outside, including the United States, before the turn of the twentieth century (and even until the last decades of the twentieth century), North Americans had, in a forgotten diaspora, arrived in the nineteenth century. The Rebels' descendants, now multiracial Afro-Brazilians, still live in Brazil today. They stage uncanny festivals in which the men dress as Confederate soldiers and the women dress in southern belle gowns. The Rebel battle flag, soldiers' uniforms, and women's dresses have meanings in these celebrations unrelated to the United States except to memorialize a diaspora.

In the context of leaving the United States because of frustrations with the lack of a continuation of progressive social change, they were fleeing another lost cause. The notion of defunct rebels, losers in history (whether deserving or not), complicates the usual celebration of displaced persons. Sometimes displaced persons engage in war, genocide, or oppression in the places they flee to or the homelands they return to conquer. Sometimes they leave so that they can practice a more repressive absolutist politics on their own communities. In addition to this mythology of the displaced as necessarily victims, histories of diasporas often portray the United States as the safe haven, the rescuer and protector (see, for example, the main exhibit at the Smithsonian Holocaust Museum); the United States is often the welcoming melting pot, rather than the nation that displaces people to other territories. Do we have names for those displaced to other lands? Is the word "expatriates" adequate to describe refugees from the States? Can we even imagine a moment in history when people illegally fled from the United States over the Mexican border and toward South America?

The Browns, who had in 1917 fled the United States with blacklisted writers and war resisters and landed eventually in Brazil, continued to

After their trip to the Amazon, the Browns donated their notable collection of ethnographic artifacts for exhibits in Brazil and at the Los Angeles Museum.

see that country as a safe haven of civilization and not as an escape to a primitive, simpler past. It was a return to civilization, not a vacation from civilization. Rose, in her study of the Brazilian ruler Dom Pedro II, describes his visit, in the late spring and summer of 1876, to an exhibit in Philadelphia that showcased the greatest technological advances and cultural achievements of the United States. Dom Pedro II also observed those achievements in the context of "how blind was the North American system of jails and penitentiaries, how cruel was their treatment of caring for the insane, and how forbidding were the half-measures taken to protect and educate freed slaves."[4] Rose made radical politics palatable for young adult readers in the United States.

In a similar way, the Browns, in their study of the supposedly savage Amazonians, commented that "it's easy to see how much more civilized they [the indigenous peoples of the Amazonian basin] are than we."[5] Comparing themselves to the indigenous people now seems in keeping

Rose and Bob mixed anecdotes about characters and places on their journey with lively cultural, political, and economic history.

with a multicultural attitude, but they wrote these comments in the early 1940s at a time when both Axis and Allied forces aggressively pursued imperialist goals often under the modern guise of a civilizing force. Their writings and adventures have some of the elements of the tourists' drive for collecting the exotic, but always with an appreciation of the unique and continuing history of the people and ecology they dealt with on their journey. They were self-aware and read the sociopolitical history back into their poetic reflections. Here is an earlier poem by Bob about Brazil from his collection of poems in his book *Nomadness*.

Saudades for Carioca
Tender tendrils of thought
fond fondling of words
lithe living of life
Color
rainbows dancing
across lacy waves
[. . .]
native raw-eyed rum
shrimps and cod-fish
mangoes and Antarctica beer.[6]

In *Amazing Amazon*, the Browns describe a young woman who graciously lends a hand to her hosts and sleeps near them; the young woman finds herself protected by "fireflies tied by their antennae to her hair; so any movement of her head during the night, would illuminate her and anyone in the hammocks around her."[7] To illuminate the traveler's every move instead of making her invisible seeks to reorient tourism, not as a punishment, but as a poetic opening. The Browns, still the life of the party, told stories, joked with the men on the boat, ate, took *siestas*, and wrote. Their memoir about their journey includes the expected anecdotes about characters they meet on their travels, but mixed unexpectedly with cultural history not of the kind of systematic boredom found in more standard travel guides. Here is the Browns' description in *Amazing Amazon* of one lunch: "Lunch at twelve consists of real meat soup with plenty of vegetables, then fish maybe caught through a hotel window, or a humpbacked turtle, although this is a rare food."[8] Of course, the image of catching lunch through the hotel window gives pause and once again suggests the Browns' strategy of including the social situation of a meal's production and consumption.[9] Then they go on to describe the actual meal. In one course, "Capybara, venison, wild duck and other occasional game come to the table, but we have chicken only two or three times a week, because the price is prohibitive [. . .] you can eat half a dozen cackleberries if you like, for 'cackle and come again' is the motto of this bounteous board where individual portions are unknown."[10] Again, personal economics and social customs of communal eating enter the conversation. The description of the last few courses connects the food to other customs. "Dessert consists of candied bananas, whipped up abacates or graviola, that heavenly fruit which our English cousins dub custard apple because it is otherwise unclassifiable to palates accustomed to Bird's custard and watery fruit salad to finish off a meal. There's other fruit, too, the best tasting mamão, papaya, in all the tropics, and that special green-skin banana you're supposed to cry for."[11]

After the meal, "having finished with fruit, coffee and toothpicks," the Browns explained how "you flop into the old string hammock for a couple of hours." They went on to explain that "Amazon travelers usually carry two different kinds of hammocks, a big cloth one from Ceara for all-night work and a lighter, cooler one for siestas. At three PM precisely, Monica, the first maid, wakes you with another demitasse."[12]

The Browns' stories meander, dense with detail, flowering into allusions and comparisons, erudite without pretension, evoking the feeling of amazing cocktail talk with multiple voices in the form of quotes from newspapers, books, songs, and passengers on their journey. The Browns sought to illuminate the lushness of the Amazon—not just the literal agricultural and biological diversity but also the cultural and racial complexity with its long history of interracial and multiracial people. The tropical ecology described by the Browns includes encounters with howling monkeys, *saracura* water birds, parrots, porpoises, egrets (*garças*), mosquitoes, and scorpions; one practical joke involved the crew's putting a live scorpion on Bob Brown's back and then rushing to get it off him before it could fatally strike. The crew and the Browns saw these parodic performances of the exotic and dangerous jungle as more about the encounter of tourists with those who stage the show. In this version, the crew made tourists and tourism the butt of the joke.

The Browns collected stuff like baby anteater skin ("we put andiroba oil on it to keep it from mildewing until we can get it tanned") or "straw covered bottles and bird-nest baskets."[13] They also recognized the exotic wonders of the place. "Parrots come in all sizes, colors and noises, from the great gaudy shrieking macaw through medium-size royal purple, mauve, and golden-headed louros who are terrific talkers."[14] They eat "salted Capybara . . . plus tapir, jaboti, alligator tail, both turtle and sea cow mixira [the manatee or sea cow's meat preserved in its own fat], parrot and smoked monkey, never did sink tooth in that mythical guanaco meat. Might as well ask for a unicorn steak . . . ."[15] At one point, a boat captain suggested a party. The menu included "a five gallon tin full of rich mixira—the kind made of sea cow, naturally, since turtle put up in toothsome mixira style is almost prohibitive in price these days."[16] Another passenger requested "a plate of toucan tongues." The captain concurred, adding how useful the tongues are "to suck up the turtle eggs." They describe eating *koro*, a "pale-colored grub" found in "rotting tree-trunks."[17] The grub is "a fat, cream colored creature, rather like a silkworm [and] the body spurted a whitish, fatty substance which I [Bob or Rose?] managed to taste after some hesitation; it has the consistency and delicacy of butter, and the flavor of coconut milk."[18] They never acted too squeamish but ate with the enjoyment of learning a new name, a new word, a new pleasure, a delicacy one longs for (e.g., *saudade*). The contemporary reader would choke on this menu for ecological and visceral reasons, but the cringe factor of eating grubs, parrots, manatees, or monkey brains might look familiar today in the context of reality TV programs.

Bob saw the adventure in terms of his research for Hollywood movies. For example, he thought about ways to consider turtle eggs, the size of ping-pong balls, as a weapon to stop villains, with an egg fight, in his potential action-adventure slapstick movie treatment. The Browns did not see their radical efforts as anathema to either writing slapstick for Hollywood or serving as "good neighbor ambassadors" in Brazil for the U.S. government. Even the Browns rarely mentioned the usually distinct aspects of their lives (e.g., the vanguardist poets and revelers, mass culture producers, and defunct rebels); when they did, they saw the avant-garde, in particular, as a reaction against popular culture. In practice, they did not position the avant-garde as completely opposed to either the popular front or popular culture. Likewise, they did not see their voracious collecting in Brazil as in conflict with their wanting to tell the sociopolitical history of the indigenous people's forced labor, diasporas, and genocides.

The Amazon River begins far inland, at the city of Manaus, where the Rio Negro and Rio Solimões meet. It is a place called the "meeting of the waters," and it is a famous natural wonder of the world. The two rivers have different colors that do not seem to mix for seven kilometers. At the mouth of the Amazon, the Browns described another mixing area where the "gray-brown Amazon pushes the blue Atlantic back in one place, and the blue rushes in to attack a charge of gray in another."[19] It is an allegorical, or at least sociopoetic, image of the way in which the Browns lived and visited Brazil and the Amazon. They flowed alongside their hosts. As if the river could talk and illustrate a sociopoetics, the river's route traced a way of traveling next to, besides, and together in very slowly giving up difference. In one of her children's books on the Amazon, Rose described how the children wait for the blue river before swimming. Instead of vainly trying to change the flow, they go with the flow.

In their cookbook on South American cuisine, the Browns include the following recipe:

> **Saudades *(Brazilian Longings)***
> Lightly beat 5 egg yolks with 1 cup sugar and knead in enough sifted *polvinho* to mold into small balls. Place these on an oiled board and bake until dry in a cool oven.

They explained, "Saudades is a word often heard in Brazil. It covers a whole lot of emotions, all the way from homesickness to a vague longing for sweets like these."[20] They offered a type of travel that allows for the longings usually effaced by the tour guide and happy tourists. The Browns' Surrealist approach to the river inflected their desire to illuminate the river's life as an involution, a web of linking practices, and masks. Brazilians call the effort to assuage an indefinable longing *matar saudades*—literally, to kill the longings.

Around the same time the Browns visited the Amazon, Claude Lévi-Strauss (1908–2009), who lived in Brazil from 1935 to 1939 while teaching sociology at the University of São Paulo, also visited, during his vacations, the people and cultures around the Amazon River and Manaus. Lévi-Strauss based all of his future ethnographic work on those visits. Lévi-Strauss may have known the Browns in Brazil. He mentions knowing a gourmand and book collector in São Paulo; the Browns were at the time well-known gourmands and book dealers and had their home in São Paulo, but Lévi-Strauss does not mention any names.[21] Whether they knew each other, or not, their works represent particularly apt examples of late modernist travelers and their concerns about diasporas. They both knew André Breton, and Lévi-Strauss exchanged letters with Breton about aesthetics and originality especially with regard to Brazil. How did the avant-garde influences change travel writing?

Just as Claude Lévi-Strauss realized that the sought-after pure encounter with the supposedly primitive folk was always already compromised, Bob's poetry, similarly, often skewers the guides, visitors, and travelers. A certain type of mainstream guide, like *Baedeker's*, is now what needs demythologizing. The Browns, much like Lévi-Strauss, see the Amazonian folk not as the primitive *Other* but as a model of diasporic civilizations. They join in the cultures, rather than romanticize a simpler life. Lévi-Strauss confessed, "I hate traveling and explorers" and explained that "Amazonia, Tibet, Africa fill the bookshops in the form of travelogues, accounts of expeditions and collections of photographs, in all of which the desire to impress is so dominant as to make it impossible for the reader to assess the value of the evidence put before him. Instead of having his critical faculties stimulated, he asks for more such pabulum and swallows prodigious quantities of it."[22]

Here is another earlier poem by Brown.

Guides

Guides with pimply faces
uncouth unbuttoned mouths and
leering lecherous slobbery eyes;
guides who spew upon the
beauty of everything seen
in their company.
Wordy, mouthy, mumbling guides:
"This is the great stone now
made of rock
right here very historic
the great stone
what they used then for that.
This is it
famous for centuries.
This is it, right here, sir!"
Guides with shifty dribbly glances
pointing smudgy fingers at
crystalline alabasters
nearly wearing out decrepit jokes
violating hallowed historic spots
sway-backed, bow-legged
sag-bellied, knock-kneed
coaxing, pleading
brow-beating, bullying
Guides
casting their bloated
hideous, besmirching shadows over all the
most beautiful places of the world.[23]

The nasty description seems more contemporaneous with our cynical era rather than from a time when mass tourism for the middle class was still considered romantic and relatively rare. One would expect a travel poem to unapologetically embrace and celebrate the important monument while cropping the image of the guide out of sight. Bob's poem gives a different view in the conventions and style of the form it parodies, as is evident in another of Brown's poems.

> ***Tourist Insurance***
> This simple instrument
> insures and guarantees
> your baggage
> or any part or parcel thereof
> properly labeled, invoiced,
> evaluated, catalogued, enumerated and
> initialed
> against any manner of accident of whatsoever nature
> which simply cannot possibly happen
> under any circumstances
> and specifically
> denies any and all responsibility
> once the baggage
> has left the
> alleged residence of the hereinbefore mentioned
> so-called believed-to-be traveler.
> Take it or leave it
> nothing whatsoever will be paid for the loss, breakage, leakage,
> theft or damage
> of/or, to/or, by/of, or/and any article in the baggage covered by
> this instrument.[24]

Modern writers, from a feminist vanguardist (Rose) and Imagist-Surrealist poet (Bob) to a radical anthropologist with strong connections to the Surrealists (Lévi-Strauss), sought to describe the politics of a situation like tourism and exploring, usually left invisible in both scientific and travelers' accounts. The experiments in poetry and art, especially in the relation to Imagism and Surrealism, led quickly, profoundly, and lastingly to a generation of poets and artists' conceiving of their lives in terms of a diasporic search for an internationalist and cosmopolitan everyday life. The Browns' writings, from the cookbooks to the visual poetry, were guides to popularize a way to eat, travel, and party: not as outsiders fascinated by quaint primitive customs but as participant-observers. They swallowed everything offered. Not as taxonomists, but poets. Not as tour guides, but hosts and guests. They traveled up the Amazon as longing *bricoleurs* looking for the poetic juxtaposition including the embedded social

Bob Brown, Hollywood story writer.

and political history, and potential futures, in the present moment. Every recipe and journey: an encounter with *saudade*.

When they returned to the United States they moved to Hollywood for less than a year to find more work writing for the movies. In 1937, Bob had sold a story treatment for the Hollywood comedy *Nobody's Baby*, and that led to interest among his old friends, now part of the fiction factory in Hollywood, for him to write more story ideas and treatments. Rose and Bob wrote five story treatments with the Amazon as the setting for potential movies, and they registered their plots with the Screen Writers Guild. They also met with Bruce Manning, whom they had known in New York and New Orleans, and who was now a writer, director, and producer at Universal Pictures of Deanna Durbin musicals. Manning offered Bob a job writing scripts and treatments, but the Browns thought they could do better freelancing. Manning at the time was starting work on a film initially directed by Jean Renoir but later credited to Manning. The movie characters' schemes, disguises, hiding, poverty (of Chinese orphans), and wealth (of a shipping magnate) make the story sound much like an adventure story—if not Bob Brown's, then from the fiction magazines like *Ladies' World* that Brown wrote for in the first two decades of the century.

Living in the Hollywood Hills, the Browns were also reminded of their friend Nathanael "Pep" West, who Bob thought would have been one of the greatest writers if he had lived longer. West had died in a car accident on his honeymoon. They had planned to have a party with Pep West (and West's soon-to-be brother-in-law S. J. Perelman). They learned of the accident two weeks before arriving in Hollywood. West had shared Brown's concern about censorship, especially after critics condemned West's language, and their letters to each other often told of the ironies of critics, who in everyday talk use the same words as West wrote, condemning the "vulgarity" in West's stories.

On their trip to the Amazon, the Browns had collected a notable collection of ethnographic artifacts and staged exhibits in Brazil (where they donated much of the collection), and at the Los Angeles Museum, where they had hoped to collaborate with Pep West on the catalogue. They published their travel book about their time in the Amazon and also compared sleeping in a hammock on the boat to sleeping in a luxurious Hollywood house. Rose had done interior decorating and design before, and in Hollywood she found a receptive market and also made their new house inviting and modern.

In Hollywood, they also partied with Sonya and Meyer Levin, the important novelist who would go on to write and produce movies, and Viola Brothers Shore, a mystery writer and scriptwriter. They had all known one another in New York. Both Meyer and Viola were also well known for publishing on Jewish themes. Bob thought of himself in his friendships with West, Perelman, the Levins, and Shore (never mind the earlier generation of radical Jewish writers like Max Eastman, Mike Gold, and others) as an honorary Jew in much the same way as he strongly identified with Brazilians, Europeans, Chinese, Mexicans, and especially African Americans. His world traveling, multiple careers, international tastes, cosmopolitanism, and elastic styles of writing all fueled his fluid identifications. In Hollywood, he saw himself once again in that mold of the Jewish radical writer even if he could never live up to Pep West's brilliance.

The Browns lived at 5816 Libby Way, a very short street off Canyon

Drive in the Hollywood Hills neighborhood. Although many involved in the film industry built their homes in the hills area, it was still relatively sparsely populated in 1941. Bob described their house as the nicest, if not the largest, one they had ever lived in anywhere in the world. It was built by a movie star in 1925, and "last occupied by John Garfield." One unnamed friend from their expatriate days joked that the house had two fine garages, but that they didn't even "own a car, not even a tire." The house had his and hers dressing rooms: Bob's done in "blue bath and cedar lined, Rose's pink tiled. There were clothes trees for both hats and shoes. Just a year before, they had slept in hammocks."[25] John Garfield, one of Hollywood's most respected actors in the 1930s and '40s, was one of Bob's favorite actors, especially in the boxing movies (e.g., *Body and Soul* and *They Made Me a Criminal*), and was a hero in the Brown household because of his Communist sympathies (he was later blacklisted). Bob and Rose Brown often described their feelings for Brazil by using the Portuguese word *saudade,* the not easily translated Brazilian emotion of haunting loss, yearning desire, and lingering emptiness that the English word "missed" fails to capture in mood, tone, or atmosphere. Even though they were able to float up and down the Amazon, they yearned to go back. When they heard about Orson Welles's planned film about Brazil and the Rio Carnival, they contacted the studio and the Washington bureaucrats organizing the film. John Hay "Jock" Whitney, millionaire and film producer, who advised the "good neighbor" programs, had approached Welles to do the film. At the same time, Nelson Rockefeller and the so-called Rockefeller Shop were also focused on projects in Latin America, and looking for writers to serve as "good neighbor ambassadors." The Browns were a perfect fit as they had already worked as "good neighbor ambassadors" on their trip up and down the Amazon, and they were recognized as authorities on the country and its culture. The program sought to prevent Brazil and other Latin American countries from allying with the Nazis (because Germans were well represented in Brazil), and on their trip a year earlier the Browns had encountered a change in the attitude of the Germans they met. The producers agreed to send the Browns along among a half-dozen researchers and advisors to Welles, but, as Bob's perhaps apocryphal story claimed, the government filled the last two available seats on Welles's plane to Brazil with a general and the general's assistant.

Nevertheless, the Browns soon moved back to their adopted homeland, where they had prospered for nearly a decade starting in the late 1910s and where they had left to travel around the world in the late 1920s. The Browns left Hollywood and moved back to Brazil. As soon as they returned to their twelve-acre jungle home in Petropolis, Brazil, which they had owned since the 1920s, a jungle home where monkeys howled at the mountain top, Rose started writing about the lush setting, history, and politics of her adopted country, and she eventually published five single-author books on Brazilian culture and history, all in the early 1940s, including three chapter books, *Two Children of Brazil*, *Two Children and Their Jungle Zoo*, and *Amazon Adventures of Two Children*; one social geography, *Land and People of Brazil*; and one biographical history, *American Emperor: Dom Pedro II of Brazil* (an Honor List Book from *Horn Book Magazine*).

In 1942, their movie treatments for Hollywood studios, registered with the Screen Writers Guild by both Rose and Bob Brown, included these synopses.

> No. 21134:—"Finger of God" (Date 2-5-42)
>
> Cadet hero, the only boy who escaped massacre of students on the Copacabana beach in the rebellion of 1922 (beginning of events that led to the present Brazilian political regime), flees to the United States, woos and marries American girl and brings her home to his family in Rio when he gets amnesty. Unknown to her he remains a revolutionary and his mysterious doings are misunderstood to her great unhappiness—story of married love with American wife trying to adapt herself to ways of her husband's country. At last all is out in the open—he goes off to fight in the final action of his political faction, is wounded and nursed back to health by wife. His side wins with present regime established, and wife at last understanding and happy. (Based on history that is now being lauded in Brazilian press and popular interest, far enough in past to eliminate any political objections. Lots of drama.)
>
> No. 21173:—"The Magic Hammock" (Date 2-11-42)
>
> Another fast Amazon comedy incorporating background of Bob Brown's "How I Sleep in a Hammock," published in December *Esquire*.
>
> No. 21399:—"the road to ruin—Mad Mary" (Date 3-18-'42)
>
> Set on the Madeira River, tributary of the Amazon. American doctor and Brazilian nurse furnish love interest against a background of the building of the Madeira-Mamore Railroad and the hospital at Porto Velho, with the lush Amazon jungle [to] furnish color and that astounding engineering accomplishment to pile up the drama. Particularly timely now, for the Brazilians are spending millions to

develop this territory through a government sponsored enterprise called *Central de Brazil.* And Colombia, Peru, Ecuador and Bolivia are all hot about their interests in Amazon transportation.

No. 21574:—"seeds of hope" (Date 4-13-42)

A story of American Civil War escapists who came to Brazil because they could still have slaves here. After a dramatic voyage they settled on wildland given to them by the Brazilian emperor, Dom Pedro II, and pioneered an alien and unexpected surroundings. An American girl and Brazilian boy carry the love story. Just as lush and romantic, but not as heroic as *Mad Mary*. Founded on historic facts.

No. 21736:—"Amazing Amazon" (Date 5-5-42)

Comedy in which an American correspondent and Brazilian girl chase each other the length of the Amazon with the [girl's] old-fashioned father, her nominal fiancé, and a second American girl furnishing the obstacles that make them miss each other everywhere, and an old foreign naturalist bobbing up between them with his eccentricities. Ending, a double wedding in Manaus. Journalist marrying Brazilian girl and her fiancé marrying American girl. We have Amazon music that could be worked into the gorgeous background.[26]

Because of the Browns' connections to the international movie industry, a Brazilian company approached Rose to make a film about their national hero Dom Pedro II, but it was never made. Dom Pedro was an intellectual emperor who sacrificed his own wealth and power to educate his people and to move the country toward democracy. Rose wrote eloquently and clearly about history and culture so that a wider audience, mostly in the States, could appreciate Brazil. Bob tended to the fruits and flowers grown on their plantation.

In Brazil, Bob and Rose described food in ways that embedded social economy and practices in the lush, detailed descriptions. They did not simply describe the food but showed how it appears in a web of relations, practices, and economies, rather than as distinct entities riven from their sociopoetic connections. Earlier they had written about the agriculture of Brazil.

A humble barefoot employee of the miracle tree's owner lops off a ripe healthy jacá bigger than our two heads and with a green hide as rough and tough as an alligator's. Like the fruit of the cacao, these jacás that look like gigantic breadfruit thrust straight out from the

Bob and Rose celebrating outside a bakery and confectionary business that their plantation supplied with fruits and sugar.

> trunk on very short stems; and as we look up the fat tree stem we see that it's studded with fruit in different degrees of ripeness.[27]

The anecdote starts with this description of picking the fruit and then moves to a description of its consumption. "A single jacá goes a long way, for it's eaten raw, seed by pulpy seed. Usually it's sold in portions of a few seeds covered with the slippery yellowish white pulp that's sickeningly sweet to our Northern palates. Deathly sweet!"[28] They connect the fruit to other tropical fruits. "It somewhat resembles the smaller chirimoya or fruta de Conde; only stickier and not nearly so parfumé, but the fruity pulp is sucked off the black shiny seeds in the same way."[29] Finally, they place the fruit at the center of a mercantile exchange, an economics lesson, and a social geography.

> If you should fall heir to a jacá weighing around fifty pounds, as we did, you could go to the nearest marketplace, sit down and sell it off three or four seeds to a clutch and end up after half a day with a pocketful of coppers. It's as popular throughout Brazil as chewing gum at home. Once in Rio we saw a sweet shop opened on a corner with one enormous jacá for its entire stock. Kids and oldsters flocked around like flies and we estimated that the take was a couple of dollars, which is a lot of money for just one fruit.[30]

Traditional travel guides might describe the look of a fruit, and cookbooks its taste, but the description of how to make money selling off parts of the fruit made the Browns' efforts something very different from a guidebook for the idle rich.

In the early 1950s, the modernist avant-garde community had dispersed with most of the writers and artists either working in isolation, passing away, or selling out. Bob had little money left, Rose had taken over the writing, and Bob began to reflect on his life filled with push and hustle. The dictator Getúlio Vargas, who had been in power since 1930, continued to run the country, either as an elected president or as an absolute dictator, in the 1940s and in the first years of the 1950s. In this context, Rose and Bob expected their waning days to end quietly with few changes planned; Bob tried to pitch an autobiography to publishers, but with no luck. The political tensions were rising, and Vargas made increasingly ultra-nationalist appeals to keep his overwhelming popular support. These nationalist moves angered the U.S. government, which likely bolstered Vargas's opponents. On top of these outside tensions, Rose became ill in 1952, and her health declined rapidly; she died in that same year. Bob had expected that Rose would outlive him. In the midst of Bob's grief, mourning, and inconsolable depression, the political situation in Brazil was deteriorating rapidly. The armed forces, with support from the United States, were looking for a way to end the decades of Vargas's power. In that climate, it would be difficult to sell the plantation and move. In the late summer of 1954, inevitably facing being forced to step down, Vargas committed suicide. This Socrates-like sacrifice and refusal to leave quietly would eventually lead to his supporters' gaining power, but in the interim the government froze major assets, like the Browns' plantation, and imposed other emergency restrictions on currency leaving the country; markets were disrupted. In a deep funk, Bob considered suicide. To assuage his longings, he wrote Rose love letters, *after* she died, in hopes that she might live on in a literary life. He felt completely alone for the first time. The political turmoil in Brazil meant that he could not sell the Petropolis plantation, and without those funds, he barely had enough money for a one-way trip to New York. Carlton, his son, wrote a relatively stiff and cold condolence letter about how bad Bob must feel, but not that Carlton felt any loss or sadness for Rose, who functioned as his mother for most of his childhood. Carlton urged Bob not to return to the United States.

Bob decided to return to Greenwich Village, as there was new interest in his potential autobiography as well as interest in his visual poetry among a new generation of experimental artists and poets. He wanted to leave his jungle home, as it was too closely associated with his memories of Rose and their happy life there. And, by his sharing the story of their lives and adventures with a younger generation in the States, Rose could live on. On his return, he was consoled by and later married to his old friend Eleanor, whom Rose and he had known since 1917 and had met again in the mid-1930s on a trip to London. When they knew Eleanor during the year at the Slackers Hotel, in Mexico City, they worked side-by-side as activists and war resisters. Eleanor was married to the famous draft resister Charles Phillips, who later changed his name and became a delegate to the Soviet Congress, and still later changed his name again and became an investment banker on Wall Street. Once Eleanor arrived at the Slackers Hotel, she soon was living with *The Masses*' editorial cartoonist, Henry Glintenkamp, and they were later married. The three continued to work together, as Eleanor, with Phillips and Glintenkamp, started to publish a radical newsletter for those fleeing the United States during World War I. The newsletter would inform them of the news back home, and the changing world situation. They also published in the *Luz!* newspaper, which sought to bring radical political ideals together with modern design and arts specifically in the context of the revolutionary movement in Mexico. The work of the exiled group began as soon as they arrived: Phillips was the political theorist and editor, Glintenkamp the visual designer and illustrator, and Eleanor the managing editor. Eleanor knew how to publish an independent operation, and Bob learned much from her. The marriage to Glint lasted only a few years, but long enough for Eleanor to give birth to Brunhilde (later known as Jean). Eleanor later met Bob and Rose on a ship to London, when the Browns were leading a summer writing group to the Soviet Union in the mid-1930s. Eleanor was traveling with her daughter to London. It is not clear if there was an onboard romance between Eleanor and Bob, or why she happened to be on the same ship as the Browns. In the twenty years between that meeting and spending time with Bob in the 1950s, she had not lost her organizational brilliance and had served as a registrar and secretary to a curator at the Metropolitan Museum of Art in New York; she also had not lost her sense of adventure. When Bob returned, Eleanor was living and working in Nassau County on Long Island, so for both of them it was a return to the neighborhood of their youth when they married, in a civil ceremony, and moved to Greenwich Village, where they rented an apartment from

Bob and Eleanor in the late 1950s.

Romany Marie, their friend and famous restaurateur for the Village's intellectual, political, and arts scene during the first two decades of the twentieth century.

Nearly forty years later, Eleanor and Bob, both experienced hands at publishing, immediately set out to restart Roving Eye Press and Bob Brown Books. They also set out to publish one more cookbook; they both desperately needed money. They ran the business (or businesses) out of the apartment at 37 West 8th Street. The small apartment quickly filled with books, coming and going, to the point that when Eleanor's daughter, then in her early thirties, or Bob's grandchildren came for a visit, they had to sleep on a cot between the shelves and shelves of books. Eleanor threw parties, poets and writers were regularly visiting, and book dealers and collectors were always calling or stopping by to buy rare books, visual poems, or modernist publications. They were once again hustling in a breathless blur of activities that seemed as disconnected, or even contradictory, and somewhat manic as always: running a business, publishing radical poetry and recollections of the avant-garde, and meeting with old friends. Bob was once again living close to where he had lived in the first two decades of the twentieth century, and they fed off of each other's manic enthusiasms and depressive crashes; today we would diagnose both as bipolar, and Eleanor did try therapy for swings in mood. Eleanor and Bob started selling off rare books through the newly reestablished Bob Brown Books; they also started publishing new editions of some of the cookbooks, but not the avant-garde projects, through Bob's Roving Eye Press. They published a couple more cookbooks with major trade publishing houses; the name Bob Brown was a brand that had a life of its own. One cookbook appeared posthumously in 1959, with no indication that it was posthumous, and the advance helped them financially. Bob had little money when he arrived from Brazil, so he was back to where he'd started, trying to sell his writing to make ends meet. Eleanor had bought a car in 1952, but she was not a good driver and preferred walking everywhere, so when they moved to the city she sold the car.

Both Eleanor and Bob knew Kay Boyle, who was, in the 1950s, forced out of *The New Yorker*, where she had worked for about six years, and blacklisted from writing for other magazines because of her political activism; this served to reinforce her determination to write about political issues of the day. When Brown returned to the States, Boyle was writing political parables in her prize-winning short stories and a novel. Bob and Eleanor visited her family at their Connecticut home; they rekindled their friendship and talked politics. Bob was able to easily reenter the United States in spite of his past associations with guilds, unions, and Communist organizations perhaps because he had also worked for the government's Good Neighbor program in Brazil, but, when he returned, he was not politically active in the public way that Boyle was in the 1950s. He was publishing recollections of his work with the avant-garde, not any memories of his work on *The Masses* or as a war resister.

The Beat generation poets, including Allen Ginsberg and Kenneth Rexroth, started to contact Bob. He published a few memories and anecdotes of Gertrude Stein's interactions with him in the late 1920s and early

Kay Boyle.

'30s for a tabloid-style culture newspaper, *Berkeley: A Journal of Modern Culture*, edited by Bern Porter, the nuclear physicist–turned–radical poet. Most important, Jonathan Williams, whose Jargon Society Press published and introduced Black Mountain College poets like Charles Olsen to a new generation of artists and poets and championed poets like Allen Ginsberg, Denise Levertov, and Louis Zukofsky, also reissued less-well-known avant-garde works, including one of Bob's collections of visual poetry, *1450–1950*, that he had first published with Harry Crosby. Williams and other poets would meet in Bob and Eleanor's apartment to talk about various projects and the current trends in poetry. The concrete poets also discovered Brown, not knowing that he had spent more than twenty years living in Brazil. Augusto de Campos, a founding leader of the Noigandres Concrete Poetry group, reissued *1450–1950* in a Brazil-

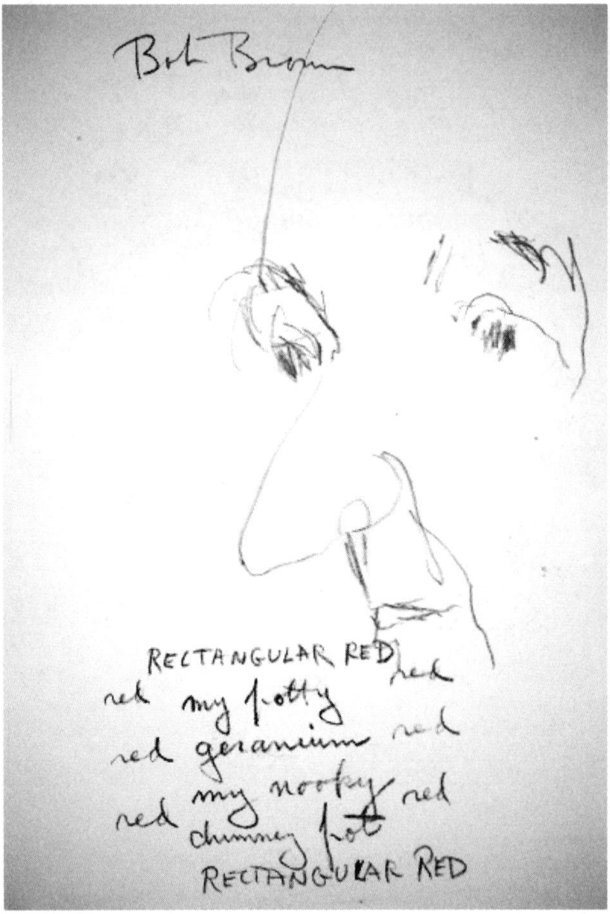

Brown's poem "Rectangular Red," with a sketch by Fielding Dawson. Dawson was the Beat poet and artist who nearly a decade later wrote an experimental biography of Franz Kline.

ian edition. Williams published an issue of *Jargon 31: 14 poets, 1 artist* in New York that included handwritten poems by Beat movement poets and with line drawings by Fielding Dawson of each poet, in colored pencil on the page where the poems appear.[31] Bob's handwritten poem "Rectangular Red" is laid out in three columns in the concrete poem style: the first and last columns have the word "red" repeated in four rows; the center column has five lines. These lines' images rhyme visually with red: "my potty / geranium / my nooky / chimney pot / rectangular." The assonance and consonance rhymes among these lines (e.g., the repeated "o," "ot," and "y") suggest some surreal connection among these apparently red images. There is also an allusion to color field paintings, characterized by abstract flat-plane paintings with large areas filled with one color or gradations of that one color, including Barnett Newman's large rectangular red painting titled *Day One* (1951–52), Josef Albers's series on *Study for Homage to the Square* (begun in 1950 and continued in iterations through the late 1970s), and Marc Rothko's red paintings, like *Four Darks in Red* (1958), and, by extension, to the work of another poet-artist included in that *Jargon 31* issue, Franz Kline.

The poem "Rectangular Red" is both evocatively alluding to images of figures or scenes involving blood in his stool, the flesh of sex, chimney soot, and flowers, and, simultaneously, a cubist-abstract composition, concrete poetry, and what we might call an example of color field poetry. The words are placed on the page in a spatial and semantic relation to create the same type of abstract illusionism in poetry that Bob's longtime friend Stuart Davis used in the 1950s. Davis created his jazz-inspired proto-pop abstract works using what he called the "europhoric method" of painting. Just as Davis offered a proto–pop cubist abstraction, Brown's poems were a type of proto-conceptual cubist-concrete poetry. Bob was not nostalgic for times gone by, or grumpy; he was keeping up with the abstraction kick of the times and the countercultural politics bubbling up during the 1950s. Bob was, like other poets at the time, visiting artists' studios and galleries and continuing to think of writing and poetry as part of the arts and with a conception of composition and form as embedded in a complicated history, biography, politics, and aesthetic theory. Bob Brown is falsely considered a dilettante only by the hopelessly parochial.

The Beats, and the art scene in the 1950s, had a fascination with machines, like Wilhelm Reich's Orgone Box or Jean Tinguely's "meta-mécaniques" of the 1950s, but they knew nothing of Bob's reading machine and were mostly fascinated with his visual poetry, satirical Imagist and lyrical poetry, and his combination of radical activism with countercultural writing. Bob represented a link to a lineage that the poets sought to extend. The Beats, who acknowledged Brown as an *éminence grise* for their own political and poetic adventures, found in his stories about the expatriate avant-garde a lineage to their own experimentation. His visual poems allowed for a free expressive verse and his visceral resistance to capitalist power made sense to the Beat poets. Brown saw himself and words as one, and he, and many who knew him, at different times in his

Stuart Davis among his jazz-inspired paintings.

life thought of words pouring forth from his typewriter like an endless flow of molten lead waiting to be set into type.

If the multiple Bob Browns were alive today, they might have contradictory reactions to this biography. The pulp fiction writer would like the appeal to a popular audience, the narrative structure, and the adventures of a hero. Like the short-story writer, the bestselling author of cookbooks and movie treatments would recognize in this biography that all literature, media, and culture depends on collective endeavor and multiple identities; the story of how marketers and academics alike invented the notion of the author's singular voice and consistent identity exceeds the scope of this biography, but Brown would know that popular writing is an industrial labor practice, not a romantic story of a hero's journey. The activist and radical editor would also embrace the fluid identities and multiplicities described here; the hugely successful publisher would smirk at the very few similarities with Orson Welles's Charles Foster Kane; and, the avant-garde poet would give a knowing wink to the poetic manna words, readie–read–Red–ready–Reddie–Reedy's–reading, as a puncept thread connecting all of the disparate aspects of Brown's lives; like the ending of Welles's *Citizen Kane*, with the revelation of one meaning of Kane's last word, "Rosebud," Bob Brown's life was guided by a poetic rhyme. In that sense, this biography used something analogous to what Stuart Davis called the "euphoric method," rather than a only a traditional biographical approach.[32] Bob would not have wanted his biography to serve as merely the slavish announcer of a series of facts and causal chronologies leading to a singular meaning of a life or oeuvre; to describe the biography, he might have preferred the new biographical methodology used here that highlights a complicated and nuanced relationship between realism, affect, and poetic abstraction. It is that Surrealist methodology that Brown embraced, and that might allow one to read Brown's story as an accurate realist biography with a twist in plain sight for those students with a careful, ready, and watchful eye open to the winking sensibility: this is a biographoem. Bob Brown's story demonstrates that we live in a poetic realm which yields to the aleatory machinations of words chirping readily, and not merely in the mundane literal world, whether we recognize it or not. Way back in 1916, in a poem called "Microscopic Things," Bob described the vision of a biography of micro-affects:

> I have never committed a single thing to memory.
> But I know what is going on in me always,
> Every minutest jot of my being,
> Each emotion, I can cut into fractions and classify.[33]

One gains access to those "minutest jots" through the "bons mots" that Brown has left for us like breadcrumbs marking his path.

A traditional biography would conclude on August 8, 1959, when, at the age of seventy-three, Robert Carlton Brown II passed away from cancer. He had entered the hospital with excruciating back pain; the surgeon cut him open and found that metastatic cancer had spread throughout his

Laughing Bob Brown in the late 1950s.

body. Bob never made it home again. Bob would not want his story to end there, and, because some of his multiplicities only now have come to fruition, the shuffling off of his body really was the start of some of his stories: As the publisher, his Roving Eye Press continued to publish books, like Michael Gold's *Life of John Brown: Centennial of His Execution* in 1960; as the machine-wise type, he would have enjoyed the roles played by typewriters, projectors, readies, and other machines, but he might have preferred a more super-condensed style with emoticons, scrolling text, and electronic multimodalities. Although Brown's proposal for a TV show that would have included segments with animated letters and words was quickly rejected by producers as unrealistic for the medium, programs like *Sesame Street*, *The Electric Company*, and *Between the Lions* later depended

An imagined portrait of Be-Bop Bob Brown!

on animated letters and words. The reading machine, beyond Brown's hopes, animated the words in absolutely particular ways with each use; so, if the goal was to use the machine as a tool for teaching generalizable linguistic rules of literacy, then it certainly failed.

Now, more than fifty years since Bob Brown passed away, the machine suggests aspects of an emerging literacy: different every time, with an affective and synesthetic physicality ready to become an app and the inspiration for a literacy well suited for what Bob called today's *electronicsniks*. Bob Brown, the avant-gardist, would have sought to run a series of experiments that would oscillate between two contradictory possibilities. At first, his experiment seems like a speed-reading machine, helping the user to read more with complete comprehension. As the speed increases, or the user reverses the direction, the texts increasingly become an incomprehensible visual artwork. This is the oscillation that Bob Brown modulated between for his entire life: a paradox focused between his "watching eye," with cultural insights, and his "winking eye," living and writing as a vanguard stunt. No doubt he would have wished that his story would close with a raised glass, a ready wink, a huzzah, and an exclamation mark!

Acknowledgments
The Making of a Biography

No one had written a biography of Bob Brown before this book, and much of the biographical information that did exist, even in archives' "finding aids" (the contextual information about the subjects covered), was incomplete or inaccurate. Even Brown's own published accounts of his life were sometimes purposefully inaccurate. Over the years I kept looking for a biography of Brown to make sense of his many publications and his reading machine. I could not find it, and so I had to write it. How does one begin to write a biography of an important cultural figure when no one has done so before? How does this making-of story begin?

One day in January 1997, as I was completing the research for my book *Networked Art* and preparing for a closely related exhibition of work from the Ruth and Marvin Sackner Archive of Visual and Concrete Poetry, Marvin Sackner asked me to follow him to the liquor cabinet in another room of the archive-museum-house. Instead of bottles of alcohol, the built-in liquor cabinet was filled with a distillation of the collection: the really good stuff. He pulled an unexceptional-looking bound book from the cabinet and handed it to me. I opened it carefully and saw a blurry photograph of an odd-looking box pasted opposite the title page. As I flipped through the pages, I saw that the book was filled with what looked like lines of single words punctuated with em dashes. Marvin insisted that I would no doubt want to write about the editor/inventor of *The Readies for Bob Brown's Machine*. Ruth and Marvin also showed me a framed pencil drawing, a scribbled visual poem by Brown, hanging in their dining room. I agreed that Brown and his machine looked like a fascinating subject, and I later included a footnote on Brown's work in my book, which was published in 2001. Ruth, who knew and cared about the people associated with their collection, often regaled me with stories about the artists, poets, and book designers, but she knew little about this fellow; his story was mostly unknown. Now, more than a decade later, just as I was writing these acknowledgments, Ruth Sackner passed away. Her death filled me with sadness and regret because I had so much looked forward to sending her and Marvin a copy of this book to thank them for their guidance, moral support, and intellectual generosity. They opened up their home and archive to help me produce three major exhibits, two books, and many chapters and articles. They gave me leads to many other projects, including the genesis of this book.

Starting in late May 2003 and over the next nine years, my family spent summers in Ithaca, New York, where my wife, Lynn Tomlinson, taught a summer course at Cornell. I decided to look again at Bob Brown. Cornell's Division of Rare Books and Manuscript Collections of the Carl A. Kroch Library allowed me to have sustained study of a few of Brown's experimental books as well as magazines he wrote for, like *Smart Set*. The director of collections for Cornell University Library and a key player in digital publication projects, Kizer Walker, introduced me to other librarians and archivists both at Cornell and around the country. At Cornell, Jeremy Braddock gave me leads into the context of Brown's work, especially during the 1910s in relation to the Imagist poets' literary magazine, *Others*, and in the late 1920s in relation to Nancy Cunard. One summer, I wandered over to the Nestlé Library in the School of Hotel Administration in search of the Browns' cookbooks, and to my surprise I noticed that the library's central campus catalogue had two unrelated entries for the cookbook-writing Bob Brown and the experimental writer Bob Brown. The mistake, soon corrected once I alerted the librarians, motivated me to think more about the now-mysterious Mr. Brown's disparate identities.

A small portion of an internal grant from the College of Arts and Humanities at the University of Central Florida (UCF) allowed me to visit the Bob Brown Papers at the Department of Special Collections, Manuscripts Division, in the Charles E. Young Research Library at UCLA. A few years earlier, I had begun writing to Simon Elliott, who, in an e-mail, described the state of the Brown collection as a "mess" when it arrived at UCLA as if "someone had thrown the entire contents off a ten-story building, and then everything had just been scooped into boxes straight off the ground," and shipped them off to the library. The papers remained in that condition for decades, from 1961, when Eleanor Parker Brown sent the "mess" of papers, until 2002, when Simon began processing the collection into 112 organized boxes. During my visit, Kathleen McHugh introduced me to N. Katherine Hayles, who asked me, "Did Brown actually construct a working reading machine?" The question helped me frame my research. The next day Michael North gave me many insights into how to design an online version of Brown's reading machine, and, over lunch, he and Jessica Pressman wanted to know if I had found any surprises in the papers. Although it was an innocent question, I had no answer, as it was all surprises to me, and at the time still an overwhelming jumble. North and Pressman both thought I should model my machine closely on Brown's readies and machine. Simon Morris, the publisher and artist, with whom I had consulted about the machine and a possible collaboration, thought the machine we built should look to Brown for inspiration but not be modeled closely on the readies. Very recently, Eric White invited me to collaborate on building an augmented-reality reading machine that will be more loosely inspired by Brown's machine. Eventually, my notes from the visit to the UCLA archives, including my follow-up requests for additional materials, grew to well over 500 pages and formed the basis for my research questions over the next few years. It was a major turning point in my research. When I was back at UCF after the visit, my colleague Bruce Janz had me deliver a talk to a humanities group; Barry Mauer enlightened me, over many years, about avant-garde music experiments; and Anna M. Jones read and commented extensively and insightfully on one of the first drafts of what would become Chapter 5 of this book.

After I wrote to book arts e-mail lists asking about Bob Brown, Rory Brown, Bob's great-grandson, now a librarian, learned of my project and encouraged me to continue. It was a crucial sign of support. Rory also introduced me, via e-mail, to Phoebe Brown, his sister and a filmmaker, who was working on a film about her great-grandfather in relation to her own coming-of-age story. Those two Browns in turn introduced me, via e-mail, to a third sibling, Eamon, an artist. A sabbatical leave from the University of Central Florida during the fall semester of 2009 allowed me to write the first complete draft of the manuscript; having that draft made me recognize that many mysteries and gaps remained in my research. Over the next few years, I reached out to a larger group of Bob Brown's grandchildren and great-grandchildren; soon I was getting inquiries from others in the extended Brown clan, including another of the great-grandchildren, Elffin Burrill, who serendipitously was living in Ithaca, New York, a few blocks from where I was staying in the summer of 2009. Elffin drew or painted the illustrations throughout this book and on the cover that all beautifully illuminate his great-grandfather's life and times in styles to match Brown's fascinations from pulp fiction adventure stories to Surrealist images.

In the summer of 2009, Fred Moody contacted me about a new book series edited by Jerome McGann and Nicolas Frankel called Literature by Design. Fred became an important guide in my thinking about the significance and importance of Brown's story and served as my editor for the publication of two of Brown's experimental books by Rice University Press. Without Fred's encouragement and, along with McGann and other anonymous reviewers, thoughtful editorial advice, my work on Brown might have ended with the publication of a new edition of Brown's *The Readies*; instead, I eventually published four new editions of Brown's avant-garde works with a new incarnation of Roving Eye Press in 2014 and 2015, as well as this biography.

Other research groups, archivists, and librarians have helped me locate materials. The fictionmags Yahoo! group was crucial in establishing a context for Brown's work in writing fiction for magazines; Dennis Lien, at the time a reference librarian at the University of Minnesota, was especially helpful. Aaron Michael Lisec of the Special Collections Research Center of the Morris Library at Southern Illinois University gave me essential help with many important and extremely rare books and documents in Bob Brown's son's papers. With the indispensable help of the Celeste Bartos Film Study Center of the Museum of Modern Art, I was able to screen all of the existing films from the *What Happened to Mary* series. It was an eye-opening experience, as few of the scholars who had written about the series had seen the actual films. I made use of many other archives during my research, including: the Eugene O'Neill Papers at Yale University's Beinecke Rare Book & Manuscript Library; the Kay Boyle Papers, Special Collections, University of Delaware Library, University of Delaware; the University of Arkansas Libraries' Commonwealth College Collection at the Special Collections Department; the Historical Society of Oak Park & River Forest; Special Collections, University of Texas; Special Collections Library at the University of Maryland, College Park; and the New York Public Library.

Davis Schneiderman invited me to Lake Forest College to deliver a public lecture on Brown's connections to the Chicago region. A few years later I also talked with Lake Forest's Robert Archambeau about Brown. Peter Krapp and Bill Tomlinson, who drove up from UC-Irvine during my UCLA trip, talked to me about machines and e-readers. The founding publisher of *Jargon*, Jonathan Williams, wrote to me late in his life to give me permission to reprint Brown's *1450–1950*. I had planned to interview him, but he passed away before we could arrange a meeting. Theo Lotz co-curated the TypeBound exhibit on typewriter poetry, and my curator's essay led me to think more about Brown's intense fascination with the machines with which we read and write. Around the time we co-curated the exhibit using materials from the Sackner Archive, I also built an online simulation of Bob Brown's reading machine at readies.org, and that project depended on the help of many undergraduate and graduate students as well as scholars; I acknowledge all of their contributions on the website. My version of the machine helped me answer some research questions by demonstrating readings of readies instead of one's having to see them as static on the page. In March 2010, Jennifer Schuessler conducted an extensive interview with me over three or four hour-long phone calls about Brown's reading machine; she had initially intended to only briefly mention Brown's machine until she heard more of his story. Her back-page essay in the *New York Times Book Review* of April 8, 2010, "The Godfather of the E-Reader," mentioned my new edition of *The Readies* and my online reading machine at readies.org. The essay led to a thousand-fold increase in traffic to the website and an increase in interest about Bob Brown.

When the University of Maryland, Baltimore County (UMBC), awarded me the Bearman Family Chair in Entrepreneurship for a three-year term, I was able to dedicate the necessary resources and time to complete the biography and restart Roving Eye Press. It was absolutely essential support, and the Bearmans encouraged me in person to write the biography rather than devote time and energy to any other potential projects. At UMBC, Jessica Berman read a much earlier draft of the book and made insightful comments on how to focus the project on Brown's modernist works. Berman, as the director of the Dresher Center, awarded me a summer stipend that helped me conduct research and awarded me a fellowship to adapt this biography into a script for film, media, or comic-graphic form. Kevin Wisniewski, my can-do graduate research assistant, whom I was able to hire with support from UMBC to investigate digital publishing, has stepped up to become the managing editor of Roving Eye Press and helped me prepare this manuscript for publication, including production of the index. Liz Steenrod went above and beyond her administrative duties in managing my grants, stipends, and funds from my endowed term chair.

Very late in the research process in the summer of 2014, I contacted

David Denison, guessing that he might be the grandson of Eleanor Parker Brown. He wrote back that I had "hit the bull's eye!" We arranged an interview with Jean Denison (born Brunnhilde Glintenkamp), who was ninety-one at the time. We started the interview online, and the in-person interview went well. Jean passed away a few months after my visit. Many months later, in the summer of 2015, David started going through her papers and sent me scans of letters, diary entries, and other documents relating to Bob Brown. The manuscript was already making its way through the publishing process, but I was able to add this new information.

The fledgling Bob Brown studies field, which focuses almost completely on Brown's important reading machine, forms part of the intellectual context for this biography, especially in the recent work of Jessica Pressman, Eric White, and Paul Stephens, as well as earlier work by Craig Dworkin and Michael North. The foundation of this focus on Brown depends on mentions, notes, and introductions to Brown's modernist works by Jerome McGann, Jerome Rothenberg, Steve McCaffery, Jed Rasula, Kate Hayles, and Augusto de Campos. In relation to the modernist Brown, Charles Bernstein and Marjorie Perloff both gave helpful comments on small portions of the manuscript. Craig Dworkin and Louis Kaplan read the entire manuscript and provided intellectually generous and insightful commentary and suggestions. Other anonymous readers made useful suggestions that I have addressed in the final version.

Very early in 2015, I sent a proposal to Fordham University Press. The Press's director, Fredric Nachbaur, greeted my proposal and sample chapters with enthusiasm, and, after we met at the College Art Association's annual meeting in New York City to talk about how the potential book would fit with Fordham's interest in studies related to New York City's cultural history, we arranged to send the completed manuscript to readers in the spring of 2015. The glowing readers' reports arrived in April, and the publication process began. Because Brown was most famous as a publisher, this part of the process should not be invisible or go unacknowledged. At the Press, Ann-Christine Racette, Kate O'Brien-Nicholson, Will Cerbone, and Katie Sweeney helped move the project along and improved it at each step. Eric Newman, the managing editor, did a brilliant job of helping me refine and correct the manuscript. Publishers, editors, designers, proofreaders, printers, and the entire scaffolding of scholarship with librarians, archivists, and collectors deserve more support and recognition.

Bob Brown was not an exemplary parent, but his work and life were all about family and long-lasting circles of friends; his was not a solitary life. It is apt that my research involved my extended family and Brown's descendants and their families as well as the many librarians, archivists, friends, and colleagues who are usually involved in helping researchers and scholars. Just as the Browns often worked in the context of travel and freelance projects, my research and writing were almost all accomplished during summer breaks, with two important exceptions. My sister-in-law and former editor for a trade publisher, Christine Bowman, read the book and made recommendations to expand the popular appeal of the biography. Over the course of the research for this book, I had many conversations with my father, Bernie, who passed away in September 2006, and my mother, Johanna, about various cultural details in the 1940s and '50s. My father-in-law, Mickey, tracked down six of the Browns' cookbooks and, with my mother-in-law, Madaline, gave them to me one Christmas; these cookbooks were key to my research. My children, Sam and Lucy, have helped my research enormously; Sam read the micrographic text as I was preparing the editorial introduction of the new edition of Bob Brown's *Words*. Sam has also read and commented on drafts of some small selections of this biography that I wanted to try out on an intelligent reader. Lucy has grown up hearing about Bob Brown and talking to me about how machines have affected, or might affect, reading. My family has grudgingly welcomed the spirit of Bob Brown, 1886–1959, into our lives as a fifth family member over the course of this past decade. All of the work on this book, both literally and figuratively, was made possible by my wife, Lynn Tomlinson, as her decade as a visiting associate professor teaching animation at Cornell allowed me to do research on Bob Brown in an idyllic setting filled with music, great food, good friends, and only a few work-related distractions. More than making it literally possible, Lynn continues to guide my thinking and inspire my passions about the arts, culture, and intimate creative collaborations.

Much earlier versions of small portions of Chapter 5 appeared in a handful of places, including in:

"Book Type Machine: From Bob Brown's Reading Machine to Electronic Simulations, 1930–2010." *Bonefolder: An E-journal for the Bookbinder and Bookartist* 6.1 (2009): 19–24

"Materiality of a Simulation: Scratch Reading Machine, 1931." *The Fibreculture Journal: Internet Theory, Criticism, and Research* 15 (2009)

"Simulating Reading: Digital Research Beyond the Database." *Research Foundations for Understanding Book and Reading in the*

Digital Age. Special issue of *New Knowledge Environments* 1.1, 2009: 1–7

"Simulating Reading," at the Futures of Digital Studies gathering in Gainesville, Florida (2010), and that piece eventually appeared as "Readies Online" in the *Digital Humanities Quarterly* 5.3 (2011)

"Bob Brown's ———" [my introduction to a selection from Brown's *Gems*], *Lost Poets Review* section. *Paul Revere's Horse, a Literary Journal* 2.2 (2010): 93–103

Very small portions of an earlier version of Chapter 1 appeared in:

"A Quick Read(ies): Speed and Formula in Bob Brown's Pulp Fiction and Avant-Garde Machines." *The Popular Avant-Garde*, ed. Renée Silverman. New York: Rodopi, 2010: 175–82

Much earlier, substantially different version of a portion of Chapter 6 appeared in:

"Saudades on the Amazon: Toward a Soft Sweet Name for Involution." *Beyond Globalization: Making New Worlds in Media, Art and Social Practices*, ed. A. Aneesh, Lane Hall, and Patrice Petro. New Brunswick, N.J.: Rutgers University Press, 2011: 250–73

Anne Reynes invited me to talk on an American Literature Association panel she organized about Kay Boyle's friendships, and my paper focused on Brown's friendship from the late 1920s through the 1950s. Anne convinced me to help her organize a Bob Brown panel in Poland, and although a back injury prevented my attending in person, I had someone deliver my paper:

"Reading Popular and Avant-Garde." European Avant-Garde Studies Conference. Ponzan, Poland. April 2010

As this book goes to press, I am planning a special Bob Brown issue of the literary journal *Jacket2* with the help of its managing editor, Michael Hennessey. My article "Concrete Poetry in America: A Story of Intermedia Performance, Publishing, & Pop Appeal," in *Coldfront* poetry and poetics magazine (October 2015), mentions Bob Brown's founding influence on modernist visual poetry.

Notes

Introduction

1. Walter Lowenfels, *To an Imaginary Daughter* (New York: Horizon Press, 1964), 82.

1. When the Artist Became a Fiction Factory, 1907–17

1. Bob Brown, *Readies for Bob Brown's Machine* (Cagnes-sur-Mer: Roving Eye Press, 1931), 159.
2. Bob Brown, "Swell Days for Literary Guys." *American Mercury*, December 1932: 480–85, 480.
3. Berton Braley, *Pegasus Pulls a Hack: Memoirs of a Modern Minstrel* (New York: Minton, Balch & Co., 1934), 139.
4. Nathanael West, *Miss Lonely Hearts* (1933) (New York: New Directions, 1962), 15.
5. Robert Carlton Brown, "Swell Days for Literary Guys." *American Mercury*, December 1932: 482.
6. William Wallace Cook, *The Fiction Factory* (Ridgewood, N.J.: The Editor Company, 1912), 150.
7. John Locke, ed., *The Ocean: 100th Anniversary Collection* (Castroville, Calif.: Off-Trail Publications, 2008), 16.
8. Cook, *The Fiction Factory*, 151.
9. Sally Ledger, *The New Woman: Fiction and Feminism at the Fin De Siëcle* (Manchester: Manchester University Press, 1997), 182.

10. Robert Carlton Brown, *What Happened to Mary: A Novelization from the Play and the Stories Appearing in the Ladies' World* (New York: Grosset & Dunlap, 1913), 200.

11. Locke, *The Ocean*, 17.

12. See Richard M. Fried, *The Man Everybody Knew: Bruce Barton and the Making of Modern America* (Chicago: Ivan R. Dee, 2005).

13. Braley, *Pegasus Pulls a Hack*, 27.

14. Hugh Merrill, *The Red Hot Typewriter: The Life and Times of John D. Macdonald* (New York: Thomas Dunne Books / St. Martin's Minotaur, 2000), 45.

15. Bob Brown, "Autobiographical Notes," 1949, The Bob Brown Papers 1844–1960. Charles E. Young Research Library, Special Collections, UCLA.

16. Robert Carlton Brown, "Swell Days for Literary Guys," 485.

17. Ibid.

18. Erin A. Smith, *Hard-boiled: Working Class Readers and Pulp Magazines* (Philadelphia: Temple University Press, 2000), 51.

19. William Wallace Cook, *Plotto: A New Method of Plot Suggestion for Writers of Creative Fiction* (Battle Creek, Mich.: Ellis Publishing Company, 1928), 22.

20. Merrill, *The Red Hot Typewriter*, 45.

21. Cook, *The Fiction Factory*, 25.

22. William Wallace Cook as quoted in Arthur E. Scott, "Hard Work: The 'Open Sesame' the Story of William Wallace Cook." *Writer's Digest*, Vol. III, No. 3 (February 1923), 8.

23. Cook, *Plotto*, 177.

24. Ibid.

25. Ibid., 179.

26. Ibid., 16.

27. Ibid., 27–28, 178, 172, 160, 148, 100, 121.

28. Ibid., 135, 182, 184.

29. Ibid., 174–76.

30. Bob Brown, "Autobiographical Notes."

31. Ibid., n.p.

32. Ron Goulart, *Cheap Thrills: An Informal History of the Pulp Magazines* (New Rochelle, N.Y.: Arlington House, 1972), 45.

33. Elizabeth Yorke Miller, "Should Woman Ride Astride?" *Munsey's Magazine*, June 1901: 553–57.

34. *The Scrap Book* magazine, Special Articles section, Vol. 5 No. 1 (The Frank A. Munsey Company, February 1908), 240–45.

35. Goulart, *Cheap Thrills*, 9.

36. Letter from R. C. Brown to W. W. Cook, August 2, 1910. Archives of the New York Public Library.

37. Frederick Arthur Dominy, "Shooting the Wily Snipe." *The Outing Magazine*, September 1911, 683–85.

38. Letter from R. C. Brown to W. W. Cook.

39. Brown, *Readies for Bob Brown's Machine*, 157.

40. Bob Brown, *The Remarkable Adventures of Christopher Poe* (Chicago: F. G. Browne & Co., 1913), 154.

41. Ibid., 218–19.

42. M. C. Rintoul, *Dictionary of Real People and Places in Fiction* (New York: Routledge, 1993), 933; see also Richard Lehan, *Theodore Dreiser: His World and His Novels* (London: Feffer & Simons, 1969); Theodore Dreiser, *A Gallery of Women* (New York: Horace Liveright, 1929).

43. *New York Times Book Review*, Volume 18: 566, October 19, 1913; *Boston Transcript*, November 17, 1913, 10.

44. Brown, *The Remarkable Adventures of Christopher Poe*, 13.

45. Christopher Breu, *Hard-boiled Masculinities* (Minneapolis: University of Minnesota Press, 2005), 115–16.

46. Ibid., 176.

47. Bob Brown, *My Marjonary* (Boston: John W. Luce, 1916), 6.

48. Brown, *The Remarkable Adventures of Christopher Poe*, 20.

49. O. Henry, "A Madison Square Arabian Night." *The Trimmed Lamp: And Other Stories of the Four Millions* (New York: McClure, Philips & Co., 1907), 26.

50. Ibid., 163.

51. Brown, *The Remarkable Adventures of Christopher Poe*, 31.

52. Charles Dwyer, "Mary and the Movies." *The Ladies' World*, August 1912, 1.

53. Roy Kinnard, *Fifty Years of Serial Thrills* (Metuchen, N.J.: Scarecrow Press, 1983), 7.

54. Elliott Flower, "Only a Woman but She Beats the Men at Their Own Game." *The Ladies' World*, September 1912: 5; Mary Atherton, "How Shall I Do My Hair?" *The Ladies' World*, September 1912: 6.

55. Roy Kinnard, *Fifty Years of Serial Thrills* (Metuchen, N.J.: Scarecrow Press, 1983), 7; Shelley Stamp, *Movie Struck Girls: Women and Motion Picture Culture after the Nickelodeon* (Princeton, N.J.: Princeton University Press, 2000), 120.

56. Ibid., 13.

57. Andrew Shail, "The Motion Picture Story Magazine and the Origins of Popular British Film Culture." *Film History: An International Journal* 20.2 (2008): 186.

58. Brown, *What Happened to Mary?*, 20.

59. Ibid., 24.

60. Ibid., 38.

61. Ibid., 46–52.

62. Ibid., 138.

63. Brown, "Swell Days for Literary Guys," 482.

64. Thomas Quinn Curtiss, *The Smart Set: George Jean Nathan and H. L. Mencken* (New York: Applause, 1997), 34.

65. Tim DeForest, *Storytelling in the Pulps, Comics, and Radio: How Technology Changed Popular Fiction in America* (Jefferson, N.C.: McFarland, 2004), 96.

66. See, for example, Pound, in a letter to James Joyce, in which Pound recommends places to publish: Ezra Pound, *Pound/Joyce: The Letters of Ezra Pound to James Joyce, with Pound's Essays on Joyce*, ed. Forrest Read (New York: New Directions, 1967), 18; see also David M. Earle, *Re-covering Modernism: Pulps, Paperbacks, and the Prejudice of Form* (Burlington, Vt.: Ashgate, 2009), 20.

2. A Pulp Nonfiction Adventure Story: Once Upon a Time, 1886–1907

1. Bob Brown, "Autobiographical Notes," 1949, The Bob Brown Papers 1844–1960. Charles E. Young Research Library, Special Collections, UCLA.

2. Jerome J. McGann, *Towards a Literature of Knowledge* (Chicago: University of Chicago Press, 1989), 71.

3. Opie Percival Read, *Glimpses and Epigrams* (Chicago: Hill, 1902), 99, 80.

4. Ibid., 80.

5. Berton Braley, *Pegasus Pulls a Hack: Memoirs of a Modern Minstrel* (New York: Minton, Balch & Co., 1934), 192.

6. Arthur Bartlett Maurice, ed., "The Nonsense Machine." *Bookman: A Magazine of Literature and Life* 1912: 13–14.

7. Brown, *The House of Content*, 1904, unpublished hand-bound book, 93 unnumbered pages. Bob Brown Papers, MSS 88. Special Collections, Morris Library, Southern Illinois University.

8. Ibid., page 10 of 93 unnumbered pages.

9. Ibid., 69 of 93 pages.

10. Paul Laurence Dunbar, *Lyrics of Lowly Life* (New York: Dodd, Mead, 1896).

11. Bob Brown, "Autobiographical Notes." 1949.

3. Free Love, Free Verse, and Free Radicals in the Avant-Garde, 1913–17

1. Federal Writers' Project Guild Committee, *New York Panorama: A Comprehensive View of the Metropolis*. American Guide Series. Ed. guild committee (New York: Random House, 1938), 172. At least three other entries mention Bob Brown, including entries on Clifton Fadiman, Alfred Kreymborg, and Burton Rascoe.

2. Bob Brown, "Autobiographical Notes," 1949, The Bob Brown Papers 1844–1960. Charles E. Young Research Library, Special Collections, UCLA.

3. Ibid.

4. Berton Braley, *Pegasus Pulls a Hack: Memoirs of a Modern Minstrel* (New York: Minton, Balch & Co., 1934), 129.

5. Ibid., 130.

6. Allen Churchill, *The Improper Bohemians: A Recreation of Greenwich Village in Its Heyday* (New York: E. F. Dutton & Company, 1959), 37.

7. Robert Carlton Brown, "City Church Bells: The Call to Worship Thought to Be Out of Date." *New York Times*, November 28, 1910: 10.

8. Neil Baldwin, *Man Ray, American Artist* (New York: Da Capo Press, 2001), 49.

9. Louis Sheaffer, "'B' Names: Sheaffer Interviews (Collective) Robert Carlton Brown," *Series VI. Name files (Correspondence, clippings, etc.)* (Waterford, Conn.: University of Connecticut, Sheaffer O'Neil Collection, 1987), unnumbered, n.p.

10. Francis M. Naumann and Man Ray, *Conversion to Modernism: The Early Work of Man Ray* (New Brunswick, N.J.: Rutgers University Press, 2003), 25.

11. Chrissie Iles, "Marcel Duchamp, Man Ray and the Desiring Machine," in *Marcel Duchamp, Man Ray: 50 Years of Alchemy* (New York: Sean Kelly Gallery, 2000), 19.

12. Brown, "Autobiographical Notes."

13. Ibid.

14. Alfred Kreymborg, ed., *Troubadour: An Autobiography* (New York: Boni and Liveright, 1925), 201.

15. Gertrude Stein, *Autobiography of Alice B. Toklas* (New York: Vintage, 1960), 197.

16. Brown, "Autobiographical Notes"; Gail Stavitsky, "Artists and Art Colonies of Ridgefield, New Jersey," in *Conversion to Modernism*, 222.

17. Workers of the Writers 9 Program of the Work Projects Administration in the State of New Jersey. *Bergen County Panorama* Ed. Series, American Guide (Hackensack, N.J.: Federal Works Agency Works Projects Administration, 1941), 260.

18. Naumann and Ray, *Conversion to Modernism*, 24.

19. Man Ray, *Self Portrait* (Boston: Little, Brown, 1963), 48.

20. *Fine Books from the Library of Robert Carlton Brown* on March 17, 1915, at the Anderson Auction Company on Madison Ave., 18–25.

21. Brown, "Autobiographical Notes."

22. Bob Brown, *Readies for Bob Brown's Machine* (Cagnes-sur-Mer: Roving Eye Press, 1931), 166.

23. Ibid.

24. Amy Lowell, *Poetry and Poets: Essays* (New York: Biblo and Tannen, 1971), 25.

25. Stavitsky, "Artists and Art Colonies of Ridgefield, New Jersey," 222.

26. Workers of the Writers 9 Program of the Work Projects Administration in the State of New Jersey, 260.

27. Bob Brown, *Let There Be Beer!* (New York: H. Smith & R. Haas, 1932), 191.

28. Ibid., 193–94.

29. Robert Carlton Brown, "Emits a Few Bubbles," in *"—and Other Poets,"* ed. Louis Untermeyer (New York: Henry Holt, 1916), 69.

30. Louis Untermeyer, *From Another World: The Autobiography of Louis Untermeyer* (New York: Harcourt, 1939), 43.

31. Churchill, *The Improper Bohemians*, 91.

32. Ibid., 90.

33. Ibid., 92.

34. Untermeyer, *From Another World*, 46.

35. William Wilson, *Stuart Davis's Abstract Argot* (San Francisco: Pomegranate Art Books, 1993), 1.

36. Reed quoted in Untermeyer, *From Another World*, 46.

37. Leslie Fishbein, *Rebels in Bohemia: The Radicals of the Masses, 1911–1917* (Chapel Hill: University of North Carolina Press, 1982), 22; see also Mark Morrison, *The Public Face of Modernism: Little Magazines, Audiences and Reception, 1905–1920* (Madison: University of Wisconsin Press, 2001), 200–1.

38. Young as quoted in Rebecca Zurier, Elise K. Kenney, Earl Davis, and Rebecca Zurier, *Art for the Masses: A Radical Magazine and Its Graphics, 1911–1917* (Philadelphia: Temple University Press, 1988), 53.

39. Fishbein, *Rebels in Bohemia*, 22.

40. Ibid.

41. Christopher Lasch, "From Culture to Politics," in *The Revival of American Socialism: Selected Papers of the Socialist Scholars Conference*, ed. George Fischer, Alan Block, John M. Cammett, and Richard Friedman (New York: Oxford University Press, 1971), 222.

42. Max Eastman, *The Masses* (New York: The Masses Editorial Board, 1913), 1.

43. Untermeyer, *From Another World*, 47.

44. Max Eastman, *Marxism, Is It Science?* (New York: W. W. Norton & Company, 1940).

45. Brown, "Autobiographical Notes."

46. Kreymborg, *Troubadour*, 200.

47. Kreymborg quoted in Works of Writers 9 Program, 1941, 260.

48. Flint's precepts quoted in F. S. Flint and Michael Copp, *The Fourth Imagist: Selected Poems of F. S. Flint* (Madison, N.J.: Fairleigh Dickinson University Press, 2007), 22. See also the identical quote from Ezra Pound, "A Retrospect," in *Literary Essays of Ezra Pound*, ed. T. S. Eliot (Norfolk, Conn.: New Directions, 1954), 3.

49. Amy Lowell, *Tendencies in Modern Poetry* (New York: Macmillan, 1917), 321.

50. Bob Brown, *My Marjonary* (Boston: John W. Luce, 1916), 3.

51. Suzanne W. Churchill, *The Little Magazine* Others *and the Renovation of Modern American Poetry* (Burlington, Vt.: Ashgate, 2006), 45.

52. Robert Carlton Brown, "*untitled* ('I am Aladdin')," *The Others* 1.2 (August 1915): 28–30.

53. Kreymborg, *Troubadour*, 162.

54. Brenda Murphy, *The Provincetown Players and the Culture of Modernity* (New York: Cambridge University Press, 2005), 103.

55. William Carlos Williams, *The Selected Letters of William Carlos Williams*, ed. John C. Thirlwall (New York: New Directions, 1984), 113.

56. Arturo Schwarz, *Man Ray: The Rigour of Imagination* (New York: Rizzoli, 1977), 27.

57. Ibid.

58. Ray, *Self Portrait*, 48.

59. Ibid.

60. Ibid.

61. Ibid.

62. Ibid.

63. Ibid., 55.

64. Churchill, *The Improper Bohemians*, 62.

65. Ray, *Self Portrait*, 53.

66. Ibid.

67. Jean V. Matthews, *The Rise of the New Woman: The Women's Movement in America, 1875–1930* (Chicago: Ivan R. Dee, 2003), 103.

68. Ibid., 110–11.

69. Man Ray, *Man Ray, 1914*. 1914. A & R Penrose Collection, England, Grantwood Village, N.J., n.p.

70. Churchill, *The Improper Bohemians*, 151.

71. Anonymous, "Clara Tice Lights Guido Bruno Garrett." *The New York Times*, May 11, 1915: 8.

72. See, for example, *Bruno's Weekly*, ed. Guido Bruno, January 1, 1916.

73. Bob Brown, *Tahiti: 10 Rhythms*, Bruno Chapbooks 1.4 (New York: G. Bruno, 1915), 41.

74. Brown, *My Marjonary*, 22.

75. Brown, "Autobiographical Notes."

76. Ibid.

77. Ibid.

78. Ibid.

79. Ibid.

80. Churchill, *The Improper Bohemians*, 109.

81. Brown, "Autobiographical Notes."

82. Ibid.

83. Ibid.

84. Ibid.

85. Ibid.

86. Ibid.

87. Eric Homberger, *New York City: A Cultural and Literary Companion. Cities of the Imagination* (Oxford: Signal Books, 2002), 122.

4. Exile, Escape, Empire, and World Travels, 1917–28

1. Bob Brown, *You Gotta Live* (London: Desmond Harmsworth, 1932), vi.

2. Hannah Arendt, "We Refugees," *The Menorah Journal* (1943) reprinted in *The Jew as Pariah: Jewish Identity and Politics in the Modern Age*, ed. Ron H. Feldman, 1st Evergreen ed. (New York: Grove Press, distributed by Random House, 1978): 55–67, 67.

3. See, for example, Donald Pizer, *American Expatriate Writing and the Paris Moment: Modernism and Place* (Baton Rouge: Louisiana State University Press, 1996).

4. Michael Gold, *Jews without Money* (New York: Carroll & Graf Publishers, 1996. Gold's book was originally published in 1930. A later edition of his novel, published in 1965, with an afterword by Michael Harrington, became a key text in the left's advocacy for a war on poverty and urban social protest in the 1960s. For example, Gold described an old, dispirited man working at "his machine in the umbrella store. He was trying to forget America. But who can do that? It roared in the street outside, it fought against him from the lips of his own children. It even reached into his synagogue, and struck at his God. It finally defeated him, this America. It broke the old man, because he could not bend" (137). The slackers wanted to forget "this America," and they would flee into exile rather than bend to the war machine, and once again it was the trope of the machine that both promised liberation and reinforced oppression. In conjunction with his fictionalized memoir *Jews without Money*, Gold published the description of this genre and coined the phrase "proletarian realism" in part as a barb to the "academic" discounting of the genre of proletarian fiction as inferior. That phrase influenced Brown and a generation of modernist writers, who according to Gold wanted to now use their skills and innovations to write about real people (working with machines), and struggling against (the machinery of) oppression, but the Browns didn't just want to write proletarian realism; they lived it as slackers repeating their mantra, "Gotta live, gotta live" with all its connotations. Gold's novel, and to a lesser extent his proclamations about the new genre, influenced Bob as he sat down to write more than a decade later, in the early 1930s, his novelized account, *You Gotta Live*, of the slackers in Mexico.

5. Floyd Dell, *Were You Ever a Child* (New York: A. A. Knopf, 1919), 151.

6. For a complete history of the strange bedfellows in the history of the adoption of the Eighteenth Amendment—Prohibition—see Daniel Okrent, *Last Call: The Rise and Fall of Prohibition* (New York: Scribner's, 2010).

7. Allen suggested they call themselves Battery J as a winking allusion to the smallest military units capable of independent operations: battalions or a battery. They were not being coordinated from a higher command, but they might be loosely thought of as part of the larger company of war resisters fleeing to Mexico. Military commands typically named battalions with an identifying letter to distinguish one from the other, like C Battery. The choice of *J* was a self-deprecating reference to the slang term, a jay, for a rube ready

to be swindled, mugged, or tricked. *Jaywalking* was a term popularized in the 1910s to denigrate pedestrian uses of streets. The term insinuated that cars had the right of way over the foolish pedestrian's thinking that cars could share the streets. In that sense, *jay* had a connotation of resistance as well as one of gullible and inexperienced. One could willfully try to take the streets back in protest. The *jay* also alluded to liveliness and a carefree perspective as a synonym for *gay* that carried over to the connotation of a happy-go-lucky rube. In any case, the name Battery J fit this small group even if Bob had already traveled widely, spent time in Mexico, and written fiction about clever criminals avoiding detection.

8. Mexico and the Americas were not simply a blank canvas on which the exiles could find their modernist voice and vision but a dynamic place with its own history involving, especially starting in the late 1910s and through the early 1930s, disjunctions and atemporal realities between the introduction of modern machines and the traditional customs of the indigenous tribes like the Yaqui.

9. Brown and his circle of comrades also started to think tentatively about new forms of writing and journalism that would address these class conflicts more directly. After the war, Michael Gold, in a speculative *Liberator* article from 1921, when Gold was the editor of that radical magazine, described what this new genre might look like; and a *New Masses* article from 1930, when Gold had become the editor of that magazine, describing what the genre had become and the scope of its international reach. Gold, now best known as the author of his own novelized memoir, *Jews without Money* (1930), knew the Browns and influenced Bob's later advocacy of a politically engaged realist memoir style in literature. Brown was not as masterful a writer as Gold, but he easily employed his knowledge of realist fiction, from years of publishing thousands of popular short-fiction adventures, to describe their real struggles.

10. Brown, *You Gotta Live*, v. The description of the hotel sets the scene for the rest of the novel. Although, after this preface, the novel does not use the style Brown developed for his reading machine, a style called "readies" that included using dashes and eliminating many words to simulate the flickering cinematic effect of the "talkies," Brown's book has other characteristics of a modernist novel, including multiple perspectives in which the main protagonist changes. The character whom we follow in the first scene, the fictionalized version of Allen Norton, later moves out of the main action completely, appearing only in third-hand rumors and reporting to the fictionalized Bob and Rose characters. Later, we sometimes follow Rose, listening in on her thoughts, and sometimes Bob. It was the last work of fiction Bob published (although three decades later he sold story treatments to Hollywood) and marked a transition to his extended essays both in more than a dozen cookbooks and other autobiographical tracts on his travels and adventures. Rose would later write a handful of books for children. These historical fiction books, about Brazil and Brazilian adventurers, explored that same creative nonfiction genre.

11. Arthur Cravan, "Hie!", trans. Paul Lenti, in *4 Dada Suicides*, ed. Roger L.

Conover (London: Atlas Press, 2005), 12. Originally published in *Maintenant*, issue 2 (1913).

12. Sandeep Parmar, "Mina Loy's 'Colossus' and the Myth of Arthur Cravan." *Jacket* 34, October 2007: n.p.

13. Charles Nicholl, "The Wind Comes Up Out of Nowhere." *London Review of Books* 28, March 2006, 8–13.

14. Brown, *You Gotta Live*, 154–55.

15. Ibid., 371, 372.

16. See Marcel Duchamp, *Affectionately Marcel: The Selected Correspondence of Marcel Duchamp*, ed. Francis M. Naumann and Hector Obalk (Ghent: Ludion Press, 2000), 81–82.

17. Brown, *You Gotta Live*, v.

5. Expatriate Avant-Garde in the South of France, 1928–32

1. Bob Brown, "Optical Balloon Juice." *Contempo: A Bob Brown Issue* (August 31, 1932), 1.

2. Bob Brown, *The Readies (1930)*, ed. and intro. Craig Saper (Baltimore: Roving Eye Press: 2014), 29.

3. Bob Brown, *1450–1950* (New York: Jargon Books, 1959).

4. Bob Brown as quoted in Augusto de Campos, "Bob Brown: Optical Poems," *Suplemento Literário de "O Estado de São Paulo" / Litterary Supplement of the newspaper O Estado de São Paulo* (9 January 1965): 126/141. Later included, with several poems by Bob Brown from the Jargon Books Edition, in de Campos, *A Margem Da Margem* [*At the Margin of the Margin*] (São Paulo, Brazil: Companhia das Letras, 1989).

5. Bob Brown, *The Readies*, ed. Craig Saper (Houston: Rice University Press, 2009), 29.

6. Hugh D. Ford, *Four Lives in Paris* (Berkeley, Calif.: North Point Press, 1987), 209.

7. Eugene Jolas, "The Machine and 'Mystic America.'" *transition: an international quarterly for creative experiment* Spring/summer (June 1930): 379.

8. All caps in original. Kay Boyle et. al., "The Revolution of the Word." *transition: an international quarterly for creative experiment* Spring/Summer (June 1929): 12.

9. Jenny Schuessler, "ESSAY: The Godfather of the E-Reader." *New York Times,* Sunday Book Review (April 11, 2010): 27.

10. Bob Brown, *You Gotta Live* (London: Desmond Harmsworth, 1932).

11. Brown, *The Readies*, 29.

12. Ibid.

13. Ibid., 28–29.

14. Ibid., 40.

15. Bob Brown, *Readies for Bob Brown's Machine* (Cagnes-sur-Mer: Roving Eye Press, 1931), 160.

16. Ibid., 180.

17. Gertrude Stein and Alice B. Toklas, *Autobiography of Alice B. Toklas* (New York: Harcourt, Brace, 1933), 178.

18. Brown, *Readies for Bob Brown's Machine,* 161–62.

19. Quoted in Sandra Whipple Spanier, *Kay Boyle, Artist and Activist* (Carbondale: Southern Illinois University Press, 1986), 94, 61.

20. Brown, *The Readies,* 1.

21. Ibid., 13.

22. Ibid., 28.

23. Ibid., 51.

24. Ibid., 40.

25. Tristan Tzara, *Faites vos jeux, Les Feuilles libres,* No. XXXI (March–April 1923): n.p., as quoted in Mary Ann Caws, *The Poetry of Dada and Surrealism: Aragon, Breton, Tzara, Eluard, and Desnos* (Princeton, N.J.: Princeton University Press, 1970), 17.

26. Alex Ross, *The Rest Is Noise: Listening to the Twentieth Century* (New York: Farrar, Straus and Giroux, 2007), 149–50.

27. Brown, *The Readies,* 2. Note Brown's typo in the title.

28. Ibid., 27.

29. Ibid., 31.

30. Ibid., 32.

31. Michael Gold with Michael Folsom, *A Literary Anthology* (New York: International, 1972); originally published in 1930 and collected and republished in 1972, 206–7.

32. Nancy Cunard, *These Were the Hours: Memories of My Proud Hours Press, Reanville and Paris, 1928–1931,* ed. and intro. Hugh Ford (Carbondale: Southern Illinois University Press, 1969), 177, 181.

33. Ibid., 9.

34. Ibid., 177; see also William Carlos Williams to Bob Brown, September 12, 1929, The Bob Brown Papers 1844–1960. Box 63. Charles E. Young Research Library, Special Collections, UCLA.

35. Cunard, *These Were the Hours,* 177.

36. Ibid., 178.

37. Hugh Ford, "Foreword," in Nancy Cunard, *These Were the Hours,* xv–xvi.

38. Bob Brown, *Words* (Paris: Hours Press, 1931), 19.

39. Cunard, quoted in Daphne Fielding, *Emerald and Nancy: Lady Cunard and Her Daughter* (London: Eyre & Spottiswoode, 1968), 188–89; Cunard, *These Were the Hours,* 183.

40. Cunard, *These Were the Hours,* 8; Lois G. Gordon, *Nancy Cunard: Heiress, Muse, Political Idealist* (New York: Columbia University Press, 2007), 142.

41. Cunard, *These Were the Hours,* 9.

42. Ibid., 10.

43. Ford, "Foreword," xii

44. Cunard, *These Were the Hours,* 182.

45. Hugh D. Ford, *Published in Paris: A Literary Chronicle of Paris in the 1920s and 1930s* (New York: Collier, 1988), 1, 286.

46. Ibid., 287.

47. Ibid., 183.

48. Cunard, *These Were the Hours*, 181.

49. Brown, *Words*, 1.

50. Cunard, *These Were the Hours*, 184, 180.

51. Bob Brown, "Letters of Gertrude Stein." *Berkeley: a journal of modern culture*, No. 8 (1951): 1–2.

52. Robert Hooke and Brian J. Ford, *Micrographia* (London: 1665). Facsimile edition in the Octavo digital rare books series (Palo Alto, Calif.: Octavo, 1998).

53. Brown, in an unpublished typed note with handwritten (in pencil) visual poems to Philip Kaplan, who was an artist collector involved in buying and trading ephemera with Brown in the 1950s; undated, no page. Brown seems to pitch the idea to the collector as suited for television. Robert Carlton Brown papers (Collection number: 72–275), Special Collections, University of Maryland Libraries, Hornbake Library, College Park, Maryland. Brown also pitched the idea in the late 1940s, but it was rejected.

54. Brown, *Words*, 19.

55. Diane Ravitch, *Left Back: A Century of Failed School Reforms* (New York: Simon & Schuster, 2000), 253.

56. Bob Brown, *Gems: A Censored Anthology* (Cagnes-sur-Mer: Roving Eye Press, 1931), 4.

57. Havelock Ellis, *More Essays on Love and Virture* (London: Constable, 1931), vii.

58. Ibid., 136.

59. Ibid.

60. Craig Dworkin, *Reading the Illegible* (Evanston, Ill.: Northwestern University Press, 2003).

61. Havelock Ellis, *Revaluation of Obscenity* (Paris: Hours Press, 1931), 125.

62. Edward Hutton, "Introduction," *Palgrave's Golden Treasury*, by Francis Turner Palgrave (London: J. M. Dent, 1906), xi.

63. Ed Halter, "Erase You." *Rhizome*, May 22, 2008: n.p.

6. Let There Be Beer, Wine, Snacks, and Radical Social Change, 1932–40

1. *Chicago Daily Tribune*, September 24, 1932: 14.

2. *Boston Transcript*, September 3, 1932: 3.

3. Bob Brown, *Let There Be Beer!* (New York: H. Smith & R. Haas, 1932), 21–22.

4. Ibid., 55

5. Ibid.

6. Ibid., 71.

7. Ibid., 143.
8. Ibid.
9. Ibid., 199.
10. Ibid., 285.
11. Ibid.
12. Ibid., 286.
13. See Cecilia Novero, *Antidiets of the Avant-Garde: From Futurist Cooking to Eat Art* (Minneapolis: University of Minnesota Press, 2010); F.T. Marinetti and Fillìa [Luigi Colombo], *La Cucina Futurista* (Milano: Longanesi, 1986).
14. Bob Brown, *Houdini*, Poetry Series Pamphlet 8 (New York: The Modern Editions Press, 1933), 2.
15. Ibid., 3.
16. Cora Brown, Bob Brown, and Rose Brown, *The European Cookbook: The Four-in-One Book of Continental Cookery: Italy, Spain, Portugal, France* (London: Arco, 1956), 220–21.
17. Bob Brown, *Can We Co-Operate?* (Pleasant Plains, Staten Island, N.Y.: Roving Eye Press, 1940).
18. "Items Forward," *Time* 25.18 (May 6, 1935): 61.
19. For example, see Mark S. Morrison, *The Public Face of Modernism: Little Magazines, Audiences, and Reception, 1905–1920* (Madison: University of Wisconsin Press, 2011); Peter Brooker and Andrew Thacker, *The Oxford Critical and Cultural History of Modernist Magazines* (New York: Oxford University Press, 2009); or *The Modernist Journals Project* (Providence, R.I.: Brown University, Department of Modern Culture and Media, 2002), http://modjourn.org/.
20. *Fortnightly* 11.1 (1935): 2.
21. *Fortnightly* 12.1 (1935): 4.
22. Michael Gold, *Change the World!* (New York: International Publishers, 1936), 39. Gold's own fictionalized autobiographical novel, *Jews without Money* (New York: Avon Books, 1965), described his childhood poverty, the dehumanizing situations, the struggles, and the make-do ingenuity necessary to survive in his emigrant ghetto neighborhood of New York City. Gold was himself a bundle of contradictions. Gold's only novel, *Jews without Money* (New York: Avon Books, 1965), exceeded, and almost countered in its eloquence and Proustian detail, his theoretical proclamations. The limited one-dimensional cookie-cutter demands of Gold's own theory, that the value of proletarian literature resided in the author's allegiance to the Communist cause against producing "merely a new *frisson*" or avant-garde "machine" that "produces nothing" and functions "only as an adult toy" (in Michael Gold, *A Literary Anthology* [New York: International Publishers, 1930, collected, republished, and edited by Michael Folsom in 1972, 206]), are no match to his moving and poetic realist fiction that places him in the company of Honoré Balzac and Upton Sinclair. Although he condemned Proust as the "master-masturbator of the bourgeois literature" and the "intellectuals" trying to make literature into a mere "confectionery," he advocated "a cinema in words" that sought to use the

fewest words possible (Gold, 1930/1972, 206, 207). A later edition of Gold's novel, published in 1965, with an Afterword by Michael Harrington, became a key text in the left's advocacy for a war on poverty and urban social protest in the 1960s. For example, Gold described an old, dispirited man working at "his machine in the umbrella store. He was trying to forget America. But who can do that? It roared in the street outside, it fought against him from the lips of his own children. It even reached into his synagogue, and struck at his God. It finally defeated him, this America. It broke the old man, because he could not bend" (Gold, 1930/1965, 137).

23. *Fortnightly* 10.23 (1934): 4.

24. Ibid., 2.

25. Anonymous, "Rich Contrasted with Poorest in Museum Exhibit." *The Lodi News* (May 9, 1935): 8.

26. *Fortnightly* 10.23 (1934): 3.

27. Cora Brown, Rose Brown, and Bob Brown, *The Wine Cook Book, Being a Selection of Incomparable Recipes from France, from the Far East, from the South and Elsewhere, All of Which Owe Their Final Excellence to the Skillful Use of Wine in Their Preparation* (Boston: Little, Brown, 1934).

28. Walter Winchell, *Things I Never Knew 'Till Now* (New York: Bibo-Lang, 1937), 4.

29. *Fortnightly* 12.1 (1935): 3.

30. Ibid.

31. William H. Cobb, *Radical Education in the Rural South: Commonwealth College, 1922–1940* (Detroit: Wayne State University Press, 2000), 142.

32. Bob Brown, "Autobiographical Notes," 1949, The Bob Brown Papers 1844–1960. Charles E. Young Research Library, Special Collections, UCLA.

33. Cora Brown, Rose Brown, and Bob Brown, *Fish & Sea Food Cook Book* (Philadelphia: J. B. Lippincott Company, 1940), 11; also see Craig Saper, "Saudades on the Amazon: Toward a Soft Sweet Name for Involution," in *Beyond Globalization: Making New Worlds in Media, Art, and Social Practices*, ed. A. Aneesh, Lane Hall, and Patrice Petro (New Brunswick, N.J.: Rutgers University Press, 2012), 162–77.

34. R. L. Pollio, Manager, The Mayflower, Washington, D.C.; The compilation of blurbs is found on the back cover of the second edition of the title: Cora Brown, Rose Brown, and Bob Brown, *The Wine Cook Book, Being a Selection of Incomparable Recipes from France, from the Far East, from the South and Elsewhere, All of Which Owe Their Final Excellence to the Skillful Use of Wine in Their Preparation*, 2nd ed. (Boston: Little, Brown, 1951).

35. Cora Brown, Rose Brown, and Bob Brown, *10,000 Snacks, a Cookbook of Canapés, Savories, Relishes, Hors D'oeuvres, Sandwiches and Appetizers for before, after and between Meals* (Garden City, N.Y.: Halcyon House, 1948), 20.

36. Ibid., 21.

37. Ibid., 23.

38. Ibid.

39. Cora Brown, Rose Brown, and Bob Brown, *Most for Your Money Cookbook* (New York: Modern Age Books, 1938), 173.

40. Ibid.

41. Sigmund Freud, *Introductory Lectures on Psycho-Analysis* (New York: Norton, 1989), 116.

42. Brown, Brown, and Brown, *European Cookbook*, 4.

43. Ibid., 1.

44. Quoted in Cora, Bob, and Rose Brown, *Salads and Herbs* (Philadelphia: J.B. Lippincott, 1938), 68.

45. Cora Lovisa Brackett Brown, Rose Brown, and Bob Brown, *The Country Cookbook; Cooking, Canning and Preserving Victuals for Country Home, Farm, Camp & Trailer*, The Country Series (New York: Farrar & Rinehart, 1937), 44.

46. Brown, Brown, and Brown, *European Cookbook*, 6.

47. Brown, Brown, and Brown, *The Country Cookbook*, 214.

48. Brown, Brown, and Brown, *European Cookbook*, 381.

49. Brown, Brown, and Brown, *Fish & Sea Food Cook Book*, 41.

50. Brown, Brown, and Brown, *European Cookbook*, 284.

51. Brown, Brown, and Brown, *10,000 Snacks*, 7.

52. See, for example, Wolfgang Schivelbusch, *Tastes of Paradise: A Social History of Spices, Stimulants, and Intoxicants* (New York: Vintage, 1993).

53. Bob Brown, *The Complete Book of Cheese* (New York: Random House, 1955), 26.

54. Novero, *Antidiets of the Avant-Garde.*

55. Cora, Rose, and Bob Brown, *10,000 Snacks*, 8.

56. Ibid., 8–9.

57. Ibid., 10.

58. Clifton Fadiman, Introduction to *The Complete Book of Cheese*, by Bob Brown (New York: Random House, 1955), ix.

59. Brown, Brown, and Brown, *Fish & Sea Food Cook Book*, 28, 113.

60. Fadiman, xi. Contextual comments added.

61. Brown, *Complete Book of Cheese*, 29–30.

62. Ibid., 26.

63. Ibid., 24–25.

64. Ibid., 25.

65. Ibid., 23.

66. Ibid., 17.

67. Brown, Brown, and Brown, *European Cookbook*, 390.

68. M. C. Phillips, "Are There Reds in the Kitchen?" *Consumers' Digest* (September 1940): 47–52, 51.

69. Ibid., 48.

70. Ibid. Italics added by Phillips.

71. Ibid.

72. Brown, Brown, and Brown, *Most for Your Money Cookbook*, 94. See also Phillips, "Are There Reds in the Kitchen?" 48.

73. Brown, Brown, and Brown, *Most for Your Money Cookbook*, 94.

74. Ibid.

75. Brown, Brown, and Brown, *Most for Your Money Cookbook*, 3; and Annette Clausen, "Despite Higher Food Prices, Percent of U.S. Income Spent on Food Remains Constant," USDA, September 1, 2008.

76. Brown, Brown, and Brown, *Fish & Sea Food Cook Book*, 187.

77. Brown, Brown, and Brown, *Most for Your Money Cookbook*, 62.

78. Ibid., 58.

79. Ibid., 97.

80. Ibid., 3.

81. Phillips, 50.

82. Ibid.

83. Ibid.

84. Ibid., 51.

85. Cora Brown, Rose Brown, and Bob Brown, *Soups, Sauces and Gravies* (Philadelphia: J. B. Lippincott Company, 1939), 128.

86. Ibid., 131.

87. Brown, Brown, and Brown, *Most for Your Money Cookbook*, 203–4.

88. Rose Brown, Bob Brown, and Consumers Union of United States, *Look Before You Cook: A Consumer's Kitchen Guide* (New York: R. M. McBride and Company, 1941), 204.

89. Brown, Brown, and Brown, *Look Before You Cook*, 174.

90. Ibid., ix.

91. Ibid., 6–7.

92. Brown, Brown, and Brown, *Most for Your Money Cookbook*, 139.

93. Ibid., 142.

94. Brown, Brown, and Brown, *Look Before You Cook*, 116.

95. Ibid.

96. Ibid., 187.

97. Cora Brown, Rose Brown, and Bob Brown, *The South American Cook Book: Including Central America, Mexico, and the West Indies* (New York: Dover, 1971), 345.

98. Ibid., 336.

99. Brown, Brown, and Brown, *Most for Your Money Cookbook*, 134.

100. Ibid.

101. Brown, Brown, and Brown, *European Cook Book*, 98–99.

102. Cora, Rose, and Bob Brown, *The Vegetable Cook Book: From Trowel to Table* (Philadelphia: J.B. Lippincott Company, 1939). [copyright held by the authors], 13.

103. Bob Brown, *Homemade Hilarity* (Weston, Vt.: The Countryman Press, 1938), 1.

104. Ibid., 1–2.

7. *Saudade* and Going Home Again: The Amazon, Hollywood, Brazil, and Manhattan, 1941–59

1. Rose Brown and Bob Brown, *Amazing Amazon* (New York: Modern Age Books, 1942).

2. Zora N. Hurston, *Dust Tracks on a Road* (New York: Harper Perennial Modern Classics, 2006), 1.

3. Brown and Brown, *Amazing Amazon*, 4.

4. Ibid., 240.

5. Ibid., 10.

6. Bob Brown, "Saudades for Carioca," in *Nomadness* (New York: Dodd, Mead, and Company, 1931), 152–53.

7. Brown and Brown, *Amazing Amazon*, 240.

8. Ibid., 240.

9. Ibid., 127–28.

10. Ibid., 241.

11. Ibid.

12. Ibid.

13. Ibid., 73.

14. Ibid., 95.

15. Ibid., 98.

16. Ibid., 116.

17. Ibid.

18. Ibid, 160.

19. Ibid, 9.

20. Cora, Rose, and Bob Brown, *The South American Cook Book including Central America, Mexico, and the West Indies* (New York, Doubleday, Doran & Co., Inc., 1939), 258.

21. Claude Lévi-Strauss, *Tristes Tropiques*, trans. John R. Ussell (New York: Vanguard Press, 1934), 100, 104.

22. Ibid., 17.

23. Bob Brown, "Guides," in *Globe-Gliding* (Diessen: Roving Eye Press, 1930), 46–47; also appears in *Nomadness*, 50–51.

24. Brown, "Tourist Insurance," in *Globe-Gliding*, 20–21; also appears in *Nomadness*, 19.

25. Rose and Bob Brown, unpublished book proposal, "Homes from Home," 1941: 13 pages, 2–3.

26. Rose and Bob Brown, unpublished one-page copy of treatments submitted to Screen Writers Guild, 1942.

27. Cora, Rose, and Bob Brown, *Fish & Sea Food Cook Book* (New York : J. B. Lippincott, 1940), 173.

28. Ibid.

29. Ibid.

30. Ibid.

31. Paul Blackburn, Bob Brown, and Allen Ginsberg et al., *Jargon 31: 14 Poets. 1 Artist* (New York: Jargon Books, 1958).

32. For explorations and definitions of the term "puncept" see Gregory L. Ulmer, *Electracy: Gregory L. Ulmer's Textshop Experiments*, ed. Craig Saper, Gregory Ulmer, and Victor J. Vitanza (Aurora, Colo.: The Davies Group Publishers, 2015), viii, xiv, 130, 204–5, 224, 229. A biography that yields to the initiative of puns hopes to trace the surreal discontinuities lurking in an otherwise chronological realist narrative. The Surrealists embraced both detailed realist narrative and the eruption of this other register, and Bob Brown sought to live and write precisely in that tension. See also Craig Saper, *On Being Red* (Madison, Wisc.: Diane Fine's Moon(kosh) Press, 1985).

33. Bob Brown, *My Marjonary* (Boston: John W. Luce & Company, 1916), 55. See also Bob Brown's untitled stories in *365 Days*, ed. Kay Boyle, Laurence Vail, and Nina Conarain (New York: Harcourt, Brace, 1936), 112, 143, 242, 381. In the Preface to *365 Days*, the editors explain that each story had the following constraints: limited to one page; instead of a title, each story has a date in the left top corner and a place name for the story's setting in the right corner; each story, the editors explained, "must not belong not an undefined period of time [not a universal story, but one firmly anchored in a specific place and time], but peculiarly to the moment of the writer had selected, the specified day and month of this particular year"; and every story is told from the perspective of an "ordinary individual's life as it was being lived" (xi). Writers like Langston Hughes, Raymond Queneau, and Henry Miller appear with the handful of entries by Bob and Rose Brown and the many one-day/one-page stories by Kay Boyle. Bob's contributions were listed in the index, without page numbers, as the following: Apr. 10 Louisiana; May 7 U.S.A.; Aug. 4 Brazil; Dec. 1 Arkansas, Rose Brown Nov. 6 U.S.A. (on page 350).

Index

absurdity 1, 17, 24, 88, 154, 168, 189, 197, 226
advertising 9–12, 38, 49, 58–59, 68–69, 79, 86, 98, 102–3, 123, 171, 209, 212–13, 229, 231, 236–37
Aiken, Conrad Potter 83, 90
Albers, Josef 263
Alighieri, Dante. *See* Dante Alighieri
allegory 134, 156
Allen, Woody 1
All-Story Magazine 7, 25, 43, 68, 188
Americana 202
American Civil War 62, 242, 255
The American Mercury 197, 202, 210, 231
American Spectator 46, 202
American Sportagraph Company 11
Amsterdam 2
The Ancient Mariner 59
Ann Arbor 15
Antheil, George 150, 161, 168, 172, 177, 180, 193
Apollinaire, Guillaume 152–53
Aragon, Louis 182–83, 205
archives 68, 160, 179, 188, 226
Arensberg, Walter 78, 90, 92, 130
Arendt, Hannah 111
The Argosy 25–26, 34, 43
artists' colony 1, 43–44, 72, 74, 76, 80, 82, 84, 147, 157, 196
Ashcan School 71–72, 74, 77–78, 87
Associated Little Magazines, 208–9, 216
Athens 2
August-Hunter Camera Composing Machine 161
Australia, 17
Auvergne Press 59, 166
avant-garde 1, 6, 12, 28, 33, 52–53, 59–61, 67, 71–73, 78, 82, 97, 109, 111, 116, 134, 144, 147–54, 157–58, 161, 163–65, 167, 170, 172, 174, 177–78, 180, 186, 190, 193, 195, 201–4, 207–11, 219, 221, 224–25, 238, 247–48, 257, 260–63, 265

Babson, Roger 104
Bad Ems 151–52, 154, 156, 158, 166
Bahia 2
Baker, Josephine 147
Baltimore 215
Banting, John 171
Barnes, Djuna 99, 239
Barranquilla 2
Barton, Bruce 11, 58, 212
Bastida, Joaquín Sorolla y 77

Battery J 110–11, 114, 117–21, 123–26, 133, 138, 140
Baum, L. Frank 59
Beach, Sylvia 148, 151
Beadle, Charles 174
Beat Generation 3, 260, 262–63
Beaumont Press 151
Beckett, Samuel 150
Begawan 2
Belgrade 2
Bell, Alexander Graham 57
Bell, Josephine 113
Bellamy, Edward 58
Benchley, Robert 227
Berkeley: A Journal of Modern Culture 261
Berkman, Alexander 109, 157–58
Berlin 2, 139
Between the Lions 266
Bevan, Tom 239
Black Cat 43, 68
Black Manikin Press 151
Black Mask 33, 47
Black Mountain College 261
The Black Riders and Other Lines 58, 66, 166
Black Sun Press 146, 151, 165
Blast 78
The Blind Man 98, 103, 107–8
Bloomberg, Inc. 140–41
Boccaccio 13
Bodenheim, Maxwell 83, 90
Bohemian 43, 68
boot-legging 118, 190
Boston Journal 24
Boswell, James 81
Bourbon Street 29
Boyle, Kay 147–51, 153, 157, 161, 164, 170–71, 177, 192–93, 216, 260–61
Brabin, Charles 36
Brackett, John S. 13, 68. *See also* Brown, Bob
Bradford, Roark 205
Braley, Berton 5, 12, 28, 30, 44, 72, 77
Brazil 140–43, 170, 174, 187–88, 211, 237–44, 247–48, 252–57, 260–61
Brazilian American 140–41, 174
Breton, André 159, 173
brewing 114, 133, 196–98, 200
British American 142
Broadway 10–11, 17, 43
Broadway Life 43
Brown, Bob: as collector, 1, 33, 44, 58, 60, 68, 77, 81–82, 106–8, 141–42, 145, 151, 180, 224, 243–44, 247–48, 252, 260; as cookbook writer, 2–3, 29, 31, 53, 57, 82, 85, 103, 151, 174, 183, 188, 195–205, 212, 216–25, 228–38, 250, 257, 259, 260, 264, 277; as editor, 44, 71, 74, 78–79, 85–89, 92–93, 103, 109, 112–13, 125, 139–41, 148, 174, 204, 206, 209, 213, 234, 258, 260; as entrepreneur, 1, 59, 67–69, 92, 102–3, 107, 116, 129, 137, 140–43, 148, 159, 161, 185, 200, 256, 259–60; as Hollywood treatment writer, 1, 3, 18, 28, 31, 205, 241, 247, 251–54, 277; as organizer, 71, 104–5, 109, 115, 140–42, 195, 206, 208, 213, 216, 251, 254, 258–60; as poet, 2–3, 6–7, 52–55, 58–60, 66–67, 82–85, 90–91, 98–102, 147–70, 174–93, 197–98, 202, 208–9, 223–24, 234, 248, 250, 258, 260–63; as printer-publisher, 3, 151, 158–61, 164–71, 175–82, 186–87, 189, 204, 208, 224, 252, 258–60, 266; as pulp writer, 1–3, 5, 7–47, 72, 123, 154, 164, 171, 174, 176–77, 184, 196, 202, 241, 264; as teacher, 3, 203, 206–8, 216; works by: *10,000 Snacks*, 218–19, 224; *1450–1950*, *viii*, 151–53, 180, 187, 261; *The Adventures of Christopher Poe*, 32; *Amazing Amazon*, 241, 245, 255; *Can We Co-operate?*, 204; *Complete Book of Cheese*, 53, 218, 226; *The Country Cookbook*, 218; *The European Cookbook*, 203, 217; "Eyes on the Half-Shell," 52, 152, 155; *Fish and Seafood Cook Book*, 218; "Foolsophy," 68, 186; *Gems*, 67, 189–92; *Homemade Hilarity*, 218–19, 238–39; *Houdini*, 202; *House of Content*, 26, 64–65; *Let There Be Beer!*, 151, 194, 196–97; *Look Before You Cook*, 218, 231; *Most for Your Money Cookbook*, 203, 218, 229–30, 234; *My Marjonary*, 91, 100; *Nomadness*, 187, 244; *The Readies*, 67, 118,

140, 150–64, 166, 168–78, 180, 183–86, 189, 190, 213, 220; *Readies for Bob Brown's Machine*, 159, 163, 170–74, 180; *Soups, Sauces and Gravies*, 218; *The South American Cook Book*, 218; *Toward a Bloodless Revolution*, 204; *The Vegetable Cook Book*, 218; *The Wine Cookbook*, 151, 203, 217–18, 222; *What Happened to Mary*, 1, 36–38, 43, 170, 184, 195; *Words*, 12, 159, 178–89; *You Gotta Live*, 111–12, 118, 128, 138, 140, 159, 196
Brown, Carlton 43, 76, 142, 156, 192, 257
Brown, Cora Louisa Brackett 23, 29, 31, 43–44, 49, 53, 57, 65, 76–77, 103, 105, 118, 142, 145, 156, 188, 192–93, 195–96, 204, 207, 212, 218, 220, 235, 238–39, 241
Brown, Cornelia 26–27, 31, 64, 139
Brown, Eleanor Parker Phillips 125–26, 129, 258–61
Brown, Robert Carlton II. *See* Brown, Bob
Brown, Robert Carlton III. *See* Brown, Carlton
Brown, Rose Watson 53, 74, 83, 93–99, 101–2, 105, 110–12, 114–29, 131–43, 145, 151, 156, 173, 188, 192, 195–96, 204–5, 207–8, 212, 216, 218, 220, 235, 239, 241, 243–44, 247, 250–58, 265
Brown, Wesley Earl 56–57
Browning, Robert 81
Bruno, Guido 92, 99
Brussels 2
Bryant, Louise 75, 83
Bucharest 2
Budapest 2
Buddy, Nathanial O. 13. *See also* Brown, Bob
Buenos Aires 2, 138–40
Buffalo Bill 14
Burgess, Gelett 60–62, 172, 239
Burr, Jane. *See* Guggenheim, Rosalind Mae
Burroughs, Edgar Rice 9, 23
Butler, Samuel 58
Cagnes-sur-Mer 157, 161, 172
Cairo 2
Caldecott Award 176
Canada 113, 117, 131
Cannell, Skipwith 83, 90
Cape Town 2, 145
Cape Verde 2
capitalism 11, 82, 97,–98, 128, 142, 209–10, 213, 231, 234, 263
Caracas 2
Carlin, George 190
Carman, Bliss 71
Carroll, Lewis 224–25
Carter, Nick 43, 140
Casanova 13
Cather, Willa 23, 36, 74–75
Cattell, Owen 125
The Cavalier 7
Caxton, William 176
censorship 35, 67, 79, 87, 103, 128, 137, 170, 182, 184–85, 189–91, 200, 214, 252
Certeau, Michel de 228
Ceylon 145
Cézanne, Paul 96
Chandler Motor 79
The Chap-Book 60, 99
Chaplin, Charlie 157–58, 161, 169
Charcot, Jean-Martin 185
Chaucer, Geoffrey 59
Chesapeake Bay 40
Chicago 5, 9, 13, 26, 49, 54–60, 63–64, 67–68, 77, 199, 239
Chicago Tribune 67, 218
China 142–45
Chopin, Kate 59
Christian Science Monitor 231–32
Cicero 185
City College of New York 216
Clark, Axton 172–73
Clemens, Samuel. *See* Twain, Mark
Cocteau, Jean 172
College World 34
Cooper, James Fenimore 226
Cologne 2
Colombo 2, 145
Columbia University 125
Columbus, Christopher 54, 198

comedy. *See* humor
Commonwealth College 203–10, 212, 214–15, 234
communal living 1, 28, 199, 203–6, 219, 245
Communism 1, 75, 171, 204, 209, 215–16, 229–31, 234–35, 237, 253, 260
Comstock, Anthony 103
conceptual art 148, 152–53, 178, 189, 191, 196, 210
Coney Island 23, 27, 56, 79, 98, 101–2, 104, 135, 167
Consumers' Digest 229–30
consumerism 24, 41, 55, 97, 213, 229–37
Contact Editions 151
Contempo 164, 171
Cook, William Wallace 14–25, 27–28, 72, 109, 176
Copenhagen 2
Copland, Aaron 147
Corfu 2
Côte d'Azur 111, 161, 193
Cowley, Peggy Baird 239
Cowley, Malcolm 239
Craig, Mary 33
Crane, Stephen 58, 66, 75
Cravan, Arthur 112, 117, 130–34, 196
Crosby, Caresse 146, 151–52, 161
Crosby, Harry 146, 151, 152, 165, 169, 187, 261
Crowder, Henry 182
Cuba 3, 30
Cummings, E. E. 147, 153, 158, 164
Cunard, Nancy 2, 79, 146, 148, 165, 169, 171, 178–84, 189, 216

Dada 92, 101, 109, 112, 130–31, 134, 149, 159, 172, 177, 180, 182, 190
Daily Mail 26
Daniel, Charles 74
Dante Alighieri, 135
Daugherty, James 176
Davies, Mary Carolyn 83, 90
da Vinci, Leonardo 185
Davis, Bob 7, 69
Davis, Stuart 72, 79, 85–89, 148–49, 166, 193, 263–65
Debs, Eugene V. 114, 136
de Campos, Augusto 261
Delineator 31
Dell, Floyd 83, 85, 88, 103, 112, 220
DeMille, Cecil B. 31
Dempsey, Jack 157
design 3, 6, 12, 35, 50, 55, 58–59, 62, 80, 98, 101, 103, 151–52, 156, 158, 161, 165–69, 175–83, 185, 189–90, 221, 252, 258
Desnos, Robert 149
The Dial 60
Diamond Dick 14, 43
Díaz, Porfirio 30
Dibden, Francis Frognall 176
Dickens, Charles 7, 81
Doctorow, E. L. 20
Domingo City 2
Dominy, Frederick Arthur 27–28
Dom Pedro II 243, 254–55
Dorsey, Emmett 66
Dos Passos, John 148
Douglass, Frederick 67
Dreiser, Theodore 31, 74–75, 205
Drucker, Johanna 61
Dubliners 78
Duchamp, Marcel 2, 73, 78, 83, 88, 91, 98, 101, 103, 107, 131, 140, 145, 147–48, 152, 154, 156, 158, 161, 169–73, 177, 180, 184, 193
Dunbar, Paul Laurence 66–67
Durham, Peter P. 13. *See also* Brown, Bob
Dworkin, Craig 190
Dwyer, Charles 36–37

Eastman, Max 44, 78–79, 85–89, 113, 127, 137, 140, 252
Eat Art Movement 225
Edison, Thomas 36–39
Edwards, John Milton 14
Egoist 78
Eiffel Tower 62
Eisenstein, Sergei 195
The Electric Company 187, 266
electricity 5, 62
Eliot, George 13
Eliot, T. S. 224, 227
Ellis, Fred 100

Ellis, Havelock 189–91
El Paso 116, 119, 125
Eluard, Paul 183
em dashes 67, 118, 156, 173, 186, 189
Emerson, Ralph Waldo 81
emoji 156
England 13, 17, 23–26, 40, 114, 130, 176, 189
e-readers 3, 154, 159, 160, 163, 169
Ernst, Max 149
Espionage Act 109, 112–13, 125
Esquire 218, 254
Evans, Donald 78
Everybody's Magazine 28
expatriate 1, 109, 111, 140, 147–50, 157, 159, 161, 163–65, 167, 170, 172, 177–78, 195, 202–3, 238–39, 242, 253, 263

Fadiman, Clifton 226
Falstaff 7
Fargue, Léon-Paul 149
Farrell, James T. 89, 147, 171, 174, 177, 213, 219
Far Rockaway 27
fascism 161, 170, 192, 211, 214, 222
fashion 25, 38, 41, 94, 102, 104, 180, 223, 253
Faubus, Orval 214
Faulkner, William 33, 77, 164, 205
Fedin, Konstantin 149
feminism 24–25, 38, 43, 74–75, 89, 93–97, 114, 116, 182, 225, 250
The Fiction Factory 5–47
film 1, 11, 18, 21, 26, 28, 33, 37–44, 56, 75, 98, 105, 118, 121–22, 134, 156, 158, 167, 170, 174–77, 184, 186–87, 195, 205, 241, 247, 251–55, 264
Fiske, Bradley A. 160
Fitzgerald, F. Scott 47, 111, 147
Fitzsimmons, Bob 11, 17
Flanner, Janet 148
Flatiron Building 8, 42
Flint, Frank Stuart 90
folklore 53, 175
food 16, 29, 34, 36, 53, 82–83, 128–29, 132, 145, 162–63, 183, 185–88, 197, 202, 208, 216–39, 245–47
Ford, Charles Henri 173, 239
Ford, Hugh 180
Ford Times 77
forgery and fraud 41, 148, 134, 140, 182, 213
Fortnightly 208–11, 215
Fox, Anna Myra 27
Fox, Cornelia Lillian 26–27, 31, 64, 139
Fox, Katrina 26–27, 31–32, 64–66
France 1, 109, 121, 142, 145, 147, 157, 161, 163, 165–66, 170, 187–88, 191–93, 201, 215, 217–18, 223, 237–38
Frankfurt 2
Fraser, Andrea 211
Freud, Sigmund 98, 185, 199, 221
fundamentalism 11
Fuller, Mary 43
Futurism 82, 109, 172, 201, 222, 225

Gaboriau, Émile 13
Gaites, Joseph M. 11
Gauguin, Paul 98
Gautier le Leu 13
Genoa 2, 222
Gershwin, George 147
Gibson, Charles Dana 38–39, 86
Gifford, Julia 17
Gillespie, Abraham Lincoln 161, 172
Ginsberg, Allen 260–61
"Give My Regards to Broadway" 17
Glaspell, Susan 100
Glintenkamp, Eleanor 129, 216, 258
Glintenkamp, Hendrik 88, 112–13, 117, 128–29, 135, 216, 258
Gold, Michael 83, 117, 178, 209–10, 252, 266
The Golden Treasury 191
Goldman, Emma 89, 93, 98, 109, 113, 115, 157–58, 161, 188, 204
Gooch, Samuel A. 215
Goodwin, Murray 149
Gorky, Maxim 26
Grand Central Station 16, 33
Grantwood Village 1, 43–44, 74–76, 79, 82, 92, 97–98, 118, 142, 150, 157, 170, 196
Graphic design 58, 175, 177, 185
The Gray Goose 23, 25–26, 43, 68

Great Depression 31, 203–4, 232
Greenwich Village 1, 7, 44, 47, 71–73, 75, 88, 92, 94–97, 99, 103, 109, 115, 117, 157, 220, 257–58
Gris, Juan 149
Guadalajara 126, 129
Guggenheim, Rosalind Mae 31, 75
Gutenberg, Johannes 153, 176
Guthrie, Woody 214

Haacke, Hans 211
Hagglund, B. C. 171
The Hague 3, 30
Halifax 2, 74
Halter, Ed 191
Hamburg 2
Hamlet 7
Hampton's 43
handwriting 61, 98, 152–54, 262
Hardy, Thomas 10–11
Harlem Renaissance 67
Harlequin 25
Harper's Weekly 43
Harvard University 172
Havana 2
Hearn, Lafcadio 29
Helsinki 2
Hemingway, Ernest 111, 150–51, 183, 196
Henri, Robert 71–72
Henry, O. 2, 9, 23, 34–36, 75
Hershey, Milton 10–11
Hibben, Sheila 227
hieroglyphic writing 98, 147, 153, 156
Hiler, Hilaire 161–63, 203
Hiroshima 2, 144
Hogarth Press 182
Hogarth, William 81
Holland 30, 74, 76
Hollywood 1, 3, 18–21, 28, 31, 41, 128, 174, 205, 210, 240–41, 247, 251–54
Holzer, Jenny 191
Home Chat 39
Hong Kong 2
Hoover, J. Edgar 112
Hoovervilles 212
Horn & Hardart Automat 36
Hours Press 146, 165, 178–80, 182, 189
Howard University 66
Hughes, Langston 171, 216, 219
humor 5, 7, 9–11, 24, 27, 50, 55, 57–60, 68, 71, 73, 75–77, 88–89, 91, 96 112, 115, 120, 124, 128, 130, 141, 158, 167, 169–70, 186, 190, 196, 199–200, 203, 205, 212–13, 241, 245–46, 249, 251, 253–55
Hurston, Zora Neal 242
Hutton, Edward 191
Huyler's 10

Imagism 1, 78–82, 87, 90–91, 93, 96, 98, 101, 132, 150, 154, 170–71, 184, 219–21, 250, 263
improvisation 30, 78, 153
International Workers of the World 115
invention 1, 3, 9–10, 15, 20, 35, 49, 51, 53, 55–56, 62–63, 91, 98 119, 137, 143, 153, 158–63, 169–70, 176, 185, 197, 201, 204, 228, 265
Irving, Washington 81
Istanbul 2
Ivanhoe 59

Japan 101, 117, 143, 145, 151, 193
Jargon Society Press 152, 261
Java 2, 117
jazz 91, 148, 182, 193, 263–64
Jesus 11, 53
Jobs, Steve 174
Johns, Orrick 83, 90, 239
Johnston, Robert 97
jokes. *See* humor
Jolas, Eugene 146–47, 151, 158
Joyce, James 78, 133, 149, 151, 158, 164, 166, 172, 177
Jude the Obscure 10

Kafka, Franz 150
Kalamazoo 15
Karfiol, Bernard 83
Kaufman, George S. 77
Kent, George 174
Kharkov 2
Kidd, Orville Updike 13. *See also* Brown, Bob
Kiel 2

Kline, Franz 262–63
Kobe 2, 144
Komroff, Manuel 80
Kreymborg, Alfred 74, 78, 83, 89–92, 99, 131
Krog, Fritz 31
Kruger, Barbara 211
Ku Klux Klan 114, 213
Kyoto 2

Ladies' Home Journal 7
Ladies' World 7–8, 36–39, 43
Laredo 119
Lark 61
Lawrence, D. H. 151
Lear, Edward 58
Léger, Ferdinand 168, 172, 193
Leningrad 2
Levertov, Denise 261
Lévi-Strauss, Claude 248, 250
Levine, Sherrie 148
Lewis, Sinclair 31
Liberal Club 95
Light in August 33
Lima 2
Lisbon 2
literacy 3, 167, 267. *See also* reading
The Little Review 78
Live Wire 25, 68
London, 2, 23–27, 141–42, 192, 195–96, 216, 227, 258
London, Jack 224, 226
Long Island 27, 258
Los Angeles 126, 243, 252
Louisiana Purchase 54
Lowell, Amy 78, 82, 84, 90
Lowenfels, Walter 1
Loy, Mina 2, 78, 83, 90 112, 130, 132, 196
Lucerne 2
Luks, George 71
Lye, Len 183

MacKenzie, Donald 175
MacLeish, Archibald 148
Macleod, Norman 171
Madison 12, 23–26, 31, 64
Madrid 2
manifesto 150–51, 154–59, 166–71, 175
Mann, William d'Alton 46
Manning, Bruce 204–5, 251–52
Marseilles 2, 145, 223
Marshall, Michigan 15, 28
Marxism 72, 89
The Masses 44, 71, 74, 78–79, 85–89, 92–93, 103, 109, 112–13, 125, 139, 148, 204, 206, 209, 213, 234, 258, 260
Mazatlán 122, 125
McArthur, Peter 71
McClure's 34, 36, 38–39
McPherson, Aimee 213
Mencken, H. L. 2, 45–47, 81, 197, 210–11, 215, 231
metaphor 72, 226
Mexican Revolution 30, 78, 117, 122, 237
Mexico City 2, 29, 122, 124, 126, 129, 133, 141–42, 258
microfiche and microfilm 160
microscopic text 12, 160, 167, 179–80, 183–86, 189, 265
Millay, Edna St. Vincent 100
Miller, Alfred 213
Miller, Elizabeth 24–25
Miller, Henry 216
Milton, John 59, 224
miniaturization 21, 102, 152, 159–60, 183–85, 223–24, 234
modernism 2, 6–7, 21, 25, 28, 30, 33, 41, 45, 47, 58–60, 63, 71–74, 77–78, 82, 84–87, 96, 101, 109, 111, 119, 123–24, 131, 134, 150–56, 158–61, 165, 167–70, 172, 174–77, 180, 182–83, 195–99, 209, 221, 250, 252, 257–58, 260
Modern Times 158
Mona Lisa 185
Montaigne, Michel de 81
Montevideo 2
Moore, George 81, 182
Moore, Marianne 83, 90
Morgan, J. P. 82, 107, 210
Moscow 2, 125, 216, 232
Moving Picture Stories 43–44
Mumme, Christian 198
Munich 2

Munsey, Frank 7, 23–26
Munsey magazines 7–9, 12, 23–26, 43
Museum of Social Change 195, 208–9
Mussolini, Benito 222
music and musicals, 11, 59–60, 80, 90, 95, 150, 167, 172, 182, 193, 214, 216, 226, 251, 255
Mydham, Martin 13. *See also* Brown, Bob
mysticism 57

Nader, Ralph 114
Nagasaki 2, 144
Nagoyn 2
Nancy Drew 33
Naples 2
Nash, Ogden 60–61, 77
Nathan, George Jean 45–47
Nation, Carrie 62
Nazis 213, 253
Neagoe, Peter 149, 161, 170–71
Newberry Award 176
New Jersey Palisades 1, 43
Newman, Barnett 263
New Orleans 28–29, 44, 73, 197, 204–5, 251
The New Quarterly 171
New Theatre League 214–15
The New York Bookman 10
New York City 10, 16, 30, 34, 38, 40, 68, 80, 121, 129, 131, 201, 206, 214, 216, 219, 232, 235
New Yorker 85, 176, 186, 227, 260
New York Sunday World 9
New York Times 73, 159, 218
New York Times Book Review 218
New York University 101
New York Weekly 14
New Zealand 17
Niger 188
Nobody's Baby 241, 251
Nogales, Arizona 119, 122
Noigandres Concrete Poetry 261
Nonesuch Press 151
non-sense 60–62, 172
Nord, Richard 30
Norton, Allen 78, 102, 104, 112, 114–16, 122, 132–34, 184, 239

Oak Park, Illinois 49, 56, 58, 166, 212
Ocean 7, 43
Odessa 2
The Oliver Company 7
Olsen, Charles 261
O'Neill, Eugene 75–76, 83, 115
Orientalism 34
Orgone Box 263
Osaka 2
Others: A Magazine of the New Verse 74, 78–79, 84, 90–92, 170
Otis Company 154
OULIPO 101
Ovid Press 151

A Pair of Blue Eyes 10
Pagliacci 153
Palermo 2
Panama 41, 133, 135
Parker, Dorothy 148
Parker, Eleanor Wilson 125
Paris 2, 26, 73, 77, 80, 105, 111, 145, 147–48, 150–52, 159, 161, 163, 166, 174, 192, 213, 215–16, 221, 223, 237
Parrish, Maxfield 59
Patriarchy 24
Paxton, Tom 214
Pearce, Richard 60, 62
Pearson's Magazine 10, 26, 34, 43
Peck, Harry T. 10
Penn Station 16
People's Magazine 14
Pepys, Samuel 81
Perec, George 101
Perelman, S. J. 252
performance 34, 36, 79, 98, 101, 130, 150, 172, 177, 180, 184, 215, 246
Pernambuco 2
Perry, Matthew C. 151
Peru 139, 142, 255
Phillips, Charles F. 125, 129, 216, 258
Phillips, M. C. 210, 229–37
Photoplay 43, 105
Picasso, Pablo 77, 149, 158, 172
plagiarism 205
Plimpton, Horace G. 36–37
plotto 14–15, 19–22

Poe, Christopher 10, 26, 29–30, 32–36, 39, 73
Poe, Edgar Allan 13, 67
Porter, Bern 261
Porter, Cole 148
Porter, William Sydney. *See* Henry, O.
Pound, Ezra 47, 78–79, 84, 90–91, 148, 170, 172, 175, 177, 182, 209–10
Prague 2
printing 3, 6–7, 12, 18–19, 26, 59, 63, 67–68, 92, 117, 137, 141–42, 151, 153, 160–61, 163, 167, 169, 171, 175–87, 189, 193, 215
Progresso 2
Prohibition 62, 114–15, 182, 189, 194, 196, 198, 200–1
propaganda 85, 87, 137–39, 184, 229–31
Proust, Marcel 175, 178
Provincetown Players 73–75, 83, 92, 115, 117
pseudonyms 9–10, 13–14, 25, 31, 34, 37, 75, 93, 115, 134, 176
pulp fiction 1–3, 5, 7–10, 12–14, 16, 18, 21, 23–24, 26, 29, 33–34, 36, 38, 43–45, 47, 60, 72, 77, 117, 123, 154, 164, 166, 171, 174, 176–77, 184, 196, 202, 218, 241, 264
puns 85, 102, 137, 152, 158, 167, 186, 199, 265
Puerto Rico 30
Pulitzer, Joseph 63, 205

Rabelais 13
radio 26, 63, 82, 150, 160, 171, 190, 212
Railroad Man's 7, 25
Ray, Man 2, 74, 79–80, 83, 90, 92–98, 109, 131, 147, 168, 170, 172, 183, 190
Reader's Digest 174
reading, 3, 9, 13, 18, 22, 38, 53, 58–63, 67, 74, 81–82, 150–56, 159–63, 166–71, 173–78, 180, 182, 184–87, 189–90, 218, 221, 224–25, 229, 237. *See also* literacy
reading machine 3, 9, 11–12, 59–60, 62–63, 67, 82, 90, 109, 146, 148, 150, 153–56, 158–64, 168–70, 174, 176–78, 180, 183–84, 187, 193, 198, 201, 222, 263, 267
recipes 29, 53, 60, 103, 145, 163, 174, 193, 200–3, 212, 217, 219, 220, 223, 225–26, 228–29, 233–39, 248, 251
Record Herald 67
Reed, John 73, 75, 78, 87, 113
Reedy's Paper 60
Reich, Wilhelm 263
Renoir, Jean 252
Renoir, Pierre Auguste 161
Republican Party 11
Rexroth, Kenneth 260
Rice, Polly 77
Rio de Janeiro 3, 141
Roberts, Carlton, 13. *See also* Brown, Bob
Rockwell, Norman 126
Rogers, Bruce 59, 176
Rogue 78, 104, 112
Rome 3
Roosevelt, Eleanor 77
Roosevelt, Theodore 105, 211
Rossetti, Dante Gabriel 59
Rostov 3
Rothko, Marc 263
Rotterdam 3
Roving Eye Press 146, 151, 165, 178, 189, 201, 204, 259–60, 266
The Royal 34
Rubin, Ben 191
Ruskin, John 81
Russian Revolution 109

Sadoul, Georges 183
Salandar, Larry 148
Salina Cruz 3, 133, 138, 140
Salvation Army 13
Sanborn, Robert Alden 83, 90
Sandburg, Carl 100, 164
Sanctuary 33
Sanger, Margaret 98
Santiago de Chile 3, 136–38
Santiago de Cuba 3
Santo Domingo 30
Santos-Dumont, Alberto 62
São Paulo 3, 140–41, 248
Sarah Lawrence College 219
Saturday Evening Post 43, 126
Schlink, Frederick 229–30

science fiction 150, 154
The Scrap Book 7, 25, 43, 99
scribbling 152–53
Scully, Frank 157
Seabrooke, Elliott 183
sedition 88, 111–14, 138–39, 215
Sedley, Charles 191
Seeger, Pete 214
Sesame Street 187, 266
Seville 3, 77
Sex in the City 41
sexuality 10, 23–25, 57, 87, 89, 97–98, 170–71, 173, 182, 189–90, 199, 213
Shadow Steve, 13. *See also* Brown, Bob
Shakespeare, William 59, 81
Shakespeare & Company 151
Shanghai 3, 142–43, 145, 193
Shaw, George Bernard 26
Sherlock Holmes, 26, 34
shorthand 32, 156, 161, 172, 174, 186
Sibthorpe, John 179, 183
Silas Marner, 59
Sims, Dorothy Rice. *See* Rice, Polly
Sinclair, Upton 26
Singapore 3, 144
Sloan, John 71, 85–86, 88
Smart Set 14, 45–47, 167, 169, 172
Smiley, Howard Dwight 28
Smithsonian Holocaust Museum 242
socialism 82, 85, 87–89, 109, 112, 115, 125–26, 139, 203
Sofia 3
Soupault, Philippe 149
Soviet Union 129, 203, 206, 210, 215–16, 219, 231–32, 258
Spooner, Phil 27
Springsteen, Bruce 214
Stalingrad 3
steampunk 168
Stein, Gertrude 2, 72, 78–80, 82, 111–12, 146, 148–49, 153, 155–58, 161, 163, 166, 169–70, 172, 175, 177, 187, 193, 195, 260
Steinbeck, John 77
Stella, Joseph 103
Sterne, Laurence 58
Stettheimer, Ettie 140
Stieglitz, Alfred 109, 131
St. Louis Post-Dispatch 63
stock market crash 193
Stockholm 3
Street & Smith Publications 12, 14, 16
Sumatra 3, 145
Sunday, William Ashley "Billy" 213
Surrealism 3, 19, 53, 55, 57, 96, 130, 134, 148–52, 156, 158–59, 162, 166, 168, 170–74, 177, 180, 182, 185, 190–91, 193, 201–3, 216, 219–21, 223–25, 227–28, 248, 250, 263, 265
Swiss Family Robinson 201

Tahiti 99–100, 133
Tangiers 3
Tanguay, Eva 115
Tanguy, Yves 183
Tarzan 9
Tehuantepec 3
Tender Buttons 72, 78, 82, 153
text messaging 63, 150, 161
Thackeray, William. M. 81
Thomas A. Edison Kinetoscope Company 37
The Thomas Hardy Company 10–11
Thomas, Theodore 60
tickertape 3, 81–82, 119, 171, 174
Times Square 17
Tinguely, Jean 263
Toklas, Alice B. 195, 222, 225
Tokyo 3
Top Notch 45
tourism 28, 30, 33, 74, 100, 123, 161, 199, 213, 244–46, 248–50
Transition (magazine) 146–50, 158–59, 165, 168, 172, 180, 193
Trieste 3
Tristram Shandy 58
Trollope, Anthony 176
Turin 3
Twain, Mark 81
Twinells, H. E. 13, 68. *See also* Brown, Bob
Tyler, Hartridge D. 13. *See also* Brown, Bob
Tyler, Parker 173, 239

Ttypography 18, 176–77
Tzara, Tristan 159, 172, 177, 182, 193

Ulysses 133
Union League Club 101
University of São Paulo 248
University of Wisconsin 58, 64
Untermeyer, Louis 84–85
U.S.S.R. *See* Soviet Union

Vail, Laurence 161
Valencia 3
Valparaiso 3, 136–39
Van Vechten, Carl 100
Vargas, Getúlio 257
Venice 3
Vera Cruz 3, 128
Victorianism 24, 50, 54, 56, 95, 169, 176, 189
Vienna 3
Villon, François 13
visual poetry 6–7, 52–53, 59–60, 98, 150–54, 158, 166, 175, 190, 222, 250, 258, 261, 263
Vorse, Mary Heaton 74

Walden 107
Walker, Jimmy 74
Walker, Mary 62, 102
Wallace, Richard Horatio Edgar 82
Wall Street 1, 80, 85, 213, 258
The Wall Street Journal 125
Warsaw 3
Washington, George 49
Washington Square 74–75, 88, 92
Watkins, Ann 31
Webster Hall 2, 70, 103–4, 106, 125, 139
Welles, Orson 253, 265
Wells, H. G. 26, 58
West, Nathanael "Pep" 5, 252
Whistler, James McNeill 58, 81
Whitman, Walt 175
Whitney, Gertrude Vanderbilt 72, 166
Whitney Museum of American Art 72
Wilde, Oscar 81, 99
Williams, Chauncey, 26, 59–64, 166
Williams, Jonathan 152, 261–62
Williams, Tennessee 209
Williams, William Carlos 2, 83, 90–92, 132, 144, 150–51, 170–71, 173, 180, 183, 217, 239
Wilson, Horatio 31
Wilson, Woodrow 109
Winchell, Walter 213
Winslow, Horatio 12
Winter Park, Florida 97
Women's World 7
Wood, Beatrice 83, 88, 101, 103
Woolf, Leonard 182
Woolf, Virginia 182, 193
World's Columbian Exposition 54. *See also* World's Fair
World's Fair 10, 12, 30, 48, 54–57, 62, 67, 102, 135
World War I 77–78, 109, 111–14, 140
World War II 144, 160
W.P.A. Writer's Project 205
Wright, Anthony 13. *See also* Brown, Bob
Wright, Frank Lloyd 50, 52, 59
Writers' Guild 71, 251, 254, 260
Wyndham, Olive 43

xenophobia 111, 114, 211

Yokohama 3, 151
Young, Art 87–88, 210
Yucatan 3

Zabaleta, Ignacio Zuloaga y 77
Zapatista 30
Zelig 1, 96
Zukofsky, Louis 261
Zululand 3, 145
Zurich 3

ESE SELECT TITLES FROM EMPIRE STATE EDITIONS

Allen Jones with Mark Naison, *The Rat That Got Away: A Bronx Memoir*

Patrick Bunyan, *All Around the Town: Amazing Manhattan Facts and Curiosities, Second Edition*

New York's Golden Age of Bridges. Paintings by Antonio Masi, Essays by Joan Marans Dim, Foreword by Harold Holzer

Daniel Campo, *The Accidental Playground: Brooklyn Waterfront Narratives of the Undesigned and Unplanned*

John Waldman, *Heartbeats in the Muck: The History, Sea Life, and Environment of New York Harbor, Revised Edition*

John Waldman (ed.), *Still the Same Hawk: Reflections on Nature and New York*

Gerard R. Wolfe, *The Synagogues of New York's Lower East Side: A Retrospective and Contemporary View, Second Edition*. Photographs by Jo Renée Fine and Norman Borden, Foreword by Joseph Berger

Howard Eugene Johnson with Wendy Johnson, *A Dancer in the Revolution: Stretch Johnson, Harlem Communist at the Cotton Club*. Foreword by Mark D. Naison

Joseph B. Raskin, *The Routes Not Taken: A Trip Through New York City's Unbuilt Subway System*

Phillip Deery, *Red Apple: Communism and McCarthyism in Cold War New York*

North Brother Island: The Last Unknown Place in New York City. Photographs by Christopher Payne, A History by Randall Mason, Essay by Robert Sullivan

Kirsten Jensen and Bartholomew F. Bland (eds.), *Industrial Sublime: Modernism and the Transformation of New York's Rivers, 1900–1940*. Introduction by Katherine Manthorne

Richard Kostelanetz, *Artists' SoHo: 49 Episodes of Intimate History*

Stephen Miller, *Walking New York: Reflections of American Writers from Walt Whitman to Teju Cole*

Tom Glynn, *Reading Publics: New York City's Public Libraries, 1754–1911*

David Borkowski, *A Shot Story: From Juvie to Ph.D.*

R. Scott Hanson, *City of Gods: Religious Freedom, Immigration, and Pluralism in Flushing, Queens*. Foreword by Martin E. Marty

For a complete list, see www.empirestateeditions.com.